THE TIMES
ATLAS OF
WORLD HISTORY

SIXTH CONCISE EDITION

THE TIMES

ATLAS OF WORLD HISTORY

SIXTH CONCISE EDITION

Edited by

GEOFFREY BARRACLOUGH

TIMES BOOKS

Sixth edition first published in 1997 by
Times Books
77-85 Fulham Palace Road
London W6 8JB

Reprinted 1998

First published in 1982
Revised editions 1986, 1988, 1992, 1994
© Times Books 1982, 1986, 1988, 1992,
1994, 1997

British Library Cataloguing
in Publication Data
"Times" Concise Atlas of World History.–
6th Rev. ed.
I. Barraclough, Geoffrey
911

ISBN 0 7230 0906 6

EDITORIAL DIRECTION   Barry Winkleman
                      Ailsa Heritage

DESIGN & ART DIRECTION   Ivan and Robin Dodd

MAP DESIGN AND ARTWORK   Swanston Graphics Ltd, Derby
                         P S G Ltd, Derby
                         Peter Sullivan
                         Ivan and Robin Dodd

PLACE NAMES AND INDEX   P J M Geelan

COLOUR SEPARATION   City Ensign Ltd, Hull
                    D S Colour International Ltd, London

PRINTED AND BOUND   Hong Kong

EDITORIAL CONSULTANTS   Dr Chris Scarre, McDonald Institute,
(Fourth, fifth and sixth editions)   University of Cambridge
                        Geoffrey Parker, Andreas Dorpalen
                        Distinguished Professor of History, The Ohio
                        State University
                        Richard Overy, Professor of Modern History,
                        King's College London

ACKNOWLEDGEMENTS   This atlas contains the work of many of the
                   contributors to THE TIMES ATLAS OF WORLD
                   HISTORY (Fourth edition, 1993) who are listed
                   in that volume. We also wish to thank:
                   Frederick W Boal, Professor of Human
                   Geography, Queens University, Belfast
                   Professor Michael Crowder, late of the
                   University of Botswana
                   Dr Elizabeth Dunstan, International African
                   Institute
                   David Hickman
                   Raymond Hutchings, Senior Editor, Abstract,
                   Soviet and Eastern European Series
                   Morton Keller, Spector Professor of History,
                   Brandeis University, Massachusetts
                   John Lynch, Professor of Latin American
                   History and Director, Institute of Latin
                   American Studies, University of London
                   Rosamond McKitterick, Professor of Early
                   Medieval European History, University of
                   Cambridge
                   W H McNeill, Robert A Millitin Distinguished
                   Services Professor of History, University of
                   Chicago
                   W H Parker, formerly Lecturer of the
                   Geography of the USSR, University of Oxford
                   Dr Jonathan Shepard, University of Cambridge
                   R L Sims, Lecturer in the History of the Far
                   East, School of Oriental and African Studies,
                   University of London
                   Peter Sluglett, Lecturer in Modern Middle
                   Eastern History, Durham University

CONTENTS

Part Four

The modern world

INTRODUCTION

The welcome given to THE TIMES ATLAS OF WORLD HISTORY, first published in English in September 1978, and now available in nine languages, shows how widespread an interest there is today in the human story. It also led us to think that there might be a place for a shorter, less elaborate atlas on a reduced scale.

The present volume is the result. Nevertheless THE TIMES ATLAS OF WORLD HISTORY, *Concise Edition* is not merely a condensed and abbreviated version of the earlier work. No fewer than 70 of the 320 maps here presented are entirely new or radically changed, and many others have been revised and redesigned. THE TIMES ATLAS OF WORLD HISTORY, *Concise Edition* is intended to stand on its own feet as a compact, easily available reference book covering the whole story of mankind from the earliest beginnings, when man's ancestors first emerged from the tropical forests of Africa, to the complex, highly articulated world in which we live.

Although the present volume incorporates new material and differs in a number of other ways from the larger work on which it is based, the principles which have guided us are the same. As in THE TIMES ATLAS OF WORLD HISTORY, we have endeavoured to make the coverage as universal as is possible in the present state of knowledge, and in particular to provide full and clear accounts of the civilisations of Asia, Africa and the Americas, both before and after the coming of the Europeans. We have paid close attention to the relations and interactions between these different regions in all their manifestations - cultural and economic, peaceful and warlike, including invasions and migrations, the spread of agriculture and the diffusion of technologies - because we believe these to be some of the main threads of world history. Although we have given more space in this volume to the intricate web of politics (war, treaties, frontier changes) and to the internal development of particular countries (e.g. England, Russia, Japan and the USA), it is our view that world history is more than a combination of national histories, and we have planned this work accordingly.

A long view and a wide historical perspective are vitally important in the world as it is constitued today. If THE TIMES ATLAS OF WORLD HISTORY, *Concise Edition* has succeeded in providing such a view, it will have fulfilled one of its objectives. Nevertheless it is important to emphasise that this is not an atlas of current affairs. We have sought, in the concluding plates, to pick out and illustrate some of the more significant trends and movements in the contemporary world, but no attempt has been made to cover the years between 1945 and 1980 in detail. That was not our purpose; but we believe that informed knowledge of the past is a key to the understanding of the present and – as the great Victorian historian, Lord Acton, said it should be – 'a power that goes to the making of the future.'

GEOFFREY BARRACLOUGH
Oxford, March 1982

This sixth edition sees many changes to Professor Barraclough's first edition and to subsequent editions overseen by Professor Norman Stone and Professor Geoffrey Parker, particularly in the final spreads dealing with the dramatic changes in eastern Europe in the 1990s. Yet the world order is changing so fast that Professor Barraclough's warning that this is not an atlas of current affairs must be repeated.

TIMES BOOKS
May 1997

Human origins

In the vast time perspective of earth history the human species is a relative newcomer. The first life on earth of which we have any trace, simple single-celled organisms, date back some 4600 million years (diagram 1). In contrast, fully modern *Homo sapiens sapiens* originated a mere 120,000 years ago. Yet within that short period of time we have become one of the most successful species ever, colonising virtually every corner of the globe, increasing enormously in numbers and manipulating the earth's resources and environment in a way never attempted by any other organism on our planet.

Study of chromosomes shows that our nearest relatives in the animal kingdom are the African apes (gorillas and chimpanzees). With them we share a common descent from various ape-like species such as the *Dryopithecines* which lived in Africa, Europe and south Asia some 20–15 million years ago. The parting of the ways, when the human line diverged from that of the chimpanzees and gorillas (diagram), may have come as recently as 8 million years ago, a tiny interval in the 4600 million years of life on earth.

The origins of the earliest hominids lie in equatorial Africa, and it is here that the oldest remains have been found (map 3). These are of a small creature known as *Australopithecus* or 'southern ape', from the first dis-

covery at Taung in South Africa in 1924. No fewer than four separate species of *Australopithecus* have now been distinguished in the fossil record, all restricted to Africa and living in the period from 5 million to 1 million years ago. We know that they walked upright on two legs from footsteps left in the mud at Laetoli in east Africa.

These *Australopithecines* were small agile creatures, only around four feet tall, and they lived almost exclusively on nuts, fruits and berries. But they already displayed some of the trends which were to lead to modern humans. The bipedal posture freed the hands for other tasks, in turn stimulating the development of a larger brain. At the same time, the jaw and snout became less prominent as hands could be used to break off foods

2 The spread of Homo sapiens

1 The origin and development of life

●———	first appearance
●– – –	mass extinction of land life
●– – –	mass extinction of marine life
＊– – –	glaciation

and bring them to the mouth.

A crucial stage in the development of modern man was the appearance of a new species, *Homo habilis* or 'handy man', in East Africa around 2 million years ago. These may have been the first hominids to make and use stone tools, and probably the first to scavenge for meat as a regular part of their diet. They were followed around 1.5 million years ago by *Homo erectus*, a larger and more intelligent creature, and the first human ancestor to spread beyond the confines of Africa to Europe, China and South-East Asia.

The colonisation of the Old World by *Homo erectus* was a considerable achievement given the environmental conditions of the period. *Homo erectus* and his descendants were able to make use of clothes and artificial shelters. They may also have started to hunt. Most important, however, was their mastery of fire. With more sophisticated tools, a larger brain, and command of fire, *Homo erectus* was able to survive north of the frost line at sites such as Chou-k'ou-tien (Zhoukoudian) near Peking around half a million years ago.

Homo erectus survived for a million years or more, but some time after 500,000 years ago new types of hominid began to develop in Europe and Africa. In Europe, these changes led c.100,000 BC to the appearance of Neanderthal man, named after a skull found in the Neander valley in Germany in 1856. The line of development leading to modern humans, however, was based in Africa. Here, a little over 100,000 years ago, developed the first members of our own species, *Homo sapiens sapiens*: larger-brained creatures, able hunters and gatherers, equipped with sophisticated language and technology. From Africa the new species spread throughout the whole of the territory which had been occupied by *Homo erectus* and its descendants (map 2), and beyond into the hitherto unsettled regions of Australia and the Americas. For a while, Neanderthals hung on in parts of Europe, as the last Ice Age gathered pace; but their days were numbered. By 30,000 years ago, of the many species of hominid which had walked the earth during the past 5 million years of human development, only one, *Homo sapiens sapiens*, was left.

3 Traces of human origins

- ● Australopithecus
- ○ Homo habilis
- ● Homo erectus
- ◗ Homo sapiens (archaic)
- ● Homo sapiens (Neanderthal)
- ○ Homo sapiens (modern)

The Ice Ages

We are well aware today that the earth's climate is not a stable, static phenomenon. Indeed, for at least 14 million years world climate has gradually been cooling. Around 2 million years ago this process intensified, and by 800,000 years ago the earth was in the grip of the first of the great ice ages which were to come and go roughly every 100,000 years, and to dominate human history until the last of them receded only 10,000 years ago.

The ice ages were periods of intense cold in northern and southern latitudes away from the equator. Temperatures fell by up to 15°C, and ice sheets advanced across the frozen wastes of northern Eurasia and North America. As more and more of the earth's water became locked into the growing ice sheets, sea levels fell, and even equatorial regions did not escape the effects of climatic adversity as rainfall diminished, turning half of all the land area between the tropics into desert.

The glaciers advanced and retreated several times, reaching a climax every 100,000 years but also giving way for short periods of 10,000 years or so to more temperate regimes. With each ice advance the plants and animals of the northern hemisphere withdrew before them to warmer latitudes waiting, perhaps several thousand years, for the ice to retreat and allow them to move northwards again. Hominids too such as *Homo erectus* must have migrated with the changing climate.

Yet despite the harshness of the coldest periods, the human species continued to develop during these millennia. It was indeed at this time that the human species spread from its original African homeland to east and south-east Asia and Europe. The mastery of fire and the invention of clothing and shelter were crucial to this achievement, but so were new social and communication skills. The human species as we know it today is the product of the long process of adaptation to the harsh conditions of the ice age.

The final phase of the ice ages began 75,000 years ago with the advance of the Würm glaciers in central Europe and the associated Weichsel and Wisconsin glacier fields in northern Europe and North America. By tying up water on a grand scale these reduced sea levels, and land bridges appeared, linking most of the major land areas and many present-day islands (including the British Isles) into one single continental mass. It was at this time, too, that a new species of human, fully modern *Homo sapiens sapiens*, began to spread from Africa, replacing or interbreeding with existing hominid populations in Europe and Asia. It was thus modern humans that were able to take advantage of the short sea crossing caused by sea-level fall and colonise Australasia in about 50,000 BC. A little later, perhaps as early as 40,000 BC, humans also colonised America (map 2), either by crossing the land bridge which joined the two sides of the Bering Straits at certain periods or by use of boats. With the onset of warmer conditions some 10,000 years ago

rising sea levels cut off these human communities in Australia and the Americas from further contact with Eurasia. Henceforward, these regions pursued their own independent lines of development.

Modern humans were relatively late arrivals in western Europe, replacing earlier Neanderthal populations only around 35,000 years ago. Yet here, as in Australia and South America, the new communities soon developed new levels of cultural expression which still impress us today (map 3). In the Dordogne area of south-west France, in the Pyrenees and in the Cantabrian region of northern Spain, hundreds of caves were decorated with paintings of symbols and animals, sometimes in rich polychrome style.

As hunting techniques and tool technology became more sophisticated, human communities became more and more able to cope with their environment. It was, however, change in the environment itself which was most important in opening up new opportunities. Around 20,000 years ago, the last ice age was at its peak (map 1); ten thousand years later, it was in its closing stages. As temperatures rose, vegetation spread and animals began to recolonise the cold northern wastes. With them went the human hunters and gatherers. By 8000 BC, in certain crucial corners of the world such as Central America and the Near East, people had begun to move beyond their existing resources to investigate new ways of producing food, manipulating plants and animals in the first experiments in farming.

1 The world 20,000 years ago

- coastline 20,000 years ago
- modern coastline
- glacier
- sea ice
- tundra
- temperate steppe
- temperate forest
- tropical forest
- desert
- tropical glacier

FENNOSCANDIAN ICE SHEET
BERINGIA
early settlements in Alaska
CORDILLERAN ICE SHEET
North Sea Lake
mammoth-hunters of S Russian plain
Black Sea Lake
Caspian Sea Lake
painted caves of SW France and N Spain
Mediterranean
Sea of Japan
early settlements of E Japan
Lake Bonneville
arid Sahara
Red Sea
TIBET
Lake Chad
Lake Makgadikgadi
painted rock shelters of S Namibia
SUNDA
SAHEL
GREATER AUSTRALIA
Koonalda Cave flint mine
settlements and painted rock-shelters of SE Australia and Tasmania
TASMANIA

Magnetic pole reversals
epochs   events
BRUNHES NORMAL
MATUYAMA REVERSED
Jaramillo
Olduvai

Temperature fluctuations based on analysis of deep sea cores
0.5
1.0
1.5
2.0
million years ago
no further data available

Climatic changes of the Pleistocene

Inset 2 — The colonisation of the Americas:

Arctic Ocean
Bluefish Cave
c. 40,000 BC?
NORTH AMERICA
Calico Hills
Clovis
Meadowcroft
Atlantic Ocean
Pacific Ocean
Caribbean Sea
SOUTH AMERICA
Pedra Furada
Monte Verde

2 The colonisation of the Americas

land bridge
route of colonisation
major site

GREENLAND ICE SHEET
LAURENTIDE ICE SHEET
Salt
ANDES ICE SHEET
painted rock-shelters of Brazil

Main map — Palaeolithic art in Europe:

Arctic Ocean
Barents Sea
Kara Sea
SIBERIA
R. Lena
R. Yenisey
R. Ob'
R. Irtysh
R. Tobol
Ural Mts
L. Baikal
Buret' Mal'ta
Maininskaya
Bérélékh
Kapovaya
80° 60° 40° 20°
SCANDINAVIA
L. Ladoga
Sungir
R. Ural
R. Volga
Caspian Sea
Gagarino
Kostienki
Khotylevo
Yeliseyevichi   Avdeyevo
Yudinovo   Mezin
Kirillovskaya   Mezhirich'
R. Don
Baltic Sea
R. Vistula
Molodovo
Maszycka
Petřkovice   Předmostí
Brno   Moravany
Dolní Věstonice   Pavlov
Willendorf
North Sea
R. Elbe
R. Oder
Carpathians
R. Danube
Black Sea
BRITISH ISLES
Oberkassel   Gönnersdorf
Goyet   Andernach
Trou Magrite   Verlaine   Vogelherd
Gough's Cave   Mauern
Petersfels   R. Drava
Gouy   Kesslerloch   Schweizerbild
Mayenne Sciences   ALPS
Savignano
Chiozza
Trasimeno
Romanelli
BALKANS
ANATOLIA
Taurus Mts
Cyprus
Crete
Caucasus Mts
R. Dniester
R. Loire
see below
Arene Candide
Grimaldi
Corsica
Sardinia
Levanzo
Sicily
Pyrenees
R. Ebro
Los Casares
La Hoz
Parpalló
Mazouco
El Reguerillo
R. Tagus
Escoural
Ardales
La Pileta
Nerja
Las Palomas
Mediterranean Sea
NORTH AFRICA
Atlas Mts

3 Palaeolithic art in Europe

site location

finds of:

mural art

portable art

female figurines

Lower map — France detail:

R. Loire
R. Rhône
Bay of Biscay
F R A N C E
La Marche   Angles-sur-l'Anglin
Teyjat   Le Placard
Roc de Sers   Montgaudier
Fourneau du Diable   Badegoule
Rouffignac   La Madeleine   Laugerie Haute
Le Gabillou   Lascaux
Pair-non-Pair   Combarelles
Laugerie Basse   Laussel
Bara-Bahau   Cap Blanc
St. Cirq   Bernifal
Le Poisson   Pech-Merle
La Mouthe   La Magdeleine
Font de Gaume   Ebbou
Cougnac   Bruniquel
L'Aldène
La Baume-Latrone
Tito Bustillo   Altamira   R. Adour
Pindal   Castillo   Brassempouy
Candamo   Isturits
Ekain   Gantes-Montespan
Herrerías   Altxerri   Lespugue   Le Mas-d'Azil
Cullalvera   Labastide   Bédeilhac
Chufin   Gargas   Niaux
Santimamiñe   Les Trois Frères
Le Tuc d'Audoubert
Gulf of Lions

From hunting to farming

Somewhere around 8000 BC human communities began to select, breed, domesticate and cultivate various species of plant and animal. This was the beginning of agriculture and is sometimes called the Neolithic or agricultural revolution. In fact, it was a slow and partial process which occurred at different times and speeds in different parts of the world and was never complete, if only because climatic and soil variations precluded agriculture in many areas. The arid zones were the home of mobile pastoralists, who domesticated sheep and horses and colonised the grazing grounds of the steppes, while the densely afforested areas, in northern Europe and elsewhere, were inhabited, as earlier, by hunters. The result, following the spread of agriculture, was a differentiated world economy, with well defined zones, cereal and root-crop cultivation being characteristic of the temperate and tropical regions respectively (map 1).

The transformation from a hunter and fisher to an agriculturalist, and from a migratory to a sedentary life, was a decisive event in world history. The increase in food resources which followed made possible a spectacular growth of human population calculated to have multiplied sixteen times between 8000 and 4000 BC. It also required co-operative effort, particularly after the introduction of irrigation c.5000 BC, leading to the establishment of settled, organised societies, at first villages, then towns and cities. Urban civilisation dates from c.3500 BC, but already before 6000 BC there were 'proto-cities' covering extensive sites (up to 30 acres) at Jericho in the Jordan valley and Çatal Hüyük in Anatolia. Here also there is evidence of long-distance trade.

There is no doubt that agriculture developed independently in different parts of the world, presumably in response to similar stimuli, but the beginnings of cereal cultivation are clearly associated with the Near East. Here, on the remote mountain uplands, were found the wild ancestors of wheat and barley, and the villages where they were first cultivated (c.8000 BC) grew up on the edge of this zone, within the critical rainfall limit of 300 mm (12 ins) a year (map 4). Only with the introduction of irrigation was it possible to extend cultivation into the adjacent dry plains. This occurred during the fifth and fourth millennia BC. At about the same time the ox-drawn plough began to be adopted throughout much of Eurasia, enlisting animal traction to increase the efficiency of farming (map 2). In much of the world, however, hoe agriculture persisted and human muscle power remained the basis of farming until relatively recent times.

Many other parts of the globe contributed their quota at different times to the supply of domesticated plants and animals (map 4). Their diffusion from their original habitat not only supplemented native food resources, but also affected human diet. Rice, which originated in South-East Asia and southern China, passed into the Near East and Mediterranean Europe, where it became a staple foodstuff. The yam and banana, later to be major African food crops, were introduced from Asia during the first millennium BC.

As farming spread, hunting and gathering was increasingly relegated to the more marginal world environments where agriculture was unable to secure a foothold (map 3). The gradual decline of hunters and gatherers can be traced across the centuries, until in recent times their sole surviving representatives have been found only in hot deserts such as the Kalahari and Australia, in the dense rain forests of the Amazon basin, central Africa and South-East Asia, and in the frozen wastes of the Arctic.

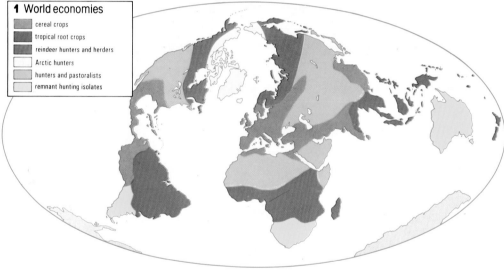

1 World economies
- cereal crops
- tropical root crops
- reindeer hunters and herders
- Arctic hunters
- hunters and pastoralists
- remnant hunting isolates

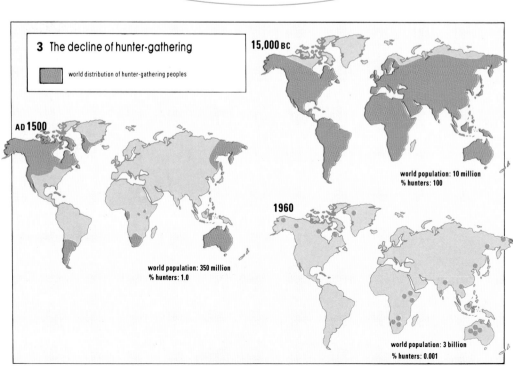

3 The decline of hunter-gathering
- world distribution of hunter-gathering peoples

AD 1500

world population: 350 million
% hunters: 1.0

15,000 BC

world population: 10 million
% hunters: 100

1960

world population: 3 billion
% hunters: 0.001

5 Centres of animal and plant domestication

alfalfa	oats
avocado	olive
banana	peas
barley	peanuts
breadfruit	peppers
cocoa	pineapple
coconut	potato
cotton	rice
cucumber	runner bean
cucurbits	rye
dates	sorghum
finger millet	soya bean
foxtail millet	sunflower
grapes	sweet potato
hemp	tepary bean
lentil	tomato
lima bean	watermelon
maize	wheat
manioc	yam

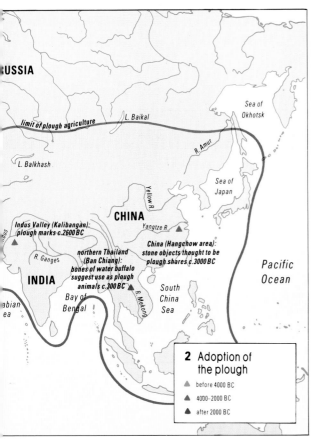

2 Adoption of the plough

▲ before 4000 BC
▲ 4000–2000 BC
▲ after 2000 BC

Indus Valley (Kalibangan): plough marks c.2600 BC

northern Thailand (Ban Chiang): bones of water buffalo suggest use as plough animals c.300 BC

China (Hangchow area): stone objects thought to be plough shares c.3000 BC

limit of plough agriculture

RUSSIA · L. Baikal · Sea of Okhotsk · L. Balkhash · R. Amur · Yellow R. · Sea of Japan · CHINA · Yangtze R. · R. Ganges · INDIA · R. Mekong · South China Sea · Bay of Bengal · Pacific Ocean

4 The agricultural revolution in the Near East

◯ natural distribution of wheat and barley
— southern limit of rain-fed agriculture
● early farming sites 9000–6000 BC
◉ farming villages 6000–4000 BC

Black Sea · Caspian Sea · ANATOLIA · L. Van · L. Urmia · Zawi Chemi · Çayönü · Nineveh · Arpachiyah · Taurus Mts · Tell Halaf · Tell Brak · Hassuna · Jarmo · Zagros Mts · Hacilar · SYRIA · Tell Abu Hureira · Samarra · Tell es-Sawwan · Chuga Mami · Ali Kosh · MESOPOTAMIA · R. Tigris · Cyprus · Khirokitia · Mediterranean Sea · Tell Ramad · Syrian Desert · R. Euphrates · Uruk · Eridu · Ur · Jericho · Dead Sea · EGYPT · Beidha · R. Nile · 30° · 30° · 40°

NORTH-WEST EURASIA · Reindeer · CENTRAL ASIA · Horse · SOUTH-WESTERN STEPPES · Cattle · Pig · SOUTHERN EUROPE · Bactrian Camal · CHINA · NEAR EAST · Yak · HIMALAYAS · INDUS · Ass · Goose · Goat · Sheep · SOUTH-EAST ASIA · Zebu · Pig · Water Buffalo · Chicken · NORTH-EAST AFRICA · WEST AFRICA · SOUTH PACIFIC · LOWLAND SOUTH AMERICA · Atlantic Ocean · Pacific Ocean · Indian Ocean · 80° · 40° · 0° · 60° · 0° · 60° · 120° · 60°

Early cultures of Asia

From an origin in Africa, *Homo erectus* or its close relatives had spread widely through Asia by the Middle Pleistocene period (400–200,000 years ago). It is not possible to establish the precise history of this colonisation process, but it is reasonable to assume that these hominids first reached India, where hand-axes, chopping tools and flakes of the early Stone Age are found not only in the foothills of the Punjab but as far east as southern Bihar and northern Orissa and as far south as Madras (map 1). It was not long before *Homo erectus* also became established in both East and South-East Asia, as shown by skeletal remains from Java and China. Here they remained until replaced some 60,000 years ago by our own fully modern species, *Homo sapiens sapiens*.

Little is known of the development of human societies in this part of the world until the advent of agriculture. At about the same time as farming communities were getting under way in western Asia, the first experiments in agriculture were also being made in East and South Asia. In China, the most important centre of early farming was the Yellow River valley in the north, where crops of millet were raised on the well-drained loess terraces of the river valleys from around 6000 BC (map 2). A little later, rice cultivation spread northwards from its original heartland in South-East Asia, giving a second productive staple crop. The early villages grew and prospered, and new technologies made their appearance: jade-carving, silk-weaving and very high quality pottery production using the fast wheel.

In about 1800 BC the thriving villages and small towns which had developed in northern China gave rise to the first Chinese civilisation. Early dynasties soon gave way to the Shang, who ruled much of the North China plain and parts of the Yangtze valley from the 16th to the 11th century BC (map 4). Great cities developed, notably at Cheng-chou and An-yang, and rulers were given lavish burial in royal tombs.

The first civilisation of South Asia developed in the valley of the Indus river. Again, this was founded on a secure agricultural base which had been developing since c.6000 BC or earlier. Large-scale settlement of the fertile river plain seems to have occurred in the 4th millennium BC, and soon afterwards the first cities appear, notably those of Harappa and Mohenjo-daro (map 5). These were highly-developed cities covering nearly 1,295,000 sq.kms, and surviving for over 1000 years. A standardised system of weights and measures was devised, and trade with the Persian Gulf brought Indus products to the great cities of southern Mesopotamia. Influences from South Asia also reached South-East Asia, where the distinctive Dong Son drums were produced by communities of village farmers from 1500–500 BC (map 3).

The Indus cities were abandoned soon after 2000 BC, overtaken perhaps by environmental change or natural disaster, and it was over 1000 years before cities reappeared in the sub-continent. The focus had by this time shifted to the Ganges, where the historic cities and states of northern India began to form in about 500 BC. By that time China too was divided between a number of major kingdoms, as the unified rule of the Shang and their successors the Chou broke down and fragmented (map 6). Yet despite the divisions, the basic foundations of Chinese and Indian civilisation had been laid.

2 Early Chinese agriculture

- area of loess soil
- redeposited loess
- early millet cultivation
- approximate northern limit of wild rice distribution
- early wet rice cultivation

Chinese settlement:
- ▲ 6000-5000 BC
- ■ 6000-4000 BC
- ● 5000-2500 BC

4 Shang China

- ● cities
- ▬ rich burials
- ▲ oracle bones
- ancient coastline
- ancient river course

6 China under the Western Chou, c.1027-771 BC

- ■ Chou capitals
- the royal domain
- fiefs allocated to Chou royal family
- Shang royal family
- fiefs allocated to other families
- ● major excavated sites

YEN

Gulf of Chihli

Lingyuan

HSING

CH'I

CHIN

CHU'

Hungchao

LU

HAN

CH'U

Icheng

Chün

TENG

TSOU

T'AN

Yellow Sea

LIANG

HSÜN

WEI

Loyang

KUAN

CH'IN

Paochi Fufeng

Loi (11th century onwards)

YEN

Mi Hsian

Lantien

CHIAO

YING

SUNG

HSÜ

Feng (before 1122)

Hao (1122)

Huaiyang

CH'EN

SHEN

FANG TAO

TS'AI

YUNG

TENG

HSI

HUANG

SHU

R. Yangtze

PAO

KU

JO

LIU

T'UNG

HUAN

LÜ

LO

SUI

YÜN

HSIEN

Tantu

WU

Chiangling

CH'U

YANGYUEH

Chichun

Tunhsi

CHOU

CHÜN

YÜEH

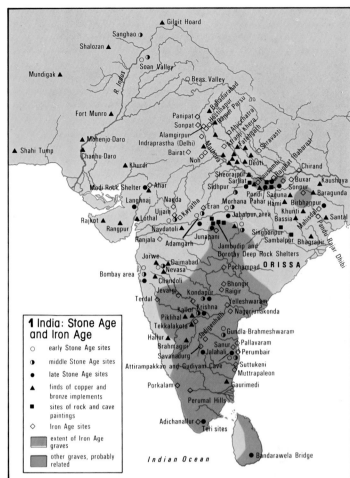

1 India: Stone Age and Iron Age

- ○ early Stone Age sites
- ◑ middle Stone Age sites
- ● late Stone Age sites
- ▲ finds of copper and bronze implements
- ■ sites of rock and cave paintings
- ◇ Iron Age sites
- extent of Iron Age graves
- other graves, probably related

Gilgit Hoard

Sanghao

Shalozan

Soan Valley

R. Indus

Beas Valley

Mundigak

Bahadarabad

Hastinapur Rupar Parsu

Fort Munro

Panipat

Ahichchatra

Atranji Khera

Sravasti

Alamgirpur

Fatehgarh

Mohenjo-Daro

Indraprastha (Delhi)

Shahi Tump

Chanhu-Daro

Bairat

Noh

Rajghat (Banaras)

Chirand

Deoti

Sheorajpur Sarnai

Buxar Kaushaya

Modi Rock Shelter

Ahar

Sidhpur

Pondi Saguna Hami

Sonpur Baragunda

Birbhanpur

Langhnaj

Nagda

Kavatha

Morhana Pahar

Eran

Jabalpur area

Mahisda

Pandu Rajar Dhibi

Ujjain

Bassia

Santal

Rajkot

Lothal

Navdatoli

Junahani

Singhanpur

Sambalpur Bhagrapir

Rangpur

Ranjala

Adamgarh

Jambudip and Dorothy Deep Rock Shelters

Pochampad

ORISSA

Jorwe

Daimabad

Nevasa

Bhongir

Raigir

Bombay area

Chandoli

Jevargi

Kondapur

Yelleshwaram

Terdal

Kallur Krishna

Nagarjunakonda

Pikhlihal

Sanur

Tekkalakota

Indigenhalli

Gundla-Brahmeshwaram

Hallur

Brahmagiri

Savanadurg

Jalahali

Pallavaram

Attirampakkam and Gudiyam Cave

Perumbair

Suttukeni

Porkalam

Muttrapaleon

Gaurimedi

Perumal Hills

Adichanallur

Teri sites

Indian Ocean

Bandarawela Bridge

3 Prehistoric sites in South-East Asia

- Neolithic/Bronze Age settlements
- Dong Son drums
- ● Early Iron Age and urn burial sites

Pacific Ocean

Moluccas

New Guinea

Banda Sea

Timor Sea

5 The Indus civilisations of Harappa and Mohenjo-Daro

- ○ pre-Harappan settlements
- principal sites of Harappan civilisation

34°

Mundigak

R. Zhob

R. Jhelum

R. Chenab

Periano Ghundai

R. Ravi

R. Beas

Kili Ghul Mohammad

Rana Ghundai

Harappa

Punjab

(Kojla Nihang Khan)

Damb Sadaat

Quetta

R. Sutlej

Chak Purbane Syal

Rupar

30°

Togau

Dabarkot

R. Indus

Alamgirpur

Siah Damb

Sandhanawala

Anjira

Judeirjo-Daro

Kalibanga

Nal

Rohri

Kotasur

11 sites in Bahawalpur State

Baluchistan

Mehi

Mohenjo-Daro

Diji-li-Takri

Nindowari

Kot Diji

Rajasthan

Nokjo Shahdinzai

Lohumjo-Daro

Nundara

Pandi Wahi

Lohri

Thar (Indian) Desert

Shahi Tump

Mitha Deheno

Ali Murad

Kulli

Ghazi Shah

Damb Buthi

Sotka-Koh

Gorandi

Chanhu-Daro

26°

Dhal

Amri

Sutkagen-Dor

Karchat

Shahjo-Kotiro

Bala-Kot

Kotrash

Othmanto Buthi

Sind

Allahdino

Tharro

Arabian Sea

Desalpur

22°

Amara

Halar

Lothal

R. Narmada

Rojadi

Rangpur

Mehgam

Kinnarkheda

Telod

Bhagatrav

Somnath

R. Tapti

Gulf of Cambay

64°

68°

72°

76°

9

Prehistoric Africa and Australasia

Climatic change, between 5–6000 years ago, profoundly influenced the early history of Africa and Australasia. North Africa developed in close association with western Asia, and by 3000 BC an advanced civilisation was established in Egypt. But Africa south of the equator, almost certainly the original home of humans, was cut off from the mainstream for centuries by the desiccation of the Sahara. Similar changes occurred in Australia which had been populated during the late Pleistocene ice age via the land bridge from New Guinea (page 4). Here the rise of the sea level drowned large areas of coastal lowland and severed the land link with New Guinea. The Australasian continent developed thenceforth in geographical isolation. The colonisation of the islands of Melanesia occurred considerably later, when settlers from New Guinea, associated with the distinctive Lapita pottery, reached Fiji (c.1300 BC) and then made their way into Polynesia via Tonga and Samoa, reaching the Marquesas Islands c.AD 300 (map 2). From here they spread north to Hawaii (c.AD 800) and south-west via the Cook Islands to New Zealand between 850 and 1100 (map 3).

Geographical isolation was an important factor in shaping the cultures of southern Africa and of Oceania. In much of Australia the aborigines remained hunters and gatherers and there was no use of iron, but they were prolific in their decoration of rock shelters with deeply symbolic designs. Elsewhere in Oceania, notably in New Zealand, a mixed hunting-farming society developed and settlement spread inland. But population remained small, about 300,000 in Australia and 100,000 in New Zealand when the Europeans arrived. The isolation of southern Africa was never so complete. In East Africa settlers spread down the Rift Valley from Ethiopia during the first millennium BC, and trans-Saharan trade increased in importance after the introduction of the camel from Asia c.100 BC (map 1).This facilitated the spread of iron tools and weapons, introduced in the north by Greeks and Carthaginians in the eighth and seventh centuries. Aided by the new iron technology, Bantu-speaking farmers and cattle-herdsmen began to colonise southern Africa in the early centuries AD. By the thirteenth century powerful Bantu chiefdoms had emerged, such as that centred on the Great Zimbabwe enclosure, cattle-raising communities already engaged in trade when the Portuguese arrived at the close of the fifteenth century.

3 The settlement of New Zealand

☐ areas of early settlement AD 850-1100

▨ areas of concentrated coastal settlement AD 1100-1300

▨ inland areas intensively exploited AD 1100-1300

1 Africa: the Stone Age to the Iron Age

- ▲ bone harpoon site
- area of Saharan rock painting c.6000–1000 BC
- ▲ early agricultural site
- limits of cattle domestication
- ○ site of cattle domestication
- area of megalithic monuments and tombs
- ➤ spread of iron   ▲ early iron-working site

major Iron Age sites
- ◐ Mediterranean
- ◐ sub-Sahara
- ◑ Sudan-Ethiopia
- area of southern African rock paintings, from 1000 BC
- ▽ late Stone Age hunters and herders of southern Africa

Mediterranean Sea

N. African megaliths 2nd and 1st millennium BC

Utica
Carthage
Capeletti

Greek and Phoenician colonists

Cyrene

Leptis (Homs)

PHOENICIA

Naucratis
Sais
Merimbe *4200 BC*
Memphis
Fayum *4300 BC*
EGYPT
Thebes

Red Sea

Atlas Mts
Sahara Desert

4500 BC

Meniet
Adrar Tiouiyne
Immidir
Uan Muhaggiag
Adrar Bous
Arlit
Hoggar Massif
Tassili Massif

3000 BC

Tibesti Massif

Jebel 'Uweinat

NUBIA
iron
Nuri
Napata
Shaheinab *3200 BC*
Meroe *500 BC*
KINGDOM OF MEROE 900 BC–AD 400
Kadero
Kadero
Adulis
Axum

2000 BC

Air
Agadez
copper working in 2nd millennium BC

Karkarchinkat
Gao

1500 BC

Ennedi

Darfur

Jebel Moya

KINGDOM OF AXUM AD 100–1000

White Nile
Blue Nile

iron

Sahel

Jenne-jeno
proto-urban settlement by 1st century AD

R. Niger

Daima

Kintampo
Ntereso *1400 BC*
Jos Plateau
Nok
Taruga *440 BC*
R. Benue
Ife
Atwetwebooso
Igbo Ukwu
shrines AD 840

1500 BC

500 BC

iron and cattle

Ethiopian Highlands

Ethiopian megaliths 1st and 2nd millennium AD
Ileret

Arab traders and colonists

possible spread of cultivation to lower Congo Basin 1st millennium BC

Urewe Iron Age groups

Rift Valley

Indian Ocean

R. Congo

Western Stream Iron Age sites

Urewe
Lake Victoria
Elmenteita
Crescent Is.
Narosura
Manda

Katuruka 5th century BC

East African 'pastoral neolithic' sites

Kwale

ports involved in Indian Ocean trade by 8th century AD. SE Asian foodstuffs (bananas, taro) introduced

Funa River *270 BC*

Lake Tanganyika

Kilwa

Eastern Stream Iron Age sites

iron and cattle

2 Early settlement in the South Seas

- ψ prehistoric rock art

The Lapita potters:
- Lapita pottery area
- • sites with Lapita pottery
- ➤ settlement of Eastern Polynesia 150 BC–AD 1000

Kalambo

Sanga
late 1st millennium AD cemetery of 144 graves

Lake Nyasa

R. Ruvuma

Madagascar
Indonesian colonists

AD 500

Lubusi

iron and cattle

Kamnama

Nkope

Kapwirimbe
Kalundu
Ziwa
Gokomere
Zimbabwe
Mabueni
Malapati

R. Zambezi

iron and cattle

Kalahari Desert

Phalaborwa

AD 1000

Castle Cavern
Shongweni
Blackburn

domestic sheep obtained by 1st century AD, perhaps from Iron Age source

Zaayfontein
Wilton
Bonteberg
Nelson Bay
Die Kelders

Drakensberg Mts

R. Orange

u Archipelago
Pitcairn I.
Easter I.
A

Peoples and cultures of the Americas

America, like Australia (page 10), was colonised from Asia during the last Ice Age more than 10,000 years ago, and like Australia was later cut off from the Old World by the melting of the ice and the rise of the sea level which submerged the land bridge across the Bering Strait (page 4). Unlike the Australian aborigines, however, who never progressed beyond a Stone Age hunting and gathering culture, geographic isolation did not prevent the American Indians from developing independently a high level of civilisation, based on agriculture (particularly the cultivation of maize), mining (particularly obsidian for tools and weapons), pottery manufacture and gold, silver and copper working. It was a civilisation distinguished not only by magnificent art and remarkable mathematical and astronomical skills, but also by monumental building on a grand scale. In its prime, around AD 600, the city of Teotihuacán in the basin of Mexico covered 20 sq. km (8 sq. miles) and had a population of 125,000.

The first civilisations arose in the climatically favourable regions of Mesoamerica and the central Andes, where maize farming, permitting a rapid increase in population, became widespread from c. 1500 BC. Between 800 and 500 BC the Olmecs on the Gulf of Mexico, the Zapotecs at Monte Albán, and the inhabitants of Chavín in Peru had developed complex societies with populations numbering tens of thousands, possibly a professional priesthood, and several social ranks including craftsmen and traders. Mesoamerica and the central Andes remained the main centres of civilisation, but the diffusion of agriculture and growing commercial exchanges soon affected other regions. In North America the introduction of maize, beans and squashes from Mexico initiated a period of rapid development between 300 BC and AD 550. Its centre was the Hopewell territory in Illinois and Ohio, but trading contacts (mainly for precious metals) extended its influence as far as Florida and the Rockies (map 3). In South America a number of separate centres, each with its own distinctive artistic style, developed in the Andes (map 4), and were fused after AD 600 into the empires of Tiahuanaco and Huari (map 5). But this precarious unity broke down after AD 800 and it was not until the fifteenth century under the Incas that Peru was once again united (page 62).

In Mesoamerica, the early Olmec and Zapotec civilisations were complemented by new influences, including the Maya in Yucatán from the fourth century BC, then the Toltecs in the ninth century and finally the Aztecs in the thirteenth century. The classic period of Maya civilisation falls between AD 300 and AD 900; but influences radiating from Teotihuacán were strong (map 2), and Maya civilisation, like all the other civilisations of the classical period, was essentially a variant of a common Mesoamerican culture pattern. Internecine warfare appears to have weakened these civilisations and left them prey to invaders or local instability. Teotihuacán was destroyed c. 750. Monte Albán allowed to go to ruin during the tenth century, and Maya civilisation collapsed between AD 800 and 900.

For all their brilliant architectural and artistic achievements, the civilisations of Mesoamerica and the Andes account for only a small area of the Americas taken as a whole (map 1). Climatic variation alone dictated disparate ways of life. Particularly in the far north and far south, where conditions were too harsh for farming, the small nomadic populations depended on hunting and fishing. Climate was also a determining factor for the desert gatherers in the interior. The continent the Europeans encountered when they arrived in the sixteenth century was at widely different levels of development; but even the simpler societies had adapted themselves to the environment and its requirements.

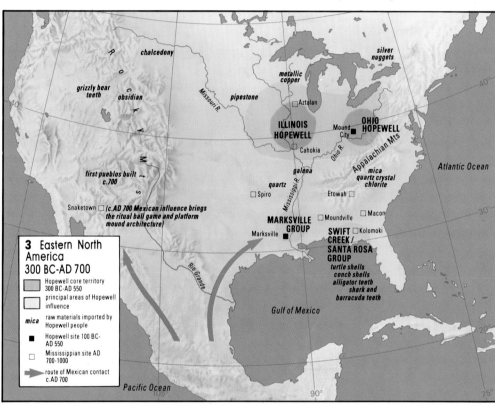

3 Eastern North America 300 BC–AD 700

Hopewell core territory 300 BC–AD 550

principal areas of Hopewell influence

mica raw materials imported by Hopewell people

■ Hopewell site 100 BC–AD 550

□ Mississippian site AD 700–1000

→ route of Mexican contact c.AD 700

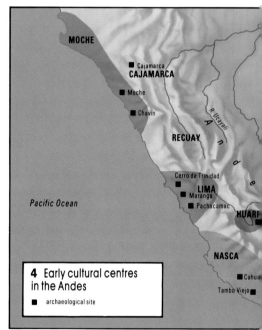

4 Early cultural centres in the Andes

■ archaeological site

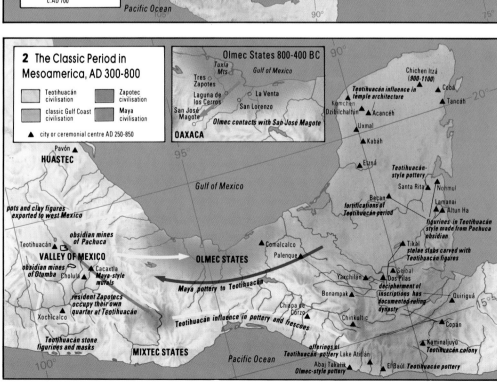

2 The Classic Period in Mesoamerica, AD 300–800

Teotihuacán civilisation

Zapotec civilisation

classic Gulf Coast civilisation

Maya civilisation

▲ city or ceremonial centre AD 250–850

Olmec States 800–400 BC

Olmec contacts with San José Magote

5 The empires of Tiahuanaco and Huari, AD 600–800

■ archaeological site

1 American peoples and cultures, c. AD 500

- farming peoples
- chiefdoms
- civilised states
- hunters and gatherers
- ■ archaeological site

ARCTIC LITTORAL HUNTERS

HUNTERS OF THE SUB-ARCTIC FOREST

(ESKIMO)

L'Anse aux Meadows
(Norse colony, founded by Icelanders AD 1001 but soon abandoned)

PLATEAU
FISHERMEN
PLANT GATHERERS
HUNTERS

Huff Village

PLAINS HUNTERS
farming introduced along river valleys from eastern woodlands

Simonsen

Hopewell

Hogup Cave
Danger Cave

FISHERMEN
MONTANE
GATHERERS

DESERT
GATHERERS

S.W.
FARMERS

PUEBLO
INDIANS

Tyuonyi

Pueblo Bonito

WOODLAND
FARMERS

Poverty Point   Hardaway

Etowah

DESERT
GATHERERS
HUNTERS

DESERT
GATHERERS

FISHERMEN
SHELLFISH
COLLECTORS

Gulf of Mexico

Atlantic Ocean

El Tajin
Teotihuacan
Monte Albán

MESOAMERICAN
CIVILISATION

MAYA

Tikal

CARIBBEAN
FARMERS

Caribbean Sea

MAIZE AND MANIOC
CULTIVATORS OF
CARIBBEAN LOWLANDS

SAVANNAH
FARMERS

NORTH
ANDEAN
CHIEFDOMS

San Agustín

FARMING TRIBES
(manioc cultivators)
of the Amazon Rain Forest

Teso dos Bichos

Pacific Ocean

Moche
Chavin
Las Haldas
La Florida
Huari
Nasca

CENTRAL
ANDEAN
CIVILISATION

SAVANNAH
FARMERS

Tiahuanaco

Pedra Furada

about AD 500 farming introduced from Amazon Basin into Brazilian forest and savannah

immigration of Tupi-Guarani tribes

HUNTERS
OF THE
CHACO
SAVANNAH

GRASSLAND
STEPPE HUNTERS

Monte Verde

MARITIME
HUNTERS

SHELLFISH
COLLECTORS

Asia

Bering Strait

WARU

Lake
Titicaca

TIAHUANACO

Tiahuanaco

Lake
Poopó

ATACAMEÑO

Piquillacta

Lake
Titicaca

Tiahuanaco

TIAHUANACO EMPIRE

Lake
Poopó

The development of Europe, 6000-300BC

It was only after farming had been established in the Near East for several hundred years that it first spread westwards to Europe. The earliest European agriculturalists settled in farming villages on the plains of Thessaly and Crete c.6000 BC (map 1). The crops of wheat and barley which these communities grew were of Near Eastern type, and they relied heavily on the Near Eastern animal domesticates sheep and goat. As farming spread north and west into temperate Europe, however, major adjustments were necessary. New types of wheat and barley replaced those of Greece and the Near East, and cattle and pig became the dominant species of livestock in forested parts of central, western and northern Europe in place of sheep and goat.

The new farming technology, including not only domesticated species of plants and animals but also pottery and polished stone tools, spread rapidly across Europe in the 6th and 5th millennia BC, reaching Britain and Denmark by 4000 BC. In the centuries of consolidation which followed, the early farmers of western and northern Europe built great burial mounds with megalithic chambers in which dozens if not hundreds of dead bodies were deposited. They also raised circles of standing stones (map 3).

By this time a new technology was spreading across Europe, supplementing the stone tools of the previous centuries: metallurgy (map 2). South-east Europe became an important centre of gold and copper-working as early as 4500 BC. By 2500 BC it had become common to alloy the copper with tin to produce bronze, an alloy of greater hardness, thus initiating the period known as the Bronze Age. The need to obtain access to the raw materials copper and tin led to the development of extensive trade networks along which other materials also travelled, such as the Baltic amber which is found as far afield as Mycenae (map 4).

Around 1200 BC a more closely articulated political organisation began to emerge, centred upon hillforts built to house and defend a warrior-aristocracy. The upper Rhine/upper Danube became an important core area where a distinctive Celtic culture emerged in the 1st millennium BC (map 5). Ironworking was introduced c.1000–700 BC, which together with population growth fuelled a period of Celtic expansion in the La Tène period (from 480 BC). Contact with the Mediterranean world stimulated Celtic civilisation, but it also prepared the way for Caesar's campaigns. Thus it was that by 50 BC most of the western Celtic world was under Roman control.

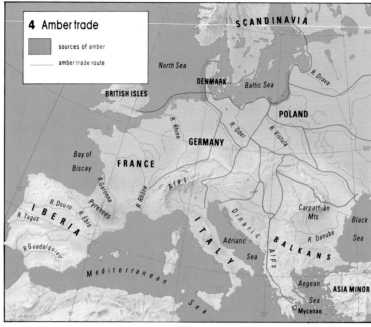

4 Amber trade
- sources of amber
- amber trade route

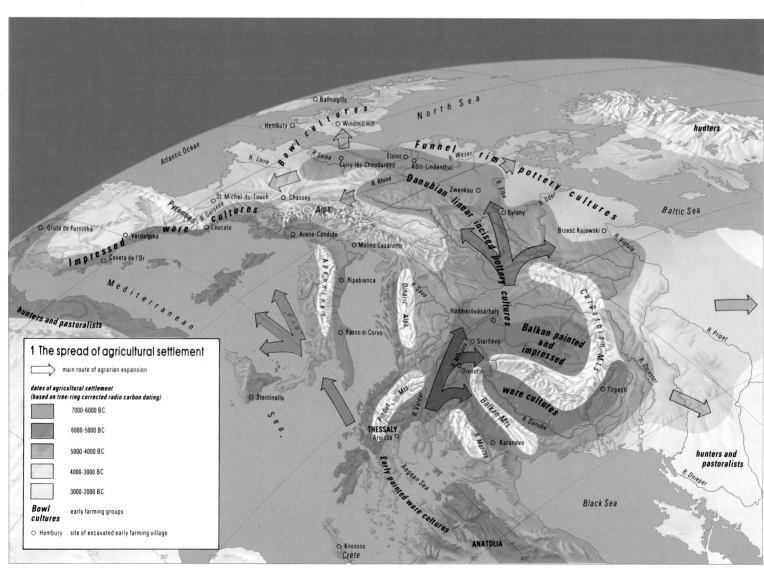

1 The spread of agricultural settlement

- main route of agrarian expansion

dates of agricultural settlement (based on tree-ring corrected radio carbon dating)
- 7000-6000 BC
- 6000-5000 BC
- 5000-4000 BC
- 4000-3000 BC
- 3000-2000 BC

Bowl cultures — early farming groups

○ Hembury — site of excavated early farming village

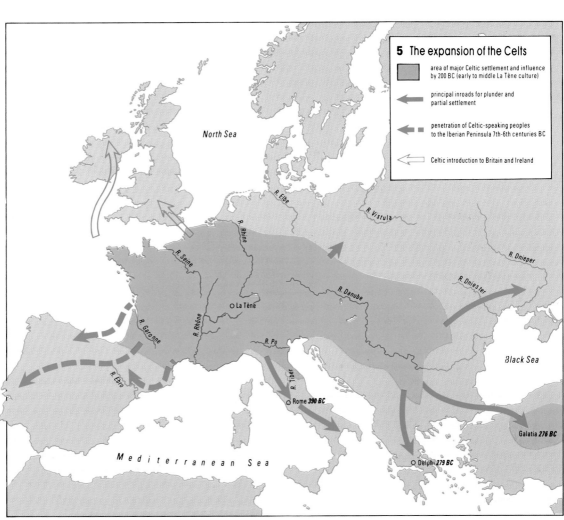

5 The expansion of the Celts

3 Megalithic monuments

2 The introduction of metallurgy to Europe

Egypt and Mesopotamia
3500-1600BC

The rise of the great riverine civilisations in the fertile valleys of the Nile in Egypt, the Euphrates and Tigris in Mesopotamia, and the Indus valley in north-west India (map 1), was a decisive stage in the development of human society. The springboard for this development was provided by the prosperous farming communities which had grown up in the hill country around the foothills of the Fertile Crescent from 8000 BC. Some of these settlements, such as Jericho and Catal Hüyük, had been of considerable size and were already small towns rather than mere villages. But the alluvial valleys of Egypt and Mesopotamia offered far greater potential, and it was here, around 3500 BC, that cities and city-states distinguished by size, planning, architecture and fortifications first appeared. It was here also, because of the need for accounting procedures in the collection and distribution of agricultural produce, that writing was first invented.

The early cities of Egypt and Mesopotamia were entirely dependent on the agricultural productivity of the alluvial plains. Water was the key to life in these semi-arid environments. In Egypt, the River Nile did most of the work, its annual flood bringing not only water but a deposit of rich alluvial silt to the farmlands of the valley and delta. In Mesopotamia, the rivers Tigris and Euphrates provided the water but to bring it to the fields an extensive network of irrigation canals was created.

Because of geographical factors political unification came early to Egypt. It was King Menes of Upper (southern) Egypt who in c.3100 BC conquered the delta kingdoms and founded a new capital at Memphis, which remained the administrative centre of Egypt for almost 2000 years. During the Old Kingdom period (map 3) (2685–2180 BC) Egyptian rulers built a series of massive pyramid-tombs along the desert edge opposite Memphis which emphasised their power and prestige and are among the greatest constructions of their age. Despite a period of setback in the political anarchy of the First Intermediate Period, the Egyptian state was sufficiently firmly established to recover and entered a second period of impressive cultural achievement under the able rulers of the Middle Kingdom (2040–1783 BC).

In Mesopotamia the basic political pattern until the second half of the third millennium BC remained one of city states, with a shifting hegemony between them but no centralised control. The Sumerians who built these cities (map 2) were also responsible for the invention of writing, at first pictographic but soon developing into the cuneiform script used on clay tablets and in inscriptions on stone. An important factor in Mesopotamian economic organisation was the need to acquire scarce resources. Southern Mesopotamia lacked stone, metals and timber, which led the Sumerians to exploit the Zagros mountains and to develop trading relations with Iran and Asia Minor. Egypt was more self-sufficient, but here also the need for timber stimulated trade with Syria, and Syria served as a link between Egypt and Mesopotamia.

The first significant attempt at empire in Mesopotamia came when Sargon (2371–16 BC), of Akkadian immigrant descent, founded the city of Agade (site uncertain) and made it his task to bring the old Sumerian city states under centralised control (map 4). From this base he and his successors, notably his grandson, Naram-Sin (2291–55 BC), undertook conquests from Elam in south-west Iran to Syria, including the recently excavated city of Ebla, and possibly also into southeastern Asia Minor. Motivated by trade, this expansion extended sea-links which reached as far east as the Indus valley.

Sargon's empire collapsed as a result of internal stresses and the invasion of hillmen from the central Zagros, and was followed by a revival of the Sumerian city-state system, in which Ur emerged as the dominant element. This was a highly bureaucratic empire, more stable than that of Agade; but it collapsed in turn (c.2000 BC) under the pressure of a new wave of Semitic invaders, the Amorites from the Syrian desert, who established control over the whole region from Syria to southern Mesopotamia, where they set up a number of small kingdoms, among which Assyria and Babylon eventually won pre-eminence. The former emerged under the Amorite Shamshi-Adad I (1813–1781 BC), who annexed the kingdom of Mari on the middle Euphrates and formed a powerful state extending from the Zagros mountains to the border of the Anatolian plateau. But the pre-eminence of Assyria was short-lived, and after Shamshi-Adad's death its place was taken by Babylon under Hammurabi (1792–50 BC). By the seventeenth century BC a new power centre was developing further north, in Anatolia, where the Hittites set up a kingdom with its capital at Hattushash. After 1650 BC they began to spread southwards and in 1595 they sacked Babylon. In the dislocation which ensued the first Babylonian dynasty collapsed; but the ideal of a single south Mesopotamian kingdom with Babylon as its capital, survived as Hammurabi's enduring legacy.

1 The spread of civilisation

centres of urban life

trading area with secondary urban centres

main trade routes of urban zone

○ early cities

principal traded commodities

ℭ copper   obsidian   ivory

grain   pearls   textiles

lapis lazuli   tin   silver

carnelian   timber   gold

Malyan

P E R S I A

Persian Gulf

28°

ancient coastline c.5000 BC

D e s e r t

Jr
Eridu
Ubaid

2 Sumerian Mesopotamia 2500-2000 BC

	fertile area
	marsh area

- - - - irrigation and ancient water courses
● city or other important site
▲ important temple
—— trade route

Mediterranean Sea

ancient coastline

Delta

LOWER EGYPT

30°

Abu Rawash ▲   ● Heliopolis
Giza ▲   ▲ Zawiyet el-Aryan
Abu Sir ▲ ● Memphis
■ ● Saqqara
● Dahshur
Faiyum Basin   ▲ ▲ Maidum
Seila ▲

S i n a i

Gulf of Suez

▲ Zawiyet el-Amwat

Bahariya Oasis

Eastern Desert

▲ Dara

R. Nile

Red Sea Hills

Red Sea

Western   Desert

Dakhla Oasis

■ ● Abydus   ▲ Tukh   ● ■ Naqada

Kharga Oasis

El-Kab
Hieraconpolis ● ■
El-Kula ▲ ● Edfu

U P P E R   E G Y P T

● Elephantine

1st cataract

Nubian Desert

3 Old Kingdom Egypt c.3000-2000 BC

● town or city c.3250-2000 BC
■ royal tomb c.3250-2650 BC
▲ pyramid c.2650-2000 BC

	cultivable land

30°
● Buhen
— *2nd cataract*

40°   50°

30°

4 Early empires of Mesopotamia

—— early Sumerian settlement
—— empire of Agade c.2360-2230 BC
—— III Ur empire c.2112-2004 BC
—— empire of Hammurabi c.1792-1750 BC

Black   Sea

C a u c a s u s   M t s

R. Cyrus

Caspian

A N A T O L I A

Ankara   ○ Hattushash
○   **H I T T I T E S**
○ Gordium   *R. Halys*   ○ Kanesh
○ Kayseri

Sea

ASIA MINOR

○ Malazgirt

Lake Van

E l b u r z   M t s

○ Konya
T a u r u s   M t s
C I L I C I A   ○ Tarsus
○ Karaman

○ Lake Urmia

○ Nusaybin
Catchemish ○   ○ Nineveh
○ Chagar Bazar   ○ Rawandiz

○ Hamadan

○ Tepe Hisar

○ Aleppo
○ Ebla
Ugarit ○   *R. Euphrates*

○ Arbailu

S Y R I A   ○ Ashur
R. Tigris

M E S O P O T A M I A

○ Sialk

○ Neyshabur

Mediterranean Sea
○ Byblos
A M O R I T E S
○ Qatna   ○ Palmyra
Mari ○

Eshnunna ○

○ Kermanshah

I r a n i a n   P l a t e a u

○ Tyre

Hit ○
Sinpar ○   ○ Der
Agade ○

○ Susa

Z a g r o s   M t s

E L A M

○ Gaza

Babylon ○
Kish ○   ○ Nippur
Umma ○
Uruk ○
Ur ○
Eridu ○

30°

EGYPT

Persian Gulf

The first civilisations of Europe
3000-600BC

The earliest civilisations in the western world arose in western Asia and the Nile valley in the fourth millennium BC, but within two thousand years new civilisations, distinctively different in character, had appeared around the shores of the Aegean in Crete, Greece, and western Asia Minor.

The first European civilisation was that of Minoan Crete, based on elaborate palaces which were both the seats of rulers and the centres of a bureaucratic administration. The most famous of the Minoan palaces is that of Knossos in northern Crete, in later Greek legend the home of King Minos. Cretan civilisation reached a level of considerable sophistication in the middle of the second millennium BC. The palaces were decorated with colourful frescoes and equipped with elaborate sanitary and drainage systems. Cretan traders visited Egypt, and spread Minoan influence among the Aegean islands. Bureaucracy flourished with the adoption of writing in around 1600 BC, using the locally-invented Linear A script. With a powerful fleet giving security at sea, the development of Minoan civilisation appears to have been interrupted only by the recurrent earthquakes of the region.

The development of civilisation on the Greek mainland owed something to contact with Crete but was nonetheless a largely independent process. Soon after 1600 BC rich graves make their appearance at important centres such as Mycenae, with sumptuous offerings of gold and jewellery, testifying to the rise of a wealthy and powerful artistocracy. These warlike rulers built themselves fortified palaces and drove to battle in horse-drawn chariots. The Mycenaeans were not only warriors, however, but also cultivated the arts and became successful traders whose products are found throughout the east and central Mediterranean (map 2).

In the fifteenth century BC the Mycenaeans conquered Minoan Crete and became the principal political and military power in the Aegean (map 1). They adapted the Minoan Linear A script and carried their modified version, Linear B, back to the mainland where it was used in the administration of their own kingdoms. Within two hundred years their ambitions had stretched still further to the coast of Asia Minor. The legend of the Trojan war is generally thought to be a memory of a successful Mycenaean campaign of c.1250 BC against a rival power, the city of Troy, strategically situated at the mouth of the Dardenelles, controlling access to the Black Sea.

The Trojan war, if indeed it really happened, must have been the final fling of the Mycenaean warlords. By 1200 BC, most of their palaces were in ruins, overthrown perhaps by civil strife, perhaps by piracy and a rebellious peasantry. With the demise of the Mycenaean kingdoms Greece entered a Dark Age which lasted some 400 years. It was only in the eighth century BC that trade and city life began to recover. The recovery was rapid, however, and two centuries later Greek colonies had been established all along the northern Mediterranean and Black Sea coasts (map 4). Writing was re-introduced, using an alphabetic script adapted from the Phoenician, and new styles of sculpture, architecture and vase-painting developed. Yet while sharing a common language and culture the Greek world of the eighth century was divided between hundreds of independent city-states, and was to remain so throughout the Classical age of the fifth and fourth centuries BC until conquered and united by Philip of Macedon in 338 BC.

3 Post-Mycenaean Greece, c.1150-950 BC

- Ionians
- Dorians
- Aeolians
- North Dorians
- Arcadians
- → Achaeans to Cyprus c. 1150 BC
- → Ionian migration c. 950 BC

2 Mycenaean trade, 1500-1150 BC

exports from the Aegean and Cyclades
- spondylus shells (Aegean)
- odsidian (Melos)
- emery (Naxos)
- silver (Cyclades)
- swords and daggers

exports from Crete
- timber
- woven wool textiles
- daggers (before 1500 BC)
- stone lamps, and vases
- fine pottery (before 1450 BC)
- metal vases (before 1450 BC)

exports from Greek mainland
- fine pottery (after 1500 BC)
- metal vases (after 1500 BC)
- Mycenaean world
- trade routes
- imports to the Aegean

1 The Aegean, 2500-1200 BC

- frontiers of Mycenaean world c.1300 BC
- ⊛ major Mycenaean palaces (c.1500-1200 BC)
- ⊡ major Cretan palaces
- ▪ smaller Cretan palaces
- ● other important settlements
- ○ finds of Linear A tablets
- ○ finds of Linear B tablets

THRACE

MACEDONIA

Troy

ANATOLIA

Lesbos

Mt Olympus

Scyros

Aegean Sea

Chios

Corcyra

Leucas

Ithaca

Iolcus

Pevkakia

Samos

Cirrha   Orchomenus

Gla   Thebes   Levkandi

Evtresis

Ayia

Zacynthus

Athens   Irini   Delos   Miletus

Ceos   Khalandriani

Mycenae

Lerna   Tiryns   Syros   Naxos

PELOPONNESE

Sparta

Pylos   Melos   Phylakopi

Trianda

Mediterranean Sea   Thera   Rhodes

Cythera   Akrotiri

Kastri   Carpathos

CRETE

Khania   Katsamba Amnisos

Monastiraki   Nirou Khani

Knossos   Arkhanes Pseira Mokhlos Palaiokastro

White Mountains   Mallia Gournia

Kanli Kastelli   Vasiliki   Zakro

Ayia Triadha Phaistos Pyrgos Mirtos

4 Greek colonisation, 750-550 BC

- extent of Greece 750 BC
- coast under Greek influence (approximate)
- coast under Phoenician influence

- ◉ Greek parent state or region
- ◎ Ionian colony
- ▲ Achaean colony
- ▼ Aeolian colony
- ● Dorian colony founded by Corinth
- ○ Dorian colony founded by Thera and Rhodes
- ⊗ Dorian colony founded by Megara or Sparta
- ⊙ other Greek colonies
- ⊞ Etruscan city
- ☐ Punic or Phoenician city
- ■ Philistine city

R. Dnieper

Tanais

Sarmatians

Scythians

Olbia   Phanagoria

Panticapaeum

COLCHIS

Ophiusa   Theodosia   Pityus   Dioscurias

Chersonesus   Phasis

Black Sea

Celts

Etruscans   Istrus   Trapezus

R. Danube   Tomi

Callatis   Cromna Sinope

R. Rhone   Odessus Tieum Sesamus Cytorus Amisus Cotyora

Herculis Monoeci   Cruni   PAPHLAGONIA   PONTUS

Nicaea   Mesembria

Antipolis   Volaterrae Arretium Apollonia

Massilia   Byzantium Chalcedon BITHYNIA

Agathe Populonia Cortona   THRACE Selymbria Astacus

Olbia Athenopolis Ilva Volsini   Abdera Aenus Perinthus Heraclea Pontica

Aphrodisias Vetulonia Volci ITALY MACEDONIA Heraeumteichos Dascylium

Emporiae   Tarquinii Caere   Apollonia Torone Lampsacus Cyzicus PHRYGIA

CORSICA Alalia   Potidaea   Thasos Sestus Abydus ASIA MINOR

Tarraco   Mende   Assus   CILICIA

Cumae Neapolis Posidonia   Lesbos   Mallus

Pithecusa Elea   Tarentum   MYSIA   Soli

SARDINIA MAGNA GRAECIA Callipolis Phocaea Aspendus Side

Saguntum   Sybaris   GREECE LYDIA PAMPHYLIA Celenderis

BALEARIC ISLANDS   Croton   Chalcis Samos Miletus CARIA Coracesium Nagidus

Mago   Hipponium Scylacium   Eretria   LYCIA   Salamis

Panormus Lipara   Corcyra Megara Xanthus Phaselis CYPRUS Citium

Hemeroskopeion Rhegium   Leucas Locris Athens Patara Idalium

Lilybaeum Himera Locri   Achaea Megara   Amathus

Selinus Messana   Corinth Rhodes   Paphos Curium

Naxos   PELOPONNESE   Aradus

Acragas Gela Megara-Hyblaea   Byblos

SICILY   Syracuse   Sidon

Camarina   Tyre PHOENICIA

Hippo Zarytus MALTA

Utica   Thera   Joppa

Carthage   CRETE   Ashdod

Hippo Regius   Ascalon Gath

Hadrumetum   Gaza Gerar

Thapsus

NUMIDIA   Mediterranean Sea

Thenae   Syrtis Minor   Cyrene Apollonia   Naucratis

Tauchira Barca

Sabrata Oea Leptis   Euhesperides EGYPT

TRIPOLIS   Syrtis Major   R. Nile

19

Near Eastern empires, 1600-330BC

Since the third millennium BC the rich lands of the Fertile Crescent had been subject to periodic invasion by warlike but less prosperous peoples from adjoining steppes and mountains, jealous of their civilisation and greedy for their riches. Egypt alone was sheltered by the desert; but even Egypt fell prey about 1730 BC to an Asiatic people known as the Hyksos, who conquered the Delta and the Nile valley as far as Cusae, and ruled there until 1567 BC. But the Hyksos occupation stimulated a great revival and, under the XVIIIth dynasty (1570–1320 BC), a policy of expansion was initiated to preclude any further occupation. Egypt advanced through Palestine into Syria and created an empire which extended almost to the Euphrates for the next four hundred years.

Egyptian control over Syria and Palestine may in part have been an attempt to shield the Nile valley from further invasions, but it in fact brought it directly into conflict with the Hittites of Asia Minor and the Mitannians of north-central Syria (map 1). In the fourteenth century BC the Hittites defeated Mitanni, which ceased to be a major actor in the struggle for the Levant. Egyptian power remained strong, however, and after the drawn battle of Kadesh in 1279 BC Hittites and Egyptians agreed to respect each other's sphere of influence.

The Egyptian pharaohs channelled the profits of empire into vast building programmes, such as the so-called 'Colossi of Memnon' built by Amenhotep III at Thebes (1391–1353 BC) or the massive rock-cut temple at Abu Simbel created by Ramesses II (1290–1224 BC). Memphis remained the administrative capital, but the power of Thebes as the religious centre of Egypt steadily grew.

The balance of power between Egyptians and Hittites in the Levant did not last long after Kadesh, since the Hittite empire collapsed around 1200 BC under internal pressure and attacks by their northern neighbours and by seaborne invaders – the so-called 'peoples of the sea'. Egypt successfully fought off similar attacks, but only with the loss of its Levantine possessions. Into the gap created by the decline of the Hittites and Egyptian empires new peoples entered; Phrygians in Asia Minor, Hebrews and Philistines in Palestine. The power vacuum enabled the Israelites under King David (c.1006–966 BC) to create a kingdom briefly controlling Palestine and Syria (map 2); but after Solomon (966–926 BC) the kingdom, inherently unstable because of its disparate tribal origins, quickly disintegrated. But change and fluidity had the effect of breaking down old geographical and cultural barriers and fusing the whole region into a single cosmopolitan society, over which, after 539 BC, Persia established hegemony.

The immediate beneficiary was Assyria, the political successor of Mitanni (map 3). Already in the thirteenth century this city-state had joined the ranks of the great powers of the ancient Near East. Early in the ninth century, the Assyrian kings again began to flex their military muscle, embarking on a policy of conquest which soon brought them to the shores of the Mediterranean (map 3). The profits were ploughed back into the construction of the successive capitals of the Assyrian empire: Nimrud, Khorsabad and Nineveh. At its greatest extent, in the seventh century BC, the empire stretched from the Nile valley to the Persian Gulf and northwards into Armenia and eastern Turkey. But during the long reign of Ashurbanipal (668–627 BC) Assyria began to lose its military dominance and soon afterwards the assault of Medes and Scythians, combined with the secession of Babylonia, brought Assyrian power to ruin. The capital Nineveh was destroyed in 612 BC, and Assyria disappeared for ever in 605 BC. After an interlude in which Medes, Chaldeans and Egyptians divided the legacy, another semi-barbarian conqueror, Cyrus the Persian, rebelled against his Median overlord, captured the Median capital Ecbatana in 550 BC, and quickly overran most of the Middle East. When his son Cambyses (529–522 BC) conquered Egypt (525 BC), the Persian empire extended from the Nile to the Oxus (map 5). The ancient world was for the first time united under one administration. Persian attempts to extend their power to the west, however, met with resistance from the Greeks and defeat at Marathon (490 BC), Salamis (480 BC) and Plataea (479 BC), and the Persian empire entered a period of slow decline. The way was opened for the ultimate triumph of Hellenism and the conquest of Persia by Alexander the Great a century and a half later.

4 The Babylonian Kingdom 604-539 BC
→ campaigns of Nebuchadnezzar
— maximum extent under Nabonidus

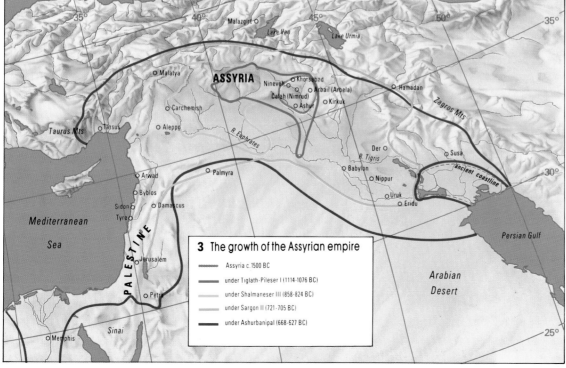

3 The growth of the Assyrian empire
Assyria c.1500 BC
under Tiglath-Pileser I (1114-1076 BC)
under Shalmaneser III (858-824 BC)
under Sargon II (721-705 BC)
under Ashurbanipal (668-627 BC)

BALKANS

GREECE

ASIA MINOR

Black Sea

Aegean Sea

Crete

Mediterranean Sea

ARAM

○ Dan
○ Hazor
○ Aphek
○ Ashtaroth
Sea of Galilee
Transjordan
■ Penuel
○ Adam
○ Jericho
○ Heshbon
AMMON
○ Rabbath Ammon
○ Dibon
MOAB
○ Kir-moab
EDOM
Arabia

○ Çatal Hüyük
○ Boğazköy
○ Alaca Hüyük
○ Alişar Hüyük
○ Kültepe
○ Karahüyük
○ Tarsus
○ Karatepe
○ Malatya
L. Van
L. Urmia
Zagros Mts
○ Weshshukanni
○ Chagar Bazar
○ Nineveh
○ Tell Brak
○ Ashur
○ Nuzi
○ Kilizi
○ Arbail
○ Carchemish
○ Aleppo
○ Emar
○ Alalakh
Tell Tayinat
○ Hamath
○ Qatna
SYRIA
MESOPOTAMIA
R. Tigris
R. Euphrates
Syrian Desert
○ Babylon
Enkomi
○ Ugarit
✕ Kadesh
Cyprus
Hala Sultan Tekke ⚓ Citium
○ Byblos
○ Damascus
○ Sidon
○ Laish
○ Tyre
○ Hazor
○ Acre
○ Taanach
○ Megiddo
○ Beth-shan
○ Tell es-Sa'idiyeh
○ Ashdod
○ Amman
○ Joppa
○ Gaza
○ Jerusalem
Pi-Ramesse
Tanis
Bubastis
Heliopolis
○ Memphis
Sinai
A R A B I A
Heracleopolis
El-Amarna (Tell El-Amarna)
Cusae
Abydus
Medinet Habu
Thebes
Karnak
Luxor
R. Nile
Red Sea
E G Y P T
○ Quban
Aniba
Qasr Ibrim
Abu Simbel
Faras
Buhen
Island of Meinarti
Island of Dorginarti
Semna
Amara
Island of Sai
Soleb
Sesebi
Tombos
Nubian Desert
Gebel Barkal
Kawa
Napata

Levantine, Miletus, Levkandi, Pylus

SAKA TIGRAKHAUDA *tribal area under loose Achaemenid control*

Aral Sea

UVARAZMISH (CHORASMIA)

SAKA HAUMAVARGA

○ Cyropolis (Krukath)

○ Maracanda

SUGUDA (SOGDIA)

○ Bactra

BAKHTRISH (BACTRIA)

○ Merv
○ Kapisa
○ Kabul
GANDARA
○ Taxila
○ Gardez
PAKTYES
○ Ghazni

HARAIVA (ARIA)

Caspian Sea

HYRCANIA

MADA (MEDIA)
Caspian Gates
○ Rhagae
○ Hagmatana (Ecbatana)
○ Bisitun

● Trapezus
Pteria 547 BC
○ Van
○ Nineveh
○ Arbela
ATHURA
○ Harran
○ Thapsacus
✕ Gaugamela 331 BC
Issus 333 BC
Alexandretta
Antioch
ABR NAHR (SYRIA)
R. Euphrates
BABIRUSH
✕ Cunaxa 401 BC
○ Opis
○ Ullais
○ Babylon
○ Susa
R. Tigris
UVJA (ELAM)
✕ Pasargadae 549 BC
○ Artacana
○ Farah
○ Zaranj
ZRANKA (DRANGIANA) (SEISTAN)
HARAUVATISH (ARACHOSIA)
R. Indus
PARSA (PERSIS)
○ Persepolis
○ Spasinou Charax
AKAUFACIYA
Persian Gulf
Arabian Sea

The Greek world
497-185 BC

The fifth century BC was the great age of Greece – the age of Pericles and Socrates, of Sophocles and Euripides, of the Parthenon and the sculptures of Phidias. It was also the century when internal strains (the growing conflict between oligarchy and democracy) and internecine war undermined the stability of the Greek city states and their ability to withstand external pressures. Colonisation had already carried Greek civilisation and Greek city life to Asia Minor (page 18). But here it came up against the Persian empire under Darius and Xerxes (page 20). Persian attempts to subdue Athens, which had been supporting the rebellious Ionians, were almost miraculously defeated at Marathon (490) and Salamis (480), (map 1). But thereafter the cities which had united against Persia fell apart, and the Peloponnesian war between Athens and Sparta and their allies (map 2) permanently weakened Greek resistance, and ensured the victory of Philip of Macedon (338). Under Philip's son, Alexander the Great, Macedonia became a world power, its dominion stretching from the Adriatic to India (map 3). Alexander's death in 323 BC at the age of 32 prevented the consolidation of his empire. In the succeeding struggles between his generals three major powers arose: Macedonia, shorn of its Asiatic conquests but still dominant in northern Greece; Egypt under the Ptolemies, with its capital at Alexander's newly founded city of Alexandria; and

the Seleucid kingdom comprising the bulk of the Persian empire (map 4). To these were added in the east the Bactrian kingdom, extending over Afghanistan into northern India, and the Parthian empire, founded in 247 BC when a dissident provincial governor broke away from the Bactrian Greeks. This Parthian state eventually stretched from the Euphrates to the Indus and successfully withstood Roman expansion until it was displaced in AD 224 by a resurgent Persia under the Sasanian dynasty.

Although politically the empire of Alexander the Great proved ephemeral, in other respects its consequences were epoch-making. Alexander himself founded some 70 cities, not merely as military strongholds but as cultural centres – a policy continued by his Seleucid successors – and thus carried Greek civilisation far to the east. Greek culture was now no longer the preserve of separate city-states but infused and Hellenised the whole civilised world (*oikoumene*) as far as India and China. Greek itself became the *lingua franca* of the whole region, though more subtly the Greek world itself was permeated by oriental influences as its contacts with the ancient civilisations of the Near East intensified. When Rome asserted control over the Hellenistic world after its defeat of Macedon at Cynoscephalae in 197 and of the Seleucids at Magnesia in 190 BC, this was its inheritance; and the longer the Roman empire existed, the greater was the part played by the Hellenic and oriental elements in its civilisation.

1 The Persian wars 490 – 479 BC

- Persian Empire in 497 BC
- Ionian rebel territory reconquered by Persia 496-493 BC
- Persian conquest 492 BC
- neutral and pro-Persian states
- Greek allies
- ✕ Persian victory
- ✕ Greek victory
- ✕ indecisive battle

3 The empire of Alexander the Great

- empire of Alexander
- states federated to the empire
- independent states
- route of Alexander the Great
- route of Nearchus
- return route of Craterus
- ✕ Alexander's major battles

4 The Hellenistic world in 185 BC

- independent Greek states
- Antigonid kingdom (and dependencies 240BC)
- Kingdom of Pergamum
- Hellenised non-Greek kingdoms

Trading links of the ancient world

Trade is as old as the beginning of settled urban life. Though ordinary needs were met by local agriculture and local manufacture, even the earliest cities had requirements that could not be satisfied locally. Jericho imported stone for tools from Anatolia (page 6); the Sumerians, who lacked timber, stone and minerals, developed trading links with Asia Minor and by sea with Dilmun on the Persian Gulf. But the formation of an intensive trading network spanning the whole Eurasian world only became possible after the rise of empires which could provide peace and security, build roads and maintain harbours. The Achaemenids made a beginning in sixth-century Persia, where Darius's Royal Road ran 1420 well-garrisoned miles (2300 km) from Sardis to Susa (page 20). But the decisive step forward was the rise, after 202 BC, of the Roman empire in the west and the Han empire in China. By the close of the first century BC Rome's conquests from the Atlantic to Syria formed a single vast trading area, gathered round a Mediterranean axis (map 2), and the expansion of Han China under Wu-ti (140–87 BC) created an economic bloc of similar

dimensions in the east (page 28). Both possessed an elaborate network of roads and a highly organised system of transport and marketing, which encouraged regional specialisation and an unprecedented interchange of goods and manufactures. In the west the requirements of the legions in the frontier provinces of Gaul and the Balkans were a further stimulus. Spain became a large-scale producer and exporter of wine and olive oil; but the most important export of all was grain from Egypt, North Africa and the Pontine provinces, upon which Rome itself and many cities of Greece and Asia Minor were dependent.

Nor did trade halt at the frontier. China sent a mission to Ferghana, Bukhara and Bactria in 128 BC, and shortly afterwards the famous Silk Route came into operation (map 1). It started at Tunhwang on China's far western boundary, and skirted north or south of the Takla Makan Desert to Kashgar, before crossing the Pamirs and debouching into Bactria, Persia and the Mediterranean coastal belt. But the Silk Route, spectacular though it was, was less important in economic terms than the sea route to India and the Far East, traffic along which increased greatly after the discovery of the monsoon around 100 BC. Previously there had been coastal traffic, mainly in Arab or Indian hands. Now up to 120 Greek vessels a year, some with a carry-

ing capacity of up to 500 tons, plied direct to the Indian ports of Barbaricum, Barygaza and Muziris, where they picked up eastern cargoes shipped by Indian merchants from Go Oc Eo in southern Cambodia, and carried them to Berenice and other Red Sea ports for transport on to Alexandria and thence to all parts of the Roman empire.

These far-flung trading links are impressive, but their economic importance should not be exaggerated. Both the Roman and the Han empires were self-sufficient in all essential commodities, and foreign trade was essentially a luxury trade, marginal to everyday needs. On the other hand, there is no doubt that foreign trade contributed directly to cultural interchange and to the spread of the great world religions (page 26). However, it also had other less happy consequences, particularly the spread of disease and pestilence (map 3). Earlier epidemics, like that which smote Athens in 430–29 BC, may have been transmitted by armies; but their incidence after about 100 BC leaves little doubt that, both in east and west, they were carried by caravans or merchant shipping from India or tropical Africa. Their precise character is not easily determined, though they seem to fall into two main groups, smallpox or measles, and bubonic plague; but there is no doubt about their devastating effects on vulnerable populations. 'One or two out of a hundred survived,' wrote the Chinese historian Ssu-ma Kuang of the epidemic of AD 317, and some later historians have attributed the failure both of China and of Rome to withstand the barbarian onslaughts of the fourth and fifth centuries to the sharp fall in manpower caused by imported pestilences.

1 Eurasian trade routes, c.AD200

- ▬ Silk Road
- ▬ trade route
- ■ trading capital
- ● trading centre

distribution of:
- ◤ Han mirrors
- ◢ Chinese silks
- ▲ Graeco-Roman objects in East AD1-300

2 The economy of the Roman Empire, c. AD 200

- ▬ boundary of Roman Empire c. AD 200
- ▬ sea routes
- ➡ land trade routes in Germany
- ➡ caravan routes
- ⸙ lighthouse
- ∿ navigable rivers (named)
- XIV Roman legion
- ⌒ fossatum Africae, fortifications
- olive-growing areas in N. Africa
- ● provincial colonial settlements
- ◉ important pottery, (modern name in brackets)
- ▬ road

- ◈ amber
- ◉ bitumen
- ◆ brass objects
- ⬜ bronzeware
- ⋈ cinnabar
- C copper
- // corn
- garum
- ⬜ glass
- ▨ gold
- horses
- ▲ iron
- ▬ lead
- + linen
- ◆ marble
- ◉ olives
- ▽ papyrus
- ⚱ pottery
- ◒ purple dye
- ◀ silk
- ⚡ silphium
- ▣ silver
- ◡ slave market
- ◱ source of slaves
- ▲ timber
- ▫ tin
- ⚥ wine
- ▱ woollen textiles
- Z zinc

3 The spread of epidemics

- AD 542-3 Plague of Justinian
- AD 165-80 Antonine Plague
- AD 251-66
- AD 312-22
- AD 162
- AD 552
- AD 251-66
- AD 430-429 BC
- SHENSI 243 BC
- AD 610
- AD 808
- AD 16
- malaria?
- measles?
- malaria?
- malaria?

Legend:
- ➡ probably smallpox or measles
- ➡ bubonic plague
- ➡ nature of epidemic unknown

25

The world religions
c.500 BC-AD 500

The period 550–500 BC saw the birth of great world religions in all the main centres of civilisation. Their appearance perhaps reflected a need in the rising empires of the old world for more universal creeds than the local tribal deities could provide, and their diffusion – particularly the spread of the great missionary religions, Buddhism and Christianity – was an important factor in linking together the different areas of civilisation (map 1). Their other major contribution – seen, for example, in the work of Anglo-Saxon missionaries in Germany or of Russian missionaries among the heathen tribes of the Urals (page 38) – was to carry civilisation to peoples outside the frontiers of the civilised world.

All the great religions shared, to one degree or another, a belief in a single spiritual reality. Not all were inspired by a missionary spirit. Hinduism, the oldest, was essentially the religion of the people of India, and Judaism, the religion of 'the chosen people of the Lord', was also exclusive. But Buddhism, originally a reformist movement within Hinduism, became perhaps the greatest of all missionary religions when it assumed its universalist, or Mahayana, form some 500 years after the death of its founder, Gautama (c.563–483 BC). Judaism also spread as a result of the persecution of the Jews by more formidable neighbours, beginning with the Babylonian exile (586 BC). After the Roman destruction of the temple in Jerusalem in AD 70 (map 3) the Jewish diaspora carried Judaism far and wide from its home in Palestine, until in time it became a worldwide religion. It also gave birth, directly or indirectly, to two of the world's great missionary religions, Christianity and Islam.

In the Far East the same period saw the rise of the ethical system of Kung Futzu or Confucius (551–479 BC) and the mystical religion of the Tao, or 'the Way', associated with the shadowy figure of Lao-tzu. Later Buddhism spread eastward along the Silk Route through central Asia and with Taoism and Confucianism became one of the 'three religions' of traditional China. Buddhism also reached Japan in the sixth century AD, where it effectively displaced spirit-worship and

traditional Shinto until the revival of the latter in the nineteenth century.

The other great religion of the period was Zoroastrianism, which originated in Persia and is associated with another shadowy figure, Zarathustra. Zoroastrianism, which sees life as a battleground between the forces of good and the forces of evil, spread rapidly through the Roman world in the form of Mithraism, with shrines as far afield as northern Britain. It was one of the many oriental cults which permeated the Roman empire when, after the beginning of the Christian era, belief in the Greek pantheon and the household deities broke down. Until the end of the third century AD it was undecided which of the oriental mystery cults would prevail; but with the conversion of the emperor Constantine to Christianity and its recognition by the Edict of Milan (AD 313), still more after it became the official religion of the Roman empire under Theodosius (374–95), the die was cast. Heathen temples were uprooted; rival cults were condemned.

Christianity had begun as a Jewish splinter-movement; its founder, Jesus of Nazareth, saw himself as the Messiah, or Saviour, sent to liberate the Jews from the Roman yoke. But when, after Jesus's condemnation and crucifixion (AD 29), Jewish orthodoxy rejected his message, his disciples, notably Paul of Tarsus, turned instead to the conversion of the 'gentiles', or people outside the law. Paul's journeys (map 2) were a turning point. Thereafter Christianity spread rapidly, both in the Roman empire and also further east. Here the great Christian centres were Antioch and Edessa, the home of the Nestorian church which carried Christ's teaching to Persia and from there to China and India (page 38). This was the situation until the rise of Islam (page 40) changed the scene.

3 Judaea 63 BC-AD 73

- area of Roman procuratorial rule in Judaea
- Agrippa II's kingdom AD 61
- area of major revolt at start of AD 66
- area of revolt at end of AD 69
- → Roman armies

1 The diffusion of religions

- → dispersion of Jews up to AD 500
- → spread of Christianity
- area converted to Christianity by AD 600
- → spread of Buddhism
- area of Buddhist missionary activity
- area of rise of Mahayana Buddhism
- • Buddhist sites
- area embracing Hinduism
- area embracing Taoism
- area embracing Shintoism
- area converted to Zoroastrianism
- → spread of Mithraism
- • Mithraic sites

2 The spread of
Christianity

- areas strongly Christian by 325
- areas largely Christian by 600
- ✠ patriarchate
- ♀ archbishopric
- ◎ bishopric
- ⊕ ecumenical council
- ⊖ council
- ◉ the Seven Churches of Asia
- → Paul's first journey
- → Paul's second journey
- → Paul's third journey
- → Paul's journey to Rome

First panel (Mediterranean and Near East) — place names:

Pityus · Mtskheta · Vagarshapat · Dvin · Artashat · Chersonesus · Trapezus · Theodosiopolis · Gondeshapur · Sinope · Amisus · Satala · Martyropolis · Arbela · Karcha · Neocaesarea · Amasia · Arbela · Rewardashur · Marcianopolis · Gangra · Melitene · Amida · Nisibis · Poetovio · Sirmium · Emona · R. Danube · Ratiaria · Constantinople 381 · Nicomedia · Ancyra · Caesarea Cappadociae · Edessa · Seleucia-Ctesiphon · Perath · Naissus · Adrianopolis · Chalcedon 451 · Nicaea 325 · Nyssa · Anazarbus · Dura-Europos · R. Euphrates · R. Tigris · Salonae · Scupi · Serdica · Philippi · Neapolis · Cyzicus · Tyana · Tarsus · Antioch · Palmyra · Scodra · Stobi · Apollonia · Amphipolis · Pergamum · Thyatira · Hierapolis · Lystra · Derbe · Seleucia · Apamea · Thessalonica · Troas · Sardes · Philadelphia · Perge · Tripolis · Damascus · Beroea · Larisa · Smyrna · Laodicea · Attalia · Salamis · Berytus · Nicopolis · Chios · Ephesus 431 · Miletus · Patara · Myra · Paphos · Sidon · Tyre · Diocaesarea · Athens · Samos · Cos · Rhodes · Ptolemais · Pella · Bostra · Corinth · Gortyna · Caesarea · Sebaste · Jerusalem · Diospolis-Lydda · Bethlehem · Joppa · Azotus · Pelusium · Petra · Neapolis · Puteoli · Vivarium · Messina · Rhegium · Syracuse · Syracusa · Melita · Alexandria · Ptolemais · Cyrene · Berenice · R. Nile · Coptus · Leptis Magna · Oea · Sabrata

? journey of Thomas to India

Second panel (Asia) — place names:

Aral Sea · R. Jaxartes · R. Oxus · CHINESE TURKESTAN · Peking · Sea of Japan · JAPAN · KOREA · Kyoto · Nara · Kyongju · Wutai Shan · Wanfohsiu · Tunhwang · Yellow River (Huang Ho) · Merv · AFGHANISTAN · Puto-Shan · Tientai Shan · Chiuhua Shan · CHINA · Pacific Ocean · PERSIA · agae · Lhasa · Himalayas · R. Yangtze · Omei Shan · Lumbini · NEPAL · Kusinagara · Brahmaputra River · R. Ganges · R. Indus · Benares · Sarnath · BENGAL · Sanchi · Bodh Gaya · BURMA · Karachi · Calcutta · Pagan · Prome · Pegu · ANNAM · South China Sea · PHILIPPINE ISLANDS · Arabian Sea · Ajanta · Bay of Bengal · Rangoon · Karli · Sukhothai · SIAM · INDIA · Angkor · Madras · Gulf of Siam · Anuradhapura · Kandy · CEYLON · Indian Ocean · MALAY PENINSULA · BORNEO · SUMATRA · MALAY PENINSULA · JAVA · Borobudur

India and China: the first empires

The fifth and sixth centuries BC were a period of consolidation in India and China. In India by the end of the fifth century the 16 political units in existence in 600 BC had been reduced to four. In China, by 400 BC, instead of the multiple feudal principalities of the Chou period (page 8) seven major states were contending for supremacy. In both countries iron tools increased both agricultural productivity and the resources of the rising states. In China the area of civilisation had expanded from the Yellow river to the Yangtze valley and beyond. In India the deforestation of the north shifted the centre of power from the Indus, the seat of the earliest civilisations (page 8), to the fertile plain of the Ganges. Here the kingdom of Magadha emerged as the nucleus of the first Indian empire.

Politically, nevertheless, it was a period of continuous strife, and the resulting social tensions were a major factor in the emergence of the great religious and ethical systems, Buddhism, Taoism, Confucianism and Jainism (page 26), which, in various ways, expressed a yearning for a more stable world order. In India the turning point came in 320 BC when Chandragupta Maurya seized the Magadhan throne, annexed the lands east of the Indus, occupied large parts of central India north of the Narmada river, and in 303 BC annexed the Seleucid province of Trans-Indus. Chandragupta's grandson, Asoka (273–236), conquered Kalinga on the Bay of Bengal, and the greater part of the subcontinent was brought under one rule. His edicts, inscribed on pillars and rocks, evidence Asoka's conversion to Buddhism (map 4).

In China the turning point came with the rise of the state of Ch'in (328–308), which finally dominated China in 221 BC (map 1). But the ruthless centralising policy of the first Ch'in emperor, Shih Huang-ti (221–206), provoked a reaction, and after his death his empire collapsed. It was revived, after a period of civil war, by the Han dynasty, which compromised between centralising policies and the feudal principalities. In India, also, the death of Asoka introduced a long period of decentralisation, punctuated by invasion from the north, which was not overcome until AD 320 when the Guptas, based again on Magadha, imposed a new imperial rule (map 5). This classical age of Indian civilisation survived beyond the collapse of the Gupta empire caused by the barbarian invasions of the fifth century (page 32).

The barbarian invasions were also a turning point in China. The Ch'in and the Han built and extended the Great Wall against the nomad Hsiungnu in the north. Under the emperor Wu-ti (140–87) the Han extended their power to central Asia (map 2). With its efficient administration, a large export trade, and an extensive network of roads and canals, Han China, with its capital at Changan was extremely prosperous (map 3). But control over south China was tenuous, while in the north feudal magnates still exercised great power, which grew with the threat of war. Crisis came in AD 9, and although Han rule was restored, disintegration set in after c.AD 160. When in 304 the Hsiungnu broke through the Great Wall, China remained divided until 589.

Map labels — Map 4: India's first empires

DRANGIANA · ARACHOSIA · CARMANIA · GEDROSIA · Ghazni · Hindu Kush · Kapisi · UDYANA · LAMPAKA · GANDHARA · Purushapura · Taxila · Harappa · R. Ravi · Mulasthana · Jalandhara · Punjab · KURUKSHETRA · Srinagara · KASMIRA · Sthanvisvara · Ahicchatra · Indraprastha · Sakhambhari · R. Yamuna · PANCHALA · Kanauj · Kanyakubja · NEPALA · Sravasti · Kapilavastu · KOSALA · Ayodhya · (Saketa) · BHOTA · Tibet · Mt. Kailas · KAMARUPA · Pragjyotisha · R. Ajayameru (Ajmer) · Mohenjo-Daro · Sind · Patalene · R. Indus · Mathura · R. Chambal · Mahotsavanagara · Kausambi · VATSA · Sarnath · Prayaga · Kasi (Benares) · Mithila · VIDEHA · Vaisali · Champa · ANGA · Nalanda · Rajagriha · Gaya · MAGADHA · Navadvipa · Bengal · R. Brahmaputra · PUNDRA · VANGA · Arbuda · Mt. Abu · Dasapura (Mandasor) · Besnagar · Vidisa (Bhilsa) · Sanchi · Khajuraho · CHEDI · Tamralipti · SAMATATA · Dvaraka · Valabhi · Lothal · Ujjayini · Dhara · Bagho · VINDHYACHALA · MAHA-KOSALA · Ramagiri · Sisupalgarh · Bhabanesar · Konarak · Puri · Girinagara · Gujerat · SURASHTRA · Barygaza · R. Narmada · AVANTI · Nasik · Ellora · Ajanta · Devagiri (Daulatabad) · Pratisthana · KALINGA conquered by Asoka 260 BC · Pishtapura · Arabian Sea · Elephanta · Bhaja · Karli · Bedsa · MAHARASHTRA · SATAVAHANA KINGDOM · R. Godavari · Kalyani · Warangal · Deccan · Manyakheta · Vengi · Amaravati · Bay of Bengal · Talikota · Vatapi · Aihole · R. Krishna · Vijayanagar · Vaijayanti · KARNATA · Belur · Dorasamudra · Sravana Belgola · Kanchi · Mamallapuram · Arikamedu · CHOLA · Kaverippattinam · Srirangam · Uraiyur · Tanjuvur · Tiruchirappalli · Indian Ocean · Muziris · CHERA (KERALA) · Madurai · PANDYA · Korkai · Anuradhapura · Polonnaruva · LANKA (SIMHALA) · Sigiriya

Legend (left box):

— routes opened to trade by Former Han
⊞ administrative centres under Later Han
⊡ centre of Later Han protectorate, 73-127 AD
▬ territory added under Later Han
← new route opened by General Pan Ch'ao for Later Han
⇐ expeditions against Hsiungnu (Huns)

conquered and put under Chinese administration 109-106 BC

4 India's first empires, 297 BC - AD 150

(approximate limits shown)

- Chandragupta Maurya's Empire 297 BC
- Bindusara's Empire 272 BC
- --- Asoka's Empire 232 BC
- ▲ rock and pillar edicts
- Western Satraps AD 150
- Kushan Empire AD 150 (eastern limit)
- Satavahana Kingdom AD 150

3 Han China in AD 2

Map labels: TUNHWANG · KIUCHUAN · CHANGI · WUWEI · SHUOFANG · WUYAN · YENMEN · PEITI · SHANG · LIAOTUNG · HSUANTU · LIAOHSI · LOLANG · ANTING · CHINCHENG · TIENSHUI · LUNGHSI · WUTU · Changan · NANYANG · JUNAN · CHIUCHANG · HUAI · KUANGHAN · HANCHUNG · SHU · PA · NAN · CHANGHSIA · TANYANG · KUAICHI · YUEHSUI · CHIENWEI · WULING · CHANGSHA · YUCHANG · MINYUEH · TAIWAN · TSANGKO · LINGLING · KUEIYANG · ICHOU · YULIN · TSANGWU · NANHAI · CHIAOCHIH · CHIUCHEN · HOPU · JIHNAN

⊞ imperial capital
■ enfiefed principalities
□ commanderies
— highways
∿∿ canals

5 Gupta India

Map labels: SASANIAN EMPIRE · KUSHAN & SAKAS · MADRAS · KARTRIPURA · YAUDHEYAS · ARJUNAYANAS · Mathura · NAGAS · NEPALA · KAMARUPA · DAVAKA · MALAVAS · MAGADHA · Ayodhya · Vaisali · Pataliputra · Dasapura (Mandasor) · Padmavati · Airikina (Eran) · PARIVRAJAKAS · UCCHAKALPAS · PUNDRA VARDHANA · SAMATATA · SAKAS · Sanchi · Girinagara (Girnar) · Ujjayini · Nandivardhana · VAKATAKAS · Ajanta · SALANKAYANAS · KADAMBAS · Vengi · Bay of Bengal · GANGAS · PALLAVAS · PANDYA · LANKA (SIMHALA)

- Empire of Chandragupta I
- added by Samudragupta
- temporarily tributary to Samudragupta
- added by Chandragupta II
- tributary tribes and states
- under Gupta influence (c. AD 380-410)

29

The Roman Empire
264BC-AD565

The rise of Rome from a collection of shepherds' huts on the hills overlooking the Tiber to a great world empire is a story of seven centuries of constant warfare. According to tradition, the city of Rome was founded in 754 BC by descendants of Aeneas, the legendary hero who had fled to Italy after the sack of Troy. Archaeology shows that it was only in the sixth century that it began to take on the trappings of a city.

In 510 BC the citizens of Rome expelled the last of the Etruscan kings and formed a republic. Over the next 300 years victories over Etruscans, Greeks and Celts gradually extended Roman control over the whole of Italy (map 1), but this expansion brought her into direct conflict with the imperialist ambitions of Carthage on the North African coast. Three fierce Punic Wars were fought for supremacy between the two powers (map 2). In the second (218–201 BC), the Carthaginians under the brilliant generalship of Hannibal inflicted a series of crushing defeats on the Romans. But Roman resolve held, Hannibal was ultimately defeated, and some fifty years later Carthage itself was destroyed in the Third Punic War (146 BC).

The Punic Wars gave Rome control over Sicily (241 BC), Spain (206 BC), and North Africa (146 BC). At the same time, conflict with the Hellenistic kingdoms of the East Mediterranean resulted in the conquest of Macedon, Greece and western Asia Minor. In this way, almost by accident, Rome became an imperial power with far-flung possessions. In the first century BC the growing power of successful war-leaders led to fierce rivalries and civil wars, culminating in the struggle between Caesar and Pompey (49–45 BC), from which Caesar emerged victorious. His assassination in 44 BC, however, initiated a further thirteen years of conflict, only ending with Augustus' victory over Antony and Cleopatra at Actium in 31 BC.

Augustus' rule initiated a period of two centuries of unprecedented peace and prosperity in the extensive lands of the Roman empire (map 3). Population increased, trade flourished, and cities grew. Civic authorities and wealthy individuals embellished their cities with theatres, baths and temples, while roads, aqueducts and harbours brought in essential supplies from outside. This vast common market was further united by Roman law and by the use of Latin.

This peace was broken in the middle of the third century AD by Germanic invasions in the west and Persian victories in the east which brought the empire temporarily to its knees (map 4). Reform and reorganisation under Diocletian (AD 284–305) and Constantine (306–337) ensured the continued survival of the eastern half of the empire, with its new capital at Constantinople (Byzantium), but Rome itself fell to the Goths in AD 410 and Justinian's abortive efforts to recover the western provinces in the mid-sixth century showed clearly that the unified empire was a thing of the past. The ghost of the Roman empire lived on in the west, however, in the continued importance of Roman law and the continued use of Latin by the Christian church.

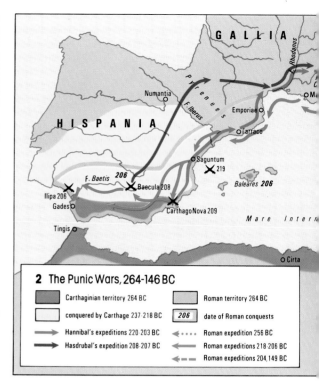

2 The Punic Wars, 264-146 BC

- Carthaginian territory 264 BC
- conquered by Carthage 237-218 BC
- Roman territory 264 BC
- *206* date of Roman conquests
- → Hannibal's expeditions 220-203 BC
- ◁···· Roman expedition 256 BC
- → Hasdrubal's expedition 208-207 BC
- ← Roman expeditions 218-206 BC
- ◁--- Roman expeditions 204,149 BC

1 Roman expansion in Italy

- Roman territory by 264 BC
- ■ Roman colonies before the Gracchi (133 BC)
- ● Latin colonies before the Gracchi
- allied states or tribal areas
- *VENETI* peoples

4 The later Empire, AD 284-565

- Praefectus Praetorio Galliarum
- Praefectus Praetorio per Orientem
- Praefectus Praetorio per Illyricum
- Praefectus Praetorio Illyrici. Italiae, Africae
- - - - - borders of Dioceses
- Empire at abdication of Diocletian AD 305
- Justinian's reconquests
- Empire at death of Justinian AD 565

3 The Roman Empire, AD 14-280

- under administration of the Senate
- imperial provinces in AD 14
- public provinces in AD 14
- provinces added after AD 14 with date
- - - - - later subdivisions of provinces

The barbarian invasions

In the fourth and fifth centuries AD the irruption of nomadic peoples from central Asia threw the civilised world into disarray. The invading nomads were under no form of central control though their movements radiated from a common centre. They were mostly Mongoloid and their languages mostly of the Turkish family; they were largely pastoralists with mobile encampments of tents and their success in war owed much to their mounted archers. All the established centres of civilisation were affected by them: China, the Gupta empire in India, Sasanian Persia and the Roman empire in the west (map 1). In 304 the Great Wall of China was breached by the Hsiung-nu, forbears of the Huns; in 367, Picts and Scots broke through Hadrian's Wall into Britain. The setbacks were lasting. China remained disunited until 589, and western Europe (if we except the short-lived Carolingian revival) only began to recover from invasion around the middle of the eleventh century (page 36).

The appearance of the Huns in Europe c.370 immediately caused a great involuntary movement among the Germanic peoples who had long been settled in northern and central Europe beyond the confines of the Roman empire. The details, beginning with the Visigoths, who defeated the Roman emperor at Adrianople in 378, sacked Rome in 410 and were settled in Aquitaine in 418, can be followed on map 2. Behind the Visigoths followed other east and west Germanic peoples: Alans, Vandals, Sueves, Alemans, Franks, and finally the Ostrogoths who, having earlier been forced into subjection, liberated themselves after the defeat of the Huns in 451, and descended into Italy, where they were in control by 493. Only the Anglo-Saxon invasion of Britain, beginning c.440, followed a different course. Here scattered bands of warriors and settlers, moving by ship up the estuaries of the Humber, Thames and the Wash, met with stubborn resistance. It was to be almost

two centuries before the invaders, following their victories at Deorham (577) and Chester• (616), established control of Britain (map 3). Here continuity with the Roman past was at a modest level at best.

In continental Europe continuity was more evident. Political control passed from Roman officials to German kings; but, except for the Anglo-Saxons and Franks, who could draw manpower from their homeland, the invaders were too few in number to change decisively the character of Roman society. Hence the success of the counter-offensive which Justinian launched in 533 (page 30). But Justinian's wars, and the havoc they wrought, left the way open for another wave of invasion from Asia, this time the Avars, and it was their onslaught, beginning c.560, that drove the Lombards into Italy (568). But they were too few in number to occupy the whole peninsula, and Italy remained divided between the Lombards, the Byzantine emperor and the Papacy (map 4). When the Lombard ruler Aistulf advanced south, seeking to establish his authority over the Lombard dukes of Spoleto and Benevento, occupied Ravenna in 751 and drove out the Byzantine exarch, the Pope, fearing for his independence, called on the Franks for aid. Thus was sealed the momentous alliance of the Carolingians and the Papacy, which resulted in Charles the Great's invasion, conquest and annexation of the Lombard kingdom in 774.

The appearance of the Avars also unsettled the Slav peoples who had greatly extended their settlement in eastern Europe following the Germanic migration westwards. Beginning c.600 Slav warbands descended into Greece and the Balkans, while the Bulgars took control of the western shore of the Black Sea (map 5). The arrival of the Slavs, cutting the landbridge between Byzantium and the west, was a cardinal fact in European history. The rise of the Bulgarian Empire and the gradual consolidation of Serbia and Croatia left a permanent imprint on the demography and historical geography of Europe.

2 Germanic invasions of Europe

→ Huns and campaigns of Attila	→ Scots and Britons
→ Vandals, Alans, Sueves	→ Slavs
→ Visigoths	⌒ boundary of Roman Empire AD395
→ Ostrogoths	
→ other Germanic peoples	▢ Anglo-Saxon settlement in England to AD626

5 The expansion of the Slavs to c.700

→ expansion of Slavs
〰 western limit of Slav expansion in 8th century AD
Sorbs Slav people
AVARS non-Slav people

North Sea

FINNISH PEOPLES

LITHUANIANS

SAXONS

Abodrites c.500

Sorbs

Bohemians c.500

R. Danube

Slovenes c.600

Croats

AVARS

Serbs c.640

BULGARS

THRACE

MACEDONIA c.600-700

Salonika

Black Sea

Pripet Marshes

Slavs 1st century AD

Kiev

c.500-700

c.400-500

3 Anglo-Saxon invasions of Britain, c.440-650

➜ lines of Anglo-Saxon advance
forest
fenland, swamp
• Anglo-Saxon burial places c.450-650
)) British fortifications

North Sea

STRATHCLYDE

LOTHIAN

BERNICIA

Bamburgh 547

REGED

Hexham 633

DEIRA

York

ELMEDSAETE (ELMET)

R. Ribble

LINDSEY

Humber

The Wash

GWYNEDD

Chester 616

R. Dee

PECSAETE

MERCIANS

WREOCENSAETE

POWYS

MIDDLE ANGLES

EAST ANGLES

R. Wye

R. Severn

DYFED

BRYCHEINIOG

GWYNLLWG

R. Thames

Bedcanford 571

EAST SAXONS

London

Chiltern Hills

Crayford 457

Ebbsfleet 449

WEST WALES

Deorham 577

WEST SAXONS

Old Sarum 552

ANDREDESWEALD

SOUTH SAXONS

HÆSTINGAS

KENT

Bindon 614

Cerdicesford 519

WIHT

Andredescester 491

GAUL

4 The Lombards in Italy

Lombard Kingdom and duchies c.600
Imperial territory c.600

LOMBARDY

Cividale

Verone

Pavia

ISTRIA

LIGURIA

Parma

Ravenna

Bologna

EXARCHATE OF RAVENNA

Rimini

TUSCANY

Siena

Adriatic Sea

DUCHY OF SPOLETO

DUCHY OF ROME

Rome

DUCHY OF BENEVENTO

Brindisi

Naples

CAMPANIA

Amalfi

CALABRIA

Tyrrhenian Sea

SICILY

Syracuse

1 Barbarian invasions of the ancient world

➜ Hsiung-nu and Huns
➜ Juan-Juan (Avars)
Goths and Vandals
━━ boundary of Roman Empire in AD454
── other frontiers as marked on map
•••• frontiers of Sasanian Empire

approximate limits of nomad belt
areas of good pasture

North Sea

L. Baikal

R. Amur

Altai Mts

R. Yenisei

R. Selenga

MONGOLIA

Gobi Desert

MANCHURIA

R. Irtysh

border of western Turkish Empire of AD600

L. Balkhash

Syr Darya

550 Juan-juan (Avars) driven westwards out of Mongolia by the Blue (Celestial) Turks

R. Tarim

Toba Wei Empire c.AD500

Ordos Desert

border of eastern Turkish Empire of AD600

Great Wall of China at AD220

Amu Darya (Oxus)

Pamirs

Takla Makan Desert

SINKIANG

KANSU

Hsien-pi invade

Hindu Kush

1st century AD Hsiung-nu broken by Han China and move westwards

R. Indus

expansion of Tibetans

TIBET

Changan

Loyang

re-unified north China under Toba (northern) Wei control

315 Hsiung-nu renew attacks on China and sack capital, Loyang

CHINA

Himalayas

Yellow River

R. Yangtze

480 White Huns destroy Gupta Empire of India

INDIA

40°

30°

Germanic kingdoms of Western Europe

Within a century of the Germanic invasions there were settled kingdoms in western Europe, except in Britain where invaders still met resistance. Among these (map 1) the Ostrogothic kingdom of Theodoric the Great (493–526) was outstanding. In Spain, the kingdom of the Visigoths was to endure from the late fifth century until the Arab conquest in 711. But monarchical institutions were still weak and religious differences divided the Arian rulers from their Catholic subjects. Justinian's attack on the Ostrogothic kingdom (page 30) destroyed equilibrium in the west and opened the way for the advance of the Franks (map 2).

The Franks also had appeared on the scene as scattered warbands, but Clovis (486–511) ruthlessly eliminated his rivals, made himself sole king, and reconciled the Gallo-Roman population by embracing the Catholic faith (497). He then turned against the neighbouring peoples, the Alemanni and Burgundians, defeated the Visigoths at Vouillé (507), near Poitiers, and forced them to withdraw to Spain and Septimania. But Theodoric's support for the other Germanic kingdoms checked further advance, and only after his death was a new phase of Frankish expansion possible. Deprived of Ostrogothic support, the Thuringians (531), Burgundians (532–4), and Alemanni (535) succumbed, and in 537 the Franks seized Provence.

Once the initial wave of conquest was spent, however, decline set in. Division of the royal patrimony, dynastic quarrels and alienation of the royal estates to buy aristocratic and ecclesiastical support, seemed after the death of Dagobert I (629–39) to presage the break-up of the kingdom. In Britain, on the other hand, the seventh century saw the emergence and consolidation of the kingdoms known as the Heptarchy. It seems that the kingdoms of the south-east (Sussex, Kent, Essex, East Anglia) were prevented from expanding by geographical obstacles, and leadership passed first to Northumbria and then to Mercia. The progress of Northumbria was helped by its early conversion to Christianity, but it was resisted by pagan Mercia under Penda (632–54), sometimes in alliance with the Britons, and by the time of Offa (757–96) the pre-eminence of Mercia, now Christian, was unquestionable. It controlled the four eastern kingdoms (map 3), and even Wessex recognised Mercian overlordship.

In the Frankish lands the turning point came with the battle of Tertry (687), when the leaders of the Austrasian aristocracy established their preponderance. This was the beginning of the rise of the Carolingian dynasty. Ruling at first indirectly, but after 751 with the royal title, the Carolingians restored Frankish fortunes and inaugurated a great surge of territorial expansion (map 4). Charles Martel (714–41) won a famous victory over the Arabs at Poitiers (732). His son Pepin (751–68) expelled them from Aquitania (752). Charles the Great, or Charlemagne (768–814), conquered Lombardy (774) and established Frankish rule in Italy. But his greatest victories were in the east, against the Bavarians (788), the Avars (796), and the Saxons (finally subdued in 804). His coronation as emperor by Pope Leo III in 800 marked the apogee of Frankish success.

However, Charlemagne's last ten years were beset by problems, the frontier marches never safe from attack; and after his death the inherent institutional weaknesses quickly became apparent. Civil war led to a first partition in 843. But the famous treaty of Verdun (map 5) was only a first step, and at Meersen (870) the 'Middle Kingdom' was eliminated (map 6) and the familiar outlines of Europe began to take shape. In 888 the Carolingian empire collapsed but its legacy to European civilisation remained.

1 Germanic kingdoms in AD 493

4 The Frankish Empire, 714–814

- Frankish realm 714
- extent of empire 814
- marches in 814 (with date of formation)
- ♔ Frankish royal residencies
- ♂ archbishoprics
- ⊕ important monasteries

GASCONY 769 province with date of acquisition

2 Early Frankish expansion

Cologne · HESSE · THURINGIA

Tournai · Cambrai · Trier · Worms · BAVARIA

Rouen · Soissons · Verdun · Strasbourg · ALEMANNIA · RHAETIA

BRETONS · Le Mans · ITALY

Tours · Vouillé 507 · OSTROGOTHS

Poitiers · BURGUNDIAN KINGDOM

VISIGOTHIC AQUITANIA

Bordeaux

SEPTIMANIA · PROVENCE (ACQUIRED 537)

BASQUES · Narbonne

VISIGOTHS

Frankish territory at the accession of Clovis 486

Merovingian territory before the battle of Vouillé 507

Merovingian territory in 560

area of Merovingian overlordship in Germany

5 Treaty of Verdun, 843

KINGDOM OF CHARLES II THE BALD

KINGDOM OF LOUIS THE GERMAN

(tributary territories)

KINGDOM OF LOTHAR I

6 Partition of Meersen, 870

KINGDOM OF CHARLES II THE BALD

KINGDOM OF LOUIS THE GERMAN

(tributary territories)

KINGDOM OF LOUIS II

XON·ARCH 8-810 · WILZI · ODRITES

Magdeburg · R. Elbe

SORBS

THURINGIAN MARCH 806 · R. Oder

BOHEMIA

ensburg · Altaich · R. Danube

Passau · OSTMARK 803

Kremsmünster · Salzburg

AVARIA 788 · CARINTHIA 788 · PANNONIA 795-6 · AVAR KINGDOM (destroyed 796)

FRIULI 776

Aquileia

VENICE under Frankish control 806-12

ISTRIA conquered by Franks 788

Ravenna

Spoleto

Adriatic Sea

Rome

Monte Cassino

3 Anglo-Saxon England c.AD 800

Mercia and subordinate kingdoms under Offa (757 - 796)

allied with Mercia

British kingdoms

STRATHCLYDE · LOTHIAN · BERNICIA

GALLOWAY · NORTHUMBRIA

Irish Sea · York · DEIRA · R. Humber · North Sea

GWYNEDD · Chester · PECSAETE · LINDSEY

R. Dee · WREOCENSAETE

POWYS · Lichfield · Tamworth · MERCIA

Offa's Dyke · R. Severn

DYFED · Hereford · EAST ANGLIA

GWENT · HWICCE · ESSEX

Bensington 779 · Dorchester-on-Thames · London

SURREY · R. Thames · Otford 776

WESSEX · Winchester · SUSSEX · KENT

WEST WALES · Hastings

English Channel

Invasion and recovery: Europe, 814-1149

The relative stability of western Europe under Charles the Great (Charlemagne) and of England under Offa of Mercia (page 34) was shattered in the ninth century by attacks by Saracens in the south, Magyars in the east, and Norwegians and Danes in the north and west (map 1). The Saracens pillaged Rome in 846, and after establishing a base at Fraxinetum in 890 raided deep into southern Gaul. Northern Italy and Germany were a prey to the Magyars who had moved into the Hungarian plain after Charlemagne's destruction of Avar power. The Vikings of Norway and Denmark also began as raiders; but in their case an initial phase of plunder was followed by settlement and colonisation, first in Orkney and Shetland, then in Ireland where Dublin was founded c.841, later (c.870) in Iceland and in England, where the Danish armies occupied the countryside round the Five Boroughs of the Midlands after 876. In France the West Frankish king conferred the lands at the mouth of the Seine – the later duchy of Normandy – on the Danish leader Rollo in 911.

The invasions were accompanied by widespread devastation and depopulation. Inevitably recovery was slow. In Germany (page 54) Otto I's defeat of the Magyars at the river Lech (955) was a turning point. In England only determined resistance by Alfred the Great of Wessex (871–99) held the Danes at bay. After 909 his successors went over to the offensive and by 939 Scandinavian England had been subjugated. But after the death of Edgar (959–75) a second wave of Danish invasion began.

In southern Europe, where most of Spain had been in Arab hands for over two centuries, the Mediterranean was by 950 virtually a 'Muslim lake'. But the collapse of Arab unity after 936 (page 40) facilitated a Christian revival. After the fall of Fraxinetum in 972 the fleets of Pisa and Genoa went over to the offensive, attacking the Muslim bases in North Africa, while Venice cleared the Adriatic (map 2). After the First Crusade (1096–99) and

the great Venetian naval victory off Ascalon in 1123, the Italian cities dominated Mediterranean trade. The period of the First Crusade also saw the beginning of the Christian reconquest of Spain under Alfonso VI (1065–1109), king of León and Castile, who actually advanced as far as Toledo in 1084 (map 4). But the first wave of reconquest was halted by the great Islamic revival under the Almoravid and Almohad dynasties. The Christian advance only resumed in the thirteenth century after the decisive victory at Las Navas de Tolosa (1212) which led to the conquest of Córdoba (1236), Valencia (1238), Murcia (1243), Seville (1248) and Cádiz (1262).

The ninth and tenth century invasions also disrupted royal authority and created political fragmentation. In Gaul the Frankish rulers virtually capitulated to the Vikings, leaving defence to the local magnates. The result was a great upsurge of feudalism. Peasant freemen virtually disappeared and society was polarised between nobles and serfs. In Germany power devolved into the hands of dukes and margraves who defended the frontiers, and in Italy only the walled cities could withstand the Magyar onslaught. The kingdom of Wessex was the exception, unique in tenth century Europe beyond the borders of Muslim Spain and Byzantium. Here the monarchy took control, creating during the reconquest of the Danelaw a system of shires and hundreds administered by sheriffs who were officials, not feudatories. But this royal government could not withstand the renewal of Danish attacks during the reign of Aethelred II (978–1016). By the beginning of the eleventh century England seemed destined to pass into a Scandinavian orbit (page 52). The Norman Conquest (map 3) decisively halted this development. William the Conqueror quickly established control in the south; but in the north, where Danish and Scottish intervention underpinned resistance, he only made his authority secure by systematic devastation (1069). Danish reconquest was still a threat until 1085; but after 1066 England was permanently aligned with the Christian and feudal civilisation of western Europe. The period of invasions had irrevocably changed the structure of Western society.

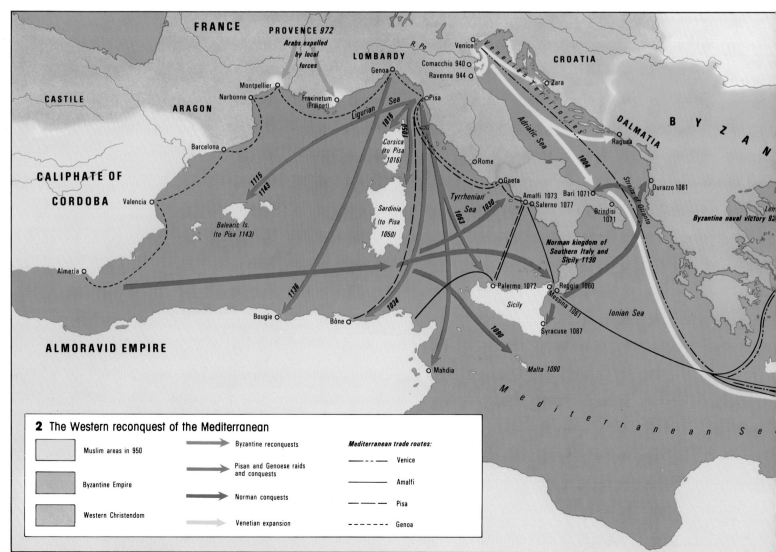

2 The Western reconquest of the Mediterranean

Muslim areas in 950

Byzantine Empire

Western Christendom

→ Byzantine reconquests

→ Pisan and Genoese raids and conquests

→ Norman conquests

→ Venetian expansion

Mediterranean trade routes:

– · – · – Venice

——— Amalfi

– – – Pisa

– – – – – Genoa

1 Viking, Magyar and Saracen invasions

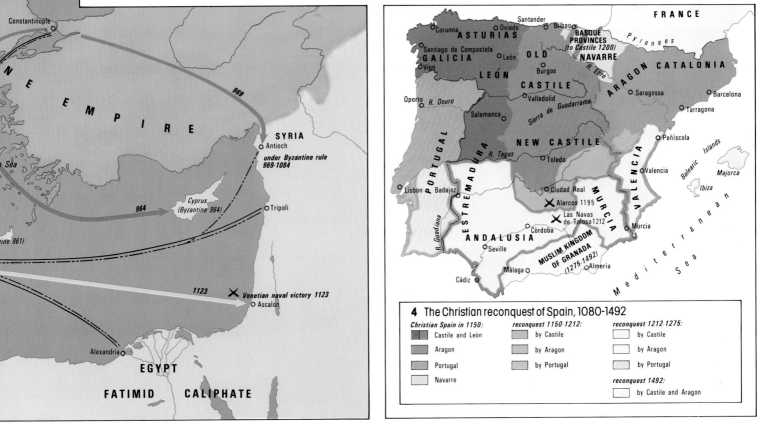

4 The Christian reconquest of Spain, 1080-1492

Christianity and Judaism, c.600–1500

By the time of Pope Leo I (440–461) an organised Christian church existed with a hierarchy of bishops and a full-scale framework of patriarchates, provinces and dioceses. But the attempt to enforce orthodoxy, particularly at the Council of Chalcedon (451), caused serious internal conflict. The Monophysite or Coptic Christians of Egypt were alienated, the Nestorians driven into exile in Persia. Here they carried on great missionary work (map 1), only halted centuries later by the advance of Islam (page 40). In the west, however, where Christianity was the official religion of the Roman empire, the church suffered from the setbacks inflicted by the Germanic invasions of the western provinces (page 32), and subsequent rivalry between Rome and Constantinople resulted after 1054 in schism between Catholicism and Orthodoxy. A period of stagnation had set in, only ended by the Irish and later Anglo-Saxon missionaries (map 3), who converted the heathen tribes of Germany, reformed the Frankish church, and inaugurated a great missionary drive to Scandinavia and eastern Europe. In addition a counter-offensive against Islam was launched in a series of Crusades beginning in 1096. The general outline of the Christian thrust, north and east from the Rhine and Danube, can be followed on map 2.

The resurgence of Christianity, particularly marked after the pontificate of Leo IX (1048–54) was a disaster for the Jewish communities which had spread throughout Europe before and after the suppression of the Jewish revolts in Palestine by the Romans in AD 66 and 132. The Jews suffered no restrictions in the Roman empire and, with their widespread international connections, were welcomed as traders by the Carolingians and other early medieval kings. But the Crusades inaugurated a wave of intolerance, and the third and fourth Lateran Councils (1179, 1215) passed discriminatory legislation. The rise of a native merchant class also made Jews less indispensable to Christian rulers, and later they became the scapegoats for the economic setbacks of the fourteenth century (page 56). The result was the series of expulsions, beginning in England in 1290. In 1492 the Sephardic Jews were expelled from Spain, in 1497 from Portugal. The Ashkenazi in the German lands took refuge in Poland and Lithuania, where they formed tight communities in what later was called 'the Pale'. Only the eighteenth-century Enlightenment brought a beginning of reconciliation, but the Nazi experience was to show that it was far from complete.

3 Irish and Anglo-Saxon missions
- Irish missions
- Anglo-Saxon missions
- Roman missions
- archbishoprics and bishoprics
- ⊕ monastery

2 Christianity in Europe
- Monophysite Christians
- Orthodox Christians
- Catholic Christians
- original Catholic core
- Celtic churches
- Islam
- heathen peoples
- ⚶ metropolitan see
- ◻ bishopric
- ⊕ monastery/hermitage
- ○ other churches
- routes of missionaries

cultural areas:

Ashkenazi

South Italian

Islamic

homeland of Spanish culture (Sephardi)

migrations

expulsions

ENGLAND
Oxford London
Southampton
1290
Paris
Troyes
FRANCE *1394*
1394
Lyons
Montpellier Arles
Narbonne
Perpignan
Marseilles
Barcelona
ossa

Amsterdam
Antwerp Cologne
Marburg
Frankfurt
Mainz GERMANIC
Trier Worms
Speyer Augsburg
Munich
R. Rhine
c.1100-1400
POLAND
Poznań R. Vistula
Breslau
Prague
Nuremberg
Regensburg
LANDS
Vienna
c.1150-1350
Budapest
c.1350-1450
R. Danube

Venice
Ferrara
Florence
c.500-800
Rome
Naples
Taranto

LITHUANIA
Minsk
Brest-Litovsk
Lublin
Cracow
Lemberg
c.1450-1500
Kiev
RUSSIA
R. Dnieper
c.1450-1500

c.700-800
Adrianople
Constantinople
Salonika

Black Sea

Caspian Sea

60°

Smyrna

Tunis
Algiers
TUNISIA

Mediterranean

Sea

40°

Aleppo
R. Euphrates
R. Tigris
PERSIA

Tripoli

Tyre
Safed Damascus
Baghdad

Alexandria
Jerusalem
Cairo
ARABIA
EGYPT

20°

40°

menians
orians
Armenians
Arbela
Bardaa
Tabriz
Karkh
Halwan
Baghdad (from 800)
Seleucia-Ctesiphon (to 800)
Rai
Jund-i Shapur
Rewardashur
Isfahan
PERSIA
Beth Katraye
Dhofar
Socotra

Caspian
Sea
Aral Sea

TRANSOXIANA
Nishapur
Merv
Bukhara
Samarkand
Herat
Balkh
Kashgar

Lake Balkhash

TURKESTAN
Almalyk Cambaluc
Kucha
Khara-Khoja
Kumul
Tunhwang
Kanchow
Sining
UICHURS

MONGOLIA

ONGUTS
Tatung Hira
Ningsia
Sianfu
Chengtu

Khanbalik
(Peking)
KOREA
Yellow
Sea
Yangchow
Chinkiang
Hangchow
CHINA
Chuanchow

Persian
Gulf

Syrians of St Thomas

Arabian Sea

INDIA

MALABAR
Cranganore
Kottayam
Quilon

CEYLON

Bay of
Bengal

Canton

South China
Sea

Indian Ocean

Christianity in Asia

Asian churches:

Nestorian churches

Coptic (Monophysite) missionary activity

Jacobite/Nestorian missions (the St Thomas church)

Metropolitan   bishopric   monastery   other churches

distribution of non-Christian religions:

Islam

Buddhism

Hinduism

GUTS pagan peoples

The Islamic world
632-1517

The rise and expansion of Islam was one of the most significant and far-reaching events in modern history. 'Islam' means 'submission to the will of God'; God's message has been conveyed to mankind through a series of prophets, culminating in Mohammed. The Koran is the Word of God; Mohammed is the Seal of the Prophets, and no others will come after him. Mohammed was born in Mecca about AD 570, and received his first revelations in 610. As his followers grew in number they aroused the hostility of the merchant aristocracy of Mecca, and the group was eventually obliged to withdraw to Medina, some 280 miles north-east of Mecca. This migration, *hijra* in Arabic, marks the beginning of the Islamic era and of the Muslim calendar. Mohammed eventually returned to Mecca in triumph in 630. He died in 632, but Islam expanded rapidly; over the next century Arab armies brought the new religion as far west as Spain and the Mediterranean islands and as far east as northern India (map 1).

In 661 the political control of the Arab-Islamic empire passed to the Umayyads, a dynasty originating from the pre-Islamic Meccan aristocracy, whose power was now centred on Damascus. In 750 the Umayyads were replaced by the Abbasids, a family claiming direct descent from Mohammed. The capital now shifted from Syria to Baghdad, and power began to pass from the Arab minority to the non-Arab Muslims, who had always formed the numerical majority in the Muslim Empire. The Abbasid period was a time of great prosperity and cultural and intellectual achievement, although the Muslim world gradually lost its political unity and split into a number of local dynastic entities (map 2). Among these were the Umayyads and Almoravids of Spain and North Africa, the Fatimids of Egypt and the Ghaznavids of north India.

In 945, the centre of the empire itself was captured by the Buyids, who ruled in the Abbasids' name for over a century. These were displaced in their turn by the Seljuks, Turks from central Asia, who gradually expanded into Anatolia. Their defeat of the Byzantine army at Manzikert in 1071 caused the Byzantines to seek the aid of Western Christendom which was to materialise in the form of the Crusades, principally in the late eleventh and twelfth centuries (map 3). The Crusades had little impact upon Arab society, but

the Norman conquest of southern Italy and the southward expansion of the Christian states of northern Spain combined to push the Muslims out of Europe by the end of the fifteenth century, and to move the centre of gravity of the Muslim world permanently further east.

In the twelfth and thirteenth centuries the Islamic world was disrupted by a new wave of invaders, the Mongols, who founded states in Iran, central Asia and south Russia (page 46). The Mongols defeated the Seljuk Turks in 1243 and sacked Baghdad in 1258, bringing about the end of the Abbasid Empire, but their defeat by the Mamelukes of Egypt at Ain Jalut in Palestine in 1260 marked their furthest westward advance. The Mongols' retreat created a vacuum which was

filled by the rise of a number of Turcoman dynasties, one of which, the Ottomans, had risen to pre-eminence by the beginning of the fourteenth century. Islam continued to expand in India (map 4), Indonesia (map 5) and in sub-Saharan Africa (page 60); today there are about 400 million Muslims, forming about one seventh of the population of the world.

5 Islam in S.E. Asia
- spread of Islam
- 13th/14th centuries
- 15th century
- 16th century

2 The Middle East and North Africa, 786-1260
- Abbasid Caliphate at greatest extent 786-809
- countries recognising Abbasid suzerainty c.1090
- territory disputed between Seljuks and Byzantine Empire
- Zaidi Imams
- Almohads 1130-1269
- line of Turkish advance
- *Seljuks* Muslim dynasties with dates

3 The Muslim reconquest of Palestine
- boundary of Crusader states
- Byzantine Empire
- *conquests of Saladin:*
  - before 1171
  - before 1187
  - 1187 to 1189

The Byzantine world, 610-1453

The history of the Roman empire was marked almost from the outset by a shift of focus to the east. The original cause was the lure of the wealth of the older oriental civilisations and the economic strength of the great commercial centres of Egypt and western Asia (page 24). Later, the loss of the western provinces to Germanic invaders (page 34) hastened the trend. Simultaneously the great Persian revival under the Sasanians forced Rome to concentrate its efforts on defence of its eastern frontier. After Justinian (page 30) the west was neglected, the Roman empire became an eastern, Greek-speaking dominion. The change is conventionally placed in the reign of Heraclius (610–641). From this time it is customary to speak of a Byzantine rather than a Roman empire.

Heraclius brought the long contest with Persia to a victorious close at Nineveh (628), but almost immediately was confronted by an even more redoubtable foe: Islam. The struggle with Islam (page 40) and with the Slavs, pressing against the European frontier in the Balkans (page 32), now became the dominant fact in Byzantine history. What is remarkable is Byzantine resilience. To meet the Arab threat, Asia Minor was reorganised into military districts, or 'themes', manned by a peasant militia (map 2). After two long Arab sieges of Constantinople had been repelled (674–8, 717–8), the new Macedonian dynasty (867–1056) launched a vigorous counter-offensive. By the death of Basil II (976–1025) the frontiers had been pushed back almost to their earlier limits. The Arabs were driven back to Jerusalem (976), and Bulgaria was finally reduced to a group of Christian provinces. Even later Manuel I (1143–80) still planned to recover the former Byzantine territories in Italy. But constant war imposed heavy financial strains, as well as profound and debilitating social change, and in spite of phases of aggressive counter-offensive and expansion, the frontiers steadily shrank (map 1).

After Basil I, the decisive fact was the appearance of a new foe, the Seljuk Turks (page 40). The crushing Seljuk victory at Manzikert (1071) induced Alexios I (1081–1118) to call on the west for help, thus initiating the sequence of events that led to the First Crusade. In retrospect, it was a disastrous move. The Franks were less concerned to aid Byzantium than to set up their own principalities in Palestine and Asia Minor. The Normans, by now in control of Sicily and Byzantine Italy, were greedy for Byzantine territory in the Morea (Peloponnese) and further east. The Italian cities, Venice to the fore, were striving to engross the oriental trade (page 36). The outcome, after a century of vicissitudes, was the Fourth Crusade (1202–4), the conquest and pillage of Constantinople, the partition of the Byzantine empire, and the establishment in its place of a Latin empire (map 3). But the Latin empire proved short-lived. The Greek-speaking population resented it, and a new dynasty, the Palaeologi, restored the Greek empire in 1261.

It was, nevertheless, only a shadow of the former Byzantine empire; and when a new Turkish people, the Ottomans, established itself in Anatolia, and then, outflanking Constantinople, advanced into Byzantium's European territories (page 48), its fate was sealed (map 4). The rest of the story is an epilogue, ending with the fall of Constantinople in 1453. Nevertheless the story of Byzantium is not without greatness and lasting achievements. For centuries it was ahead of the west in government and in the arts of civilisation. It also passed on its culture and its religion to the Balkan peoples and to Russia. 'Two Romes have fallen,' a Russian monk wrote shortly after 1453, 'but the third is standing, and there shall be no fourth.' He was speaking of Moscow. Russia, gradually consolidated under its Varangian rulers and their Muscovite successors (page 44), now emerged as heir to the Byzantine inheritance. This was to be a fact of lasting importance in world history.

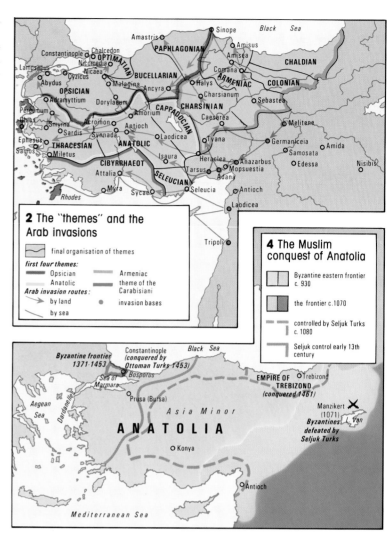

2 The "themes" and the Arab invasions

final organisation of themes

first four themes:
Opsician
Anatolic

Armeniac
theme of the Carabisiani

Arab invasion routes:
→ by land   ● invasion bases
→ by sea

4 The Muslim conquest of Anatolia

Byzantine eastern frontier c. 930

the frontier c.1070

controlled by Seljuk Turks c. 1080

Seljuk control early 13th century

1 The Byzantine Empire, 628-1143

imperial frontier c. 628
imperial frontier c. 1025
imperial frontier c. 1143

special areas:
Exarchate of Ravenna
to Lombards 751

Exarchate of Africa
to Arabs from 670
to Franks from 754
to Arabs from 815

Catapanate of Italy
to Normans from 1071

general territorial losses:
to Arabs 636-641
to Arabs after 641

to Seljuk Turks from 1065
Sultanate of Rum from 1071

temporary reconquests:
Africa 685-710
Syria 975
Sicily 1038-1043
Ani 1054
Edessa 1052
Rum c. 1118

3 The Crusades and the decline of Byzantium

Legend:
- the Norman attack 1084-5
- routes of the First Crusade 1096-7
- the Norman attack 1147
- the Norman attack 1185
- route of Fourth Crusade 1202-4
- imperial frontier 1180
- imperial territory in 1214
- Despotate of Epirus
- Latin Empire in 1204
- Venetian territory in 1214

*Upper map labels:*

PECHENEGS · WALLACHIA · SERBIA · DALMATIA · *Adriatic Sea* · Vidin · *R. Danube* · Mesembria · Serdica · Philippopolis · Ragusa · Ochrida · Prilep · Adrianople · Constantinople · Dyrrhachium · Vodena · Tzurulum · Nicomedia · *Black Sea* · Sinope · Kastamuni · Theodosiopolis · Sebastea · Manzikert · *L. Van* · Bari · Brundisium · Avlona · Castoria · Berrhoea · Thessalonica · Cyzicus · Prusa · Nicaea · EMPIRE OF NICAEA · Ancyra · SELJUKS OF RUM · *R. Halys* · Caesarea · Samosata · NORMANS · Corfu · Nicopolis · Larissa · *Lemnos* · *Aegean Sea* · *Lesbos* · Adramyttium · Pergamum · Dorylaeum · Amorium · Philomelium · Tyana · Marash · Edessa · Cephalonia · Athens · *Negroponte* · *Chios* · Sardis · Smyrna · *R. Meander* · Chonae · Sozopolis · Iconium · Heraclea · Tarsus · Carrhae · *R. Euphrates* · MOREA · *Zacynthus* · Corinth · Attalia · Antioch · *R. Orontes* · Aleppo · Modon · *Cos* · RHODES · CYPRUS · Tripoli · Homs · Monemvasia · *Cerigo* · CRETE · Tyre · Acre · *Mediterranean Sea*

*Lower map labels:*

Caspian Sea · Bosporus · Cherson · ABASGIA · IBERIA · Tiflis · Singidunum · Dorostolon · Marcianopolis · *Black Sea* · Phasis · LAZICA · ALBANIA · *R. Danube* · Nicopolis · ...ESIA · DACIA · Serdica · THRACE · Anchialus · Arcadiopolis · Sinope · Trebizond · PONTUS · Kars · Ani · *R. Araxes* · Scupi · Philippopolis · Adrianople · Melantias · PAPHLAGONIA · Neocaesarea · Manzikert 1071 · Dyrrhachium · Ragusa · Pylae · Nicomedia · Heraclea · Constantinople · Helenopolis · *Van* · NEW EPIRUS · MACEDONIA · Gallipoli · Prusa · Malagina · Ancyra · Sebastea · Bitlis · Avlona · Thessalonica · BITHYNIA · GALATIA · *L. Urmia* · Troy · Abydus · Cotiaeum · Caesarea · CAPPADOCIA · Arabissos · Samosata · PERSIA · ANCIENT EPIRUS · Larissa · LYDIA · Germanicea · Edessa · Mosul · Nineveh · Kirkuk · THESSALY · Demetrias · Sardis · PHRYGIA · Carrhae · *R. Tigris* · *Aegean Sea* · Thebes · Ephesus · PISIDIA · CILICIA · Zeugma · Callinicum · Zenobia · Dastagord · Patras · Athens · Miletus · Iconium · Adana · Hieropolis · Circesium · *R. Euphrates* · Corinth · Halicarnassus · PAMPHYLIA · Attalia · Tarsus · Antioch · Aleppo · Ctesiphon · Seleucia · Lacedaemon · ISAURIA · *Rhodes* · Laodicea · Emesa · Palmyra · Hira · *Ionian Sea* · CYPRUS · Tripoli · Damascus · CRETE · Tiberias · PALESTINE · Bostra · Apollonia · Jerusalem · Gaza · Hebron · Maan · Petra · PENTAPOLIS · Damietta · Alexandria · Pelusium · TRIPOLITANIA · Mareotis · Memphis · ARABIA · Arsinoe · EGYPT · Tabuk · *R. Nile* · *Red Sea* · *Ionian Sea*

Early Russia
862-1245

Three factors shaped the early history of Russia: the movement eastward of Slav tribal settlers; the impact of the Vikings or Varangians, seafaring raiders and traders from Sweden who entered northern Russia c.850 (page 36) and imposed tribute on the neighbouring Slavs and Finns; the basic geography of the region, particularly the division between the forests of central and northern Russia and the treeless steppes of the south through which successive waves of invaders from Asia poured into Europe. Fierce Pechenegs controlled the fertile steppelands. To avoid them Slav colonists moved into central Russia, where they settled in the river basins, clearing the forests and living by agriculture, hunting, trapping and by the fur trade.

At first the Slavs resisted the Varangians. But in 862 they called in 'Rurik the Viking' to restore order and protect them from Pecheneg raiders. Rurik occupied Novgorod, but the Varangians immediately pushed south to Smolensk and then along the Dnieper to Kiev (882). They thus controlled the trade route from the Baltic to the Black Sea. At the same time they imposed their rule over the Slav tribes on both sides of the river (map 1). It was nevertheless only a loose tributary overlordship, and it was not until the time of Vladimir I of Kiev (980–1015)

that the tribal regions were welded together into a single state.

The reign of Vladimir's son, Yaroslav I (1019–54) was the high point of Kievan Russia. Converted to Christianity under Vladimir and in close contact with Constantinople, Kiev ranked high among European cities. But the new state had grown too quickly and after 1054 its decline was rapid. Dynastic conflict was incessant, and the administration ineffective. At the same time the destruction of the Khazar empire by Svyatoslav (965) opened the way for a new wave of Asiatic nomads, the Polovtsy, who broke through the defences erected by Vladimir I and sacked Kiev in 1093. The result was a great exodus of peasants northwards to the region between the Oka and the Volga, where many new towns were founded including Vladimir, Suzdal, Rostov, Moscow and Tver. Novgorod-Seversk, and in the west, Galich and Vladimir-Volynsk broke away from Kiev. After 1125 the axis of Russian life shifted north and the state broke up into warring principalities (map 2), among which Vladimir-Suzdal was outstanding.

The final blow to the old order was the Mongol invasions, which fell upon the Volga region before turning south against Kiev which was sacked in 1240 (map 3), while Novgorod was exposed simultaneously to German and Swedish attack. Mongol control was only indirect, but its results were far-reaching. Kievan Russia, already debilitated, disappeared for ever, and the way was open for the rise of Moscow.

2 Kievan Russia, 1054-1242

- ○ towns and places of significance 1054
- □ towns and places of significance 1054-1200
- *MARI* tribes
- ➡ movement of steppe nomads in 11th century
- ▬▬ defensive works built against nomads
- ≈ boundaries of Russian principalities c. 1200
- ⇢ Prince Igor Svyatoslavich's campaign against Polovtsy 1185
- ⋯ waterway trade routes
- ▬ tundra
- ▬ coniferous and deciduous forest
- ▬ steppe and desert
- ▬ mountain vegetation

SAMOYED

YUGRA

R. Pechora

Ural Mts

Arctic Circle

White Sea

R. Mezen

Pinega

Northern Dvina

CHUD

R. Onega

R. Vychegda

PERM

KARELIA

L. Onega

NOVGOROD EMPIRE

R. Surkhona

VYATKA TERRITORY

L. Ladoga

Beloozero

Gulf of Finland

Ladoga

R. Neva 1240

ESTS

R. Volkhov

Novgorod

L. Ilmen

Galich

MARI

Baltic Sea

L. Peipus 1242

Yuriev

ORDER

Gulf of Riga

Pskov

Izborsk

Yaroslavl

Rostov

Kostroma

R. Kama

KURS

Riga

Kukeynoys

Torzhok

Tver

VLADIMIR-SUZDAL

LIVONIAN

Gertsike

R. Lovat

Volok-Lamsky

Pereyaslavl

Suzdal

Nizhniy Novgorod

ZHMUD

Western Dvina

Toropets

Dmitrov

Moscow

Vladimir

R. Klyazma

TEUTONIC ORDER

Polotsk

SMOLENSK

R. Moskva

Bolgar

Bilyar

LITVA

POLOTSK

Vitebsk

Smolensk

R. Oka

Kolomna

Murom

VOLGA BULGARS

Orsha

Kopys

Ryazan

Suvar

Gorodno

Minsk

Koselsk

MUROM-RYAZAN

MORDVA

Nesvizh

Klechesk

CHERNIGOV

Bryansk

R. Desna

Karachev

Novosil

Berestye

Drogochin

VLADIMIR-VOLYNSK

TUROV-PINSK

Pinsk

Turov

Rechitsa

NOVGOROD-SEVERSK

Kholm

Vladimiro

Listem

Novgorod-Severskiy

R. Ural

Cherven

Vruchy

Lyubech

Rylsk

Kursk

Belz

Korosten

Chernigov

Peremyshl

Gorodets

KIEV

Kiev 1093

Terebovl

Pereyaslavl

R. Don

Galich

Rodnya

Donets

PEREYASLAVL

R. Volga

GALICH

Kolomyya

Kamenets

Poltava

POLOVTSY (in 1054)

R. Prut

PECHENEGS

P O L O V T S Y

T O R K I

Peresechen

Southern Bug

in 1200

R. Donets

SAKSINY

HUNGARIAN KINGDOM

Belgorod

R. Dniester

R. Dnieper

Sarkel

Itil

Carpathian Mts

Pereslavets

Oleshe

Sea of Azov

R. Danube

Dristov

Khersones

Sugdeya

Tmutarakan

Caspian Sea

BULGARIA

Kasogi

R. Kuban

R. Kuma

Black Sea

KASOGI

YASI

R. Terek

45

The Mongol Empire, 1206-1696

The Mongols, a primitive nomadic people from the depths of Asia, had tremendous influence on the course of world history. Few in number, but augmented by Turcoman auxiliaries, they threw themselves against the old centres of civilisation in east and west (map 1). After overrunning the Ch'in empire in north China between 1211 and 1234, they defeated the Sung army and ruled over the whole of China from 1280 to 1367 (page 50). They even launched seaborne expeditions against Java and Japan, though neither was successful. In the west their first victim was the Muslim empire of Khwarizm (1220), after which they turned against the Abbasid caliphate, sacking Baghdad in 1258. But the decisive Mameluke victory at Ain Jalut (1260) halted their advance in this direction. Meanwhile, they had thrown themselves against Christian Europe, overrunning the northern Russian principalities in 1237-8 and sacking Kiev in 1240 (page 44), before advancing into Hungary and Poland and destroying a German-Polish army at Legnica in 1241 (map 2).

The architect of these amazing victories was a certain Temujin, known to history as Genghis Khan, son of a Mongol chief, who united the different Mongol tribes under his leadership (1206) and subdued other neighbouring, mainly Turcoman, tribes, before turning against China in 1211. Genghis died in 1227, but his wars of conquest were continued by his sons and grandsons, among whom Ogedei, elected Great Khan in 1229, and Möngke, who succeeded in 1251, were outstanding. But the vast empire lacked coherence and stability, and the Mongols failed to develop appropriate institutions. Genghis himself divided his empire among his four sons, like earlier Frankish rulers in the west (page 34), and with similar results. Already on the death of Ogedei (1241), Genghis' grandson Batu, commander-in-chief in the west, withdrew his army from Poland to the base on the lower Volga, in order to take part in the choice of a successor. It never returned and western Europe was spared, though Russia remained a Mongol tributary for over two centuries. Finally, on the death of Möngke (1259), the brittle unity dissolved. Kublai (d. 1294) was elected Great Khan, but instead of a general overlordship, his authority was confined to the east, and the western khanates (Chagatai, Il-Khan and the Golden Horde) went their own way (map 3). By the sixteenth century only the eastern khanate survived: in Persia the Ilkhanids were displaced by a local Turcoman dynasty in 1353, and later the successors of the Golden Horde, which had broken up into a number of smaller khanates at the time of Tamerlane the Great, were mopped up by a resurgent Russia.

It was, paradoxically, Timur, or Tamerlane (1336-1405), traditionally the last great Mongol conqueror (though he was in fact a Turcoman from Transoxiana), whose victorious career initiated the decline. Timur's vast empire (map 4) fell apart rapidly after his death while leading an expedition against China; but in the course of his conquests he destroyed the Chagatai khanate, which ceased to exist in 1405, and dislocated the

Golden Horde. Henceforward the Mongols were under attack from all sides, increasingly at a disadvantage as the introduction of firearms weighed the balance on their adversaries' side. In the west Russia absorbed the former territories of the Golden Horde (page 84). In the east, the Mongols threw back a major Chinese assault in 1449 (page 50) and resumed their offensive under Altan Khan (1507-82); but in the end Mongolia itself was brought under Chinese dominion in 1696 by the new Ch'ing dynasty (page 106). Nevertheless the Mongol impact had lasting results. All the older civilisations were affected; faced by the Mongol challenge, their history took a new course.

1 The Mongol Empire before 1259

- the Mongol Empire before 1259
- ← campaigns under Genghis Khan
- ← campaigns of his successors
- ‖‖‖‖ incursions and loose Mongol control
- *OIROTS* Mongol tribes around 1220

2 The Mongol invasion of Europe, 1237-42

3 The break-up of the Mongol Empire after 1259

- successor states to the Mongol Empire

The Muslim resurgence
1301-1639

The revival of Islam after 1300 and the great wave of Muslim expansion that followed, dominated the next four centuries, far more so than European expansion, which had only marginal effects before 1700. After 1354 the Christian west stood on the defensive, while the Turks conquered the whole of Europe east of the Adriatic and south of the Danube. The progress of Islam in the east was equally remarkable. By 1500 northern India was under Muslim rule, and most of the south after 1565 when the last surviving Hindu state, Vijayanagar, succumbed. It prevailed also in the oases of central Asia, in the outlying provinces of Ming China, and was making rapid headway in Java.

This amazing revival was the more remarkable because in 1258, when the Mongols sacked Baghdad and overthrew the caliphate (page 46), the Muslim world was in disarray. The Seljuk sultanate (page 40) had broken up after half a century, and only the Mamelukes of Egypt and Syria maintained any sort of political stability. Two factors transformed the situation. One was the revitalisation of Islam itself under the impact of Sufi mysticism. The other was the infiltration, with or in the wake of the Mongols, of Turkic peoples from central Asia, who, after conversion and assimilation, became the spearhead of Muslim advance. It was they who, in 1206, set up the Delhi Sultanate, the leading Indian state until the appearance in 1526 of Babur, another warrior from inner Asia. In the west Turkish warriors settled around 1265 in north-west Anatolia, and here in 1301 their leader, Osman, founded a state which became the core of the future Ottoman empire (map 1). By 1354 the Turks had crossed the Dardanelles to Gallipoli, and their victory at Kosovo (1389) and repulse of a Christian counter-offensive at Nicopolis (1396) left them masters of the Balkans. Only the invasion of Timur (page 46) and his destruction of the Turkish army at Ankara (1402) gave hard-pressed Byzantium respite. But the renewal of expansion under Murad II (1421–51) and Mehemmed II (1451–81) sealed its fate. In 1453 Constantinople fell, and Mehemmed went on to extend control over Moldavia, the Crimea and Trebizond, turning the Black Sea into an Ottoman lake.

By the time that Suleiman the Magnificent (1520–66) succeeded to the throne, the Ottoman empire was one of the world's leading powers, comparable with Ming China or Charles V's empire in the west. But now two other empires arose to share pre-eminence in the Muslim world. The one was the Mughal empire, founded by Babur in 1526, but only consolidated by his grandson, Akbar (1556–1605). The other was Persia, which had been in a state of chaos ever since it was overrun by Timur. Here, in 1500, the leader of a fanatical Shi'i sect, Ismail Safavi, seized Tabriz, crowned himself shah as Ismail I (1500–24), and quickly reunited the country. Safavid Persia reached its peak under Abbas I (1587–1629), by which time the three Muslim empires controlled a wide belt of territory from the frontiers of Austria and Morocco to the borders of China, the foothills of the Himalayas and the Bay of Bengal (map 2). But their divisions and rivalries, particularly the clash between Sunni Turkey and Shi'i Persia, drove a wedge into the Muslim world, comparable to the conflict between Catholics and Protestants in western Europe. Shi'ism had originated centuries earlier over the question of the true succession to the Prophet Mohammed; but wider issues, religious and political, were involved. In Persia a resurgent nationalism certainly played a part. The Safavids were the first native Persian dynasty since Sasanian times, and Ismail I's decision to make Shi'ism the Persian state religion was a challenge to the Sunni Turkish sultan. The Ottoman reaction was swift. In 1514 Ismail's armies were defeated at Çaldiran, and in 1516–17 the Ottomans captured Syria and Egypt from the Mamelukes. These successes enabled Suleiman to resume the Ottoman advance in Europe. After the battle of Mohács (1526) Hungary was overrun and Vienna was besieged (1529). But Persia remained a thorn in the Ottoman side. The long wars against the Safavids (1534–35, 1554–55, 1577–90, 1603–19) were not the only reason for the Muslim decline which became apparent after 1560, but they certainly hastened it. This was a great age of Islamic art and architecture, particularly in Persia and India. But in a changing world Islam remained static. All three Muslim empires were essentially land-based; but now hegemony was passing to the sea, and to the peoples on the fringe – the Dutch, the French, the English – who knew how to master and exploit it.

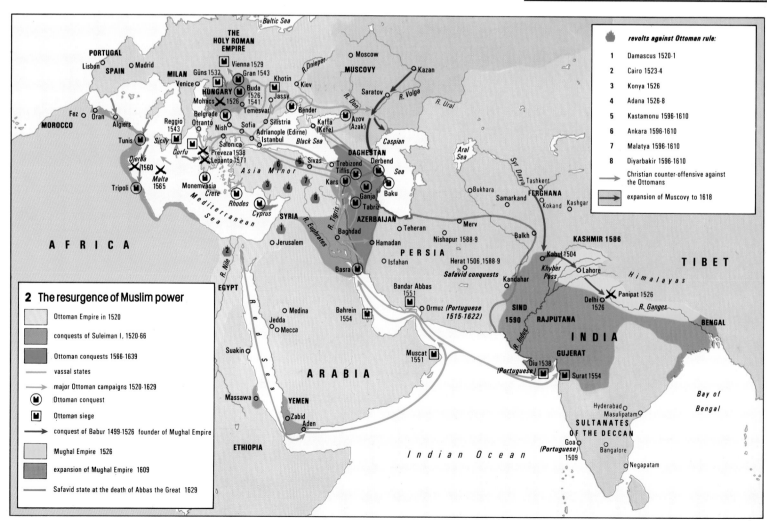

2 The resurgence of Muslim power

- Ottoman Empire in 1520
- conquests of Suleiman I, 1520-66
- Ottoman conquests 1566-1639
- vassal states
- major Ottoman campaigns 1520-1629
- Ⓜ Ottoman conquest
- ▣ Ottoman siege
- conquest of Babur 1499-1526 founder of Mughal Empire
- Mughal Empire 1526
- expansion of Mughal Empire 1609
- Safavid state at the death of Abbas the Great 1629

revolts against Ottoman rule:

1. Damascus 1520-1
2. Cairo 1523-4
3. Konya 1526
4. Adana 1526-8
5. Kastamonu 1596-1610
6. Ankara 1596-1610
7. Malatya 1596-1610
8. Diyarbakir 1596-1610

- Christian counter-offensive against the Ottomans
- expansion of Muscovy to 1618

A R Y

TRANSYLVANIA

Carpathian Mts

MOLDAVIA (1455)
(BOĞDAN)

○ Suczawa

○ Jassy (Yaş)

R. Dniester (Turla)

R. Prut

COSSACK SETTLEMENTS

R U S S I A

R. Dnieper (Ak Su)

50°

○ Tergoviste

WALLACHIA (1396)
(EFLÂK)

(1484)

BUJAK

KHANATE OF THE CRIMEA (VASSAL 1475)

dre 1444

○ Bucharest (Bükreş)

○ Giurgiu (Yergöğü) ○ Silistria

○ Akkerman

R. Don

○ Azov (Azak)

○ Vidin

S

DOBRUJA

Kilia ○

Sea of Azov

○ Nicopolis
1396

Bakhchesaray
(Bahçesaray) ○

Kerch (Kerç) ○

ELIA (1393)

LGARIA)

○ Sofia

○ Trnovo

1444

○ Varna

Black   Sea

Kaffa
(Kefe) ○

45°

○ Philippopolis
(Filibe)

CIRCASSIA
(ÇERKES)

○ Adrianople (Edirne)
1361

Bosporus

○ Sinop

Istanbul (Constantinople)
⊙ 1453

CANDAR
(KASTAMONU)1393 1461

○ Kastamonu

○ Samsun

C a u c a s u s   M t s

○ Gallipoli
(Gelibolu)
1354

Dardanelles

nucleus of
Ottoman state c. 1281

⊙ Bursa
1326

○ Amasya

Trebizond
(Trabzon)
1461

○ Tiflis

KARASI 1345

Söğüt 1265

EMPIRE OF TREBIZOND

Eskişehir 1289

Ankara
1402 ✕

hios
noa

○ Manisa

A N A T O L I A

○ Smyrna
(Izmir)

SARUHAN 1390
1405

GERMIYAN 1380
1428

Sivas ○

Otluk-Beli 1473 ✕

Erzurum ○

Samos

SIVAS 1398

K u r d i s t a n

40°

AYDIN
1396
1426

HAMID
1381-90

○ Konya

Kayseri ○

KARAKOYUNLU

MENTEŞE
1396

TEKE 1391
1427

KARAMAN

AKKOYUNLU

Lake Van

Çaldiran
1514 ✕

○ Rhodes

KNIGHTS OF ST JOHN

1390 1468

Taurus Mts

DHU'L-KADR
1398 1515

○ Adana

○ Diyarbakir

Lake Urmia

Tabriz
1514

✕ Marj Dabik 1516

R. Tigris

M e d i t e r r a n e a n   S e a

Cyprus
(Venetian 1489,
Ottoman tributary 1517)

○ Aleppo 1516

○ Rakka

○ Mosul

○ Tripoli

S A F A V I D   E M P I R E

(from 1501)

35°

○ Beirut

○ Damascus 1516

O T T O M A N   E M P I R E   (1517)

○ Alexandria

○ Jerusalem

○ Baghdad

M A M E L U K E

✕ Al-Raydaniyya

○ Cairo 1517

SHARIFS OF MECCA

R. Nile

R. Euphrates

Red   Sea

to 3rd cataract
of the R. Nile

1 The Ottoman advance, 1300-1520

☐ probable extent of Ottoman state c. 1300	☐ reduced frontiers of Ottoman state after Timur's invasion and civil war of 1403-13
← main routes of Ottoman advance	● Emirates restored by Timur in 1402
⬚ conquests of Osman c. 1300-26	1468 date of final reincorporation into Ottoman Empire
⬚ conquests of Orkhan 1326-62	✕ European counter-offensive against the Ottomans
⬚ conquests of Murad I, 1362-89	▨ conquests and re-conquests 1413-51 (Mehemmed I.1413-21, Murad II, 1421-51)
1390 absorbed Emirates with date of first absorption	☐ boundary of Ottoman state at the accession of Mehemmed II, 1451
⬚ conquests of Bayezid 1389-1402	⬚ vassal states 1451
(1389) other places and dates of Ottoman conquest	▨ vassal states 1512
⬚ vassal states of Bayezid 1402	▨ Ottoman empire in 1512
▨ Venetian territories	☐ western frontiers of Safavid state in c. 1512 including tributary states
← invasion of Timur (Tamerlane) 1402	◄ major campaigns of Selim I, 1512-1520
⊙ successive centres of Ottoman state, with dates of conquest	☐ Ottoman sphere of influence c. 1520

China and its neighbours
618-1644

The recovery of China from the barbarian invasions of the fourth and fifth centuries (page 32) was the work of the Sui dynasty (581–617). But it was the T'ang (618–907) who ushered in one of the great ages of Chinese history. Under the T'ang and their successors, the Sung (960–1279), China attained a level of prosperity, social stability and civilisation far ahead of contemporary Europe; and it was only another wave of invasion from inner Asia, this time the Mongols (page 46), that brought this era of wellbeing to a temporary halt. During the period of Mongol domination (1280–1368) much of the land was devastated, particularly in the north, and the population, which in 1280 probably topped 100 million, was reduced by 1393 to 60 million. The Ming dynasty (1368–1644) reversed these setbacks and put China back on the course charted by its T'ang predecessors.

T'ang China (map 1) was a centralised empire with a uniform administrative organisation of prefectures, in which the old ruling aristocracy was replaced by officials recruited by an examination system which lasted into the twentieth century. A massive movement of population into the fertile Yangtze valley and southern China produced large agricultural surpluses which stimulated trade and urban development. The T'ang also embarked on an ambitious programme of external expansion which carried them in the north-west to the Tarim Basin before they were halted by the Arabs at the Talas river in 751. By 649, the end of the reign of T'ai-tsung, 88 Asiatic peoples recognised Chinese overlordship. But the widespread military expeditions over-extended the empire's resources, many of the gains proved only temporary, and after 1127 even north China was lost and only recovered after the fall of the Mongol dynasty in 1386. Their successors, the Ming, also engaged in an active foreign policy, particularly against the Mongols in the north (map 4), but these ventures proved too costly and sparked off a series of rebellions which, coupled with external pressures from the Manchus in Liaotung and Japanese raiders, toppled the dynasty.

Military and political reverses did not impede the expansion of Chinese culture and political institutions to all her neighbouring states. Those most directly affected were Korea, under Chinese rule from 668 to 676 and a vassal state after 1392, Japan and South-East Asia, though in the latter region, where they came into contact with Indian and (from about AD 1300) Islamic influences, they were largely confined to north Vietnam. In South-East Asia the small temple states of the ninth to twelfth centuries (Prambanan, Angkor, Pagan), established under Hindu and Buddhist influence, gave way after the thirteenth century to new political centres (Ava, Pegu, Phnom Penh), while in Vietnam, where Chinese attempts at reconquest failed, a new kingdom of Dai Viet arose. But behind the fluctuating political fortunes the outstanding fact was the formative influence of Hinduism, Buddhism and Confucianism; their assimilation defined the distinctive character of South-East Asian civilisation (map 2).

In Japan Chinese influence was more direct. As early as AD 645 the whole administration had been re-modelled on the pattern of T'ang China. The two capitals, Nara (710) and Kyoto (794), were copied from the T'ang capital of Changan, and Buddhism was introduced from China. But after 1192 the bureaucratic state was displaced by a feudalised society, until finally, between 1467 and 1590, the country broke up into a series of warring Daimyo clans (map 3). It was the work of Oda Nobunaga (1534–82) and Hideyoshi Toyotomi (1535–98) to bring the anarchy under control, and prepare the way for the Tokugawa shogunate which gave Japan 250 years of internal peace and prosperity until, in the middle of the nineteenth century the western powers forced Japan into the modern world (page 126).

2 South-East Asia, AD 500-1500

- ▲ Hindu-Buddhist remains and temples AD 500-1300
- ⊡ major political centres of c.AD 1200-c.1300
- ← Mongol attacks 1257-92
- Dai Viet Kingdom: independent from 10th century
- Champa Kingdom: gradually absorbed by Dai Viet (11th-15th centuries).
- Khmers: their temple kingdoms united under Angkor (9th-14th centuries).
- Thai-Lao-Shan region: the Thai peoples expanded southwards from the 12th century, conquering the Mons of Dvaravati. Shan states later fell under Burmese domination.
- Mons: their kingdoms of Thaton (11th century) and Pegu (14th-15th centuries) were later absorbed by the Burmese, and their kingdom of Dvaravati (7th-13th centuries) by the Thais.
- Burmese: their empire of Pagan (11th-13th centuries) was succeeded by Ava and other states (14th-16th centuries)
- Arakanese: their Muslim kingdom independent in 14th and 15th centuries; later absorbed by Burma.

In maritime S.E. Asia temple kingdoms are found in Java and seafaring trading states flourished, notably the Srivijayan empire of Sumatra and the Malay Peninsula (7th-13th centuries).

3 Civil war in Japan 1467-1590

spheres of influence of the most powerful Daimyo clans

—— boundaries of Daimyo domains

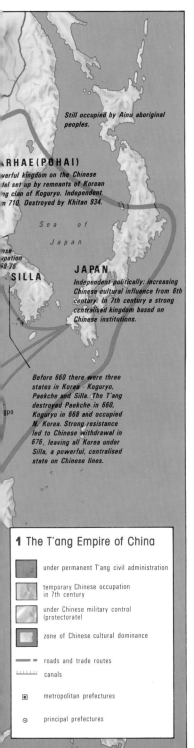

Still occupied by Ainu aboriginal peoples.

...RHAE (POHAI)
...werful kingdom on the Chinese
...del set up by remnants of Korean
...ng clan of Koguryo. Independent
...n 710. Destroyed by Khitan 934.

JAPAN
Independent politically: increasing Chinese cultural influence from 6th century. In 7th century a strong centralised kingdom based on Chinese institutions.

Before 660 there were three states in Korea - Koguryo, Paekche and Silla. The T'ang destroyed Paekche in 660, Koguryo in 668 and occupied N. Korea. Strong resistance led to Chinese withdrawal in 676, leaving all Korea under Silla, a powerful, centralised state on Chinese lines.

1 The T'ang Empire of China

- under permanent T'ang civil administration
- temporary Chinese occupation in 7th century
- under Chinese military control (protectorate)
- zone of Chinese cultural dominance
- —— roads and trade routes
- canals
- ⊡ metropolitan prefectures
- ⊙ principal prefectures

4 China under the Ming, 1368-1644

- major post roads
- Great Wall
- canals
- ⊙ provincial capital
- ☐ the nine frontier defence areas
- ⊡ National capital
- guard units
- Japanese pirate invasions before 16th century
- Japanese pirate invasions after 1550
- Chinese expeditions against the Mongols

The 'Willow palisade' surrounding area of Chinese settlement in Liaotung

Ming counter attack to defend Korea

Japanese invasions of Korea under Hideyoshi Toyotomi 1582, 1592, 1597-98

Northern and Western Europe, 930-1314

Two features marked the period following the Viking and Magyar invasions in northern and western Europe: the emergence of settled states and the spread of Christianity. The two went hand in hand. Both in Scandinavia and in the Slavonic east the Christian church, introduced in Denmark by Harold Bluetooth in 965, in Norway by Olaf Tryggveson (995-1000), in Bohemia by Boleslav II (967-99), and in Poland by Miesko I (960-92), contributed substantially to political cohesion. The rise of powerful kingdoms in Poland and Denmark was also in part a response to German pressure. In Poland (map 1) the Piast dynasty united the tribes of Great (or northern) Poland. Boleslav Chrobry (992-1025) not only added Little Poland, Silesia and Lausitz but also temporarily Bohemia and Moravia. In Denmark Harold Bluetooth (940-86) defended Slesvig from German attack, strengthening and extending the fortified Danevirke (map 3). In Norway and Sweden development was hampered by formidable geographical obstacles (map 5). Under Sweyn I, who also became king of England in 1013, both countries were under Danish control; and Sweyn's son Canute the Great (1014-35) ruled a great but short-lived Anglo-Scandinavian empire (map 4). Following an interlude under Edward the Confessor (1042-66) England passed under Norman rule (page 36). Norway achieved independence and was united under Magnus the Good (1033-47). Sweden (except for the southern provinces which remained under Danish rule) was welded together by the kings of Uppland, and Denmark itself settled down within its frontiers after the death of Sweyn II (1047-74).

Nevertheless all countries were plagued by dynastic conflict and aristocratic resistance. In Poland Boleslav Chrobry's ambitious foreign policy provoked a sharp reaction after his death. In England William the Conqueror was faced by baronial unrest as early as 1074. But it was France that suffered most from feudal disruption. The Capetian kings, who displaced the Carolingians in 987, were confined to the Ile de France, and even here royal authority was insecure until the reign of Louis VI (1108-37). Even then the Capetians lagged behind the feudal princes. The continental possessions of Henry II of England (the so-called Angevin Empire) far outmatched the French royal domain (map 2). When Philip Augustus (1180-1223) conquered Normandy (1204) and the Angevin Empire collapsed, English rule was confined to Gascony, and the Capetians embarked on a policy of expansion which carried them to the Mediterranean by 1229.

In England expansion had begun on the morrow of the Conquest when Norman barons invaded Wales and set up extensive marcher lordships. A century later they moved on to Ireland. By 1250 two-thirds of the country had been occupied, but Ireland remained divided and rebellious. So also did Wales which had seen a remarkable national resurgence under Llewellyn the Great (1197-1240). But Edward I (1272-1307) would not brook Welsh independence. After a first campaign (1276), followed by systematic castle building to enforce English control, a second campaign in 1283 (map 7) placed the principality directly under royal administration in 1284. Edward's attempt in 1296 to repeat the process in Scotland was a costly failure, culminating in the English defeat at Bannockburn in 1314. Like his French contemporary, Philip the Fair (1285-1314), defeated by the Flemings in 1302, Edward had overreached himself. The great baronial families, still firmly ensconced (map 6), forced him in 1297 to confirm the charters wrested from King John in 1215. It was a prelude to the aristocratic reaction and the setbacks of the fourteenth century.

1 The rise of Poland

- Polish territory 960-92
- lands added by Boleslav Chrobry 992-1025
- lands temporarily in Polish occupation
- Hungarian territory
- German territory
- ⊡ bishoprics with date foundation
- ⚓ archbishoprics
- wasteland (forest and swamp)

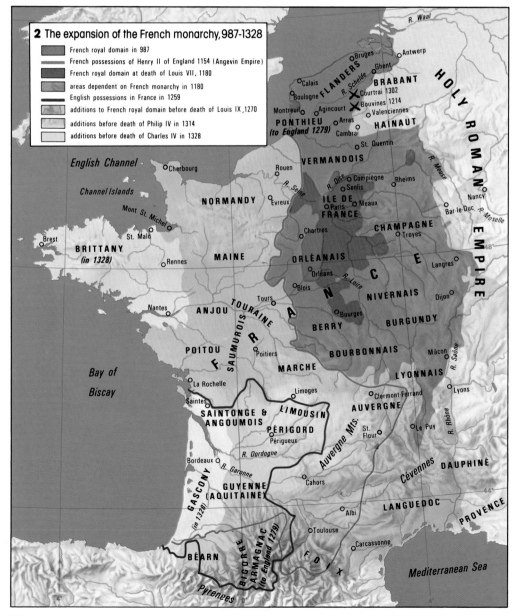

2 The expansion of the French monarchy, 987-1328

- French royal domain in 987
- French possessions of Henry II of England 1154 (Angevin Empire)
- French royal domain at death of Louis VII, 1180
- areas dependent on French monarchy in 1180
- English possessions in France in 1259
- additions to French royal domain before death of Louis IX, 1270
- additions before death of Philip IV in 1314
- additions before death of Charles IV in 1328

6 The British Isles, 1215-1307

- boundary of England and Scotland 1157
- land claimed by Scotland 1139-57
- English Marcher lordships in Wales
- Principality of Wales 1284
- County Palatine of Chester with Flint
- Edward I's Scottish campaign 1296
- meetings of Edward I's Parliament
- *Clare* great landowners c.1307

Ireland
- Norman conquests 1169-1215
- Norman conquests 1215-1307
- Irish lands 1307
- Norman castles

4 The empire of Canute the Great, 1014-1035

5 The Northern Kingdoms c.1035

3 The rise of Denmark

- bishoprics
- archbishoprics
- northern extent of Danish territory
- circular fortifications
- Haervej - the main land route through Jutland

7 The conquest of Wales, 1283-4

- Principality of Wales in 1282
- Edward I's Welsh castles
- Edward I's campaigns 1283-4

53

The medieval German Empire
962-1356

Germany, or the eastern half of the Frankish empire, was the first country in Europe to recover from the setbacks of the ninth century invasions (page 36). This fact assured its predominance for upward of three centuries. German rulers never sought to assert control over the West Frankish lands, but, as heirs to the Carolingians, they claimed the imperial title and the right to rule over Italy and the lands of the former 'Middle Kingdom.' Germany's control of the Alpine passes between Lombardy and the Rhinelands assured not only its political preponderance but also gave it a leading place in the cultural exchange between Mediterranean and northern Europe.

There was, at first, no sense of a common German, or East Frankish, identity, and the effective control of the first German ruler, Henry I of Saxony (919–936), scarcely extended beyond Saxony and Franconia (map 1). But his son, Otto I (936–973), brought the other German duchies under royal control. Also, by defeating the Magyars at the battle of Lechfeld (955), he freed Germany from external threats and was able, in 951 and 961, to intervene effectively in Italy. His coronation as emperor (962) sealed the historic connexion between Germany and Italy. As heir to the Carolingian tradition, he also inaugurated a Christian drive against the pagan Slavs on the eastern frontier. But the great Slav revolt of 983 halted this advance until the twelfth century, and German efforts were concentrated instead on the south and south-west. The result, in 1034, was the addition of Burgundy to the imperial domains.

In spite of these successes, aristocratic resistance to royal centralisation was never overcome, and an opportunity to renew it came in 1075, when the outbreak of conflict between the emperor Henry IV (1056–1106) and the papacy, which saw imperial power in Italy as a threat to its independence, played into the German princes' hands. The ensuing civil war (1076–1122) was a turning point in German history. Although the monarchy emerged successful, its position was permanently weakened. German power was apparently restored during the reign of Frederick I (1152–1190), but it depended increasingly on the riches of Italy, and this embroiled Frederick not only with the papacy but also with the Italian cities. The marriage of his son, Henry VI, with Constance, the heiress of Sicily (1186), held out new possibilities. But the prospect of the union of Sicily and the empire alarmed the papacy, which saw itself being encircled, and led to the final struggle between Frederick II (1212–1250), and Pope Innocent IV (1243–1254).

Meanwhile Germany was being overtaken by the western monarchies (page 52). The empire under Frederick II was still the most imposing political body in Europe (map 3), but by 1200 Paris was the intellectual and cultural centre of Europe, and by comparison with England and Sicily Germany's financial organisation was antiquated. Eastward expansion had begun again after 1138 (map 2). It added two-thirds to the German territories and shifted the seat of power from Rhine to Elbe. But the beneficiaries were the princes on the eastern frontier, not the monarchy. Later, the Teutonic Knights conquered heathen Prussia (map 4), but within the empire the tendency was to fragmentation rather than expansion, and gains in the east were offset by loss of control over Italy which now went its own way (page 56). In default of royal authority local leagues were formed to resist princely encroachments and to preserve the peace. The most famous and enduring was the Swiss Confederation, formed in 1291 (map 5). The Golden Bull of 1356, formally recognising the autonomy of the princes, marked the beginning of a new era in German history; but the age of German preponderance in Europe had already ended a century earlier.

2 German eastward expansion

SORBS west Slav tribes most affected by German expansion

expansion to 1250

expansion 1250 to 1300

expansion during 14th century

5 The rise of the Swiss Confederation

original cantons 1291-1315

cantons added to 1389

✕ battles for independence

— main roads

4 The conquest of Prussia

→ advance of Teutonic Knights

swamp and wilderness

occupied before 1309

occupied 1309-1382

occupied 1382-1411

Riga 1201 foundation date of town

1 The East Frankish Kingdom of Otto I

▲ royal mint under Otto I

← Otto's main campaigns

← main Magyar raids

North Sea

Baltic Sea

Utrecht

Bruges
Ghent
Brabant
Brussels
Hainaut
Cambrai
✕ Bouvines 1214

Lower
Lorraine
Aachen
Cologne
Liège

Holstein
Hamburg
Bremen
Lüneburg
✕ Bornhöved 1227
Lübeck
Schwerin

S a x o n y
Münster
DUCHY OF
WESTPHALIA
(after 1180)
Dortmund
Paderborn
Goslar
ANHALT
(After 1180)

Altmark
DUCHY OF BRUNSWICK
(after 1235)
Magdeburg
Havelberg
Brandenburg

Pomerania

Cammin
Stettin

Gdansk
(Danzig)

Gniezno
Poznań

K I N G D O M

Trier
Kaiserslautern
Verdun
Metz
Trifels
Toul
Hagenau
Strassburg

Thuringia
Hersfeld
Erfurt

Frankfurt
Mainz
Worms
Speyer
Gelnhausen
Würzburg
Bamberg

Naumburg

Meissen
Altenburg

Lusatia
Meissen
Freiberg

Eger
Prague

Silesia
Wrocław (Breslau)

K I N G D O M

O F   B O H E M I A

F r a n c o n i a
Nuremberg
Regensburg

O F

Moravia

Upper
Lorraine

Alsace

Hohenstaufen
Ulm
Augsburg

Swabia

B a v a r i a
Munich

Austria

Vienna

Besançon
Basel
Constance
Zurich

G E R M A N Y

Salzburg

Styria

Semmering ⴷ

Burgundy

Brenner ⴷ

Tyrol
Brixen
Bozen

Carinthia
Pontebba ⴷ

St. Gotthard ⴷ   Septimer ⴷ

Friuli

Carniola

K I N G D O M

St. Bernard ⴷ

Lyons

A
L
P
S

Como
Bergamo
Novara
Milan
Brescia
Vicenza
Verona
Padua

Trient
Verona

Aquileia

Venice

Mont Cenis ⴷ

O F

Vercelli
Lodi
Crema
Cremona

Treviso

V E N E T I A N

Turin
Pavia
Piacenza
Mantua

Asti
Savoy
Alessandria
Tortona
Parma
Reggio
Modena

T E R R I T O R I E S

A R L E S

K I N G D O M
Lombardy
Genoa

Ferrara
Bologna
Imola

Ravenna

O F

Faenza
Rimini

Provence

I T A L Y

*expansion of Papal
States under Innocent III*

Pistoia
Lucca
Pisa

Florence
Arezzo

Ancona

Adriatic Sea

Arles

Marseilles

T u s c a n y
Siena
Perugia
Assisi
Orvieto

Spoleto

Viterbo
Rieti
✕ Tagliacozzo
1268

PAPAL
PATRIMONY
Rome
Tivoli
Ostia
Tusculum
Anagni

1190
Apricena

1193   San Germano
Lucera
Troia Foggia

1191/1194
Gaeta
Capua
Benevento

Barletta
Bari

1194
Melfi

Naples
Salerno
Amalfi

K I N G D O M

Taranto

Brindisi
Lecce

Cosenza

O F

Palermo
Monreale
Trapani   Cefalù
S I C I L Y
Messina
Reggio

Catania

Syracuse

Baltic Sea

Hedeby
Oldenburg 948
WAGRIANS
ABODRITES
Hamburg
955
POLABII   WARNABI
March of the Billungs
c. 937-82
Lenzen
929
REDARII
VELETIANS
Nordmark
Havelberg 948
936

Pomerania

Gniezno 1000
Poznań 968

axony
Magdeburg 967
Werla
Brandenburg 948
Quedlinburg

Pöhlde
Wallhausen
Merseburg 968
HEVELLI
R. Elbe
Lusatia
LUSIZZI

vey
Erfurt
Fulda
Salz
SORBS
Zeitz 968
Meissen 968
Mark
Zeitz DALEMINZI
MILIZI
Meissen

P O L A N D

kfurt
933
ranconia
950
938
Prague 975

937   954

Bohemia
(tributary from 950)

abia
Regensburg
951   961

✕ Augsburg
feld 955

955
Ostmark
Pressburg

Bavaria
Wels 943

Pitten

H U N G A R Y

Styria

Carinthia
(Duchy 976)

✝ new bishopric with
date of foundation

♀ bishopric destroyed in
Slav rising of 983

✕ visited more than
once by Henry I

MILIZI Slav tribes

⌒ frontier c.950

---

3 The Hohenstaufen Empire
1152-1250

▨ eastward spread of German
peasant settlement 12th century

▨ German settlement by 1200-1250

◉ city with over 10,000 inhabitants

◎ member of Lombard Leagues
of 1167 and 1226

◑ member of 1167 League only

◐ member of 1226 League only

→ German invasions 1190-94

⇢ Henry VI's Genoese and Pisan fleet
1194

◼ main Hohenstaufen palaces
and castles

ⴷ mountain pass

Fourteenth century Europe

After the rise and consolidation of national monarchies in Spain, France and England in the thirteenth century (page 52), the fourteenth century was a period of setbacks on all fronts in western Europe. In part, this may be attributed to a sudden climatic deterioration (the onset of the 'little ice age') which brought to an end the agricultural boom that had been virtually continuous since 1150. Already in 1315–17 Europe experienced a 'great famine', and the weakening of human powers of resistance induced by inadequate nourishment may have been one factor accounting for the rapid spread of the Black Death, or bubonic plague, which first appeared in the Crimea in 1346 and spread from there first by ship to Italy and then to the west (map 1). But there were also other factors. All the western monarchies had over-extended themselves financially, and the economic setback accentuated their difficulties. Philip IV's unsuccessful attempts to subdue Flanders played after his death (1314) into the hands of the aristocracy; so also

did the involvement of Catalonia in Italy after the death of James II (1285–1327); and in England the attempt to subdue Scotland (map 4) proved to be a running sore. Ireland also virtually went its own way until Tudor times (page 72), and Wales, conquered but not subdued by Edward I (page 52), had a great national revival under Owain Glyndwr (1400–1409). Germany broke apart into rival principalities after the extermination of the Hohenstaufen dynasty (page 54), and Italy went the same way once Hohenstaufen rule was removed, breaking up into a number of local lordships or *signorie* (map 3). In the end, even the Catholic church was affected by the economic and fiscal stringency. From 1378 to 1417 it was divided by schism (map 6), which undermined its authority, while its financial extortions gave impetus to the anti-papal, reformatory movements of Hus in Bohemia and Wyclif in England.

Eastern Europe, on the other hand, was in process of recovery from the Mongol incursions of the thirteenth century (page 46). Bohemia under Charles IV (1333–78), Poland under Casimir III (1339–70), and Hungary

under Louis the Great (1342–82), all made rapid strides, helped perhaps by the fact that the impact of the Black Death was less severe in the east than in the west, and also by exploitation of their natural resources, such as the silver mines of Kutna Hora (map 2). In the west, on the other hand, the setback was lasting. Two English kings, Edward II (1327) and Richard II (1399) were murdered. The Hundred Years' War between England and France (map 5) resulted in widespread devastation. Overall, the Black Death reduced the population of Europe by roughly one-third. Further, the misery caused by economic recession and military ravages sparked off a series of popular risings, the Jacquerie in France and the Peasants' Revolt in England being best known (map 1), although urban discontent – the weavers' rising in Flanders under Artevelde, or the Ciompi in Florence – was no less significant in the long run. It was not until after c.1450 that recovery began (page 82); but even then under-currents of popular resentment persisted, which found their outlet in the Peasants' War of 1524–5 and the messianic movements of the Reformation.

3 Italy, c.1310

Papal states

◑ Republican communes

○ cities under Signorial domination c.1310

the Signorie:

1 Avvocati	5 Da Camino	9 Este	13 Malatesta
2 Bonacolsi	6 Da Correggio	10 Fissiraga	14 Robert of Anjou
3 Brusati	7 Da Polenta	11 Langosco	15 Scotti
4 Cavalcabo	8 Della Scala	12 Maggi	16 Visconti

2 Eastern Europe 1278-1389

growth of Lithuania 1300-1377:

to 1300

under Gedymin 1316-41

under Olgierd 1345-77

Lithuania under Jagiello and Witold from 1377

Poland-Lithuania after union of 1386

Habsburg lands

Bohemian lands

5 The Hundred Years' War

● English bases in 1380

acquired for Burgundy 1363-1404

acquired for Burgundy 1419-67

4 The Anglo-Scottish Wars, 1296-1402

route of Edward I's campaign 1298

route of Edward I's campaign 1303-4

route of Richard II's campaign 1385

boundary of land acquired by Edward III in 1334

border between England and Scotland in 15th century

abbreviations:

B. OF D. BISHOPRIC OF DURHAM

F. OF T. FRANCHISE OF TYNEDALE

F. OF H. FRANCHISE OF HEXHAMSHIRE

1 Europe at the time of the Black Death

extent of spread of Black Death:
- 1346
- 1347
- mid 1348
- end 1348
- mid 1349
- end 1349
- 1350
- c. 1351
- c. 1353
- little or no plague mortality

political change:
- union of Kalmar 1397
- Milanese territory under Giangaleazzo Visconti 1378-1402
- territory under Florentine control, end 14th century
- Luxembourg lands
- Wittelsbach lands
- Habsburg lands

social unrest:
- areas of disturbance during Great Peasant Revolt in England 1381
- ⊙ centre of urban revolt
- rural uprisings
- ⊗ defeats in battle of lower class   ✗ battle

religious unrest:
- spread of Lollardry in England to death of Richard II, 1399
- area of Hussite influence
- ■ Hussite centre

the Western Schism (inset map right):
- areas giving allegiance to Pope in Rome
- areas giving allegiance to Pope in Avignon
- allegiance officially to Rome but shifting local allegiances

6 The Western Schism, 1378-1417

Avignon
Rome

RUSSIAN STATES

Orkneys
Hebrides
SCOTLAND
Edinburgh
Armagh
Carlisle
Newcastle
York
ENGLAND
WALES
Chester Lincoln
Bristol Norwich
Bury St Edmunds
Winchester London

Oslo
Uppsala
NORWAY SWEDEN
Stockholm
Visby
Baltic Sea
North Sea
DENMARK
Copenhagen
Riga
Königsberg
Danzig
PRINCIPALITY OF MOSCOW
Novgorod
Smolensk

ORDER
TEUTONIC

LITHUANIA
Kiev
R. Dnieper

Lübeck
Hamburg
Bremen
POMERANIA
FRIESLAND
Amsterdam SAXONY
HOLLAND Brunswick BRANDENBURG
Antwerp Magdeburg
Bruges Aachen
Ghent Cologne
Ypres Liège
FLANDERS Trier Frankfurt
Agincourt Mainz
Crécy Rouen HOLY
Amiens FRANCONIA
Paris Rheims ROMAN
Chartres Meaux 1358 LORRAINE
Troyes Strasbourg
BRITTANY Mello 1358

Warsaw
POLAND
Cracow
R. Oder
R. Elbe
SILESIA
Prague
BOHEMIA
MORAVIA
Tabor

R. Dniester
UKRAINE
MOLDAVIA

Regensburg
BAVARIA Passau
Augsburg
Munich Vienna
SWABIA AUSTRIA
Basle Constance Salzburg
SWISS CONFED.
Lausanne CARINTHIA
Geneva EMPIRE
Lyons SAVOY
Milan Venice Trieste
Turin REPUBLIC OF VENICE
Genoa Ravenna

Buda Pest
HUNGARY
R. Danube
Belgrade
WALLACHIA
Bucharest
Black Sea

FRANCE
Poitiers
BURGUNDY
R. Loire
Orléans

Bordeaux
ENGLISH GASCONY
AQUITAINE R. Dordogne
Cahors
Toulouse R. Rhône
Montpellier Avignon
Narbonne PROVENCE
Marseilles
NAVARRE
Saragossa
CATALONIA
ARAGON Barcelona
Valencia
Balearic Islands

DAUPHINÉ
Pisa Florence Ancona
Siena
PAPAL STATES
Rome
Corsica
Sardinia

BOSNIA
SERBIAN PRINCES
Ragusa
PRINCIPALITY OF ALBANIA
BULGARIA
Adrianople
Constantinople
Salonica
OTTOMAN TURKS

Adriatic Sea

KINGDOM OF NAPLES
Naples
Amalfi

Palermo Messina
KINGDOM OF SICILY

DUCHY OF ATHENS
ACHAEA ATHENS
Rhodes
Crete

Mediterranean Sea

Medieval trade routes
c.1000-1500

Trading connexions had been remarkably widespread during late antiquity, and they had brought with them important cultural interchanges (page 24). The barbarian invasions, beginning c.300 AD and lasting some 200 years, had disastrous results. The Silk Route from Rome to China was cut, and even within the Roman empire communications broke down. There was a short-lived recrudescence in Carolingian times, involving trade in the North Sea, centred on Dorestad and Quentovic; but it was only after c.1000, with the restoration of relatively stable conditions, that trade picked up. In particular, the Italian cities, already in contact with the Near East (page 36), established connexions with north-west Europe, where the fairs of Champagne were becoming clearing-houses for trade between Italy and the rising industrial centres of Flanders (map 1).

The consolidation of the German empire under the Saxon and Salian dynasties gave impetus to trade from west to east, along a line running from the Low Countries via Cologne to Magdeburg, and along the Main valley to Bamberg and Prague. German control of the Alpine passes, particularly after the opening of the Septimer and St. Gotthard passes during the Hohenstaufen period, stimulated trade with Italy, which contributed to the growing wealth of the south German cities, among them Augsburg, which later became a major commercial and financial centre after the rise of the Fugger merchant family in the fifteenth century. In the north the most important city was Lübeck (founded 1158), the key point controlling trade between the North Sea and the Baltic and the seat of the Hanseatic League, an association of German merchants which took shape in 1259 and was formally constituted in 1358. With its far-flung network of associated cities, and with branches in London, Bruges and Bergen, the Hansa dominated the trade of northern Europe in the fourteenth and fifteenth centuries. It also had connexions with Venice and Genoa, the cities which dominated Mediterranean and Levantine commerce (map 2).

Levantine trade fell into two broad categories: the spice trade, in which Venice predominated, and the silk trade, largely in the hands of Genoa and its merchant colonies in Constantinople and at Kaffa, Tana and Trebizond. The latter profited greatly from the restoration of order and settled government in central Asia by the Mongols (page 46), which allowed a resumption of overland trade, and for a time there was extensive east-west traffic, exemplified by the famous journeys of Marco Polo between 1271 and 1295 (map 3). But the roads opened by the rise of the Mongol empire in the thirteenth century were closed by its decline in the mid-fourteenth century. The important spice trade from Ormuz to the Black Sea was also badly affected; but the trade via the Red Sea and Alexandria to Venice continued without interruption until the Ottoman conquest of Egypt in 1517 (page 48).

Spices were indispensable, easy to handle and highly profitable, and they were the staple of intercontinental trade in this period. Both Europe and China were dependent for supplies on the spice-producing regions of Asia, particularly the Moluccas and the Malay archipelago, and the resultant transactions, largely in the hands of Arab and Indian middlemen, created a complicated network of sea routes, hinging on Malacca, which stretched from the Red Sea and the Persian Gulf to the South China Sea (map 3). In the early fifteenth century, between 1405 and 1433, the Chinese sent seven expeditions through the Strait of Malacca to the Indian Ocean and beyond; but this enterprise ceased abruptly after 1440. Meanwhile, Portugal was probing down the west coast of Africa (page 64) in search of gold; but later, when Genoa, which had lost its eastern markets after the fall of Constantinople in 1453, provided financial backing for the Portuguese ventures, the main objective became the search for an alternative route to the east, to cut out Genoa's rival, Venice. When the Portuguese reached India in 1498, and Columbus, despatched by Portugal's rival, Spain, reached America, a new era had begun. The thousand-year-old pattern, centred on the Mediterranean, gave way to an Atlantic economy (page 82), and the whole economic and political balance in Europe shifted dramatically.

3 Eurasian trade routes, c.1000 - 1500

- ——— principal Eurasian routes
- ——— principal Eurasian sea routes
- ——— principal Hanseatic routes
- ——— trans-Saharan trade routes
- ▨ area of Muslim domination in the mid-15th century
- – – – Marco Polo's routes (1271-95)
- · · · · Chinese Admiral Cheng-ho's routes (1405-33)

major commodities:

- ● camphor
- ▷ cottons
- ⊝ drugs
- ⬗ dyestuffs
- ▨ gold
- ● ivory
- ◆ linen
- ⊞ metalware
- ▤ pepper
- ⬣ perfumes
- ⬢ porcelain
- ◇ precious stones
- ◀ silks
- ◩ silver
- ℧ slaves
- ◺ soap
- ▥ spices
- ⊞ sugar
- ♈ wine
- ◣ woollens

1 Trade routes in Western Europe, c.1000 - 1150

- ——— trade routes
- ▨ areas of forest
- ▲ fairs

2 Hanseatic trade

- ▫ site of important fair
- ⊙ site of lesser fair
- —— Hanseatic trade routes

The Hanseatic League:
- ● Wendish and Pomeranian circle
- ◆ Saxony, Thuringia, Brandenburg circle
- ▼ Prussia, Livonia, Sweden circle
- ■ Rhine, Westphalia, Netherlands circle

- ◉ ◈ ▽ ▣ chief city
- ● ◆ ▼ ■ associated city
- ◖ kontore
- ◐ subsidiary kontore
- ○ other important city

note: places that are important fairs as well as Hanseatic cities have red symbols

African states and empires, c.900-1800

By the end of the first millennium AD great changes had taken place in Africa. The rise of a culture based on iron-working (page 10) led to a large-scale displacement of Khoisan-speaking Bushmen and Hottentots by settled Bantu-speaking agriculturalists (map 3) and to the appearance of extensive states and empires based on trade. In the south, Zimbabwe, with its monumental stone buildings, exported gold and copper to the Orient via the port of Sofala, and the impressive Kongo state on the west coast had an important trade in ivory. Further north, the Arab conquest of the Maghreb and the rise of the Almoravid and Almohad empires (page 40) marked a watershed. The Arabs, great traders, developed and extended the trans-Saharan caravan routes, and there is no doubt that trade was an important factor in the development of the great empires which arose in the sub-Saharan savanna. The early history of Ghana (some 500 miles north-west of the modern state with the same name) precedes the Islamic era; but its successors, Mali and Songhay, owed much of their wealth and civilisation, described in glowing terms

by Arab travellers, to the Islamic impact. So also did the Kanem-Borno empire around Lake Chad and, after the fifteenth century, the city states of Hausaland (map 1). Arab merchant colonies also spread far down the east coast from Mogadishu to Kilwa. The staples of trade in all cases were gold, ivory and slaves. According to a conservative estimate, the trans-Saharan slave trade before the coming of the Europeans amounted to almost 5 million.

The arrival of the Portuguese on the African coast and the building in 1448 of a first European fort and warehouse at Arguin, followed (1482) by a second at Elmina on the Gold Coast, had at first little impact on Africa. The immediate objective was to share directly in the gold trade, hitherto dominated by Muslim middlemen, and the slave trade was a secondary by-product. But with the development of sugar plantations in Brazil (page 68) and later in the West Indies, the slave trade became a major source of profit, particularly after Dutch and British traders ousted the Portuguese. Along the length of the Gold and Slave Coasts, from Axim to the Niger Delta, fortified trading stations (or 'factories') were set up as bases for this trade (map 2, inset), and the Portuguese continued to export slaves further south in Angola. Of some 15 million Africans shipped aboard between 1450 and 1870, some 90 per cent

went to South America and the Caribbean, most of them between 1700 and 1800. The effects on Africa of this appalling trade in human beings are not easy to quantify, though the effects on the victims themselves need no description. Furthermore, the loss of population was not evenly divided and some areas suffered disproportionately. Others profited from the trade. After the invasion and destruction of the great Songhay empire by Morocco in 1591, the forest states of Asante, Dahomey and Benin, having direct access to the Atlantic and to European trade, increased in importance and political power (map 2). The Europeans remained largely ignorant of the African interior, and their influence was limited. In the far south the Dutch were established in the Cape Colony; but, in a continental perspective, its extent was still minimal. In the north-east Islam was spreading; but the Christian kingdom of Ethiopia, despite a serious setback in the 1520s, still held its own. By 1800, with the exception of the Ottomans in the north (and even their power was more nominal than real), Africa remained independent of foreign control. Nevertheless there is little sign that it was ready to meet the European challenge that developed in the nineteenth century (page 102). It was a world unto itself, but in no position to compete with the technological dynamism of the West.

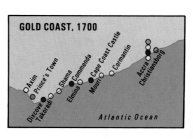

GOLD COAST, 1700

Axim · Prince's Town · Shama · Commenda · Cape Coast Castle · Cormantin · Accra · Christiansborg
Discove · Takoradi · Elmina · Mouri
Atlantic Ocean

Cape Bojador 1434
Arguin (Portuguese 1482) · Wadan
KAARTA 18thC
BERBERS (MOORS) · Awdaghost
St Louis
Cape Verde Is.
Gorée · SENEGAMBIAN STATES · Gambia
James Island
Cacheu
Bunce Island
Freetown
Windward Coast
Vasco da Gama to India
July 1497-Dec. 1498
Atlantic

1 Africa, 900-1500

- state nucleus and sphere of influence
- spread of Islam
- Islamised North and East Africa
- Muslim colony
- major gold producing region
- Ghana 8th-12th century
- Mali 12th-15th century
- Songhay c.1500

gold		cattle	
musk		copper	
slaves		salt	
bananas		millet	
rice		ivory	

Map labels: SPAIN · Cordoba · Ceuta · Fez · Tlemcen · Bougie · Algiers · Tunis · Mediterranean Sea · Marrakesh · ALMORAVID EMPIRE 1050-1140 · ALMOHAD EMPIRE 1140-1250 · Sijilmassa · Wargla · Tripoli · Barca · Alexandria · Cairo · Ghadames · Augila · FATIMIDS 960-1171 · AYYUBIDS 1171-1250 · MAMELUKES 1250-1517 · Murzuk · Medina · Tuat · Ghat · Kufra · EGYPT · Arabia · Persian Gulf · Sahara Desert · Taghaza · Taodeni · Idjil · Wadan · Awdaghost · Walata · Timbuktu · Takedda · AIR · Tadmekka · Agades · Bilma · KANEM-BORNO 15thC · Dongola · NUBIA · MAKURRA · Napata · Merōe · ALWA · Adulis · Dahlak Is. · Aden · Red Sea · Jedda · Mecca · Aidhab · Awlil · TAKRUR 9thC-11thC · Kumbi Saleh · Galam · R. Senegal · Gao · HAUSA STATES · Katsina · Kano · Zaria · El Fasher · WADAI · DARFUR · Ain Farah · AXUM 3rdC-8thC · Soba · Sennar · CHRISTIAN KINGDOMS · FUNJ EMPIRE 15thC · DAMAKIL · AGAU · ETHIOPIA · ADAL · Zeila · Berbera · Ras Hafun · Boure · Niani · Jenne · MOSSI STATES · NUPE · KWARARAFA · Ngazargumu · Lake Chad · R. Niger · OYO · IFE · BENIN · AKAN · YORUBA STATES · SIDAMA · GALLA · SOMALI · Mogadishu · DUALA · NGBANDI · MANGBETU · RIVER LAKE NILOTES c.1400 · PLAINS NILOTES · HIGHLAND NILOTES c.1000 · MASAI · Lamu · Malindi · Mombasa · Pemba Is. · Zanzibar · Indian Ocean · PYGMY · MONGO · KUBA · LATE IRON AGE PASTORALISTS · VILI · KONGO · MBUNDU · LUBA · LUNDA · Ivuna 13th C-15th C · Sanga 800 · Kilwa Kisiwani · CHOKWE-LUENA · OVIMBUNDU · LOZI · MANGANJA · R. Zambezi · Comoro Is. · Ingombe Ilede · TONGA · SHONA · Sofala · MADAGASCAR · Zimbabwe 1200-1850 stone buildings · Muslim colony 13th C · migrations of Bantu speakers to Madagascar bringing cattle and millet · cattle-keeping Khoisan peoples · Mapungubwe stone buildings · Phalaborwa · Iron Age peoples · Indonesian expansion from East Coast into interior bringing bananas and rice · Atlantic Ocean

3 African languages

c.3000-2000 BC (right):

- Niger-Kordofanian
- Nilo-Saharan
- Afro-Asiatic
- Khoisan
- unoccupied

c.AD 1000 (above):

- Niger-Kordofanian (including Bantu)
- Nilo-Saharan
- Afro-Asiatic
- Khoisan
- Malayo-Polynesian

SPAIN

○ Granada

OTTOMAN EMPIRE

2 Africa, 1500-1800

movement of peoples

spread of Islam

area of Islamic influence by 1800

trade routes

slave trade routes

Spanish offensives against Algiers and Tunis in the 16th century

Moroccan military expeditions

Saladian extension of Moroccan territory c. 1591

Portuguese voyages to Africa and India

areas of Ottoman control

coastal settlements:
○ Dutch
◑ French
○ Portuguese
◑ Danish
● Ottoman
● British
◑ Spanish
◑ Brandenburger

○ Tangier
○ Fez
Atlas Mts.
MOROCCO
Morocco ruled by Sharifian dynasties 1553-1912
○ Sijilmassa

Algiers ○ *Corsair cities under Ottoman suzerainty 1516*
ALGIERS
○ Wargla

Tunis
Mediterranean Sea

○ Jerba
Tripoli

○ Ghadames

Alexandria ○

Cairo ○

Ottoman conquest 1517

R. Nile

Red Sea

○ Suakin

○ Massawa

○ Taghaza
T u a t

○ Ain Salah

○ Ghat

○ Murzuk

Arab trans-Saharan slave trade route

E G Y P T

Sahara Desert

○ Tamanrasset

○ Bilma

SONGHAY

○ Tadmekka

AIR
○ Agades

Central Sudan

FUNJ
16th C

Nilotic Sudan

○ Sennar

ETHIOPIA
16th C

○ Zeila
ADAL
○ Berbera

○ Timbuktu
○ Gao

SEGU
18th C

○ Jenne

Western Sudan

○ Katsina
HAUSA STATES
○ Kano
○ Zaria

Lake Chad
KANEM
BORNO

WADAI

DARFUR

White Nile

SHOA

SOMALI

GALLA

MOSSI STATES
15th C

R. Volta

DYOLA TRADERS

BORGU STATES
NUPE

DAHOMEY 18th C
Badagri
ASANTE 18th C
Accra
see inset above

Ife
OYO 17th C
Lagos
BENIN
Whydah
Slave Coast
IBO
Brass

R. Benue

KWARARAFA

NIGER DELTA STATES 18th C

OLD CALABAR

TIKAR BAMUM BAMILEKE

BANDA

NZAKARA

AZANDE

PARANILOTES

NILOTES

MANGBETU

Mogadishu ○
Brava ○

West Africa - arrival of Portuguese 15thC and 16thC. Dutch, English and French 17thC

Fernando Po ○

Principe ○

São Tomé ○

NGBANDI
BABWA
R. Congo

BUNYORO
BUGANDA

ANKOLE

Lake Victoria

KIKUYU
Lamu ○

Ocean

PYGMY

TEKE

MONGO

KARAGWE

RWANDA
BURUNDI

Mt Kilimanjaro ▲

Malindi ○
Mombasa ○

Vasco da Gama to India
April 1498 · Dec. 1498

Pemba
Zanzibar

Arab slave trade

KUBA
TETELA
LUANGO
LULUA
KETE
KONGO

CHOKWE
LUBA
15th C - 16th C

Lake Tanganyika

Kilwa Kisiwani ○

Ambriz ○
Luanda ○
MBUNOU

LUNDA
16th - 17th C

LUENA-LOVALE

BEMBA

SANGA
BEMBA

BISA

Lake Nyasa

Comoro Is. ○

Benguela ○

OVIMBUNDU

LOZI

LAMBA

LENJE

MARAVI

Mozambique ○

OVAMBO

SAAN

TONGA

R. Zambezi
Tete ○
Sena ○

MWENEMUTAPA 16th C

Quelimane ○

Sofala ○

settlements of mainland African slaves

ROZWI
○ Great Zimbabwe
KARANGA

Portuguese slave trade

M A D A G A S C A R

HOVA MERINA

HERERO

TSWANA

SOTHO

KHOISAN

R. Orange

SOTHO
NGUNI

Delagoa Bay

Fort-Dauphin ○

I n d i a n

O c e a n

CAPE
KHOISAN

NGUNI

○ Cape Town

Cape of Good Hope

Cape established by Dutch East India Company in 1652. Gradual spread of white settlers inland. Occupied by Britain 1798.

61

America on the eve of European conquest

Two great and wealthy civilisations confronted the Spaniards when they arrived in America at the beginning of the sixteenth century: the Aztec empire in Mexico and the Inca empire in Peru. The former had a population of 10–12 millions, the latter 6 millions or possibly considerably more. A few other centres of civilisation existed, such as the Chibcha state in modern Colombia; but the remainder of the continent was sparsely inhabited (perhaps 1 million north of the Rio Grande and 1 million in the rest of South America) and divided among more than a thousand small tribal societies, with distinct, often unrelated languages (map 1). Few regions, particularly in the north, had reached the stage of settled agriculture (map 4).

The Aztec and Inca empires were different in character, and there is no evidence of any contact between them. The Aztecs, like the Toltecs who controlled much of Mexico in the eleventh and twelfth centuries, were raw warriors from the north who entered Mexico during the thirteenth century and settled on islands in Lake Texcoco, where c.1325 they founded the town of Tenochtitlán, which was to become their capital. The Inca empire was created by one of the numerous tribes of Quechua stock inhabiting the central Andes, which established itself in the Cuzco valley in the twelfth century. The expansion of both came late and only reached its full extent on the eve of the Spanish conquest. In the case of the Aztecs (map 2) the first step was to ally with the neighbouring tribes in Texcoco and Tlacopán against their overlords in Azcapotzalco, and then to turn against their allies. This aggressive policy began c.1427 under Itzcoatl and was continued by Montezuma I. It reached its peak under Montezuma II (1502–20), when the Aztecs, in control of the greater part of Mexico, were beginning to enter Maya territory in Yucatán. Inca expansion began under the eighth emperor, Viracocha, and his son Pachacuti (1438–63), whose son Topa subdued the coastal civilisation of Chimú (1470), and then, after his accession as emperor (1471), pushed south into Chile and northern Argentina (map 3). Huayna Capac (1493–1525) advanced north into modern Ecuador, where he founded a second capital at Quito. By now the Inca empire was some 200 miles wide and 2500 miles long, held together by an impressive system of highways and post-stations, with relays of runners who conveyed imperial orders to all parts of the empire.

The Incas created a genuine imperial system, with an hereditary dynasty, a Quechua aristocracy and a highly trained bureaucracy. All land was state-owned, and there was a complex system of irrigation. The ordinary Indian spent nine months of the year working for the state, but in return was protected from famine by large state-owned food repositories and provided for in sickness and old age. The Aztec empire, on the other hand, rather like that of the Mongols in Europe (page 46), was essentially a harsh military dominion over vassal peoples, who were left to rule themselves on condition that they paid heavy tribute to Tenochtitlán in food, textiles, pottery and other goods, but increasingly in human beings for sacrifice to the Aztec gods. The number of sacrificial victims rose from 10,000 a year to 50,000 a year at the time of the Spanish conquest. This was certainly one reason why the Totonacs and Tlaxcalans welcomed the Spanish invaders of Mexico (page 68), and resentment against Inca oppression probably played a similar role in Peru. Neither empire was as stable as it seemed. Nevertheless their collapse at the hands of small bands of adventurers (Cortés had only 600 men, a few small cannon, 13 muskets and 16 horses when he invaded Mexico in 1519, and Pizarro had only 180 men, 27 horses and 2 cannon when he attacked the Inca empire in 1531) is not easily explained.

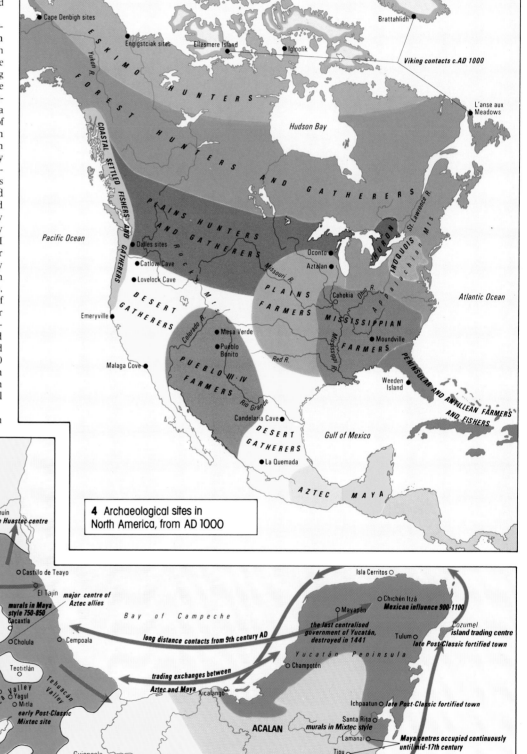

4 Archaeological sites in North America, from AD 1000

2 The Aztec Empire in Mexico

- Maya cultural area
- Postclassic Maya kingdoms
- area of Aztec domination 1519
- spread of Toltec influence from 9th century AD
- Postclassic trading routes

1 The American peoples, c.1500

culture areas:

North America
- Arctic
- Sub-Arctic
- Northwest coast
- Plateau
- Great Basin
- California
- Southwest
- Great Plains
- Northeast
- Southeast

Mesoamerica
- Mesoamerica

South America
- Circum-Caribbean
- Savanna-Orinoco
- Andean
- Tropical forest
- Atlantic
- Southern

3 The Inca Empire in Peru

growth of the Inca Empire:
- under Pachacuti 1438-63
- growth under Pachacuti and Topa Inca 1463-71
- growth under Topa Inca 1471-93
- growth under Huayna Capac 1493-1525
- imperial roads

North America labels:
ESKIMO, ALEUT, KOYUKON, INGALIK, TANANA, HAN, KUTCHIN, HARE, TUTCHONE, DOGRIB, KASKA, CHIPEWYAN, CREE, TSIMSHIAN, TLINGIT, CARRIERS, BEAVER, HAIDA, SARCEE, SHUSWAP, BLACKFOOT, KWAKIUTL, NOOTKA, CHINOOK, NEZ PERCÉ, ROCKY Mts, MANDAN, CROW, OJIBWA, MONTAGNAIS-NASKAPI, BEOTHUK, YUROK, KAROK, MODOC, SHOSHONE, CHEYENNE, SIOUX, MENOMINEE, OTTAWA, ALGONQUIN, MICMAC, POMO, YOKUTS, PAIUTE, UTE, ARAPAHO, PAWNEE, SAUK, POTAWA-TOMI, FOX, HURON, ERIE, IROQUOIS, ABENAKI, MASSACHUSET, NARRAGANSET, CHUMASH, MOHAVE, NAVAJO, HOPI, KIOWA, WICHITA, OSAGE, ILLINOIS, MIAMI, SUSQUEHANNA, DELAWARE, PAPAGO, APACHE, COMANCHE, CADDO, SHAWNEE, CHICKASAW, CHEROKEE, CATAWBA, POWHATAN, COCHIMI, PIMA, TARAHUMARA, TEPEHUAN, COAHUILTEC, NATCHEZ, CHOCTAW, CREEK, CORA, HUICHOL, HUASTEC, OTOMI, TIMUCUA, CALUSA, TARASCO, TOTONAC, NAHUATL, MIXTEC, ZAPOTEC, MAYA, CIBONEY, ISLAND ARAWAK, LENCA, PAYA, CIBONEY, ISLAND CARIB, NICARAO, MISKITO

Central/South America labels:
GUAYMÍ, CUNA, GOAJIRO, CHOCÓ, CHIBCHA, PAEZ, GUAHIBO, YANOMAMO, WARRAU, ARAWAK, CARIB, TUCANO, MACÚ, WAIWAI, TRÍO, TUMBEZ, CHIMÚ, JÍVARO, WITOTO, YAGUA, OMAGUA, MUCHIC, SHIPIBO, CAWAHIB, MUNDURUCÚ, TEREMEMBE, TENETEHARA, CAMPA, PIRO, TIMBIRA, CAYAPÓ, SHAVANTE, QUECHUA, NAMBICUARA, CARAJÁ, NAZCA, AYMARA, MOJOS, BORORÓ, SIRIONÓ, GUATÓ, TUPINAMBÁ, ATACAMA, MATACO, CAIGUÁ, DIAGUITA, Chaco, GUARANÍ, KAINGANG, TUPINAMBÁ, ABIPON, ARAUCANIAN Andes, PUELCHE, CHARRÚA, ALACALUF, TEHUELCHE, YAHGAN, ONA, ANDES

*Inca inset labels:*
Quito, Cuenca, R. Japurá, R. Amazon, R. Marañón, R. Ucayali, R. Purus, Cajamarca, Chan Chan, Huánuco, R. Mamore, Bombón, Vilcashuamán, Machu Picchu, Pachacamac, Ollantaytambo, Incahuási, Cuzco, Tiahuanaco, Limatambo, Lake Titicaca, Lake Poopó, Pacific Ocean, R. Maule, R. Salado, CHIMÚ, Andes

Oceans:
Atlantic Ocean, Pacific Ocean, Caribbean Sea

63

European voyages of discovery
1487-1780

The European voyages of discovery opened a new era in world history. They began early in the fifteenth century when Portuguese navigators advanced southward, round the coast of Africa, in search of gold, slaves and spices, until in 1487 Dias and de Covilhã brought them into the Indian Ocean (map 1). Thenceforth voyages of exploration multiplied, particularly after the resurgence of Islam made the old route to the east via Alexandria and the Red Sea precarious.

While the Portuguese explored the eastern route to Asia, the Spaniards sailed west. Once in the Indian Ocean the former quickly reached their goal: Malabar (1498), Malacca (1511), and the Moluccas (1512). The Spanish search for a western route to the Spice Islands was less successful. Its unintended but momentous result was Columbus' discovery of the New World in 1492 (map 2), followed by the Spanish conquest of America (page 68). But it was not until after 1524, when Verrazzano traced the coastline of North America as far north as Nova Scotia, that the existence of a new continent was generally accepted, and meanwhile the search for a western route to Asia continued, leading to extensive exploration of the Caribbean (map 3). Finally, in 1521, Magellan rounded South America, entered the Pacific, and reached the Philippines, but the route was too long and hazardous for commercial purposes. In 1557 the Portuguese occupied Macao, and after 1571 Spanish galleons traded between Manila and Acapulco in Mexico; but otherwise the exploration of the Pacific was delayed until the eighteenth century (map 4). This was the work of British, Dutch and Russians seeking a navigable passage via the Arctic between the Atlantic and the Pacific, and hoping also to locate a hypothetical southern continent. Both proved illusory; but the result was the charting of New Zealand and the eastern coast of Australia, both in a few years opened to European colonisation (page 112).

Meanwhile England and France, unwilling to recognise the monopoly claimed by Spain and Portugal in the Treaty of Tordesillas (1494), had embarked on a series of voyages intended to reach Asia by a northern route (map 2). All these proved abortive and were abandoned after 1632, but they resulted in the opening of North America to European settlement. The English, French and Dutch were also unwilling to abandon the profitable trade with South and South-East Asia to the Portuguese and Spaniards, and the later years of the sixteenth and first half of the seventeenth centuries saw a determined and ultimately successful effort to breach their privileged position (page 66). After 1500 direct sea contact was established between continents and regions which hitherto had gone their own way in isolation. It was necessarily a slow process, and for long the European footholds in Asia and Africa remained tenuous and precarious. But by the time of the death of the last great explorer, James Cook, in 1779, the worldwide network of relationships had been formed which characterises the modern era and differentiates it from all preceding times.

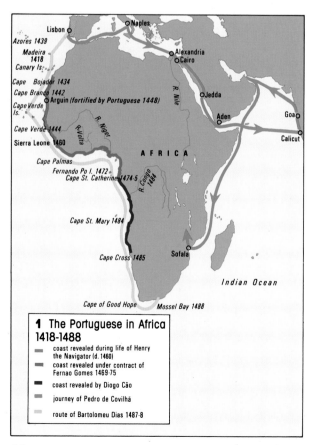

1 The Portuguese in Africa 1418-1488

- coast revealed during life of Henry the Navigator (d. 1460)
- coast revealed under contract of Fernao Gomes 1469-75
- coast revealed by Diogo Cão
- journey of Pedro de Covilhã
- route of Bartolomeu Dias 1487-8

Voyages intended for S. Asia by S.E. Route:
1/Dias 1487/88 (outward) discovered open water S. of Cape Agulhas; entered Indian Ocean; reached Great Fish River.
2/Vasco da Gama 1497–99 (outward) discovered best use of Atlantic winds on way to Cape of Good Hope; reached India, navigated by local pilot.
3/Cabral 1500 (outward) the second Portuguese voyage to India, sighted coast of Brazil at Monte Pascoal, probably accident

2 Voyages of discovery, 1480-1630

→ voyages intended for Southern Asia by South East route

→ voyages intended for China and Southern Asia by West or South West route

→ voyages intended for Asia by North West and North East routes

⇨ approximate prevailing winds (shown for the first quarter of the year)

⇨ alternating monsoons

Voyages in the Caribbean:
29/Bastidas & La Cosa 1501–02 explored coast from Gulf of Maracaibo to Gulf of Urabá.
30/Pinzón & Solís 1508 sent from Spain to find strait to Asia, coasted E. coast of Yucatán.
31/Ponce de León 1512–13 sailed from Puerto Rico, explored coast of Florida from N. of Cape Canaveral to (possibly) Pensacola. May have sighted Yucatán on return. First explorer to note force of Gulf Stream.
32/Hernández de Córdoba 1516 sailed from Cuba, explored N. and W. coasts of Yucatán. First report of Mayan cities.
33/Grijalva 1517 followed S. and W. coasts of Gulf of Mexico as far as Pánuco River.
34/Pineda 1519 explored N. and W. coasts of Gulf of Mexico from Florida to Pánuco River. Finally ended hope of strait to Pacific in that region.

Voyages in the Pacific:
35/Roggeveen 1721–22 discovered Easter Island and some of the Samoan group. Circumnavigation.
36/Bering 1728 sailed from Kamchatka, discovered strait separating N.E. Asia from N.W. America.
37/Wallis 1766–68 discovered Society Islands (Tahiti), encouraged hope of habitable southern continent. Circumnavigation.
38/Cook 1768–71 charted coasts of New Zealand, explored E. coast of Australia, confirmed existence of Torres Strait. Circumnavigation.
39/Cook 1772–75 made circuit of southern oceans in high latitude, charted New Hebrides, ended hope of habitable southern continent. Circumnavigation.
40/Cook & Clerke 1776–80 discovered Sandwich Islands (Hawaii), explored coast of N. America from Vancouver to Unimak Pass, sailed through Bering Strait to edge of pack ice, ended hope of passage through Arctic to Atlantic.

4/First Portuguese voyage to Malacca, 1509.
5/Abreu 1512–13 visited Moluccas.
6/First Portuguese visits to Canton River, 1514.

Voyages intended for China and S. Asia by W. or S.W. Route:
7/Columbus 1492–93 (outward and homeward) discovered islands in Bahama group, explored N. coasts of Cuba and Hispaniola; interpreted discoveries as part of Asia; found best return route.
8/Columbus 1493–94 (outward) explored S. coast of Cuba; reported it as peninsula of mainland China.
9/Columbus 1498 (outward) discovered Trinidad and coast of Venezuela; recognised coast as mainland, surmised it to be

terrestrial paradise.
10/Columbus 1502–04 explored coast of Honduras. Nicaragua and the Isthmus. Believed Honduras to be Indo-China.
11/Ojeda & Vespucci 1499–1500 (outward) reached Guiana coast, failed to round Cape São Roque, coasted W. to Cape de la Vela. First report of Amazon.
12/Coelho & Vespucci 1501 (outward) coasted S. from Cape São Agostinho to (possibly) 35°S.
13/Solis 1515 entered Plate River estuary and investigated N. bank.
14/Magellan & Cano 1519–22. Discovered Strait of Magellan, crossed Pacific, reached Moluccas via Philippines. Revealed Pacific as separate ocean of immense size. First circumnavigation.
15/Saavedra 1527 discovered route from coast of Mexico across Pacific to Moluccas.

16/Urdaneta 1565 found feasible return route Philippines to Mexico in 42°N. using W. winds.
17/Schouten & Le Maire 1616 discovered route into Pacific via Le Maire strait and Cape Horn.

Voyages intended for Asia by Northern Route:
18/Cabot 1497 (outward) rediscovered Newfoundland, first sighted by Norsemen in 11th century; took it for N.E. extremity of Asia.
19/Corte-Real 1500 rediscovered Greenland.
20/Verrazzano 1524 traced E. coast of N. America from (probably) 34°N. to 47°N.; revealed continental character of N. America.
21/Cartier 1534 and 1535 explored Strait of Belle Isle and St. Lawrence as far as Montreal.

22/Willoughby & Chancellor 1553 rounded North Cape and reached Archangel.
23/Frobisher 1574 reached Frobisher Bay in Baffin Island, which he took for a 'strait'.
24/Davis 1587 explored W. coast of Greenland to the edge of the ice in 72°N.
25/Barents 1596–97 discovered Bear Island and Spitsbergen and wintered in Novaya Zemlya.
26/Hudson 1610 sailed through Hudson Strait to the S. extremity

of Hudson Bay, which he and others took to be the Pacific.
27/Button 1612 explored W. coast of Hudson Bay, concluded Bay land-locked on the W.
28/Baffin & Bylot 1616 explored whole coastline of Baffin Bay and decided that no navigable N.W. passage existed in that area.

3 Voyages in the Caribbean, 1493-1519

▬▶ voyages intended for China and Southern Asia by West or South West route

▬▶ voyages exploring the Caribbean

4 Voyages in the Pacific, 1720-1780

European expansion overseas, 1493-1713

The Portuguese were the first to exploit the European voyages of discovery. Theirs was essentially a trading empire, and by the middle of the sixteenth century they had more than fifty forts and factories reaching from Sofala on the Zambezi to Nagasaki in Japan (map 1). In 1557 they occupied Macao on the Chinese mainland. The Spaniards, on the other hand, set out on a deliberate policy of conquest and settlement, first in Hispaniola and, a decade or so later, in Mexico and Peru. The result was the foundation of the great Spanish colonial empire (page 68). But the Iberian preponderance did not go unchallenged. Particularly after the foundation of the English and Dutch East India Companies, in 1600 and 1602 respectively, Portuguese trade came under attack (map 2). With the acquisition of Batavia (1619) as an eastern headquarters and of the Cape of Good Hope (1652) as a station on the route to the east, Dutch commercial pre-eminence in Asian waters was assured.

While there was no direct attack on Spain's mainland empire the islands of the Caribbean, coveted as a prime source of sugar for the European market, became an object of intense rivalry and competition, in which all the leading powers engaged (map 4). Furthermore, whatever Spanish pretensions may have been, it was unable to make its presence felt much north of the Rio Grande. There was a slow advance in the west into California; but on the east coast Spanish power was limited to a tenuous foothold in Florida. Here the states of northern Europe, led by England and France, took the lead. France, in particular, advancing down the St. Lawrence estuary, penetrated deep into the interior, exploring the whole Mississippi valley (1682) and establishing fortified posts all the way to the Gulf of Mexico (map 3). The English, on the other hand, established a series of settlements along the eastern coast, beginning with Virginia in 1607. The clash of commercial and colonial interests which ensued ushered in the first age of imperial rivalry and conflict (page 86). Its prelude was the Anglo-Dutch wars of 1652-73 (page 80) which resulted in the British seizure (1664) of the Dutch settlement of New Amsterdam, subsequently renamed New York. It marked the decline of the Netherlands and the rise of England and France to the paramount position in the overseas world.

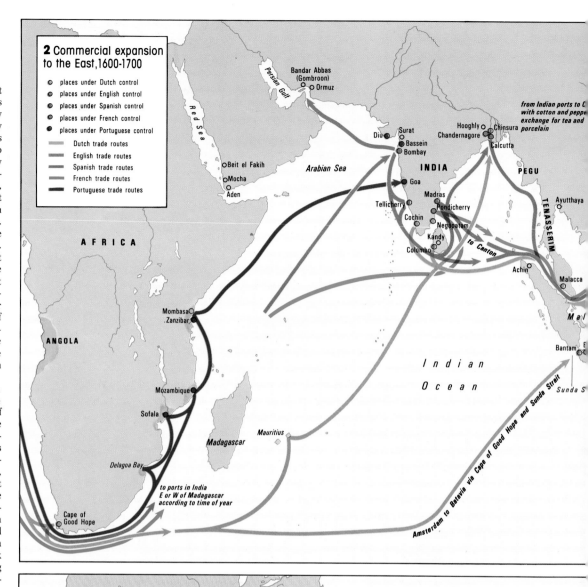

2 Commercial expansion to the East, 1600-1700

- places under Dutch control
- places under English control
- places under Spanish control
- places under French control
- places under Portuguese control

Dutch trade routes
English trade routes
Spanish trade routes
French trade routes
Portuguese trade routes

4 The West Indies

Spanish settlements
French settlements
English settlements
Dutch settlements

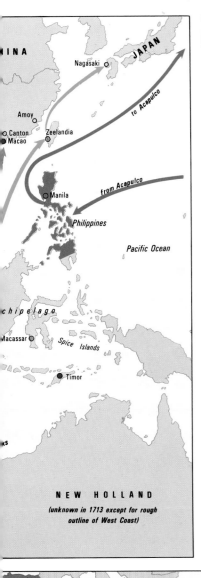

JAPAN
Nagasaki
Amoy
Canton
Macao
Zeelandia
to Acapulco
from Acapulco
Manila
Philippines
Pacific Ocean

Archipelago
Macassar
Spice Islands
Timor

NEW HOLLAND
(unknown in 1713 except for rough outline of West Coast)

RUPERT'S LAND
Fort Albany (Hudson's Bay Company's trading post) 1679
Rupert House (Hudson's Bay Company's trading post) 1668
NEWFOUNDLAND
ILE ST. JEAN
ILE ROYALE
Fort Tadoussac (1600)
NOVA SCOTIA
L. Superior
Quebec (1608) *capital of New France*
Trois Rivières (1634)
Penobscot 1628
NEW FRANCE
Sault Ste. Marie (1639)
Fort Frontenac (1673)
NEW YORK
Fort Niagara (1679)
Portsmouth 1653
Boston 1630
MASS
Plymouth 1620
Albany 1664
Providence 1636
CONN.
New Haven 1640
L. Huron
L. Michigan
L. Ontario
L. Erie
Fort Pontchartrain (1701)
PENNSYLVANIA
New York (New Amsterdam 1624-1664)
Fort St. Joseph (1680)
Philadelphia 1682
Chester 1682
NEW JERSEY
Fort St. Louis (1682)
Fort Crèvecoeur (1680)
Ohio R.
DELAWARE
Annapolis 1709
MARYLAND
Missouri R.
Cahokia (1698)
VIRGINIA
Atlantic Ocean
Kaskaskia (1703)
Tennessee R.
NORTH CAROLINA
SOUTH CAROLINA
Fort Prudhomme (1682)
LOUISIANA
Mississippi R.
Pensacola (1696) *founded to counter French claims*
Fort Maurepas (1699)
Gulf of Mexico

3 European settlement in North America
- English settlements
- French settlements
- Spanish settlements

BRITISH TERRITORIES
Carolina Settled from 1663; separated into two colonies 1713.
Connecticut Settled 1635–38; separately incorporated 1662.
Delaware Settled by Swedes from 1638; separate proprietary colony 1704.
Maine Settled from 1622; effectively part of Massachusetts Bay from 1651, formally annexed 1691.
Maryland Settled as proprietary colony from 1632.
Massachusetts Bay Settled 1629 by Massachusetts Bay Co.
Newfoundland Claimed for England by John Cabot 1497; British sovereignty recognised 1713.
New Hampshire Part of Maine 1622; separate province from 1698.
New York Settled as New Netherland from 1624. Seized by English 1664.
Nova Scotia Settled by French (as Acadia) 1604; ceded to English 1713.
New Jersey Part of New Netherland; English proprietary colony 1664.
Pennsylvania Settled as proprietary colony from 1681.
Rhode Island Settled by dissident groups from Massachusetts Bay from 1636; separately incorporated from 1644.
Rupert's Land Fur trading area claimed by Hudson Bay Co. from 1670; claim recognised by France 1713.
Virginia Settled by Virginia Company from 1607; crown colony from 1624.

FRENCH TERRITORIES
New France Settled from c.1608.
Louisiana After exploration of Mississippi by La Salle (1682), France claimed whole Mississippi drainage. Fortified trading posts established at strategic points from Great Lakes to Gulf of Mexico.

SPAIN
Seville
Balearic Is.
MOROCCO
SYRIA
Alexandria
Cairo
KUWAIT
EGYPT
SINKIANG
Sea of Japan
Ormuz
BAHRAIN
R. Indus
R. Yangtze
R. Ganges
CHINA
JAPAN
Nagasaki
Ryukyu Islands
Manila galleons with silk
Bonin Islands
Canton
Macao
Taiwan
R. Nile
Red Sea
A F R I C A
Diu
Arabian Sea
Hooghly
Hainan
R. Mekong
Luzon
Mariana Islands
Bab el Mandeb
Aden
Goa
Laccadive Islands
Calicut
Andaman Islands
Manila
Manila galleons with silver
Philippines
Cochin
Ceylon
Nicobar Islands
Cebu
Guam
R. Benue
Guato
Caroline Islands
Elmina
Colombo
Malay Archipelago
Malacca
Brunei
Gulf of Guinea
São Tomé
Ternate
Tidore
Maldives
Borneo
Moluccas
Indian Ocean
Sumatra
Celebes
Malindi
Chagos Arch.
Mombasa
Pemba
Zanzibar
Amboina
Banda Is.
Kilwa
Java
Seychelles
Luanda to Bahia with slaves
Luanda
Christmas Island
Timor
ANGOLA
...d sugar
St. Helena
R. Congo
R. Zambezi
Mozambique
Comoro Is.
Agalega Islands
Sofala
Madagascar
Réunion
...stan da Cunha
Lisbon to Goa (alternative route, second half of year)

1 Spanish and Portuguese trade and settlement by c.1600
- principal Spanish trade routes
- principal Portuguese trade routes
- areas under effective Spanish control
- areas under effective Portuguese control
- ☐ important towns in the 16th century
- ● Spanish towns
- ◉ seat of *Audiencia* (Spanish administrative division)
- ● Portuguese towns

Colonial America
1519-1783

The conquest of Mexico by Hernán Cortés in 1519–20 (map 1), and of Peru by Francisco Pizarro in 1531–33 (map 2), laid the foundations of the Spanish colonial empire in America. With the help of rebellious tribes, oppressed by their Aztec and Inca conquerors (page 62), both were amazingly successful. By 1535, when vice-regal government was set up in Mexico and Lima was founded as the capital of Peru, the first dramatic phase of conquest was over. By 1550 all the chief centres of settled population were in Spanish hands, though the task of pushing forward frontiers into unexplored territory continued until the end of the colonial period (map 3). New viceroyalties were set up in New Granada (1739) and Rio de la Plata (1776), and new military governments in Texas (1718) and California (1767). But none of the later, sparsely inhabited conquests compared with Mexico and Peru in wealth and importance. Potosí in Upper

Peru and Zacatecas in Mexico became the biggest sources of silver in the world, and by 1560 silver was the chief export from the American colonies to Spain.

Elsewhere on the American mainland colonisation was slower to take effect. The Portuguese, on the eastern coast of South America, were only goaded into action by fear of the French. But in 1549 they founded Bahía as an administrative capital, and sugar plantations and mills, worked by slaves from Africa, were introduced. Between 1575 and 1600 coastal Brazil became the foremost sugar-producing territory in the western world, and attracted many land-hungry immigrants from Portugal and the Azores. But the vast Brazilian interior remained largely unexplored and in the hands of native Indian tribes (map 4). The same was true of the whole of North America at this date, beyond the frontier of New Spain. With its harsh climate and poor soil, the eastern seaboard of North America was uninviting territory, and for the first century after its discovery the great Newfoundland fisheries were its main attraction. There was also a fur trade with the natives, and by 1535 French explorers

had penetrated far up the St. Lawrence river in the quest of skins and furs. When, after 1670, the English also built up a fur-trading empire, based on Hudson Bay (map 5), the result was a rivalry which erupted in the colonial wars of the eighteenth century (page 86). Nevertheless, fish and furs were the original staple of North America, and settlement, strongly opposed by fishing interests, only began in the seventeenth century, with the foundation of Acadia, or Nova Scotia, by the French in 1604, of Virginia (1607) and Massachusetts Bay (1629) by the English, and of New Netherland, later New York, by the Dutch in 1623. Even so, progress was slow. As late as the end of the seventeenth century, the total population of the twelve English colonies was a mere 250,000.

The pattern of settlement was also different in the north. The English colonists wanted land for farms and plantations, expelling or exterminating the native population. The history of the British colonies in the eighteenth century is punctuated by savage Indian wars. In Virginia, and later in the Carolinas, where tobacco was introduced as a cash-

crop from Guiana, the plantations were worked by Negro slaves, numbering well over 100,000 by the time of the American War of Independence. The Spaniards, on the other hand, relied on Indian labour, both in ranching and mining, and readily intermarried; hence the extensive *mestizo* population, particularly in Mexico and Peru. At the same time, all the colonies were firmly administered in the interests of the mother country. This inevitably provoked resentment on the part of the colonial élites, and lay behind the demand for independence which erupted in the north in 1775 (page 92) and in Latin America in 1808 (page 96).

3 The development of colonial America

- French territory
- Spanish territory
- Portuguese territory
- Dutch territory
- Russian territory
- British by 1763
- ceded by France to Britain 1763
- ceded by France to Spain 1763
- United States 1783
- — — — international boundary
- ··········· provincial boundary
- ➙ major exports
- *colonisation routes:*
  - Spanish
  - Portuguese
  - British
  - Russian
  - French

Arctic Ocean

GREENLAND

unexplored

RUPERT'S LAND
(Hudson's Bay Company)

Hudson Bay

furs

disputed by Russia and Spain

NEWFOUNDLAND

ceded to Britain 1763

QUEBEC
St. Lawrence R.
Québec
Montreal
NOVA SCOTIA
whale products, fish

UNITED STATES OF AMERICA 1783

San Francisco

LOUISIANA

INTERIOR PROVINCES

Los Angeles (1780)

Boston
New York
Philadelphia
THE THIRTEEN COLONIES
Jamestown

naval stores, furs, fish, grain

Ohio R.
Mississippi R.

tobacco, grain

North

WEST FLORIDA
New Orleans
EAST FLORIDA (Br. 1763-83)

skins

Zacatecas

NEW SPAIN

silver

Mexico

Gulf of Mexico

BAHAMA ISLANDS (Br. 1783)

sugar, tobacco

CUBA

WEST INDIES

Atlantic

SANTO DOMINGO

JAMAICA (Br. 1655)
SAINT-DOMINGUE

GUADELOUPE (Fr.)
MARTINIQUE (Fr.)

silver

Belize (Br. 1683)

CENTRAL AMERICA

Caribbean Sea

CURAÇAO (Dutch 1634)

cochineal, gold

gold

Caracas

VENEZUELA
R. Orinoco

tobacco, cocoa beans, hides

Paramaribo
Cayenne
GUIANA

Panama

Pacific

Santa Fé de Bogotá

NEW GRANADA

Quito

drugs, rare plants

gold, naval stores

R. Amazon

B R A Z I L

Ocean

QUEBEC

slave trade from Africa

Venezuela

NEW GRANADA

PERU

B R A Z I L

PERU

CHILE

RIO DE LA PLATA

silver, drugs

Lima
Cuzco

UPPER PERU

Potosí

Paraguay R.
R. Paraná

Treaty of Tordesillas 1494, 1506

R. São Francisco

dyewoods, sugar, tobacco, cotton
Bahía

gold, diamonds

Rio de Janeiro

copper, grain

beef

RIO DE LA PLATA 1776

Indian frontier

Buenos Aires

hides, silver

South

Atlantic

Ocean

FALKLAND IS.

Spanish American population in 1800
(total 16.9 millions)

Whites 3.3
Indians 7.5
Negros 0.8
Mestizos 5.3

Population of the United States and Canada, 1820
(total 11.6 millions)

Whites 9.0
Mulattos 0.1
Negroes 1.9
Indians 0.6

South-East Asia, 1511-1826

When European traders and adventurers broke through into the Indian Ocean at the close of the fifteenth century (page 64), the great prize, drawing them forward, was the spices of South-East Asia. Here was untold wealth to be tapped. But here also, at one of the world's main crossroads, where cultural influences from China and India intermingled, they found themselves in a region of great complexity, divided in religion between Buddhism, Hinduism and Islam, and politically fragmented and unstable (map 1). On the mainland, rival peoples and dynasties competed for hegemony. In the Malayan archipelago the empires of Srivijaya and Majapahit (page 50) had disappeared, leaving behind scores of petty states, with little cohesion. This was the situation when Albuquerque conquered the great international emporium of Malacca for the king of Portugal in 1511.

The Portuguese presence changed little at first. Albuquerque and his successors were there to dominate the spice trade through a chain of fortified trading-stations, linked by naval power. Provided this was accepted, they had no wish to interfere with the native potentates. Far more important, after the arrival on the scene of the Dutch and English (page 66), was the challenge to their trading monopoly by their European rivals. For most of the seventeenth century this rivalry was the dominant factor (map 3). The Dutch, in particular, began a systematic conquest of the Portuguese settlements, capturing Malacca in 1641, and then turned against the British. But in doing so, they were inevitably drawn into local politics. After establishing a base at Batavia in 1619, they interfered in succession disputes among the neighbouring sultans, to ensure their own position, and in this way gradually extended control over Java, expelling the British from Bantam in 1682 (map 4). Already earlier they had driven them out of the Spice Islands by the 'massacre of Amboina' (1623) and the seizure of Macassar (1667), in this way forcing the English East India Company to turn instead to the China trade. With this in view the British acquired Penang on the west coast of Malaya in 1786, the first step in a process which was ultimately to make them masters of the Malay peninsula.

But this was still exceptional. European activities encroached on the outlying islands, but had little impact on the mainland monarchies, which had no direct interest in European trade and were mainly concerned with extending their power at the expense of their neighbours. This is a complicated story, because all the main centres were also under pressure from the hill peoples of the interior, always waiting to assert their independence; but the main lines of development are indicated on map 2. They include the advance of Annam at the expense of Cambodia, the rise of a new Burmese empire under Alaungpaya (1735-60), after a Mon rebellion in 1740, and successful Siamese resistance to Burmese encroachment, in spite of Burmese conquest in 1767. These events occurred for the most part without European involvement, but during the struggle for empire between England and France in the eighteenth century (page 86) some states were implicated. Already under Louis XIV France had intervened in Siam against the Dutch. During the Anglo-French war in India after 1746 it supported the Mon rebellion in Burma, and in reply the English East India Company seized the island of Negrais at the mouth of the Bassein river. Later, when the Burmese, foiled in their attempt to conquer Siam, switched their efforts to the north, the British, fearing for the security of Bengal, again intervened. The result was the first Anglo-Burmese war (1824-26) and the British annexation of Assam, Arakan and Tenasserim.

In Malaya there was similar encroachment on the independent rulers when the British, after acquiring Penang in 1786, established Singapore in 1819 as a free trade port after its acquisition by Raffles. This led to a conflict of interests with Holland which was only settled by the Anglo-Dutch treaty of 1824 when the British withdrew from Sumatra in return for Dutch withdrawal from Malacca (map 5). The future Dutch and British colonial empires in South-East Asia were taking shape. But their control was still loose and indirect. Only after the Industrial Revolution in Europe, and the expanding demand for raw materials and markets, were the lives and fortunes of the peoples of the region seriously affected.

1 South-East Asia in 1500

distribution of major religions:

Theravada Buddhism

Mahayana Buddhism mixed with Confucianism and Taoism

Hindu-Buddhism

Islamic states

● places sending tribute to China between 1370 and 1440

3 European rivalries 1511-1682

→ English expeditions

→ Dutch expeditions

→ Spanish expeditions

→ Portuguese expeditions

first Dutch voyage to Bantam and Batavia 1595

Portuguese expedition to Malacca 1511; to Bandas 1512; to Moluccas 1513

English East India Company's first voyage to Atjeh and Bantam 1601-2

Malacca 1511 captured by Portuguese 1641 captured from Portuguese by Dutch

1571 Spanish capital Manila

abortive Spanish expedition to Tidore 1524

Spanish expeditions from Manila to aid the Portuguese against Ternate begin 1582; against the Dutch from 1606

Francis Drake calls at Ternate 1579

1513 Portuguese arrive at Ternate and Tidore

1623 massacre of English factors by Dutch

Bantam 1602-82 English factory

Batavia 1619 founded by Dutch

1667 captured by Dutch.

4 Dutch expansion in Java

1619 – date of Dutch control

Dutch expansion

Bantam
1684-1809
1619
Batavia
BANTAM
PREANGER
DISTRICTS
1677
CHERIBON
1679-
1813
Cheribon
Pekalongan
Japara
Rembang
Semarang
Demak
Tuban
N.E. COASTAL DISTRICTS
1743
MADURA I.
1705-1743
MANCHANAGARA
Gresik
Surabaya
Sampang
SURA
KARTA
1830
Madiun
Pasuruan
JOGJAKARTA
Kediri
Malang
BALAM
BANGAN
1777

Java Sea

Indian Ocean

5 The Malay states in 1826

Malay states tributary to Siam in 1826

British possessions

SIAM
PERLIS
KEDAH
PENANG
PERAK
KELANTAN
TRENGGANU
PAHANG
South China Sea
SELANGOR
NEGRI SEMBILAN
MALACCA
JOHORE
Straits of Malacca
SUMATRA
SINGAPORE

2 Trade and politics

- principal trading centre
- Vietnamese border in 1500
- expansion to 1611
- further acquisitions from Cambodia in early 18th century
- Vietnamese expansion in 19th century
- Kingdom of Luang Prabang 1707
- area which broke away under Vientiane in 1707
- major Burmese conquests
- Siamese conquests

trade routes:
- routes developed by Dutch and English East India Companies
- routes developed by Arab and Gujerati traders
- route developed by the Dutch in the 17th century
- routes used by English shipping after 1786
- route used by the 'Manila Galleon'
- local trade routes

European possessions in 1826:
- British
- Dutch
- Spanish
- Portuguese

Labels on main map:

ASSAM
MANIPUR
Imphal
R. Brahmaputra
Naga Hills
Myitkyina
Mogaung
YUNNAN
CHINA
Bhamo
R. Chindwin
Tagaung
R. Shweli
BURMA
Chin Hills
Shwebo
Mandalay
Ava
Amarapura
SHAN STATES
Teknaf
Akyab
Myohaung
Minbu
Magwe
Pagan
R. Sittang
KARENNI STATE
1564
1767
1785
An Pass
Chiang Saen
Chiang Rai
Luang Prabang
Thanh Hoa
TONGKING
Hanoi
Bac Ninh
Haiphong
Thayetmyo
Prome
Toungoo
Chiengmai
Lamphun
Lampang
Vientiane
Paksane
Ha Tinh
Porte d'Annam
Taungup Pass
Pegu
Rangoon
Syriam
Thaton
Martaban
Sawankhalok
Sukhothai
Savannakhet
Hue
Tourane
Bassein
C. Negrais
(from 1755)
(to 1755)
Moulmein
MONS
R. Ye
1767
Lop Buri
SIAM
Champassak
Binh Dinh
Tavoy
Thon Buri
Korat
Ayutthaya
Bangkok
Sisophon
Mongkol Borey
Angkor
Siem Reap
Stung Treng
Qui Nhon
TENASSERIM
Mergui
Battambang
Chanthaburi
Kompong Thom
CAMBODIA
Kratie
Kompong Cham
Nha Trang
Andaman Is.
Mergui Archipelago
Isthmus of Kra
Phnom Penh
COCHIN CHINA
Bien Hoa
Saigon
Gulf of Siam
Kampot
Chau Doc
Ha Tien
Cho Lon
R. Mekong
Nakhon Si Thammarat
Phuket
Trang
Songkhla
Pattani
Penang
MALAYA
Straits of Malacca
SUMATRA
Malacca
(Portuguese Malacca 1511-1641)
Singapore
Tiku
Fort de Kock (Bukit Tinggi)
Padang
Painan
R. Rokan
R. Kampar
Benkulen
Djambi
Bangka
Palembang
Billiton
Sukadana
Pontianak
R. Sambas
R. Kapu
Borneo
R. Barito
Karimata Strait
Bandjarmasin
Sunda Strait
Bantam
Batavia (Jakarta)
MATARAM
Surabaya
Jogjakarta
Java
Bali
Lombok
Sumbawa
Flores
Sumba
Timor
Indian Ocean
to Madras and Calcutta
Java Sea
South China Sea
LAOS
ANNAM
Canton
Macao
TAIWAN
contested by Dutch and Spanish in 1620s and 1630s
to Japan
from Canton to all major S.E. Asian ports
Luzon
PHILIPPINES
Manila
to Acapulco
from Acapulco
Sulu Sea
Balambangan
Mindanao
Manado
Brunei
SARAWAK
Sulu Archipelago
Strait of Macassar
Halmahera
Tidore
MOLUCCAS
Celebes
Macassar
Buru
Ceram
Amboina
Banda Is.
Banda Sea

New monarchy in Europe, 1453-1547

In Europe revival after the setbacks of the fourteenth century (page 56) began around 1450. The whole continent was affected. In the east Ivan III (1462-1505) profited from the decline of the Mongol khanates (page 46) to inaugurate a rapid expansion of the territory of Muscovy (page 84) and to attack the independence of Tver, Novgorod and the landowning aristocracy. In the west endemic civil war in Spain was ended after the union of Castile and Aragon in 1479. The ending of the Hundred Years' War between England and France (1453) and the expulsion of the English from French territory saw a rapid extension of the area controlled by the French monarchy (map 2), while in England Edward IV (1461-83) began a restoration of royal power which was carried further by the new Tudor dynasty after 1485. Through the Council in the North with its seat at York, and the Council in the March of Wales, with its seat at Ludlow, the turbulent outlying regions were brought under control, while Wales itself and the palatinates of Chester and Durham were integrated into the parliamentary and judicial systems from 1536 (map 4). But an attempt to integrate Ireland by Poynings' Law (1494) had little effect, and although Henry VIII was proclaimed King of Ireland (1541), English power was effectively limited to the Pale around Dublin. Scotland also resisted successfully.

Not all attempts at state-building were a success. The efforts of the dukes of Burgundy to erect an independent state in the rich lands between France and the Empire collapsed when the ambitious Charles the Bold was killed at Nancy in 1477 (map 3). The empire of Matthias Corvinus of Hungary (1458-90) also proved ephemeral. Italy remained divided, in spite of a marked strengthening of government under rulers such as Lorenzo de' Medici (1469-92) at Florence and Ludovico Sforza (1460-99) at Milan (map 5), and after the French invasion of 1494 internal divisions left Italy a prey to foreign intervention. The main legatee in all instances was the house of Habsburg, which succeeded to the Spanish possessions in 1516 and emerged, under Charles V (1519-56) as the preponderant power in western Europe (map 1). But the diversified Habsburg empire lacked cohesion, and when the Ottoman advance, halted on the middle Danube since 1456, was resumed after 1520 (page 48), and at the same time the emperor was involved in the religious wars in Germany (page 74), the strain was too great. In 1556 Charles V abdicated and the empire was divided between the Austrian and Spanish Habsburgs. Only ten years later the Dutch revolt began.

The Dutch revolt, although the most formidable uprising (page 76), was not exceptional. In England, from Henry VII to Elizabeth I, the Tudors were faced by repeated rebellions, and elsewhere, even in Russia, resistance to centralisation became a powerful force after 1550. The rise of the new monarchies was less a new beginning than the culmination of the long struggle of aristocracy and monarchy. Their financial and administrative machinery was not enough to raise a modern system of government in place of the feudal order, and the decisive change from the old to the new was not made until after another century of strife and turmoil.

2 The reunification of France, 1440-1589

- frontier of France 1493
- Royal Domain c.1475
- lands annexed from Burgundy 1477
- lands of René of Anjou, annexed 1481
- lands of the Duke of Brittany, annexed 1491
- lands brought to the crown by Louis XII, 1498
- lands brought to the crown by Francis I, 1515
- lands of the Duke of Bourbon, annexed 1527
- lands brought to the crown by Henry IV, 1589
- other fiefs annexed with date
- fiefs still independent at end of 16th century
- lands recognising English suzerainty 1429

1 The new monarchies

- Habsburg territory
- Ottoman territory
- Muscovy and territories
- Venetian territories
- Empire of Casimir IV, 1447-92
- Empire of Matthias Corvinus, 1485-90
- *1483* date of conquest

3 The Low Countries, 1467-1548

- Charles the Bold's possessions, 1477
- Burgundian possessions lost after the death of Charles the Bold, 1477
- Emperor Charles V's Burgundian possessions, 1548

1 FRIESLAND	14 CAMBRAI
2 GRONINGEN	15 NAMUR
3 OVERIJSSEL	16 LUXEMBOURG
4 GELDERLAND	17 PONTHIEU
5 UTRECHT	18 AMIENS
6 HOLLAND	19 VERMANDOIS
7 ZEELAND	20 BAR
8 BRABANT	21 LORRAINE
9 LIMBURG	22 BURGUNDY
10 FLANDERS	23 FRANCHE-COMTÉ
11 BOULONNAIS	24 ALSACE
12 ARTOIS	25 TOURNAI
13 HAINAUT	

M. METZ
T. TOUL

LINGEN 1543
RAVENSBURG
CALAIS
LIÈGE
Nancy 1477
Morat 1476
Grandson 1476

4 Extension of Tudor power in Britain

- The Pale 1537
- The Pale 1596
- Principality of Wales before 1536
- new Welsh counties after 1536

- Council of the Marches of Wales 1525-1642
- Council of the North 1537-1641
- Council of the West 1539-40
- X English attempts to subdue Scots

- rebellions against Henry VII, 1485-1509
- rebellions against Henry VIII, 1509-47
- rebellions against Edward VI and Mary 1547-58
- rebellions against Elizabeth I, 1558-1603

KINGDOM OF SCOTLAND
North Sea
Leith 1560
Pinkie 1547
Haddon Rig 1542
Edinburgh 1544
Flodden Field 1513
Ancrum Moor 1545
Naworth Castle 1569
Solway Moss 1542
Hexham 1569
Newham
Carlisle
PALATINATE OF DURHAM
Barnard Castle 1569
Durham
Kirkby Stephen
Richmond
Northern risings 1536-7, 1569-70
Pilgrimage of Grace 1536-7
Yorkshire rising 1489
York
PALATINATE OF LANCASTER
Bramham Moor 1569
PALATINATE OF CHESTER
Pontefract
Lincolnshire rebellion 1536
under Council of Wales to 1569
Lincoln
ULSTER
Derry
Coleraine
O'Neill's rebellion 1593-1603
Yellow Ford 1598
Curlew Mts 1599
Clontibret 1595
Newry
O'Donnell's rebellion 1594-1601
IRELAND
PRESIDENCY OF CONNAUGHT 1569
Galway
Athlone
THE PALE
Dublin
Kildare's rebellion 1534
Irish Sea
Caernarvon
Shrewsbury
Ludlow
Mousehold Heath 1549
Norwich
Radnor
WALES
Kett's rebellion 1549
Cardigan
ENGLAND
Limerick
Kilkenny
PRESIDENCY OF MUNSTER 1571
Waterford
Smerwick 1579
Fitzmaurice's rebellion 1579
Kinsale 1601
Monmouth
Gloucester
Sudbury 1525
Pembroke
Cardiff
Bristol
London 1554
Blackheath 1497
Maidstone
Western rebellion 1549
Wells
Guildford 1497
Wyatt's rebellion 1554
Launceston
Sampford Courtenay 1549
Exeter 1549
Okehampton 1549
Portsmouth
Bodmin
Cornish rebellion 1497
English Channel

LITHUANIA
NOVGOROD acquired by Ivan III 1462-1505
PSKOV
LIVONIA
ESTONIA
TVER
1462
Moscow
MUSCOVY
acquired by Vassily III 1505-33
TRANSYLVANIA 1541
1504
1504
TARTARS
1459
OTTOMAN EMPIRE in 1451
Black Sea
1453
ANATOLIA
MOREA 1460
Chios 1566
1470
Rhodes 1522
CRETE (Venetian)
20°
30°

5 Renaissance Italy, 1454

- boundary of Holy Roman Empire

R. Adige
Pieve di Cadore
DUCHY OF SAVOY
Trent
REPUBLIC OF VENICE
R. Piave
Trieste
Como
Bergamo
Vicenza
R. Po
Istria
Turin
Milan
Brescia
Verona
Padua
Venice
Pola
Asti
MONT FERRAT
Pavia
Piacenza
Cremona
Parma
MANTUA
DUCHY OF FERRARA
REP. OF GENOA
DUCHY OF MILAN
Reggio
Ferrara
Ravenna
to Savoy
Modena
DUCHY OF MODENA
Bologna
Faenza
Rimini
PR. OF MONACO
Genoa
LUCCA
REP. OF
Urbino
Sinigaglia
Ancona
to Savoy
Pisa
FLORENCE
Florence
Arezzo
PAPAL STATES
Elba
REP. OF SIENA
Siena
Assisi
Ascoli
Spoleto
Corsica (to Genoa)
DUCHY OF PIOMBINO
R. Tiber
Atri
Ajaccio
Rome
Adriatic Sea
Aquino
Fossanova
KINGDOM
Tyrrhenian Sea
Capua
OF
Naples
NAPLES
Sardinia
Cagliari

73

The Reformation in Europe, 1517-1648

The closing years of the fifteenth century saw a great revival of popular religion in Europe, but the established church, which never fully recovered from the effects of the schism of 1378–1417 (page 56), was ill equipped to satisfy its needs. Except in Bohemia and Moravia, where the Hussites comprised over half the population, and in England, where small groups of Lollards survived, heresy was virtually dead by 1500; but the materialism of the Renaissance popes and the self-seeking of the higher clergy discredited the hierarchy in the eyes of many laymen. Some, like Erasmus of Rotterdam (1466–1536) and Sir Thomas More (1478–1535), still pinned their hopes on spiritual renewal; but elsewhere, particularly in Germany and German-speaking Switzerland, financial and other abuses fired revolt. In 1517 Martin Luther (1483–1546) posted his 95 theses on the church door at Wittenberg. In 1520, under the impulse of Huldreich Zwingli (1484–1531), Zurich renounced allegiance to Rome. Their denunciations of the clergy and the supremacy of the pope and their demand for a return to the standards of early Christianity exercised a vast appeal. By 1560 (map 1) seven out of ten of the Emperor's subjects were Protestants, and the reformed faith prevailed in Scandinavia, Baltic Europe and England. Further impetus came from the teaching of John Calvin (1509–64). In France over one hundred Calvinist churches existed by 1559 and perhaps 700 by 1562, and Calvinism also made rapid progress in Poland, Hungary and Scotland, where it became the official religion in 1560. In addition, a number of more radical sects

2   The European sectaries, 1525-1620

- Mennonites
- Hutterites
- other Anabaptist groups 1525-49
- other Anabaptist groups 1550-1620
- boundary of Holy Roman Empire c.1620
- boundary of Habsburg lands 1620

3   The French wars of religion

- greatest extent of Roman Catholic League (1590)
- area under Huguenot control (1598)
- area disputed by Roman Catholics and Huguenots
- ○ Huguenot towns recognised by Edict of Nantes 1598-1629
- □ towns with courts for trying Huguenot cases after 1598
- ● main towns experiencing St. Bartholomew Massacre 1572

4   The Thirty Years' War in Germany 1618-48

- route of the Spanish Army 1634
- route of Gustavus Adolphus 1631-2
- ✕ imperial (Catholic) victory
- ✕ imperial (Catholic) defeat
- boundary of Holy Roman Empire
- areas affected by Edict of Restitution 1629
- ■ date region became Lutheran
- ▲ date region became Calvinist

the religious position in 1640:
- Lutheran
- Calvinist
- Catholic
- regained by Roman Catholics

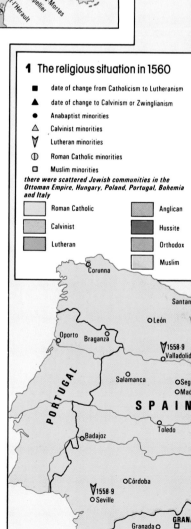

1   The religious situation in 1560

- ■ date of change from Catholicism to Lutheranism
- ▲ date of change to Calvinism or Zwinglianism
- ● Anabaptist minorities
- △ Calvinist minorities
- ⩔ Lutheran minorities
- ◐ Roman Catholic minorities
- ▣ Muslim minorities

there were scattered Jewish communities in the Ottoman Empire, Hungary, Poland, Portugal, Bohemia and Italy

- Roman Catholic
- Calvinist
- Lutheran
- Anglican
- Hussite
- Orthodox
- Muslim

sprang up, Anabaptists, Mennonites and others (map 2), which rejected theology, ritual and clerical order in favour of Biblical simplicity and often combined evangelism with social protest. They even proclaimed an Anabaptist republic at Münster in 1534, but it was brutally suppressed the next year.

However, the Reformation was soon entangled in politics. Princes and kings, including Henry VIII of England, saw an opportunity to despoil the church of its wealth. Some German princes espoused Protestantism out of fear of imperial power. Luther himself, dependent on princely support, turned against the more radical sectaries and condemned the peasants' revolt of 1525. Foreign policy

also played a part. The Valois kings of France, though combating the protestant Huguenots at home, supported the German Protestant princes against the Habsburg emperor. Although the French Huguenots won toleration by the Edict of Nantes (1598), their numbers were severely reduced during the religious wars between 1562 and 1598 (map 3), and elsewhere in Europe the second half of the sixteenth century saw a great Catholic revival, led by the Jesuit Order, founded in 1534 by St. Ignatius Loyola (1491–1556), and inspired by the reforms of the Council of Trent between 1545 and 1563. Using the Jesuits as their spearhead, Catholic rulers went over to the offensive. Protestants were expelled

from Bavaria (1579) and Styria (1600), and in Poland the number of Protestant churches decreased from 560 in 1572 to 240 in 1650.

The decisive phase of the struggle between Protestants and Catholics, the Thirty Years' War, took place in the Holy Roman Empire (map 4). It began in 1618–21 when the emperor Ferdinand II defeated the Bohemian Protestants at the battle of the White Mountain (1620) and won back Bohemia and Moravia for Catholicism. When he turned against the Protestant princes of Germany, Denmark, England and the Dutch intervened on the Protestant side, but the imperial forces were initially successful and in 1629 an Edict of Restitution was promulgated

which reclaimed large areas of church lands held by Protestant princes. Only the intervention of Gustavus Adolphus of Sweden saved the Protestant cause from collapse. But the Swedish victories at Breitenfeld (1631) and Lützen (1632) brought in Spain on the imperial side, while France allied with Sweden and declared war on Spain (1635). The war was now a struggle in which it seemed that neither side could hope for outright victory, until in 1648 the Peace of Westphalia brought a compromise solution. Lutherans and Calvinists retained the lands they held in 1624, and the wars of religion were over. But Germany, the scene of battle, suffered a lasting setback.

Western Europe, 1558-1648

The second half of the sixteenth and the first half of the seventeenth centuries were a time of turbulence throughout Europe. In Russia the 'time of troubles' after the death of Ivan the Terrible (1584) lasted until 1613. Northern Europe was embroiled in almost continuous war from 1561 to 1658, as Sweden, independent since the time of Gustavus Vasa (1523–60), struggled with Denmark, Russia, Poland and Brandenburg for control of the Baltic and its important trade. The rise of the Swedish empire (map 3), leading to Gustavus Adolphus' intervention in the Thirty Years' War (page 74) and the Swedish acquisition of western Pomerania, Wismar and the bishoprics of Bremen and Verden at the Peace of Westphalia, vitally affected the balance of power in Europe and was one of the most significant developments of the period. In western Europe developments were more confused. The new monarchies of the preceding period (page 72) had over-reached themselves, and from around 1530 reaction set in, particularly when rising prices, recession and widespread unemployment reinforced existing discontents. The Elizabethan Poor Law and other legislation of 1563 was no remedy: indeed, the reign of Elizabeth I (1558–1603), was less auspicious than often painted, and Elizabeth, whose relations with parliament deteriorated sharply at the end of her reign, left her Stuart successors on the English throne a legacy of unsolved problems with which they failed to cope.

From around 1530, sometimes earlier, the history of France and England was punctuated by revolts. As in Germany (page 74), they reflected a combination of religious, social and political grievances. In England the northern risings of 1536 and 1569 (page 72) were Catholic protests against the suppression of the old faith, but they also embodied the resistance of the northern gentry to centralisation and control from London. On the other wing the unrest of radical dissenters combined dissatisfaction with Henry VIII's and Elizabeth's conservative church settlements with resistance to the enclosure of common lands for the benefit of grasping landlords. A similar mixture of motives permeated the frequent uprisings, 500 in all, in France (map 2). These were largely revolts of the common people, driven to extremes by economic hardship; but in the end the most influential factor, visible in France in the revolt of the judges and nobility which drove the king from Paris in 1649, was resistance to autocracy, centralisation and taxation. The Dutch revolt, which began in the North Netherlands in 1572 and ended in 1648 (map 1),

was inspired by fear that the central government, controlled from Spain, intended to override the traditional liberties of the Netherlands. Similar motives underlay the Catalan and Portuguese revolts against Castile (1640).

In the British Isles, united from 1603 under a single monarch, the efforts of Charles I (1625–49) to change the traditional religious and political structure resulted in rebellions in Scotland (1638) and Ireland (1641). The king's innovations were no more popular with many of England's political leaders, called to Parliament to vote the taxes required to restore royal control in the other two kingdoms: their refusal provoked a civil war in England (1642). In a complex sequence of political and military moves (map 4), a small Parliamentary faction not only contrived the defeat and execution of the king (1649), creating an English Republic under the Lord Protector Oliver Cromwell, but went on to establish London's direct control over the entire British Isles (1649–51). Even though the Monarchy was restored in 1660, power was now shared between the crown and Parliament (in constant existence from 1689).

In continental Europe the sequel was different. In France the failure of the Fronde broke the power of the aristocracy and cleared the way for the absolutism of Louis XIV (page 80). Only in Germany was the disarray caused by a century of religious and political conflict enduring. Here the devastation of the Thirty Years' War resulted in a decline of population from some 21 millions in 1618 to around 13 millions in 1648 (map 5), and though some regions were spared, the setback was undeniable. The outcome was a major shift in the European balance. The Habsburgs, who had dominated the previous period, were in retreat, and the future in the West was in the hands of a resurgent France and its rivals, the maritime powers.

The English Civil War (below)

1/Edinburgh 1638: National Covenant signed.

2/Newcastle 1640: Scottish Covenanters invade England and force Charles I to buy them off.

3/Kilkenny 1641: centre of rebellion by Irish Catholics (to 1649).

4/Antrim 1641: massacre of Catholics by Protestants.

5/Westminster 1642: English Parliament raises army against Charles I.

6/Edgehill 1642: first battle of English Civil War, indecisive.

7/Westminster 1643: alliance of English Parliament and Scottish Covenanters against Charles I (to 1648).

8/Nantwich 1644: Parliamentary army defeats Irish Catholic invasion in support of Charles I.

9/Marston Moor 1644: Scots and Parliamentary army defeat Charles I and occupy N. England.

10/Lostwithiel 1644: Parliamentary army loses control of SW England to King.

11/Tippermuir 1644: Montrose and Scottish royalists defeat Covenanters.

12/Philiphaugh 1645: Montrose defeated by Covenanters and forced to flee.

13/Naseby 1645: Parliamentary army defeats Charles I and wins control of all England.

14/Burford 1647: Oliver Cromwell suppresses mutiny of Parliamentary troops (the 'Levellers').

15/Preston 1648: Cromwell defeats Covenanters' invasion of England in support of Charles I.

16/Whitehall 1649: Parliament tries and executes Charles I.

17/Drogheda and Wexford 1649: Cromwell overruns Ireland and ends rebellion there; occupied to 1660.

18/Dunbar 1650: Cromwell defeats Covenanters and occupies Scotland (to 1660).

19/Scone 1651: Charles II crowned king of Scotland by Covenanters.

20/Worcester 1651: Cromwell defeats invasion of Covenanters in support of Charles II who is forced to flee abroad (to 1660).

21/Whitehall 1658: death of Oliver Cromwell (Head of State since 1654).

22/Westminster 1660: coronation of Charles II as king of England.

1 The Dutch revolt, 1572-1648

- boundary of Netherlands 1548
- rebel areas in 1572 (December)
- furthest extent of Dutch revolt (July 1577)
- rebel areas December 1588
- rebel areas December 1606
- Dutch conquests 1621-48
- the Dutch Republic 1648

4 The English Civil War, 1642-45

- area controlled by Parliament August 1642
- Parliamentary gains 1643
- Parliamentary losses 1643
- Parliamentary gains 1644
- area controlled by the King 1644
- area controlled by the King December 1645
- Parliamentary and pro-Parliamentary forces
- Royalist and pro-Royalist forces

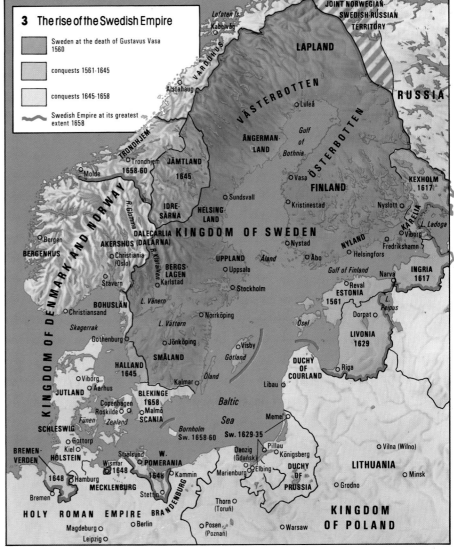

Germany and its neighbours
1648-1806

The Peace of Westphalia (1648), besides bringing to a close the wars of religion (page 74), was a milestone in German history. The failure of the emperor to impose his will on the Protestant princes confirmed the political fragmentation which had gathered pace since the fourteenth century (page 54). After 1648 Germany was a patchwork of some 300 small, petty states and free cities (map 1). In addition, the independence of Holland and Switzerland was formally recognised. Theoretically the rights of the princes were limited by the rights of the Holy Roman Empire, but in practice every prince was emperor in his own lands, with full sovereign powers including the laws to make foreign alliances. Political disruption was also compounded by a sharp economic setback, due partly to the devastation and depopulation resulting from the Thirty Years' War, but also to a long-term shift in the European economy. The great south German banking houses of Welser and Fugger went bankrupt in 1614 and 1627 respectively. The Hanseatic League, in disarray since the closing years of the sixteenth century, was dissolved in 1669. Everywhere the towns were in decline, particularly in Austria, Prussia and

Bavaria, but even worse was the plight of the peasantry. In Bohemia and Moravia their legal rights were abolished; in the north and north-east they were ejected from their holdings to permit the consolidation of Junker estates, and reduced to serfdom (page 82). Impoverishment and stagnation were the result. A modest economic recovery occurred after 1750; but with its resources dissipated on ostentatious building and the upkeep of princely households Germany was an economic and social backwater. It was also a pawn in great power politics. Divided among themselves and fearful of Habsburg ambitions, the princes were clients of foreign powers, including Britain and Sweden, but particularly of France, which used its position to make inroads on German territories in the west (page 80), annexing the Franche-Comté of Burgundy (1678), Strassburg (1681), most of Alsace (1697) and Bar and Lorraine (1766).

After 1648, apart from Austria, only Saxony, Bavaria and Brandenburg could claim even the status of second-rate powers. Saxony, with the mineral resources of the Erzgebirge and its varied industries, was the most advanced, while Bavaria was falling behind; but Brandenburg-Prussia was beginning, under the Great Elector (1640–88) the long climb which made it by 1786 the second German power and the rival of Austria. The rise of Prussia (map 2) is a story of tenacity, unscrupulous diplomacy, but above all of single-

2 The rise of Prussia

- Brandenburg in 1648
- Prussian acquisitions 1648-1707
- acquisitions 1715, 1720
- acquisitions 1742, 1744, 1772
- X battles between Austria and Prussia

3 The growth of the Habsburg Empire

- hereditary Habsburg lands 1525
- acquisitions 1526-1648
- acquisitions 1648-99
- acquisitions 1699-1772
- acquisitions 1772-1805
- boundary of the Holy Roman Empire 1789
- military frontier

minded devotion to building a strong military and administrative apparatus to weld together the scattered territories stretching from the Vistula to the Rhine. The Hohenzollern domains lacked internal and external cohesion. Prussia itself was until 1657 a Polish fief; and it was only in 1772, after the first partition of Poland (map 4) that Frederick the Great (1740–86) succeeded in creating a continuous Prussian territory from Memel to Magdeburg. More impressive, and a cardinal fact in eighteenth-century history, was the recovery of Austria after its setbacks in the Thirty Years' War and the creation of a vast new Austrian empire (map 3). This was largely the work of the great field marshal, Prince Eugene of Savoy (1663–1736). As late as 1683 Vienna itself was besieged by Turkish armies. Eugene turned the tide and by 1699 they had been thrown back and the whole of Hungary brought under Habsburg rule. Austria was now a major power in eastern Europe, while in the west the peace settle-

ment of 1714 brought it the Spanish Netherlands and the Spanish inheritance in Italy. But it was a giant with feet of clay, with weak finances and an inadequate army. Serbia and Belgrade, acquired in 1718, were lost again in 1739, Lombardy and southern Italy in 1734–5. When, on the death of Charles VI (1711–40) and the accession of Maria Theresa (1740–80), Frederick II of Prussia seized Silesia, Austria's inherent weaknesses were exposed. Although the struggle went on until 1763, it proved impossible to dislodge the Prussians. Later both Prussia and Austria took advantage of the disarray of Poland to enlarge their territories in the east. But in the three partitions (map 4) they had to share the spoils with Russia, and their mutual suspicions and rivalry left the west exposed to France. When the French revolutionary armies marched into Germany in 1793 the old order was doomed, and in 1806 the Holy Roman Empire passed unmourned from the map of Europe.

France and Europe
1648 – 1715

Under Louis XIV who succeeded to the throne in 1643, France became the leading country of Europe. His long minority, during Cardinal Mazarin's rule, saw the last major revolts of the aristocracy in defence of its prescriptive rights. When in 1661 Louis became effective ruler, the ground had been prepared for a new regime of centralisation and absolutism. This was the work of Mazarin, who had broken the aristocratic revolts and who turned the *intendants* into permanent representatives of the royal will in the provinces; of Louvois, who reformed the army; and particularly of Colbert's programme of financial reform. At the same time Vauban encircled France with a chain of defensive fortresses (map 1). All this was accompanied by great public works,

including the Languedoc canal, connecting the Atlantic and the Mediterranean, the palace of Versailles, and much building in Paris which became the centre of the cosmopolitan civilisation of Europe.

But Louis XIV's wars, inspired by an almost neurotic fear of the revival of the empire of Charles V and the encirclement of France by Habsburg power, seriously damaged this solid achievement. Beginning with his attack on the Spanish Netherlands in 1667, they imposed a growing burden of taxation and gradually united Europe against him (map 4). England and Holland, maritime and colonial rivals since 1652 (map 3), settled their differences by the Treaty of Breda (1667) and in alliance with Sweden compelled Louis to make peace at Aix-la-Chapelle in 1668. Thereupon Louis detached England from the anti-French alliance by the Secret Treaty of Dover (1670), won over Sweden, and turned against Holland in 1672; but he was halted by an alliance between Austria, Spain and Brandenburg (which

defeated his Swedish allies at Fehrbellin in 1675), and at the Peace of Nimwegen (1678) Holland emerged unscathed.

These inconclusive results convinced Louis that there was little hope of major territorial acquisitions by direct conquest, and after 1679 he turned to a policy of indirect aggression, nibbling away at German territory in the east, particularly in Alsace (map 2), the object being to absorb the remainder of the Burgundian territories which had been partitioned between France and Austria after the death of Charles the Bold in 1477 (page 72). Strasbourg was annexed in 1681, the Palatinate burnt and ravaged in 1689. But these provocative and often brutal actions united German opinion against him, and the revocation of the Edict of Nantes (1685) and the persecution of the French Huguenots incensed the Protestant powers. The result was the formation of the Grand Alliance (1689), led by William of Orange, who had succeeded to the English throne after the revolution

1 France under Louis XIV

frontiers and administration:
- 〰 frontier of France 1713-14
- administrative units of Louis XIV's reign, the *généralités* (generalities)
- ⊙ seat of intendants, Louis XIV's royal commissioners
- ⊕ *parlement* (law courts)

defence:
- ▣ fortifications (the so-called *barrière* or *frontière de fer*)
- ▣ fortifications built by Vauban but ceded during reign of Louis XIV
- ➤ fortification gap, possible invasion route *(porte)*
- ⚓ galley port
- ⊞ naval port

economic:
- ⚓ commercial harbours

major manufactures:
- ▢ brandy
- ⚔ cloth
- ▢ glass
- ⊞ iron
- ◔ madder dye
- ▱ paper
- ▱ pottery
- ⚓ printing
- ▤ salt
- ◔ silk
- ◔ soap
- ⊠ tapestry and carpets
- ▼ wine

of 1688 and the deposition of James II. Louis' attempts to foment rebellion in Ireland failed after the defeat of the French navy at La Hogue (1692), but fighting continued inconclusively on the continent until 1697, when the Peace of Ryswick registered Louis' first serious setback.

A new phase opened with the death without heirs of Charles II of Spain in 1700. This event had long been anticipated, but plans to divide the Spanish dominions in such a way as to maintain the balance of power were thwarted not only by the rivalry of France and Austria, but also by the maritime powers (England and Holland), which feared French ascendancy in overseas trade if it acquired the Spanish overseas empire. The result was the long War of the Spanish Succession (map 5), ended, in spite of the victories of Prince Eugene of Savoy and the Duke of Marlborough, by the compromise Peace of Utrecht in 1713. The French candidate retained the Spanish throne as Philip V, and France kept most of its gains on its eastern frontier (map 2). But the ruinous expense of Louis' wars left France in a desperate situation, with a legacy of financial disorder and internal discontent from which his successors never fully recovered.

4 The wars of Louis XIV 1667-1697
- main lines of French advance
- main theatres of operation
- ■ towns occupied by France
- ✕ French victory
- ✕ Allied victory
- ✕ English victory

Triple Alliance 1668

Coalition of 1673

The Grand Alliance 1689

2 The north-east frontier, 1648-1714
- —— French frontier 1713/14
- French gains to 1659
- gains to 1679
- gains to 1679 later lost
- gains by Treaty of Ryswick 1697

3 The Anglo-Dutch wars, 1652-1673

First Anglo-Dutch War:
1 Kentish Knock, 1652
2 Dungeness, 1652
3 Three Days' Battle, 1653
4 Gabbard Shoal, 1653
5 Scheveningen, 1653
Second Anglo-Dutch War:
6 Lowestoft, 1665

7 Four Days' Battle, 1666
8 St James's Day Fight, 1666
9 'Holmes's Bonfire' (Terschelling), 1666
10 Chatham Raid, 1667
Third Anglo-Dutch War:
11 Sole Bay, 1672
12 Schooneveld I, May 1673
13 Schooneveld II, June 1673   14 Texel, 1673

✕ English victory
✕ Dutch victory

5 The War of the Spanish Succession 1702-1713
- to Spanish House of Bourbon
- to Great Britain
- to Austria
- to Savoy
- to France
- to Prussia
- ✕ Allied victory
- ✕ Bourbon victory
- ✕ indecisive

The European economy
c.1500-1815

Recovery from the economic setbacks of the fourteenth century (page 56) began around 1450, and Europe's population expanded rapidly, though the fast growth of the sixteenth century was interrupted by war, rebellion, famine and plague in the seventeenth century and not resumed until the middle of the eighteenth century. Overall it increased from an estimated 69 million in 1500 to 188 million in 1800, but the increase was uneven and most marked in Britain and the Netherlands, by 1700 the greatest textile producers of Europe, the most active traders, with the largest merchant fleets and rapidly growing shipbuilding and metalware industries. The result was a shift in the economic axis. In 1500 industry was concentrated in the narrow corridor running north-south from Antwerp and Bruges through Ulm and Augsburg to Milan and Florence. By 1700 the axis ran west-east from England and Holland through the metal and woollen districts of the lower Rhine to the industrial concentrations of Saxony, Bohemia and Silesia, and thence to Russia, now beginning to build up an industrial base (map 4). The great expansion of overseas trade, particularly after 1700, also favoured the maritime powers (map 5). A consequence was the decline of the great trading cities of northern Italy, dominant two centuries earlier. In 1500 only four cities – Paris, Milan, Naples and Venice – had more than 100,000 inhabitants. By 1700 this number had trebled, and the majority of the rising urban centres lay west of the Rhine. London and Paris had already passed the half-million mark.

Significant as these developments were, agriculture was still Europe's most important industry. As late as 1815 three-quarters of its population were employed on the land, though here again there were sharp regional differences. In most of Europe farmers were subsistence peasants, whose smallholdings of 2–10 hectares produced only about 20 per cent more than their immediate needs. But in the west the need to feed growing urban populations led, first in Holland and then in Britain, to an agricultural revolution. The Dutch poured capital into land reclamation, recovering some 180,000 hectares between 1540 and 1715 (map 3), and developed intensive cultivation, eliminating the need to leave land fallow by means of a rotation of crops, which was later taken over in England. The growing population was also sustained by the introduction of new, more productive crops, mainly from America, including maize, which gave a far higher yield than the old regional cereals of southern Europe, and the potato, introduced in c.1565, which spread slowly until it became a key field crop after 1700 (map 2). Urban demand also stimulated specialisation (Holland was exporting 90 per cent of its cheese by 1700), and generated a massive demand in western Europe for wheat and rye from Pomerania, Prussia, Poland and Russia, greatly to the profit of Holland which virtually monopolised the Baltic carrying trade in the sixteenth and seventeenth centuries.

The profitable grain-export trade of eastern Europe adversely affected the position of the peasant population which had enjoyed relative freedom before 1500 but now was reduced to a state of abject serfdom on large commercial estates. Only on the frontiers (e.g. in Hungary and on the Volga) where they performed military service, did the peasants retain freedom. Otherwise emancipation (postponed in Russia until 1861) only came slowly after the French Revolution, and the same was true in western Germany where, following the savage repression of the great peasant revolt of 1525, feudal relationships persisted (map 1). A few rulers, notably the emperor Joseph II (1780–90), realised that improvement of productivity depended on breaking the old feudal relationships; but they were frustrated by landed interests. The position in north-west Europe was very different. Serfdom had disappeared in the Low Countries by 1300. In France and England feudal services had been replaced, even before 1500, by money rents; and although, when prices rose after 1700, French lords sought to recoup themselves by reviving ancient dues (only abolished in 1793), peasant ownership was protected by the courts. Rising prices led, in England, to enclosure of the common fields, a precondition for agricultural improvement. Rich peasants benefited, but poor peasants, driven off the land, flocked to the towns, where they provided the labour force for the new industries.

1 The emancipation of the peasantry

- free settlement
- freed early during transition from labour services to payment of money rents
- in process of achieving freedom in 1789
- completely freed during French Revolutionary period (1789-1815)
- personally free 1799-1815 after surrendering land in exchange
- emancipation starting 1807 (smaller holdings excluded)
- emancipation beginning 1815
- peasants remaining unfree 1815
- great German peasant revolt 1525

4 Trade and industry in the 18th century

population per sq. km.:

under 20

20 to 40

40 or more

town population:

⊙ 500,000+

⊕ 200,000+

○ 100,000+

○ 30,000+

○ less than 30,000

● financial centres

metallurgical industries

textile industries

⬤ wool

+ linen

▶ cotton

◀ silk

3 Land reclamation in the Netherlands

— the Dutch Republic in 1648

before 1600

1600-1800

North Sea

FRIESLAND

HOLLAND

Zuider Zee

ZEELAND

2 The introduction of the potato

FINLAND 1735

SWEDEN 1726

Edinburgh

from Chile 1580

Dublin

1599

London

1621

1708

Breslau 1708

BELGIUM 1566

Frankfurt 1580

Paris

Vienna 1580

Budapest

HUNGARY 1654

Lyons

Milan

Venice

from Peru 1565

1600

1625

Rome 1566

Madrid

5 The main trading flows c. 1775

⟶ exports to Britain

⟶ exports to Spain

⟶ exports to United Provinces

⟶ exports to Portugal

⟶ exports to France

Glasgow

Liverpool

Bristol

Amsterdam

London

Nantes

La Rochelle

Bordeaux

Lisbon

Cádiz

£5.6 million

£5.2 million

£4.9 million

£1.8 million

all Asiatic trade: value unknown

£1.4 million

£2.4 million

£2.2 million

St Petersburg

Moscow

Vilna

Sofia

Adrianople

Constantinople

Salonica

S W E D E N

FINLAND

Stockholm

St Petersburg

Baltic Sea

Riga

PRUSSIA

Königsberg

Danzig

POLAND

Warsaw

Moscow

R U S S I A

Kiev

Saratov

Lemberg

AUSTRIA – HUNGARY

Vienna

Budapest

Odessa

R. Volga

The Military Frontier

Bucharest

OTTOMAN EMPIRE

Sofia

Black Sea

Salonica

Constantinople

Athens

Mediterranean Sea

65°

60°

55°

50°

45°

40°

20°

30°

35°

40°

45°

The expansion of Russia, 1462-1905

The rise of modern Russia dates from the reign of Ivan III (1462–1505). During the preceding century the principality of Moscow had expanded at the expense of its immediate neighbours; but it was still a tributary of the Mongols (page 46), and in the west it was hemmed in by the great Polish-Lithuanian state, which extended deep into the Ukraine (page 56). Ivan III threw off the Mongol overlordship (1480), and in the west his conquest of the ancient republic of Novgorod (1478) opened the way to Livonia and the White Sea. Under his son Vassily (1505–33) and his grandson Ivan IV (1533–84) the advance continued. The subjection of the Khanate of Kazan (1552) opened the way across the Urals into Siberia; the conquest of the Khanate of Astrakhan (1556) gave Moscow control of the Volga to the Caspian Sea. But in the west Lithuania and Poland, joined after 1560 by Sweden, fought back vigorously, and during the 'time of troubles' following the death of Ivan IV made substantial gains at Russian expense (map 1). This, on the other hand, was the time of the great Russian thrust across Siberia, which, beginning in 1582, reached the Sea of Okhotsk by 1639 (map 2).

Siberia, where the population in 1720 was only about 400,000, still counted for little. The axis of Russian expansion was in the west, its thrust symbolised by Peter the Great's foundation of the new capital, St. Petersburg (1703). His long Swedish wars, concluded by the Peace of Nystad (1721), brought him Estonia, Livonia and part of Karelia. Russia now had free access to the Baltic. Under Catherine II (1762–96) it won control of the northern shore of the Black Sea, where Odessa (founded 1794) became a main outlet for Russian exports. But the question of secure access from the Black Sea to the Mediterranean remained unsolved. It was to be a central concern of Russian policy in the nineteenth century, and when it was thwarted by the other European powers in 1856 and again in 1878 Russia turned from

Europe to Asia, securing control of the Caucasus (1857–64) and then of the Khanates of Tashkent (1865), Samarkand (1868), Bukhara (1868), Khiva (1873) and Kokand (1876), while in the Far East it conquered the Amur and Ussuri regions at the expense of China (map 3). But defeat in the Crimean War (1854–56) convinced Russia of its backwardness, and in 1861, as a first step to modernisation, the serfs were liberated. Some went to Siberia, far more to the towns, where they provided a working force for industrialisation which began in the 1870s and was especially rapid 1893–1904 and 1909–13, when it exceeded the American growth rate. A metallurgical industry was developed in the Ukraine (map 4) producing mainly rails for the expanding railways. But the achievement was unstable. Russian ambitions in the Far East excited British and Japanese fears, and the result was the Anglo-Japanese alliance (1902) and the Russo-Japanese war of 1904–5 (page 126), which halted Russian expansion until 1945. At home the consequences were even more ominous. An urban proletariat had been formed which became the mainstay of the revolution of 1905 and more fatefully still in 1917.

4 The industrialisation of the Ukraine, 1861-1913

1861-1890   1890-1913
raw materials:
● coal
▲ iron
industry:
■ metals
◆ machinery
▮ chemicals
✚ textiles
◗ food (mainly sugar refining)
M miscellaneous
—— railways

3 Russia in Asia, 1815-1900

The Russian Empire in 1815
acquisitions 1816-56
acquisitions 1856-76
acquisitions 1877-1900
vassal khanates
—— railway

2 Russian expansion in Siberia, 1581-1800

Russian territory in 1581
territory added 1581-98
territory added 1598-1618
territory added 1618-89
territory added in 1650s; returned to China 1689
territory added 1689-1725
territory added 1725-62
territory added 1762-1800
YAKUTS native peoples
○ Bratsk 1630 forts and trading posts (with date of foundation)

Barents Sea

Obdorsk 1595

Kola Peninsula

White Sea

Berezov 1593
1501

FINLAND
1809

R. Pechora
PECHORA

R. Mezen

1478

Archangel 1584
Kholmogory

YUGRA

Ural Mts.

1743
Vyborg *1721*
L. Ladoga
Gulf of Finland
Kronstadt 1704
St. Petersburg 1703
Narva

NOVGOROD TERRITORY

Kargopol

Solvychegodsk
Ustyug

R. Vychegda

1472
Solikamsk

R. Kama

R. Belaya

Nizhniy Tagil 1724
Perm 1724
Yekaterinburg 1725
Kungur

1478

ESTONIA
1721

LIVONIA
1478

Pskov
Novgorod
L. Ilmen

1362-89
1393-1425
Vologda
Soligalich
1364
Galich

1393-1425
1489

MARI

UDMURTY

KHANATE
OF
KAZAN
1552

SIBERIA

Riga
1510
COURLAND
LITHUANIA

1772

Memel

Baltic Sea

R. Niemen

R. Western Dvina
Polotsk
1514-21
Vitebsk

Velikiye Luki
1503
1389-1425
Tver
1494
Vyazma
1364
1302
Mozhaysk
Dmitrov
Smolensk
1634
Moscow
1301
Serpukhov
1353-59
Kaluga
1425-62
1494
Bryansk
Orel 1564
1503
Gomel
Chernigov
1503
Belgorod
1593
1634

Kovno
Vilna
Grodno
Minsk
Mogilev
1772

R. Volga
1451
1364
Yaroslavl
Kostroma
Vladimir
1364
1393-1425
Murom
1393
Nizhniy Novgorod
Arzamas

Kazan
R. Volga

Ufa 1586

BASHKIRS

CHUVASHI
MESHCHERA

Kolomna
Ryazan
1393
MORDVA
Tula
1521

Simbirsk 1648
Samara 1586
Syzran
1683

R. Sura
Penza 1650
Tambov 1636
Voronezh 1586
Saratov 1590

R. Khoper
R. Don

NOGAI
TARTARS

Orenburg 1743

R. Ural

Kalish
Warsaw
1807

R. Vistula

POLAND
1795

Pinsk
Lublin
Lemberg

R. Pripet

1793

R. Dniester
Kamenets
Bratslav

AUSTRIA
MOLDAVIA
BESSARABIA

Kishinev
Nikolayev 1789
Ochakov
Akkerman
1812
Odessa
1794
R. Danube

1791
ZAPOROZHYE
Sech
1774
Kherson 1774

1793

Kiev
Pereyaslavl
1667

R. Dnieper

Yekaterinoslav
(Kodak) 1786

1783

Kharkov 1654
Poltava

R. Donets
DON
COSSACKS
1739

Kamyshin

Tsaritsyn
1589

KHANATE OF
ASTRAKHAN
1556

KALMUKS

Guryev 1645

Novograd-Volynskiy
Kursk 1586
Yelets
1592

R. Oka

Belgorod

KHANATE OF
CRIMEA

Yevpatoriya
Karasubazar
Sevastopol 1783
Bakhchisaray
Simferopol 1784

Kerch
Feodosiya (Kaffa)

OTTOMAN EMPIRE

Black Sea

Taganrog
Azov
Cherkassk
1783
KUBAN
COSSACKS
Stavropol

R. Kuma

R. Don

KALMUKS

Sea of Azov

Astrakhan

Caspian

1810
Sukhum-Kale
Poti
1804
Kutaisi
1801
Tiflis
GEORGIA
1805
AZERBAIJAN
1813

Pyatigorsk
R. Terek
Vladikavkaz
1806
1784
DAGHESTAN

Derbent

Sea

Baku

R. Kura

ceded temporarily by Persia 1723-32

Inset (upper left)

Chertkovo
Millerovo
Kramatorsk Lisichansk
Lugansk
Ruzhkovka
Kadiyevka
Gorlovka
R. Donets
Makiyevka (Makeyevka)
Yuzovka (Donetsk)
Aleksandrovsk-
Grushevskiy
R. Don
Novocherkassk
Taganrog
Rostov
Mariupol (Zhdanov)
Sea of Azov
Novorossiysk
yansk
Yekaterinodar (Krasnodar)

Legend

1 **Muscovy and the Russian Empire, 1462-1815**

~~~ boundary of Russian territories in 1462

— boundary of Lithuania in 1462

the expansion of Muscovy :

Moscow territory at end of 13th century

1478 date of acquisition by Muscovy

acquisitions to 1462

acquisitions under Ivan III, 1462-1505

acquisitions during 16th century (1505-86)

acquisitions during 17th century

acquisitions during 18th century

acquisitions 1801-15

territory ceded to Sweden 1617 and Poland 1618

recovered from Poland 1634

recovered from Poland 1667

area affected by Pugachev uprising 1773-4

route of Pugachev rebels

Orel 1564 date of foundation of new town

85

The struggle for empire
1713-1805

The Treaty of Utrecht (1713), which ended the War of Spanish Succession (page 80), sought to establish stability in Europe and overseas on the basis of a balance of power. But owing to commercial disputes and colonial rivalries, particularly in America, peace remained precarious. In 1739 war broke out between England and Spain; in 1740 Frederick II of Prussia, supported by France, seized Silesia (page 78); and when France, supporting Spain, declared war on England in 1744, the European and overseas wars were fused into a single global conflict. It also quickly turned into a duel between England and France, particularly when, after the inconclusive Treaty of Aix-la-Chapelle (1748), fighting again broke out in North America in 1754. Here the French, with their strategically situated forts, were initially successful. But the whole situation changed when William Pitt the Elder, later Earl of Chatham, became British prime minister in 1756. By allying with and subsidising Prussia, struggling to retain Silesia against an overwhelming French-Austrian-Russian coalition, Pitt compelled France to concentrate on the continental war. Naval victories at Quiberon Bay and Lagos in 1759 assured British control of the Atlantic and prevented reinforcements reaching Canada (map 1). The result was the loss of the French and, when Spain entered the war on the French side in 1761, of the

1 The North Atlantic and North America, 1754-63

- → British operations and date
- → French operations
- ✕ British victory
- ✕ French victory
- British fort
- French fort
- Spanish fort
- British naval base
- French naval base
- Spanish naval base
- British capture and date
- French capture of fort and date
- British possessions
- French possessions
- Spanish possessions

Spanish colonial empires in North America. At the Peace of Paris (1763) the French and Spanish possessions in the West Indies were restored, but England retained the North American mainland east of the Mississippi, including Florida which was ceded by Spain.

The British triumph was nevertheless short-lived. When the thirteen colonies rebelled in 1776 (page 92), France, which had rebuilt its navy, supported the rebels and by naval action compelled Great Britain to recognise American independence in the Treaty of Versailles (1783). In India, on the other hand, Britain built an empire which lasted until 1947. Here again, sea-power was decisive, enabling the English East India Company to checkmate the ambitions of the able French governor, Joseph Dupleix, to expand French influence in south India (map 2). By 1763 France was eliminated as a rival in India. An important determinant of the pace of British expansion was the decline of the Mughal Empire (page 48) after the death of Aurangzeb in 1707. Some states, the Marathas and the Sikh Punjab for example, asserted their independence, while former Mughal provinces, such as Oudh, Bengal and Hyderabad, achieved virtual autonomy. The British both feared, and profited from these developments. By the end of the governor-generalship of Richard Wellesley (1797–1805) British supremacy was an acknowledged fact. Revolutionary France attempted a comeback, and Napoleon planned an invasion of India (page 90). But once again sea-power was decisive, and in 1815 Great Britain occupied an unrivalled position in the colonial world.

3 The growth of British power in India to 1805

territory ceded to Britain by 1805

2 The Franco-British conflict in India

- territory under British control by 1783
- territory under British control by 1815
- Indian states in subsidiary alliance with Britain by 1815
- ● gained by British 1815
- ◉ gained by British from French 1815
- ▭ gained by British from Dutch 1815
- ● French towns and territory
- ○ Portuguese towns
- → French attacks with date
- → British attacks with date
- ✕ British victory
- ✕ French victory
- ✕ Afghan victory over Marathas

abbreviations:
S. Seringapatam
AR. ARCOT
A. ANANTAPUR
B. BELLARY
C. CUDDAPAH
K. KURNOOL

The age of revolution
1773-1810

1755, 1793 Corsica Local clans led by Paoli rebelled against Genoese rule and established independent democratic government. France bought island from Genoa in 1768, crushed revolt. Second attempt by Paoli to secure independence from (revolutionary) France, 1793, resulted in brief British occupation; rise of Bonaparte, himself a Corsican, put an end to separatist movement.

1768 Geneva Middle-class citizens of small city-state rebelled against domination by few patrician families; with French support the latter stayed in control.

1773 South-East Russia Serfs, Cossacks and Asiatic tribes rebelled in Volga and Ural region under leadership of Pugachev, a Don Cossack. Russian army put down revolt in 1774.

1775 America Resistance by Britain's Thirteen Colonies to her financial policies resulted in open warfare and Declaration of Independence, 1776.

1784 Dutch Netherlands Three-cornered struggle for power between Stadtholder, patrician families who controlled Estates General, and middle class Patriot party which aimed to democratise government. In 1787 Prussian troops defeated Patriot army and restored Stadtholder with greater powers.

1787 Austrian Netherlands (Belgium) Revolt against centralising policy of Emperor Joseph II, leading to proclamation of the Republic of the United Belgian Provinces (1790). Fights broke out between aristocratic and middle-class rebels; Austrian Emperor reconquered area, 1790.

1789 France (See main text). Risings by peasantry and Parisians overthrew feudal social and political order; Louis XVI's opposition and attempted flight led to abolition of monarchy (1792). King and Queen were guillotined as traitors (1793). Threat of invasion led to Jacobin 'reign of terror', ended by fall and execution of Robespierre (1794). Following weak and corrupt rule of Directory (1795-99) power passed to Napoleon Bonaparte.

1789 Liège Middle-class citizens supported by workers and peasants expelled prince-bishop and abolished feudalism. Bishop restored by Austrian troops, 1790.

1790 Hungary Magyar nobles rejected edicts of Austrian emperor and demanded greater independence for Hungary within Habsburg Empire; later, frightened by peasant disturbances, accepted compromise with the monarchy.

1791 Poland King, supported by lesser nobles, adopted new constitution designed to strengthen Poland against Russian encroachment. Catherine II of Russia, at invitation of greater nobles, invaded, destroyed constitution and divided large areas of Polish territory between Russia and Prussia. Attempt by Kościuszko and lesser nobles to strengthen surviving Polish state (1794) crushed by Russia and Prussia; Poland partitioned and ceased to exist as a separate state.

1791 Haiti Slave rising in western (French) part of island (Saint Domingue) resulted in rise of black leader, Toussaint l'Ouverture; by 1801 had conquered rest of island from Spaniards and secured virtual independence. Island then seized by the French, rising suppressed, and independence not fully secured until 1825.

1793 Sardinia In return for expelling French revolutionary invaders, islanders demanded autonomy within combined kingdom of Piedmont-Sardinia. King reasserted his authority when French threat subsided in 1796.

1798 Ireland Rebellion of United Irishmen seeking independence from England, put down by British army. Suicide of Wolfe Tone.

1804 Serbia Peasant rising against local garrison developed into demand for autonomy within Ottoman Empire. Under Karageorge Serbs fought fiercely for three years before revolt crushed by Turks.

1808 Spain After Napoleon placed his own brother, Joseph, on throne, a peasant rebellion gave assistance to British expeditionary force under Wellington. Middle-class intellectuals proclaimed constitution, but it did not survive restoration of Bourbon king in 1814.

1809 Tyrol After Austria renewed war against Napoleon, the peasants of Tyrol, whose territory had been taken from Austria by Napoleon in 1805 and given to Bavaria, rebelled under Hofer against new rulers. Revolt was crushed by Bavarian and French troops.

1810 Spanish America (See page 96).

1 Revolts and revolutions in Europe and America

— boundaries at 1789   █ areas affected by revolution

The second half of the eighteenth century was a time of revolutionary ferment throughout the western hemisphere, from the Volga, where a great peasant insurrection under Pugachev in 1773 took Kazan and threatened Moscow, to Haiti, where the black population rose in rebellion in 1791 under Toussaint l'Ouverture and won control of the island by 1801. The character of the many rebellions of the period (map 1) was varied, but all derived, directly or indirectly, from the Enlightenment, with its assertion of the rights of man, its rationalism and rejection of traditional authority. Paradoxically, it was enlightened rulers, such as Catherine II of Russia (1762–96) and Joseph II of Austria (1780–90), searching for more modern and efficient foundations for government, who gave practical expression to the new ideas, thus provoking the opposition of vested interests, aristocratic and provincial. Provinces like the Austrian Netherlands (1787) and Hungary (1790) rose in rebellion against the centralising policies and reforming edicts of progressive rulers; colonial peoples resisted dictation by the home government and demanded autonomy or

at least no taxation without consent, as in North America in 1775 (page 92) and in South America after 1808 (page 96). The demand for independence was the commonest motive for revolt, and lay behind the risings in Ireland (1798), Corsica (1755, 1793), Sardinia (1793), Spain (1808), Serbia (1804), and the Tyrol (1809). Sometimes they were underpinned by social unrest; but this was exceptional. Serfdom was abolished in Savoy (1771), Austria (1781), Baden (1783) and Denmark (1788), and peasants had more to hope for from reforming monarchs than from nobles who were their oppressors. Hence their failure to support the gentry in the Polish revolts of 1791 and 1794. Revolts against patrician oligarchies occurred in Geneva (1768) and the Netherlands (1784–87); but usually it was only when concerted aristocratic opposition to the monarchy opened the flood-gates that the peasants and the labouring class took a hand. This was what happened in France after 1787.

The immediate cause of the French revolution was the financial crisis arising from the American war (page 86). By

1786 the government was faced with bankruptcy, and after a vain attempt to persuade an Assembly of Notables to tax the privileged classes, Louis XVI was forced by a rebellious aristocracy to summon the Estates-General which had not met since 1614. When the Estates-General turned itself into a National Assembly on June 17, 1789, the revolution had begun, but it was still a middle-class revolution, and the constitution drawn up in 1791 showed their distrust of the masses by limiting the right to vote. But they counted without the workers, exasperated by a serious economic crisis and by fear of counter-revolution. In Paris, a popular rising stormed the Bastille (July 14, 1789); in the provinces peasants burned châteaux and murdered landlords. Matters now proceeded apace (map 2), particularly when Austria and Prussia threatened invasion. This sealed the fate of constitutional monarchy. In 1792 a republic was proclaimed; in 1793 Louis XVI was executed and a Committee of Public Safety set up, first under Danton and then under Robespierre, which instituted a reign of terror against enemies at home, while Carnot mobilised an army

of 770,000 men against enemies abroad.

By 1795 the French armies were victorious and the revolution had spent itself. Spain and Prussia made peace; French troops held Belgium and the left bank of the Rhine, while William V of Holland was deposed and his country turned into a Batavian republic, closely bound to France, forerunner of other similar republics from Naples to Switzerland (map 3). French influence was spreading far and wide, a victory not simply for French arms but for the ideas and achievements of the revolution, equality before the law, the abolition of feudalism, and the 'rights of man' as defined in the famous declaration of October 2, 1789. When French troops entered the Rhineland in 1792 they were welcomed as liberators and 'brothers' by the educated middle classes. Except among the conservative peasantry, who fought the revolution in France itself from 1793 to 1802, the principles of the French revolution had immense appeal; and though their appeal was later dimmed, they lighted a torch which was never extinguished, even during the reaction which set in after 1815.

3 The expansion of revolutionary France, 1793-99

- frontier of France 1789
- frontier of France 1799
- areas annexed by France
- areas occupied by France
- Venetian territory given by France to Austria 1797
- states established by revolutionary France

2 The French Revolution 1789-94

- starting point of the 'Great Fear' (July-Aug. 1789)
- main currents of the 'Great Fear' ('reign of terror')
- centre of execution during terror, with number of victims
- federalist stronghold
- area of federalist revolt
- republican victory over internal dissidents
- rural disturbances, with dates
- area of Vendée revolt, 1793-4
- area of 'chouannerie' (guerrilla resistance to republicans) 1793-4
- offensives of French armies over European allies, 1792-4
- offensives of European allies against revolutionary France, 1793-4
- X French victory
- X French defeat

Napoleonic Europe

In 1799 the 31-year-old general Napoleon Bonaparte seized power in France and was to rule until 1814, first as First Consul and then, after 1804, as emperor. His reign was a watershed in the history not only of France but of the whole of Europe. Napoleon had won his reputation by his spectacular victories over Sardinia and Austria in the Italian campaign of 1796; but after 1799, particularly during the Consulate, he proved as brilliant a statesman and administrator as a general. In 1799 Frenchmen, particularly the urban and rural middle classes, wanted peace and security. Napoleon gave them both. The wars were ended by the treaties of Lunéville (1801) and Amiens (1802); for the first time in ten years there was general peace in Europe. At home he gave the citizens who had supported the 'Thermidorian reaction' of 1794 the stability which the Directory (1795–99) had

failed to provide. But he was no reactionary. He made it his task to mould the essential achievements of the revolution into permanent institutions. In 1800 the 83 *départements* into which France had been divided in 1789 were reorganised under prefects responsible to the First Consul. The new civil code of 1804 confirmed the property rights created by the revolution and won him the lasting support of the peasant proprietors who were the backbone of the country. At the same time a career open to talents was provided for men of ability rising through the system of state schools and universities established in 1802.

These achievements outlived Napoleon himself, but peace proved elusive. A durable settlement might have been reached with the continental powers, Prussia and Austria; but the issues between France and England were too deep-seated for compromise, and in 1803 Great Britain declared war on France.

Thereafter war continued almost without interruption until 1815. In essence it was a continuation of the Anglo-French conflict of the eighteenth century (page 86), complicated by the traditional British fear, ever since the French occupation of the Austrian Netherlands in 1792, of a hostile great power on the Scheldt. From that time Great Britain was the moving spirit behind the anti-French coalitions which it kept going, as in the Seven Years' War, by subsidies. France, on the other hand, had not abandoned the hope of recovering the overseas empire lost in 1763. Napoleon's expedition to Egypt (1798–99) was intended to open the back door to India, and there were other plans for recuperating France's position in the Caribbean and on the American mainland. They were foiled by British control of the sea. Nelson's destruction of the French fleet at Aboukir sealed the fate of the Egyptian expedition (map 2), and elsewhere the French navy was no

match for the British, which thwarted French attempts to intervene in Ireland (1797–98) and a projected invasion of England in 1804 (map 3). After Nelson's victory at Trafalgar (1805), British control of the seas was assured, and Napoleon had no alternative except to turn against Britain's continental allies, hoping in this way to seal off Europe and bring Britain to heel by economic pressure.

Napoleon's campaigns against Austria, Prussia and Russia in 1806 and 1807 were brilliantly successful, and 1810 saw him at the peak of his power, directly controlling the whole of western Europe from Catalonia to Lübeck as well as Italy west of the Apennines, with satellite kingdoms and duchies in Spain, the remainder of Italy and Westphalia (map 1). But so long as Britain held out, Napoleon's position was insecure. Control of the sea enabled the British to land an expeditionary force under the future Duke of Wellington in Spain (1808). His attempt to close the continent to British trade led to his breach with Russia. The invasion of Russia (1812) was an act of desperation, a gamble which failed, and after the retreat from Moscow and the battle of Leipzig (1813) Napoleon's fate was sealed. In the reaction which followed much, but not all, of his system perished. In Germany, in particular, the Napoleonic settlements of 1797–98 and 1803 reduced the 234 territories of the old empire to 40 (map 4), and after 1815 there was no going back. Equally important were the institutional changes introduced on the French model. A society based on wealth and merit rather than prescription and privilege was introduced in the Netherlands, the Rhinelands and north-east Italy, and even countries like Prussia reformed to meet the French challenge. The political geography of Europe was rationalised and the modern national state was born, fragile at first but destined to command the future.

4 Napoleonic Germany 1806

—— Confederation of the Rhine 1806

1 Württemberg
2 Baden
3 Würzburg
4 Thuringian states
5 Electorate of Hesse
6 Swedish Pomerania
7 Oldenburg
8 Hesse
9 Berg

1 The empire of Napoleon

- French territories ruled directly from Paris c.1810
- states ruled by members of Napoleon's family c.1810
- other dependent states c.1810
- British or British occupied territory

✕ French victory ✕ French defeat

- ✕ battles of the Italian campaign
- ✕ battles of the War of the Second Coalition
- ✕ battles of the War of the Third Coalition
- ✕ battles in the Austrian War of 1809
- ✕ battles in the Peninsular War
- ✕ battles of the Russian campaign
- ✕ battles of the War of Liberation from French Rule
- ✕ battles in the defence of France
- ✕ battles in the War of the 100 Days

The United States
1783-1865

The disputes and difficulties leading to the American War of Independence and the foundation of the United States began almost immediately after the English victory over France and the acquisition of Canada at the Peace of Paris in 1763 (page 86). When the British government reorganised its vastly expanded North American possessions, establishing a huge Indian reserve west of the Alleghenies (1763) and extending the boundaries of Quebec to the Mississippi and Ohio rivers (1774), its measures were bitterly resented by the colonists in New England, Virginia and Pennsylvania as a check to westward expansion. This resentment, combined with resistance to English tax demands and trade controls, was one of the factors behind the revolt of the American colonies. The War of Independence (map 1) began at Lexington and Concord in Massachusetts in April 1775 and was ended, after the British surrender at Yorktown (October 1781), by the Treaty of Versailles (1783), which extended the frontiers of the newly independent United States to the Great Lakes in the north and the Mississippi in the west.

Once independence was achieved, expansion proceeded rapidly. In 1783 the new republic comprised some 800,000 square miles of territory. The purchase of Louisiana from France (1803) more than doubled its extent. Thereafter expansion in the south and west was largely by conquest at the expense of Mexico (map 2), though the Oregon question, finally settled in 1846, looked for a moment as though it might bring war with Great Britain. In the north settlers moved into the 'back country' in increasing numbers after 1800, but it was the arrival of a new wave of European immigrants, predominantly German and Irish, which populated the Midwest. By 1850 the frontier of settlement had reached the 100th meridian, the dividing line between sparse and adequate rainfall.

This vast territorial expansion, which raised the population from approximately 3,000,000 in 1783 to 31,000,000 on the eve of the Civil War, had important political consequences. By 1860 the original 13 states had increased to 34. The result was a deterioration in the relative position of the Southern states with their plantation economy and black slave population, as a result of which the plantation aristocracy saw itself being swamped by the industrialising North and the growing Midwest. This, rather than the simple issue of slavery, was the underlying cause of the American Civil War, but the issues were in fact inseparable because, with over 90 per cent of the black population living in the South (map 3), the moral question was also a regional question. Abraham Lincoln, elected President in 1860 by a northern vote, was right when he said that the nation could not permanently remain 'half-slave and half-free.'

The North fought at first to preserve the Union; but, significantly, it was over the question of whether slavery should be permitted in Kansas and Nebraska that the conflict came to a head. Soon after Lincoln's election South Carolina seceded from the Union and was quickly joined by ten other states (map 4) which came together as the Confederate States of America with their capital at Richmond, Virginia. The course of the war, which opened with an attack on Fort Sumter in April 1861, can be followed on map 5. Northern strategy was to deny the South vital resources by a naval blockade, to gain control of key river routes and forts in the west and to capture the Confederate capital of Richmond. In spite of the preponderance of the North in manpower and resources, the South held out for four years, a fact which heightened the bitterness and resentment during the subsequent period of Reconstruction. The outcome has been called 'the Second American Revolution'; by crippling the Southern ruling class and liberating its labour force, it determined that the thrusting, urban, industrialised North, with its creed of competitive capitalism, would stamp its pattern – for good or ill – on the entire post-bellum United States.

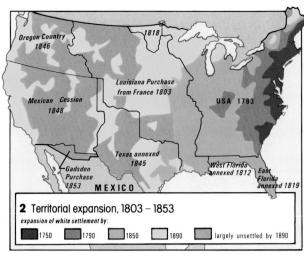

2 Territorial expansion, 1803 – 1853

expansion of white settlement by:

| 1750 | 1790 | 1850 | 1890 | largely unsettled by 1890 |

1 The American War of Independence, 1775 – 1783

	the Thirteen Colonies
	Indian Reserve 1763
	Quebec 1763-74
····	Quebec under Quebec Act 1774
	other British possessions
	Spanish territory

American War of Independence 1775-83:

✗ U.S. victory
✗ British victory
━━ 1763 Proclamation Line

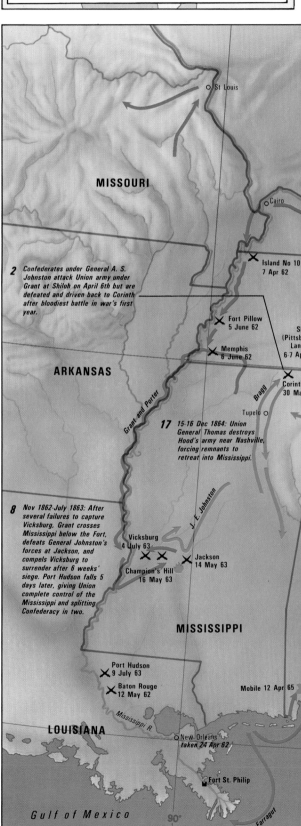

2 Confederates under General A. S. Johnston attack Union army under Grant at Shiloh on April 6th but are defeated and driven back to Corinth after bloodiest battle in war's first year.

17 15-16 Dec 1864: Union General Thomas destroys Hood's army near Nashville, forcing remnants to retreat into Mississippi.

8 Nov 1862-July 1863: After several failures to capture Vicksburg, Grant crosses Mississippi below the Fort, defeats General Johnston's forces at Jackson, and compels Vicksburg to surrender after 6 weeks' siege. Port Hudson falls 5 days later, giving Union complete control of the Mississippi and splitting Confederacy in two.

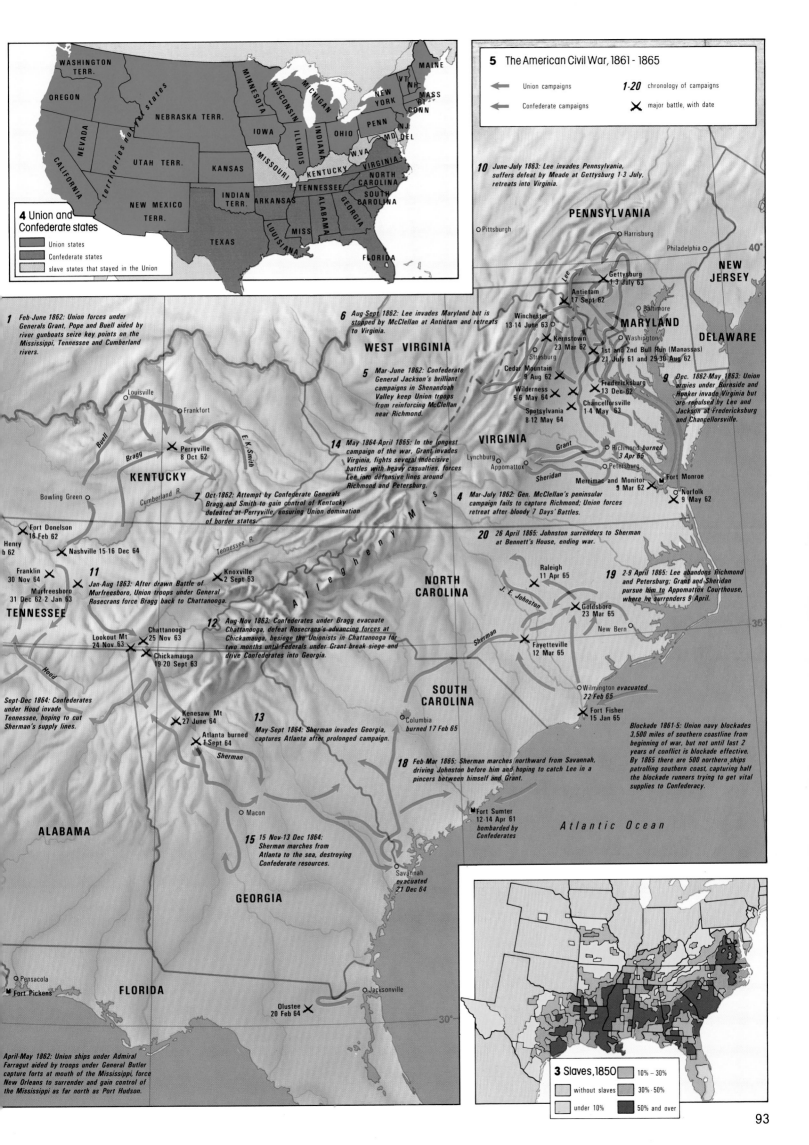

4 Union and Confederate states

- Union states
- Confederate states
- slave states that stayed in the Union

5 The American Civil War, 1861 - 1865

- ← Union campaigns
- ← Confederate campaigns
- *1-20* chronology of campaigns
- ✕ major battle, with date

10 *June-July 1863: Lee invades Pennsylvania, suffers defeat by Meade at Gettysburg 1-3 July, retreats into Virginia.*

1 *Feb-June 1862: Union forces under Generals Grant, Pope and Buell aided by river gunboats seize key points on the Mississippi, Tennessee and Cumberland rivers.*

6 *Aug-Sept 1862: Lee invades Maryland but is stopped by McClellan at Antietam and retreats to Virginia.*

5 *Mar-June 1862: Confederate General Jackson's brilliant campaigns in Shenandoah Valley keep Union troops from reinforcing McClellan near Richmond.*

14 *May 1864-April 1865: In the longest campaign of the war, Grant invades Virginia, fights several indecisive battles with heavy casualties, forces Lee into defensive lines around Richmond and Petersburg.*

9 *Dec. 1862-May 1863: Union armies under Burnside and Hooker invade Virginia but are repulsed by Lee and Jackson at Fredericksburg and Chancellorsville.*

7 *Oct-1862: Attempt by Confederate Generals Bragg and Smith to gain control of Kentucky defeated at Perryville, ensuring Union domination of border states.*

4 *Mar-July 1862: Gen. McClellan's peninsular campaign fails to capture Richmond; Union forces retreat after bloody 7 Days' Battles.*

20 *26 April 1865: Johnston surrenders to Sherman at Bennett's House, ending war.*

11 *Jan-Aug 1863: After drawn Battle of Murfreesboro, Union troops under General Rosecrans force Bragg back to Chattanooga.*

19 *2-9 April 1865: Lee abandons Richmond and Petersburg; Grant and Sheridan pursue him to Appomattox Courthouse, where he surrenders 9 April.*

12 *Aug-Nov 1863: Confederates under Bragg evacuate Chattanooga, defeat Rosecrans's advancing forces at Chickamauga, besiege the Unionists in Chattanooga for two months until Federals under Grant break siege and drive Confederates into Georgia.*

Sept-Dec 1864: Confederates under Hood invade Tennessee, hoping to cut Sherman's supply lines.

13 *May-Sept 1864: Sherman invades Georgia, captures Atlanta after prolonged campaign.*

18 *Feb-Mar 1865: Sherman marches northward from Savannah, driving Johnston before him and hoping to catch Lee in a pincers between himself and Grant.*

Blockade 1861-5: Union navy blockades 3,500 miles of southern coastline from beginning of war, but not until last 2 years of conflict is blockade effective. By 1865 there are 500 northern ships patrolling southern coast, capturing half the blockade runners trying to get vital supplies to Confederacy.

15 *15 Nov-13 Dec 1864: Sherman marches from Atlanta to the sea, destroying Confederate resources.*

April-May 1862: Union ships under Admiral Farragut aided by troops under General Butler capture forts at mouth of the Mississippi, force New Orleans to surrender and gain control of the Mississippi as far north as Port Hudson.

Battle labels

- Perryville 8 Oct 62
- Fort Donelson 16 Feb 62
- Henry b 62
- Nashville 15-16 Dec 64
- Franklin 30 Nov 64
- Murfreesboro 31 Dec 62-2 Jan 63
- Knoxville 2 Sept 63
- Lookout Mt 24 Nov 63
- Chattanooga 25 Nov 63
- Chickamauga 19-20 Sept 63
- Kenesaw Mt 27 June 64
- Atlanta burned 1 Sept 64
- Olustee 20 Feb 64
- Savannah evacuated 21 Dec 64
- Columbia burned 17 Feb 65
- Fort Fisher 15 Jan 65
- Wilmington evacuated 22 Feb 65
- Fayetteville 12 Mar 65
- Goldsboro 23 Mar 65
- Raleigh 11 Apr 65
- Antietam 17 Sept 62
- Gettysburg 1-3 July 63
- Winchester 13-14 June 63
- Kernstown 23 Mar 62
- Cedar Mountain 9 Aug 62
- Wilderness 5-6 May 64
- Spotsylvania 8-12 May 64
- 1st and 2nd Bull Run (Manassas) 21 July 61 and 29-30 Aug 62
- Fredericksburg 13 Dec 62
- Chancellorsville 1-4 May 63
- Richmond burned 3 Apr 65
- Merrimac and Monitor 9 Mar 62
- Norfolk 9 May 62
- Fort Sumter 12-14 Apr 61 bombarded by Confederates
- Fort Pickens

3 Slaves, 1850

- without slaves
- under 10%
- 10% – 30%
- 30% - 50%
- 50% and over

The expansion of the United States
1803-1898

The dominant fact in the history of the United States during the nineteenth century was the opening of the continent. In 1783 the effective frontier of the new Republic was the Allegheny Mountains (page 92). The Louisiana Purchase (1803) opened vast new areas for explorers, led by the famous expedition of Lewis and Clark (1804–8), and for settlers who quickly followed in their wake (map 1). After the Mexican wars (1846–8) and the discovery of gold in California (1848) prospectors, miners, speculators and settlers pushed west across the mountain chains from Salt Lake City and Santa Fe or by the Overland Trail from San Antonio. The great westward movement, bolstered by a confident belief in America's 'manifest destiny', could not, however, proceed without brutal disregard for the native population. The destruction of the North American Indians had begun much earlier in New England in the Pequot war of 1636, and the Delaware Indians were uprooted and driven west before the end of the eighteenth century; but it was in the 1830s, when the land-hunger of the white planters and settlers became insatiable, that the expulsion of whole tribes, Cherokee, Chocktaw, Creek and Chickasaw, and their deportation to the Midwest (and later to Indian reservations) got underway. By 1850 the frontier had reached the 100th meridian, and it was here, in the Midwest and West, that the great battles of the 1860s and 1870s took place, which reduced the Indian population to scarcely more than 200,000 by the end of the nineteenth century (map 2).

In their place, and usurping their lands, poured in a flood of immigrants, mainly from Europe, which reached its peak in the last decade of the century (diagram 4). In the later phases most of the immigrants (from southern and eastern Europe) remained in the cities on the eastern seaboard, where they swelled the industrial proletariat; but by mid-century Germans and Scandinavians had formed a preponderant element on the farming frontier of Wisconsin, Iowa and Minnesota, and in the last quarter of the century British and Irish settlers, as well as native Americans, played an important part in the development of cattle ranching and stock raising in Texas, Wyoming and New Mexico. British capital and British land companies also contributed. But the most important area of European investment before 1914 was the financing of American railways, particularly the transcontinental lines. Railroads in operation in 1840 were confined to a few industrial regions in the east. British capital provided the finance to double the mileage between 1866 and 1873 and to carry it west, and this westward shift of transport and population was accompanied by a similar shift of agricultural production (map 3). The effects were dramatic. By 1890, when the rail network was larger than that of the whole of Europe, including the British Isles and Russia, a population moving onto virgin lands, with improved mechanisation, such as the steel plough, new strains of cotton, wheat and maize, and the ubiquitous barbed wire fence, had made the United States the world's leading agricultural producer.

By 1890 the frontier was closed, the prospect of indefinite opportunities within the boundaries of the United States becoming a thing of the past. West of the 100th meridian population was still sparse, and urban and industrial development negligible (page 110); the great upsurge in the colonisation and development of California and the Pacific seaboard was still to come. Nevertheless 1890 marked a turning point, registered in 1898 when the United States, denying its own past refusal to involve itself in other continents, turned from the American continent to the wider world of Asia. In 1898 American history merged into world history, with incalculable consequences for the future.

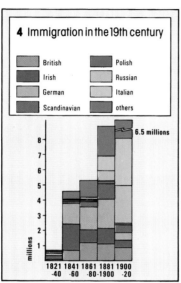

4 Immigration in the 19th century

- British
- Irish
- German
- Scandinavian
- Polish
- Russian
- Italian
- others

6.5 millions

millions

1821 -40 | 1841 -60 | 1861 -80 | 1881 -1900 | 1900 -20

2 The Indian wars

major Indian battles:
- ✕ 1601-1700
- ✕ 1701-1800
- ✕ 1801-1845
- ✕ 1846-1890
- ☐ Indian reservation 1875
- ✚ Indian reservation 1930
- ▲ village of the Delaware Indians
- → route of retreat of the Delaware Indians
- → removal of the southern tribes (the Trail of Tears)

1 The opening of the continent

- → explorers' routes
- → settlers' routes
- cattle trails
- ○ cow town
- fur traders' routes
- ■ fur station
- ⟍ pass
- ⟈ mining area
- ⚲ Catholic mission
- ⚱ Protestant mission

Independent Latin America
1808-1910

Napoleon's invasion of Spain and Portugal in 1808 (page 90) enabled their colonies to assert their independence. The revolt began in Argentina in 1810 and Venezuela in 1811, and was later helped by Great Britain and the United States which prevented intervention by the Iberian powers. After the fall of Lima (1821) and Bolívar's victory at Ayacucho (1824) Spain's fate in South America was sealed. In the north, early revolts in Mexico were suppressed, but in 1823 a republic was proclaimed, and a last Spanish attempt at reconquest in 1829 was defeated by Santa Ana. Only Brazil made the transition to nationhood peacefully. Here Portugal agreed to a constitution, and in 1822 the Portuguese king's eldest son became ruler of an independent Brazilian empire, as Pedro I. Only in 1889 when, following the abolition of slavery (1888), disgruntled plantation-owners rose in revolt, was the empire replaced by a federal republic.

Independence essentially was a political movement in the hands of the colonial aristocracy, who wanted a transfer of authority but a minimum of social upheaval. After 1826 the old colonial division between a privileged minority, monopolising land and office, and a barely subsisting mass of peasants, grew sharper. Though the period was rarely without civil strife, the *caudillos*, or military dictators, who dominated the scene during the 50 years following independence, ruled in the interests of the privileged classes, and there was only marginal reform before the Indian, Benito Juárez, took over in Mexico in 1861 (map 1). There were also repeated territorial disputes between the different republics, the fiercest being the War of the Pacific for control of the Atacama Desert nitrate deposits (map 4), to say nothing

of the wars with the United States (page 92) which deprived Mexico of 40 per cent of its territory. Bolívar had plans for an all-encompassing South American Union, but they came to nothing at the Congress of Panama (1826). Instead, such federations as existed (e.g. Great Colombia, 1819–30) quickly fell apart into their constituent elements, usually representing former Spanish administrative units.

For most of the century there was virtually a subsistence economy in most republics. Brazil, with its coffee plantations based on slave labour, was an exception. Elsewhere the *hacendados* treated their estates more or less as self-supporting and self-sufficient, and had little interest in production for the market. Change only came after about 1880 when foreign investment, hitherto modest, increased rapidly (map 3). Even so, it was highly selective, concentrated mainly in Argentina, Brazil, Mexico and Chile. Except in Mexico, where the United States predominated, Britain had the lion's share.

much of it in railways. The stimulus was undoubted but it also shifted the economy sharply to the export o primary products. Argentina's 'revolution on the pampas' made it a main supplier of grain and meat; Chile was the world's leading producer of nitrates; Brazi exported coffee and rubber, and American food corporations invested heavily in the so-called 'banana republics.' The economic 'take off' also attracted a new wave of European, mainly Italian and Spanish, settlers, notably in Argentina, which greatly altered the population profile (map 2). Urbanisation increased apace, and with it came the beginning of a new urban and industrial proletariat and a middle class growing rich on the export trade. But unbalanced growth also produced new problems. The dictatorship of Porfirio Díaz (1877–1910) brought spectacular economic progress to Mexico, but the mass of the people were left in abject poverty. The result was the Mexican revolution of 1911, the harbinger of a new era in the history of Latin America.

2 Population and immigration

	population	
	1825	**1900**
Cuba	700,000	1.6 m
Mexico	6.8 m	13.6 m
Guatemala		1.4 m
El Salvador		1.2 m
Honduras		400,000
Nicaragua		400,000
Costa Rica		300,000
Brazil	4.0 m	17.0 m
Colombia	1.3 m	4.1 m
Peru	1.4 m	3.8 m
Venezuela	800,000	2.3 m
Ecuador	550,000	2.0 m
Bolivia	1.1 m	1.7 m
Argentina	630,000	4.7 m
Chile	1.0 m	2.9 m
Uruguay	50,000	800,000
Paraguay	180,000	690,000

slave trade from Africa to Cuba 1822-67 400,000

3 Exports and foreign investment

commodities exported
major US company
major UK company

Foreign investment in Latin America (1913) about £2000 million

Foreign investment in Mexico (1911) £388 million

Total British investment in Latin America

1913 total £999 million
1890 total £427 million
1880 total £179.5 million

Foreign investment in Argentina (1913) £650 million

Immigrants to Argentina: country of origin
1857-1924

1 Political development

- boundary of Mexico 1824
- Mexico 1867
- **1821** date of independent statehood
- Republic of Colombia, 1819-30
- United Provinces of Central America, 1823-38
- later Brazilian acquisitions
- areas affected by Mexican revolution from 1910
- dispute between Ecuador and Peru
- disputed area, Bolivia and Paraguay
- ▽ caudillismo (military dictatorship)
- ○ revolutionary movements
- ◇ constitutionalism
- □ radical reformism
- French territory
- British territory
- Dutch territory
- Spanish territory

CALIFORNIA

UTAH

UNITED STATES

ceded to USA by Mexico 1848

sold by Texas to USA 1853

NEW MEXICO

Texas 1850

San Diego

sold to USA 1850

TEXAS

LOWER CALIFORNIA

SONORA

CHIHUAHUA

COAHUILA

Independent 1838-45

MEXICO

Pancho Villa 1914

DURANGO

ZACATECAS

TAMAULIPAS

N

Carranza 1913

BAHAMA IS.
(British 1783)

SINALOA

TEPIC

A S G Q H

JALISCO

Ten Years' War 1868-78

Santa Ana 1834-55 ▽

COLIMA

MICHOACÁN

ME (T) V

P

GUERRERO

Liberal reform 1855-7
War of Reform 1857-60
Benito Juárez 1867-72

CUBA 1898
US Protectorate

Madero 1911

OAXACA

CHIAPAS

TABASCO

YUCATÁN

Caste war of Yucatán 1848

JAMAICA *British*

REPUBLIC OF HAITI 1804

DOMINICAN REPUBLIC 1844
*to Spain 1808-22
to Haiti 1822-44*

PUERTO RICO *Spanish to USA 1898*

VIRGIN IS.

ANTIGUA *(east) British (west) Danish, to USA 1917*

Zapata 1910

BRITISH HONDURAS

GUATEMALA 1838

HONDURAS 1838

SABA *Dutch*

ST EUSTATIUS *Dutch*
ST CHRISTOPHER *British*

GUADELOUPE *French*
MARIE GALANTE *French*
DOMINICA *British*
MARTINIQUE *French*
ST LUCIA *British*

Morelos 1811-15

EL SALVADOR 1838

NICARAGUA

MOSQUITO COAST
1860 to Nicaragua

ARUBA *Dutch*
CURAÇAO *Dutch*

NEVIS *British*
BONAIRE *Dutch*

ST VINCENT *British*
BARBADOS *British*
GRENADA *British*
TRINIDAD *British*

A	AGUASCALIENTES
C	CAMPECHE
G	GUANAJUATO
H	HIDALGO
ME	MÉXICO
M	MORELOS
N	NUEVO LEÓN
P	PUEBLA
Q	QUERÉTARO
S	SAN LUIS POTOSÍ
T	TLAXCALA
V	VERA CRUZ

COSTA RICA 1838

Cartagena

Maracaibo

PANAMA 1903

Panama

Mompas

Caracas

Páez 1830-48 ▽

Guzmán Blanco 1870-88 ▽

Antioquia

R. Orinoco

Angostura

Georgetown

Cabanagem 1835-40

◇ violent constitutionalism

NEW GRANADA 1831

Bogotá

VENEZUELA 1830

to Britain 1904

BRITISH

DUTCH

FRENCH

GUIANA

Cayenne

Balaiada 1839

Confederation of Equator 1824

COLOMBIA 1886

Quito

to Ecuador 1890

R. Amazon

Manaus

PARÁ

MARANHÃO

CEARÁ

RIO GRANDE DO NORTE

Immigrants to Brazil:
country of origin

ITALY

ECUADOR 1803

Guayaquil

Oriente

García Moreno 1860-75

Iquitos

Tabatinga

RIO NEGRO
(later Amazonas)

PIAUÍ

PARAÍBA

PERNAMBUCO

ALAGOAS

OTHERS

PORTUGAL

SPAIN

to Ecuador 1890

PERU *to Peru 1867*

Castilla 1845-62 ▽

Lima

Callao

1821

to Peru 1902

to Peru 1909

Cuzco

EMPIRE OF BRAZIL
(kingdom 1815, empire 1822, republic 1889)

BAHIA

million people

3.0
2.5
2.0
1.5
1.0
0.5

racial profiles 1825:

Whites

Mestizos, Mulattos

Indians

Blacks

1854 date of abolition of slavery

unconquered Indians

Ayacucho

Tacna *to Peru 1929*

Arica

GOIÁS

Santa Cruz

MATO GROSSO

BOLIVIA 1825

La Paz

Potosí

Corumbá

MINAS GERAIS

Diamantina

Minas Novas

ESPÍRITO SANTO

slave trade from Africa 1800-55 1.2 million

Chilean gains

Melgarejo 1864-71 ▽

GRAN CHACO

Concepción

PARAGUAY 1811

Asunción

Ciudad Real

SÃO PAULO

São Paulo

RIO DE JANEIRO

Rio de Janeiro

Sabinada 1837

SANTA CATERINA

Praieira 1848-9

PERU

Puno

L. Titicaca

La Paz

Moquegua

BOLIVIA

Jujuy

Córdoba

Mendoza

San Luis

Rosario

RIO GRANDE DO SUL

URUGUAY 1828 *part of Brazil 1816-28*

Montevideo

Rio de la Plata

Liberal Revolution 1842

Farroupilha Revolution 1835-45

Tacna

Arica

R. Camarones

TARAPACÁ
(former Peruvian province)

Iquique

Pozo Almonte

La Central

Oruro

Valparaíso

Santiago

Constitución

Buenos Aires

Batlle 1903-15 ○

Rosas 1829-52 ▽

◇ aristocratic presidentialism

Valdivia

ARGENTINA 1810

conservative republic 1862-1910 ◇

Calama

ANTOFAGASTA
(former Bolivian province)

Pacific Ocean

Atacama Desert

ARGENTINA

CHILE 1818

Patagonia

War of the Desert 1880-81

FALKLAND IS. (ISLAS MALVINAS)
*1770-1820 Spanish
1820-33 Argentine
1833 British*

Taltal

Miraflores

CHILE

4 The War of the Pacific, 1879-83

Chilean gains

nitrates

South Atlantic Ocean

The Industrial Revolution in Europe, 1760-1914

The Industrial Revolution, which began in England in the reign of George III (1760–1820), was the catalyst of the modern world. Nevertheless the speed of change should not be exaggerated. Even in continental Europe its impact was limited before 1850 to a few industrial enclaves, and it was not until the last quarter of the nineteenth century – in the case of France, Italy and Russia only after 1890 – that the great surge forward occurred. Outside Europe, with the sole exception of the United States, its impact was delayed for much longer (page 108). Even in Germany 35 per cent of the population was engaged in agriculture in 1895, and most of eastern Europe (Poland, Romania, Bulgaria) and much of southern Europe (Spain, Greece, southern Italy) was virtually untouched by industry. Until 1900, when it began to be challenged by Germany and the United States, the United Kingdom was the workshop of the world, and its industrial strength, which enabled it to dominate world markets, accounts for its pre-eminence in the age of imperialism (page 100).

population of main towns 1801:

London: 959,000
Liverpool: 82,000
Manchester: 77,000
Glasgow: 77,000
Birmingham: 71,000
Bristol: 61,000
Leeds: 53,000
Sheffield: 46,000
Newcastle upon Tyne: 33,000
Hull: 30,000
Nottingham: 29,000
Bradford: 13,000

time taken for fastest mail coach from London to:

Carlisle: 41 hours
Liverpool: 32 hours
Manchester: 28 hours
Great Yarmouth: 21 hours
Birmingham: 16 hours

1 The beginning of the Industrial Revolution: Great Britain, c.1750-1820

population per sq. mile in 1801 (data based on county divisions):

under 50
50 to 100
100 to 150
150 to 200
200 to 260
260 to 390
390 to 800
river
narrow canal
broad canal

○ town connected with water transport system
□ expanding port
○ expanding town
•:• coalfields
▲ iron ore mining
c copper mining
▬ lead mining
⊡ tin mining
⊟ salt mining
↙ slate mining

3 The economic unification of Germany, 1828-88

Prussian Customs Union 1828
Deutscher Zollverein (German Customs Union) 1834
New Zollverein 1867
additions to 1888

Many factors account for the precedence of Great Britain. It was not only that it was well endowed with coal, iron, and other basic materials; so were many other countries. It was also spared the ravaging effects of warfare on its own soil, unlike most of continental Europe during the revolutionary and Napoleonic wars (pages 88, 90). Unlike France and Germany, where markets and trade were limited by a multiplicity of customs barriers and internal and external frontiers, Great Britain after the union of England and Scotland in 1707 was a single economic unit, where men and goods moved freely. It also enjoyed an advantageous position in Atlantic trade, from which capital flowed into industry. In an age of sailing ships, ports like Liverpool, Glasgow and Bristol had obvious advantages over Hamburg and Bremen. The English social structure was also favourable. In contrast to continental Europe, where most peasants were still tied to the soil (page 82), the early disappearance of serfdom in England meant that the surplus labour released by the enclosure of common land during the eighteenth century could move, without legal obstacles, to the growing industrial centres. Finally, England had a unique network of navigable rivers and canals (map 1), which was of inestimable importance before the railway age for moving both raw materials and finished goods.

In its earliest phase English manufacture had relied on water power; hence the location of the early cotton and woollen mills on the slopes of the Pennines. But

essentially the Industrial Revolution, in the century to 1870, was a revolution of coal and iron. Its basis was the application of steam power to machinery, and a series of technical innovations – Watt's rotative engine (1782) and Cartwright's power loom (1792) among others – quickly demonstrated the superiority of steam-power driven machines. In continental Europe, apart from Belgium, where industrialisation proceeded rapidly after 1820, the use of steam power came more slowly. The famous German steel firm of Krupp, later to be a giant of German industry, was founded in 1810 in green fields outside Essen, where a stream provided water power; it had only 7 employees in 1826 and 122 in 1846. Here, and elsewhere, large-scale industry was held back by political fragmentation, lack of capital, and, above all, by poor communications, which severely limited markets. What changed this, above all else, was railway development, beginning in the 1830s. By 1860 the railway networks of Britain, Belgium and Germany were virtually complete, although in Austria-Hungary and Russia large-scale construction was only beginning (map 2). With their demand for rails, sleepers, engines and carriages, railways also provided immense impetus to heavy industry. A second factor was the dismantling of obstructions to trade. In France internal tariffs had been demolished in 1790 as part of the revolutionary reorganisation. In 1818 Prussia followed suit, setting up free trade between its provinces, followed by a Prussian Customs Union (1828) including other smaller

German territories, and finally (1834) the German Customs Union, or *Zollverein*, comprising 17 states and some 26 million people (map 3). Here was a solid basis for the development of German industry.

A new period, sometimes called the Second Industrial Revolution, opened after 1870. The new German Empire, founded in 1871, was in the forefront. Coal and iron were still basic, and here Germany forged ahead, increasing its coal output from 38 million tons in 1871 to 279 million tons in 1913 and its iron output from 1.5 million tons to 15 million tons. But it was in the new branches of industry – steel, electricity and chemicals – that Germany outpaced all other nations. German steel production leapt from 1.5 million tons in 1880 to over 13 million tons in 1910, by which time Krupps was employing 70,000 men. Steel, electricity and chemicals were the index of the new industrial society, and at a time of growing international tension (page 116) Germany's headstart was bound to produce a defensive reaction among its rivals. The intensive industrialisation which occurred in France after 1895 and in northern Italy after 1905 represented a deliberate national effort not to be left behind. The same was true of the great upsurge of Russian industry after 1890, particularly the massive development of the iron and steel industry of the Donets basin (page 84). By now much of heavy industry was keyed to armaments. Industrialisation had changed the face of Europe by 1914; but it had also made it more dangerous and more explosive.

2 The Industrial Revolution in Europe, 1860-1914

areas of industrial concentration 1870-1914

+ centres of textile industry

I centres of chemical industry

⚓ centres of shipbuilding industry

⚙ coalfields

⚙ centres of engineering, armaments and metal industries

▲ iron ore fields

◑ lignite fields

⬠ potash fields

▲ centres of petroleum industry

European railway network 1870 (largely complete)

railway development 1870-1914

canals

European imperialism
1815-1914

Between 1815 and 1914, under the impact of the Industrial Revolution, the character of European imperialism changed. Earlier the motivating force had been the search for the riches of the Orient, and the European stake in Asia and Africa was confined to trading stations and the strategic outposts necessary to protect the trade. In 1815, with the important exception of India, this was still the situation. But in the nineteenth century two new factors came into play. The first was the enforced opening of the world – Turkey and Egypt (1838), Persia (1841), China (1842), even Japan (1858) – to European, particularly British, commerce; in short, the breaking down of barriers to European penetration. The second, setting in around 1880, when a new phase of the Industrial Revolution got under way (page 98), was the search for the raw materials without which industry, in its new form, could not exist. Tin and rubber from Malaya, nickel from Canada, copper from Australia and South America were now the sinews of European industry; and so the scramble for natural resources began, providing a new impetus for colonial expansion. Between 1880 and 1914 Europe added over 8½ million square miles, or one-fifth of the land area of the globe, to its overseas colonial possessions.

Nevertheless no clear line divides the period before and the period after 1880. Criticism of imperialism was certainly strong in the first half of the century. Free traders of the so-called 'Manchester School' argued cogently that empire was unnecessary, even detrimental,

to commerce, and the burgeoning trade with the ex-colonial countries of North and South America seemed to prove their point. Nevertheless imperial expansion was continuous after 1815. Both Great Britain and France – particularly France, which had lost its first empire in 1815 and was determined to constitute a new empire – steadily advanced (map 1). The French conquered Algeria in the 1830s, annexed Tahiti and the Marquesas in the 1840s, expanded their colony in Senegal in the 1850s, and began the conquest of Indo-China in 1859. Great Britain, which had retained the Cape of Good Hope, the maritime provinces of Ceylon and other strategically important footholds (Malta, Mauritius, the Seychelles) in 1815, also continued to expand. Fearing a French challenge, it claimed sovereignty over Australia and New Zealand (page 112). It built up its power in India (page 104), acquired Singapore (1819), Malacca (1824), Hong Kong (1842), Natal (1843), Lower Burma (1852) and Lagos (1861). Many of these acquisitions were defensive reactions against France; most were intended to secure its position in India which, with its army of 150–200,000, made Britain the strongest territorial power in the east. Even so, except for India, imperialism still only touched the outer fringes of Asia and Africa. Even the Russian empire, which by 1886 was to engross much of central Asia (page 84), still only affected the periphery.

After 1880 a fundamental change came about. Its causes were partly economic, but still more important were the rivalries of the European powers, each of which feared that its competitors would steal a march on it. Comparison of maps 1 and 2 points out the difference. Even as late as 1870 colonial penetration was

marginal. By 1914 the European powers had engrossed nine-tenths of Africa and a large part of Asia. Between 1871 and 1914 the French empire grew by nearly 4 million square miles and 47 million people, mainly in north and west Africa and Indo-China, but also in the Pacific islands and Madagascar. But a significant factor was the entry of new claimants, particularly Germany and Italy, challenging the old imperial powers. Germany acquired an empire of 1 million square miles and 14 million colonial subjects in South-West Africa, Togoland, the Cameroons, Tanganyika and the Pacific Islands. Italy obtained Tripoli and Libya, Eritrea and Italian Somaliland, but failed in 1896 to conquer Abyssinia. But the greatest gains of all were made by Great Britain, which secured control over Nigeria, Kenya, Uganda, Northern and Southern Rhodesia, Egypt and the Sudan, as well as areas in the Pacific including Fiji and parts of Borneo and New Guinea. The keystone of the British empire was India, and its acquisitions were made with a view to bolstering British control over access to India and the Indian Ocean via the Suez Canal and East Africa, but also via Singapore and the south Pacific (map 3). So long as it was assured of control of the Indian Ocean, the British imperial position was secure.

In retrospect, the fragility of the European empires so hastily assembled between 1884 and 1914, is obvious. None of the imperial powers had the resources to govern them adequately. European imperialism was more ephemeral than anyone, at the close of the nineteenth century, could have believed; and yet it left an indelible impression on the peoples of Asia and Africa, propelling them willingly or unwillingly into the twentieth century.

3 British control of the Indian Ocean
— British controlled sea routes
British controlled territory

1 Colonial expansion, 1815-70

CANADIAN CONFEDERATION

(TO USA 1867)

B.C. 1871   M. 1870

O.1867   O. 1867

1846   N.B. 1867

USA   N.S. 1867

1848

1853

1845

MEXICO 1821

CUBA (Spanish)

provinces of Canadian Confederation:

O. Quebec
N.B. New Brunswick
N.S. Nova Scotia
B.C. British Columbia
M. Manitoba
O. Ontario

CENT. AMERICAN REPUBLICS 1821

VENEZUELA 1830

COLOMBIA 1830

ECUADOR 1830

PERU 1821

BRAZIL 1822

B. 1825

P. 1811

abbreviations:
P. PARAGUAY
B. BOLIVIA

CHILE 1818

URUGUAY 1828

ARGENTINA 1816

Tahiti 1842

Falkland Is (Islas Malvinas) **British 1833**

RUSSIAN EMPIRE

ALGERIA 1830

SENEGAL 1854-65

GAMBIA

PORTUGUESE GUINEA

SIERRA LEONE

GOLD COAST

Lagos 1861

SPANISH GUINEA

GABON

Ascension I.

St. Helena

OBOCK   ADEN 1839

Suez Canal opened 1869

OTTOMAN EMPIRE

Seychelles 1815

Indian Ocean

MOZAMBIQUE

Mauritius 1815

Réunion

CAPE COLONY   NATAL

CHINA

INDIA

1852

CEYLON 1815

COCHIN CHINA

treaty ports:
S. Shanghai
N. Ningpo
F. Foochow
A. Amoy
C. Canton

Macao   Hong Kong 1842

Malacca 1824

Singapore 1819

SUMATRA

LABUAN 1846

BORNEO

JAVA   TIMOR

NEW GUINEA

PHILIPPINES (Spanish)

Pacific Ocean

AUSTRALIA

WESTERN AUSTRALIA

S. AUST.

QUEENSLAND

N.S.W.

VICTORIA

TASMANIA

NEW C. 1853

NEW ZEALAND 1840

RUSSIAN EMPIRE

MONGOLIA

MANCHURIA

GERMANY

OTTOMAN EMPIRE

CYPRUS (leased by UK 1878)

MALTA

RUSSIA 1881

LYBIA 1912

Suez Canal opened 1869

EGYPT 1882

Ottoman Dominions under British control

ANGLO-EGYPTIAN SUDAN 1898

AFRICA

ERITREA 1889

ITALIAN SOMALILAND 1893

BRITISH SOMALILAND 1884

ABYSSINIA

Aden

Socotra 1876

OBOCK 1884-8

ARABIA

OMAN

KUWAIT

PERSIA

TURKESTAN

1895

1873

1884-5

CHINA

TIBET

Port Arthur

Weihaiwei 1898

Tsingtao

KOREA (to Japan 1910)

JAPAN

Shanghai

Ningpo

Foochow

FORMOSA (to Japan 1895)

Amoy

Canton

Hong Kong (UK)

Pescadores

Macao (Portuguese)

PHILIPPINES (to USA 1898)

major raw materials exported to Europe:

⁄⁄ grain		⊖ veg. oil	
◖ meat		◗ copra	
⁄ tea		◇ wool	
⊞ cane sugar		◇ diamonds	
⊞ dairy produce		▨ gold	
▶ cotton		◨ silver	
▭ jute		⬚ tin	
◀ silk		C copper	
○ rubber		◆ nitrates	

Diu (Portuguese)

Goa (Portuguese)

INDIA

Hyderabad

BURMA 1886

TONKIN

LAOS

ANNAM

SIAM

CAMBODIA

INDO-CHINA 1859-93

Andaman Islands

Pondicherry

Karikal

Nicobar Islands

Penang

CEYLON

Maldives

MALAYA 1875-95

SARAWAK 1888

BRUNEI 1881

Singapore

DUTCH BORNEO

SUMATRA

JAVA

TIMOR

NEW GUINEA

PAPUA (to Australia 1906)

Marianas (Ladrones) 1899

Guam (to USA 1898)

Marshall Is. 1888

Caroline Is. 1899

Pacific Islands (to Germany)

BISMARCK ARCHIPELAGO 1885

Nauru

Gilbert Is. 1892

Ocean I.

Solomon Is. 1893

CAMEROONS 1884

CONGO FREE STATE 1885

FRENCH CONGO 1875-92

(BELGIAN CONGO) 1908

RUANDA URUNDI

UGANDA

BRITISH EAST AFRICA (KENYA) 1886

GERMAN EAST AFRICA (TANGANYIKA) 1886

Zanzibar 1890

NYASALAND

ANGOLA

NORTH RHODESIA 1891

SOUTH RHODESIA 1890

PORTUGUESE EAST AFRICA

BECHUANALAND 1884-8

GERMAN SOUTH WEST AFRICA 1884

UNION OF SOUTH AFRICA 1910

BASUTOLAND 1871

SWAZILAND 1907

MADAGASCAR 1895-6

Seychelles

Chagos Archipelago

Comoro Is.

Mauritius

Réunion

Cocos Islands

Indian Ocean

COMMONWEALTH OF AUSTRALIA

New Hebrides 1906

NEW CALEDONIA

Norfolk Island

Ellice Is. 1886

Samoa 1888-99 (to Germany) (to UK)

Fiji 1874

Tonga 1900 (to USA)

TASMANIA

NEW ZEALAND

2 The colonial empires in 1914

(for 1815-70 see inset maps above)
colonial powers:

British		Dutch	
French		Italian	
German		Spanish	
Portuguese		Belgian	
Ottoman		Russian	

1883 date of European control

1822 date of independence

Princely states of India

spheres of influence

proposed spheres of influence

major sea routes

Nineteenth century Africa

Although European exploration began in the eighteenth century (map 1), its impact on Africa was limited until after 1870, except in the far south where Dutch settlers, or Boers, in Cape Colony, who had been brought under British rule in 1806, moved north in the Great Trek (1835) in search of land and freedom, and founded settlements which eventually became the republics of the Orange Free State and Transvaal (map 2). The only other area of European settlement was Algeria, conquered by France between 1830 and 1847 after fierce resistance under Abd al Kadir. Nevertheless this was a period of great change and instability in Africa. In the north-east the dominating fact was the advance of Egypt under Mohammed Ali, who conquered northern Sudan in 1820, founded Khartoum as its capital in 1830, and inaugurated the attempt to build a great Egyptian empire reaching the length of the Nile and east to the Horn of Africa. In the north-west a great Muslim religious revival, beginning around 1804 under Uthman dan Fodio, carried the Fulani south into Hausaland, where they founded the Sultanate of Sokoto. Later, another empire was carved out further west, between the Ivory Coast and the Upper Niger, by a Mandingo Muslim leader, Samory. In the south, the outstanding event was the rise of the Zulus, which resulted in a great political and demographic revolution (the so-called *Mfecane* or 'time of troubles'), as the local tribes were driven west and north into Rhodesia, Malawi and Zambia.

This was the situation when the European 'scramble for Africa' got under way after 1882 (page 100), and the countries named above were leaders of African resistance (map 3). The Zulus, hard pressed between British and Boers after the British annexation of Natal (1845), held out fiercely until the war of 1879–81, when their country was annexed (map 2). Resistance elsewhere was equally strong. Samory was only defeated by the French in 1898; Sokoto only fell to the British in 1903. In the north the British established a *de facto* protectorate over a bankrupt Egypt after 1882 (turned into a full-scale protectorate in 1914); but they were only able to secure control of the Sudan in 1898 after the slaughter of some 20,000 Sudanese. Nowhere was occupation unchallenged, as the great Herero and Maji-Maji revolts of 1904–6 against German colonialism showed. But the only lasting success was the Ethiopian defeat of Italy at Adowa in 1896. Morocco kept a precarious independence until 1912 before being divided between France and Spain, and Libya and Cyrenaica were occupied by Italy in the same year. By 1914 the European powers were in full control (map 5). Apart from Ethiopia, only Liberia could claim independence.

The position of the Boer republics in the south was different. Transvaal also had been annexed by Great Britain in 1877 and then restored to independence in 1881. But the discovery of diamonds at Kimberley and of gold on the Witwatersrand (1886) sealed their fate. The entry of foreign speculators (*Uitlanders*) sparked Boer hostility, and when an attempt by Cecil Rhodes (Prime Minister of Cape Colony, 1890–96) to stage a take-over failed dismally (Jameson Raid, 1895), the outcome was the Boer War (1899–1902), in which, after initial Boer successes, ruthless British suppression forced the Boers to capitulate (map 4). Nevertheless the Afrikaners secured favourable terms after the Peace of Vereeniging (May 31, 1902), including the use of their own language and the exclusion of blacks from the franchise, and this compromise made possible the formation (1910) of the Union of South Africa as a dominion of the British Commonwealth. It was nevertheless a betrayal of black Africans by Britain which led step by step to the policy of *Apartheid* (1948) and to the radical conflicts which bedevilled South Africa after the rest of the continent had won its independence.

5 Africa after partition, 1914

- French
- British
- German
- Portuguese
- Belgian
- Spanish
- Italian
- Anglo-Egyptian Condominium

1 European exploration in Africa 1769-1887

- Bruce 1769-72
- Mungo Park 1795-97
- Mungo Park 1805-06
- Mollien 1818
- Clapperton 1822-27
- René Caillié 1828
- Livingstone 1841-56
- Barth 1850-56
- du Chaillu 1855-65
- Burton and Speke 1857-59
- Livingstone 1858-64
- Livingstone 1866-73
- Nachtigal 1869-74
- Stanley 1871-72
- Stanley 1874-77
- Brazza 1875-79
- Wissmann 1880-87

India under British rule, 1805-1947

By 1805 the hegemony of the English East India Company in the Indian sub-continent was an established fact. With the conquest of Sind (1843) and the Sikh kingdom of the Punjab (1849) its dominion became co-terminous with the country's natural frontier in the north-west, while in the north a war with Nepal (1814–16) extended it to the Himalayan foothills (map 1). To the east the British clashed with the Burmese empire and in 1826 and 1852 annexed most of its territories, including Assam. Upper Burma itself was brought under British rule in 1886 (map 2). Within India Dalhousie's Doctrine of Lapse led to the absorption of several small kingdoms in central India, and in 1856 the kingdom of Oudh was annexed following charges of 'misgovernment'. Not surprisingly, this policy provoked disaffection which found a violent outlet in the rebellion of 1857. Beginning as a mutiny of the Company's Indian sepoys, the revolt soon involved princes, landlords and peasants throughout northern India, but the loyalty of the Sikhs and the passivity of southern India enabled the British to crush it after fourteen months of bitter fighting.

The mutiny was a watershed in the history of British India. It discredited the Company and in 1858 the British government assumed direct control, though the autonomy of the Indian princes was respected. The impetus to economic development was immediate. First-class roads were built, totalling 57,000 miles by 1927, but it was the railways which made possible the exploitation of raw materials and the profitable introduction of export crops, such as tea. Between 1869 and 1929 India's foreign trade increased sevenfold. How far this benefited the rural masses is a moot question; but modern industries brought into existence an Indian entrepreneurial class. After 1919, when protective tariffs were introduced, industrial expansion made further progress (map 3).

With the rise of a new middle class, partly through industry but more through the recruitment of educated Indians into the colonial administration, came a reawakened political consciousness. The Indian National Congress (1885) accepted British rule, though in 1905 there were periodic outbreaks of terrorist violence. But it was only after 1919 that Congress, under Gandhi's leadership, fought actively for Home Rule and, after 1929, for independence (map 4). Gandhi's civil disobedience campaigns galvanised the Indian masses; but Congress's claim to represent all Indians, Hindu and Muslim alike, alienated the Muslim minority and led to conflicts which resulted in 1947 in partition (map 5). Faced by mounting unrest and the naval mutiny of 1946, the Labour government in Britain realised that a transfer of power could not be delayed; but in 1946–7 the gradual breakdown of law and order, including communal riots, forced its hand. Plans for partition were hastily drawn up. But the boundary award in Kashmir, Punjab and Bengal resulted in large-scale disturbances in which some 500,000 lost their lives and many millions became refugees, leaving a tense situation which erupted in wars between India and Pakistan (1965, '71) and separatist violence in Kashmir since 1977.

1 India, 1805-57

territory under British rule in 1805

boundary of Ranjit Singh of Lahore's territories 1835

territory under British rule at close of Lord Dalhousie's administration 1856

main area affected by Indian mutiny 1857

○ main centres of rebellion

2 The annexation of Burma, 1826-86

British India 1826

area annexed by British 1826

area annexed by British 1852

area annexed by British 1886, pacified by 1890-1915

— boundary of modern Burma

India's Road to Independence (right)
1885 creation of Indian National Congress
1906 Muslim League formed
1915 Gandhi returns to India. Following death of Gokhale (1915) and Tilak (1920) emerges as leader of Congress
1916 Lucknow Pact: Congress and Muslim League agree to co-operate in demand for home rule (swaraj)
1917 Montagu Declaration: Britain's goal is 'responsible government for India as an integral part of the British Empire.' But
1919 Government of India Act: some Indian ministers, but central admin. and power in British hands
1919 Amritsar Massacre: troops fire on demonstrators and kill 379 Indians
1920 Khilafat Committee of Hindus and Muslims adopts Gandhi's programme of peaceful non-cooperation (satyagraha)
1920 First Civil Disobedience campaign
1922 after violence at Chauri Chaura and Moplah rising in South India
1922–29 Gandhi (in prison 1922–24) withdraws from active politics
1928 Revival of political activity; rise of Jawaharlal Nehru (President of Lahore Congress, 1929). Widening rift between Congress and Muslim League
1929 Lahore Congress demands immediate independence
1930 Gandhi's march to the sea opens Second Civil Disobedience campaign, 90,000 arrests
1930–32 Round Table Conference breaks down over question of separate electorates for Muslims, Sikhs and Untouchables
1935 Government of India Act. Denounced by Nehru as 'satanic', but main provisions accepted by Bombay Congress which agrees to participate in provincial elections
1937 Congress wins 8 out of 11 provinces in elections, but Muslim opinion alienated
1938 Jinnah reorganises Muslim League
1939 resignation of Congress ministries after Viceroy declares war without consulting Indian leaders
1940 Lahore resolution of Muslim League in favour of independent Pakistan
1942 Congress rejects British offer of Dominion Status after war. Gandhi launches 'Quit India' campaign. 'August Revolt' suppressed and Congress leaders imprisoned
1946 Second British Cabinet Mission fails. Communal violence in Calcutta, E. Bengal, Bihar and Punjab; half-million deaths
1947 partition and independence

4 The Indian Nationalist Movement, 1915-47

British India and Ceylon

Princely States

3 The Indian Empire in 1931

- territory under British rule
- territories permanently administered by Government of India (mostly tribal)
- states and territories under Indian administration
- Portuguese enclave
- French enclave
- Hindu majority provinces
- Muslim majority provinces
- area of large Sikh population
- area of Buddhist predominance
- ⊙ important town
- ▶ cotton textiles
- ▭ woollens
- ▲ tea
- | chemicals
- ⌀ tobacco
- ▥ sugar
- ━ railways
- ◆ rice mills
- ■ iron and steel (large-scale)
- ◆ metals
- ⊞ machinery and transport material
- ⌖ shipping
- ⫽ mills (various grains)

RUSSIA

AFGHANISTAN

CHINA

JAMMU AND KASHMIR

N. WEST FRONTIER PROVINCE
Peshawar
○ Srinagar
○ Rawalpindi

○ Quetta
Lahore
Amritsar
Simla

BALUCHISTAN AGENCY
○ Kalat

PUNJAB
Multan
PUNJAB STATES

TIBET

KALAT

RAJPUTANA
Delhi

R. Indus

R. Brahmaputra

Hyderabad
Karachi

SIND

AGENCY
Jodhpur
○ Jaipur
Ajmer

UNITED
Lucknow
Oudh
PROVINCES

Cawnpore
Agra

SIKKIM
Darjeeling
TARAI
R. Tista

BHUTAN
ASSAM

KUTCH
Gulf of Kutch
STATES OF W. INDIA
Ahmedabad
KATHIAWAR

R. Chambal
GWALIOR
BUNDELKHAND
CENTRAL INDIA AGENCY

Allahabad
Benares
Patna
R. Ganges
Bhagalpur

CACHAR
Shillong

BENGAL
Dacca

NORTHERN SHAN STATES

Baroda
R. Narmada
Indore

CHOTA NAGPUR
BIHAR
Jamshedpur
AND
ORISSA

Chandernagore
Chittagong
Calcutta

BURMA

SOUTHERN SHAN STATES

DIU
Surat
Daman

R. Tapti
BERAR
CENTRAL

Nagpur

R. Salween

ARAKAN

Arabian Sea

Bombay
Poona

HYDERABAD
SATARA
Sholapur
Kolhapur

PROVINCES
BASTAR

Sambalpur
R. Mahanadi
Cuttack

ORISSA

Yanaon

Bay of Bengal

Rangoon
Gulf of Martaban

R. Godavari
Hyderabad
R. Kistna

Deccan

Masulipatam

Nova Goa (Panjim)
GOA

MYSORE
Mangalore
Bangalore
Mysore

Madras
Pondicherry

Mahé
NILGIRIS
Coimbatore
Calicut
Trichinopoly
Karaikal
Negapatam
Cochin
Madura

Andaman Islands

Trivandrum

Gulf of Mannar
CEYLON (CROWN COLONY)

Nicobar Islands

Colombo

---

5 The partition of India, 1947

- India in 1947
- Pakistan in 1947
- Radcliffe Award line 1947
- ━ state borders 1947-55

abbreviations:
SY. Sylhet
T. Tripura

Maharaja forced to join India, Oct 1947 in face of tribal invasion; conflict ended by ceasefire under UN, Jan 1949

tribal invasion 1947

AFGHANISTAN

Gilgit
Aksai Chin

JAMMU AND KASHMIR (disputed)

Peshawar
NORTH WEST FRONTIER PROVINCE
Islamabad
Rawalpindi
Srinagar

IRAN

WEST PUNJAB
Lahore
Amritsar
HIMACHAL PRADESH

○ Quetta

Multan
Chandigarh
EAST PUNJAB

CHINA

BALUCHISTAN

BAHAWALPUR
DELHI

Himalayas
TIBET

NEPAL

the 'Chicken's Neck': sole means of communication between Bihar and West Bengal and Assam

R. Brahmaputra

to Pakistan by plebiscite

GWADAR
ceded to Pakistan by Muscat, 1956
KARACHI
R. Indus
KHAIRPUR
SIND

Thar Desert
RAJASTHAN

Jaipur
Agra
R. Ganges
UTTAR PRADESH

Lucknow
Benares
R. Yamuna

SIKKIM
BHUTAN
ASSAM

SY.

EAST PAKISTAN
Dacca
MANIPUR

Rann of Kutch

KUTCH
GUJERAT

Ahmedabad
SAURASHTRA

R. Narmada
BHOPAL

VINDHYA PRADESH
BIHAR

MADHYA PRADESH

WEST BENGAL
Jessore
T.
EAST BENGAL
Chittagong

Calcutta

Kutch border conflict, exact boundary resolved by international arbitration, 1968

Diu (Portuguese)
Daman (Portuguese)

BOMBAY
○ Nagpur

Jamshedpur

R. Tapti

ORISSA

BURMA

Arabian Sea

Bombay

Bay of Bengal

CHAMPARAN
Indigo tenants campaign 1917

Chaura violence 1922

Partition of Bengal 1905

Dacca
1930 1941
1947

BIHAR
1946

APORE
Moirang

BURMA

Indian National Army advances into Indian territory

1926, 1946
Calcutta
naval mutiny 1946

NOAKHALI AND TIPPERA 1946

Bay of Bengal

Rangoon

Independence campaigns:
- Hartal and Punjab disturbances 1919
- Non-cooperation campaign 1920-22
- major areas affected by Civil Disobedience campaign 1930-31
- Quit India campaign 1942
- areas of widespread communal riots 1946-7
- major riots and political disturbances, with dates

China under the Ch'ing Dynasty, 1644-1911

A new era in Chinese history opened in 1644 when the Ming dynasty, beset for a century by Mongol invasions, Japanese raids and civil war, was displaced by a line of foreign, Manchurian, emperors which ruled China until 1911. The Ch'ing, or Manchu, dynasty was resisted in south China for half a century but it quickly established good relations with the dominant Chinese gentry (*shen-chin*) and with its support began a successful policy of territorial expansion which went on until late in the eighteenth century (map 1).

At the same time there was a great economic upsurge (map 2) and a huge increase in population, from 100 million in 1650 to 300 million in 1820 and 420 million in 1850. There was also a considerable export trade in tea, silk and porcelain with the West from Canton and with Russia from Kyakhta. But the financial strain of the wars of expansion and the pressure of the growing population on the land imposed hardships which led to recurrent unrest and revolts, not only among the minority peoples who were harshly exploited by Chinese and Manchus alike, but also in the heart of China itself. Of these the most serious was the White Lotus rebellion between 1795 and 1804. Meanwhile the export surplus was converted after 1825 into a net outflow as a result of the opium trade. Manchu China was still the world's largest and most populous empire. But its growing economic difficulties, coupled with the failure to expand the administration to match the rapid growth of population, and the pressures of the Western powers, seeking to open the China market for their manufactures, resulted in a crisis which came to a head after Chinese attempts to halt the illicit opium trade were decisively defeated by the British in the Opium War of 1839–42.

The Opium War had two major consequences. First, it resulted in the cession of Hong Kong to the British and in the opening of the first five Treaty Ports (their number was thereafter steadily in-creased) in which foreigners enjoyed extra-territorial rights. Secondly, it weakened imperial authority and led to the great Taiping rebellion (1850–64), the most serious but only one of many rebellions which shook Manchu power to its foundations (map 3). The Taiping and Nien rebellions alone left 25 million dead and vast areas, including the wealthy region around Nanking, were devastated. They also convinced the Western powers that Ch'ing China was on the point of collapse and inaugurated a scramble for concessions (map 4).

The response of the Manchu court and bureaucracy was hesitant and half-hearted, more intent on maintaining traditional institutions and Confucian values than on modernisation. Foreign powers had taken advantage of the situation: the British and French occupied Peking in 1856 and forced open more treaty ports, the Russians occupied the Amur region in 1858 and the Maritime Province in 1860 and China was defeated by France in a war over Indo-China in 1884–85. But it was the overwhelming success of Japan in the war of 1894–95 that convinced a section of the Chinese intelligentsia that only a break with the past could save China, and they secured the support of the young emperor Kuang-su. But the reform movement of 1898 was defeated by the dowager empress Tzu-hsi whose reaction was to turn the popular discontent against the foreigners. The result was the Boxer Rising of 1900, an outburst of xenophobia savagely suppressed by the Western powers, who imposed a heavy indemnity and wrung still further concessions from China. By now even the imperial government realised that modernisation was imperative; but, in spite of a number of reforms, its attitude was still essentially conservative. Convinced that the imperial government was the main obstacle to change, revolutionary groups sprang up everywhere after 1901, and when in 1911 a small-scale army mutiny broke out in Wuchang, disaffection spread throughout the whole country (page 122). The imperial government fell, almost without fighting; but China had still to undergo more than forty years of tribulation before it finally made the transition to the modern world.

furs, gold, ginseng

Peking

SHANTUNG

Lintsing

Tsining

raw cotton, grain

Hwaian

Yangchow

Nanking

Soochow

Sian

HUPEH AND
HUNAN

Hangchow

copper

R. Yangtze

Changsha

Nanchang

tea, porcelain,
silk, cotton

FUKIEN

limited Dutch trade

Amoy

KWANGSI

Canton

KWANGTUNG

overseas trade with West
tea, silk, fine cottons,
porcelain, lacquer

3 Rebellions and foreign attacks 1840-1901

- Taiping control early period 1853-7
- Taiping control late period 1857-63
- routes of Taiping rebels
- other areas of rebellion (named on map)
- British attacks
- French attacks

North-Western Muslim rising 1863-73

JEHOL

FENGTIEN

Peking

principal area affected by Boxer uprising 1900-1901

Tientsin

K A N S U

Lanchow

CHIHLI
Boxer uprising
1900-01

Nien invasion
1868

SHANSI

Taiping northern
expedition
1853-54

Grand
Canal

mouth of Yellow
River after 1855

SHANTUNG

SHENSI

Kaifeng

Nien rebels
1853-68

mouth of Yellow
River to 1853

HONAN

main
Nien centre

KIANGSU

Yangchow

Anglo-French campaigns 1858-60

S Z E C H W A N

HUPEH

Nanking
Taiping
capital

Chinkiang

Shanghai

route of
Taiping advance
to Szechwan 1856-63

R. Yangtze

Hankow

ANHWEI

Hangchow

Ningpo

Sungkiang

Y U N N A N

Yunnanfu

KWEICHOW

Kweichow Miao
tribal rising
1854-72

HUNAN

Taiping
advance
1856-53

KIANGSI

Opium War
1839-42

Yunnan
Muslim
rebellion
1855-73

KWANGSI

outbreak of
Taiping rebellion 1850

Chintien

FUKIEN

Foochow

Chinese attacks during
Sino-French war
1883-85

Hanoi

Hakka-Cantonese
war 1855-57

Canton

KWANGTUNG

Amoy

Tamsui

Hong Kong

Sino-French war 1883-85

---

4 The dismemberment of the Chinese Empire, 1842-1911

R U S S I A N   E M P I R E

Russian protectorate 1912

TANNU
TUVA

MARITIME
PROVINCE

Manchouli

Aigun

to Russia 1858

R. Amur

M O N G O L I A

autonomous 1912

occupied by Russia 1897-1905
Japanese influence after 1905

Harbin

Changchun

Mukden

KOREA

R. Ussuri

Suifen

Vladivostok

to Russia
1864

Ili

to Russia
1871-81

Yellow River
(Huang Ho)

Kalgan

Newchwang

Hunchun

40°

S I N K I A N G

Peking

Antung

Tientsin

Port Arthur

Dairen

to Russia 1898
to Japan 1905

C H I N A

Taiyuan

Chefoo

Tsinan

Weihaiwei
British 1898

Tsingtao
German 1898

Japanese
1910

J A P A N

80°

T I B E T

autonomous after 1912
under British influence

Pukow

Chinkiang

Nanking

Wusung

Shanghai

Ichang

Hankow

Wuhu
Soochow

Chungking

R. Yangtze

Hangchow

Ningpo

Kiukiang

NEPAL

Yochow

Changsha

Wenchow

Ryukyu Is

to Japan 1872

BHUTAN

SIKKIM

British protectorate
1817

ASSAM

British 1826

Santuao

FUKIEN

Foochow

B R I T I S H   I N D I A

Kunming

Tengyueh

Tamsui

Amoy

Taiwan
to Japan 1895

BURMA

British 1886

Mengtze
Manhao

Lungchow

Nanning

Canton

Swatow

Szemao

Pakhoi

Macao
Portuguese 1557

Kowloon British 1898
Hong Kong British 1842

New Territories British 1898

LAOS

French 1893

FRENCH
INDO-
CHINA
1884

Haiphong

Kwangchowan
French 1898

Kiungchow

SIAM

Hainan

boundary of Ch'ing Empire in 1850

colonial possessions:	spheres of influence:	railways:
		Russian
		British
		Japanese
		French
		German
states formerly tributary to China		Chinese

Treaty ports and towns:
- 1842 Treaty of Nanking
- 1858 Treaty of Tientsin
- 1860 Peking Convention
- 1876 Chefoo Convention
- 1897 Sino-French Trade Convention
- additional ports opened by 1911

The world economy, 1850-1929

After the middle of the nineteenth century the Industrial Revolution, which had radiated from Great Britain to north-west Europe and the eastern seaboard of the United States, spread to the rest of the world. The result, by 1914, was the formation of a single interdependent world economy. But the impact was extremely varied. Though the United States after 1890 was becoming an important subsidiary centre, the focus throughout was on Europe, and most of the development was keyed to the needs of European industry for raw materials and fed by European capital. In 1914 Great Britain was the largest source of foreign investment, with overseas assets totalling nearly £4,000 million, while the United States, like Russia, was still a net borrower (map 3); but in world trade it was losing the predominance it had enjoyed in 1860 to Germany and the United States (diagram 5).

One factor behind these developments was the vast, unprecedented flow of population, mainly from Europe to the New World, but also from China and India to South-East Asia and East Africa (map 2). Between 1850 and 1920 over 40 million Europeans emigrated overseas or to Siberia, carrying with them European institutions and skills which they used to exploit the vast overseas territories. Much foreign investment went into building the infrastructure of railways, ports and shipping and creating the network of communications upon which the functioning of the world economy depended. Outside Europe and the United States there were only 9,100 miles of railroad track in 1870. By 1911 it had increased

to 175,000 miles. Equally important was the expansion of world shipping and the replacement of sailing ships by ocean-going steamships of large capacity. The opening of the Suez Canal (1869) and the Panama Canal (1914) gave a great fillip to world trade (diagram 4). Traffic via Suez rose from 437,000 tons in 1870 to over 20 million tons in 1913, and foreign trade increased threefold in volume during the same period.

Nevertheless the effects of industrialisation were distinctly one-sided. The main shipping routes (map 3) were between the advanced countries and the white dominions, or between them and the producers of raw materials. Even as late as 1929 the world was still a white man's world. A few countries such as India (page 104) and China had begun to develop their own industries; but, with the exception of Japan, they were small enclaves in a vast rural population. In 1914 there were still only 900,000 factory workers in the whole of India, and 69 per cent of cotton operatives in 1919 were in Bombay province. Nowhere outside the United States and Europe was the income produced by manufacturing substantial in 1930 (map 1) and in most cases it accrued to foreign investors. This was true of Malaya, which by 1900 was producing nearly half the world's tin and by 1910 was a major exporter of rubber, and of Katanga, where copper production rose from nothing in 1900 to 305,000 tons (including Northern Rhodesia) in 1930. Here, as elsewhere, the bulk of the population benefited only marginally, and per capita income in most countries seems actually to have declined. This was the situation which led, a generation later, to the conflict of rich nations and poor nations (page 150) and the demand for a New International Economic Order.

2 Population movements 1820-1910

emigration from Europe
emigration from Japan
emigration from China
emigration from India

Upper left map (Asia/migration):

J A P A N

C H I N A

A S I A

BURMA SIAM

MALAYA

INDIA

CEYLON

550 000 Russians 1860-1900

illion ssians USA

slaves to Arabia

A

Mauritius

2 million British to Australia and New Zealand

NATAL

PE LONY

Map 3 — Trade and investment:

3 Trade and investment

— major sea routes
— international telegraph cables

concentration of investment 1914 (in $ million):

UK   German
French   USA

UNITED STATES

C A N A D A   2800 880

850 4250 950 200

400 400

MEXICO

Gulf of Mexico

500

Pacific Ocean

CUBA 340

Panama Canal (1914)

COLOMBIA VENEZUELA

ECUADOR

PERU BOLIVIA

DUTCH GUIANA

CHILE 1550

B R A Z I L 700

400 200

300

ARGENTINA URUGUAY 200

700 500

Straits of Magellan

Atlantic Ocean

investment in the rest of Europe 3180 535

1050 UNITED KINGDOM

420 GERMAN EMPIRE 750

FRANCE AUSTRIA HUNGARY

OTTOMAN EMPIRE

650 450

200

ALGERIA EGYPT

LIBYA

Suez Canal (1869)

100

FRENCH WEST AFRICA

NIGERIA FRENCH EQUATORIAL AFRICA

200

500

600

SUDÁN

UGANDA BRITISH EAST AFRICA

GERMAN EAST AFRICA 500 (all of Africa)

GERMAN SOUTH WEST AFRICA 1550

UNION OF SOUTH AFRICA

MOZAMBIQUE

Cape of Good Hope

R U S S I A

500

J A P A N

C H I N A 600

200

200 SIAM

1850 INDIA 200

Indian Ocean

300

1700 AUSTRALIA

NEW ZEALAND

Foreign investment box:

Foreign investment in 1914 (in $ million)

Russia 500
Belgium 900
USA 3510
Holland 4100
Germany 5650
France 9280

United Kingdom 19935

---

1 Industrialisation outside Europe

ALASKA

$1100M

CANADA

$1330

Vancouver

Iceland

Atlantic Ocean

Indianapolis Milwaukee Montreal

Chicago Cleveland Pittsburgh Boston

Denver Cincinnati New York

Memphis Richmond Philadelphia

Birmingham Knoxville Washington Norfolk

Charleston Savannah

New Orleans

$15000M

MEXICO

Gulf of Mexico

Mexico City

Cuba

Haiti Dominican Republic

Caribbean Sea

$1380

Pacific Ocean

VENEZUELA

BR DUT/FR GUIANA

$350 COLOMBIA

ECUADOR

PERU

BRAZIL

$115M

BOLIVIA

$40M

$350

PARAGUAY

CHILE

URUGUAY $45M

Valparaiso Montevideo Buenos Aires

ARGENTINA

$105M

$550 $325M

$1000

Rio de Janeiro Santos

$435

ALL OTHER LATIN AMERICAN COUNTRIES

$350

$650

% working population engaged in non-agricultural occupations in 1930:

over 90%
81%-90%
71%-80%
61%-70%
51%-60%
41%-50%
31%-40%
21%-30%
10%-20%
unknown

$45M net income produced by manufacturing 1920-30 ($M = millions of US dollars)

$200 gross national product per capita 1930

major industrial regions (excluding Europe)

● major coalfield
■ iron and steel works
⊞ machinery and hardware
| chemicals
‸ woollen industry
▶ cotton spinning
▣ cotton textile industry

---

5 Balance of world trade, 1860 and 1913

		Europe	N. America	S. America	Asia	Africa
UNITED KINGDOM	imports 1860	419	252	96	143	80
	exports	358	132	74	139	36
	imports 1913	1,548	848	393	458	220
	exports	917	265	272	620	248
USA	imports 1860	217	–	80	29	–
	exports	249	–	46	11	–
	imports 1913	893	199	381	298	26
	exports	1,479	469	294	140	29
FRANCE	imports 1860	234	47	41	16	34
	exports	293	49	53	3	45
	imports 1913	880	187	183	192	148
	exports	937	89	94	36	181
HOLLAND	imports 1860	92	5	3	32	–
	exports	87	2	1	14	–
	imports 1913	624	190	87	274	14
	exports	1,131	57	9	73	14
GERMANY	imports 1913	1,402	423	290	250	118
	exports	1,828	184	183	130	50
RUSSIA	imports 1913	556	–	–	–	–
	exports	719	–	–	–	–

figures in million dollars US

---

4 Shorter journeys via the Suez and Panama Canals

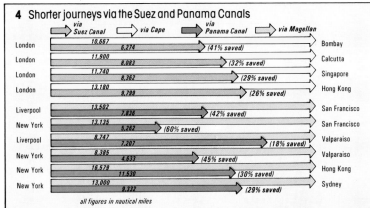

via Suez Canal   via Cape   via Panama Canal   via Magellan

London	10,667 / 6,274	(41% saved)	Bombay
London	11,900 / 8,083	(32% saved)	Calcutta
London	11,740 / 8,362	(29% saved)	Singapore
London	13,180 / 9,799	(26% saved)	Hong Kong
Liverpool	13,502 / 7,836	(42% saved)	San Francisco
New York	13,135 / 5,262	(60% saved)	San Francisco
Liverpool	8,747 / 7,207	(18% saved)	Valparaiso
New York	8,385 / 4,633	(45% saved)	Valparaiso
New York	16,579 / 11,530	(30% saved)	Hong Kong
New York	13,000 / 9,332	(29% saved)	Sydney

all figures in nautical miles

The United States and Canada, 1865-1920

The rise of the modern United States dates effectively from the Civil War, but development was very uneven. For the defeated South the period of Reconstruction (1865–77) was a bitter experience. South Carolina had ranked third in the nation in per capita wealth in 1860; ten years later it was fortieth, and Mississippi, Alabama and Georgia fared no better. Worst of all was the position of the 4 million liberated slaves, who found themselves (as the black leader Frederick Douglass said) without money, property or friends. The great upsurge in population, from 31 million in 1860 to 92 million in 1910, by-passed the South and concentrated wealth and power in the north-east where, with the exploitation of the rich ore reserves of the Mesabi Range in Minnesota and the vast coal reserves of the Appalachians, industry spread rapidly from the original manufacturing belt between Boston and New Jersey to Pitts-

burgh, Detroit and Chicago. Only around 1920 did cheap labour attract the textile industry from New England to the South (map 2).

The Civil War itself had stimulated Northern industry. After 1865 it forged ahead. But the most striking achievement of the immediate post-war period was the opening of the Great Plains, made possible by the railroad boom after 1870. In 1860 some 30,000 miles of railway were in operation, but few lines extended beyond the Great Lakes. By 1870 the mileage had reached 53,000, by 1880 93,000 and by 1890 163,000 miles (page 94). Land grants of more than 132 million acres encouraged railway promoters, and homestead grants of 285 million acres attracted settlers. The number of farms rose from 2 million in 1860 to 6 million in 1910, and grain exports, which the rail network made possible, were an important source of capital for industrial development. The population west of the Mississippi rose from 6 million in 1870 to 26 million in 1910. Nevertheless the bulk of the population was concentrated

in the north-east (map 5), and most of the 25 million immigrants between 1870 and 1914 remained there, providing cheap labour for American industry. Their miserable conditions, and those of the southern blacks, lay behind the unrest which erupted in the 1890s (map 2).

In Canada railway development was even more important than in the United States. Hitherto the 'small and unimportant' eastern colonies (as Lord Durham described them in his famous Report of 1839) had gone their separate ways, more closely linked to the United States, which made no secret of its hope to absorb them, than with each other. After the acquisition of Alaska from Russia (map 4), United States' pressure grew, and to meet it the Canadian Federation was formed in 1867 and completed by the adhesion of Manitoba (1870) and British Columbia (1871). The great transcontinental railways – the Great Western and Canadian Pacific (completed 1885), followed by the Canadian Northern and Grand Trunk Pacific – were the lifeblood of the new Dominion and

changed the axis of Canadian life. Railway development opened Manitoba and Saskatchewan, and made Canada into one of the world's leading wheat producers (map 1). It also led to the discovery of rich mineral deposits, particularly copper and nickel (1883). The other major industry in 1914 was lumber and the manufacture of paper and newsprint. In general, however, industrialisation was only beginning, though the value of Canada's industrial output increased from $190 million in 1890 to over $500 million in 1914.

In the United States, on the other hand, the 1880s and 1890s saw an astounding industrial upsurge. Output of coal and iron increased twenty times between 1870 and 1913, by which date steel production exceeded that of Britain and Germany combined. But the 'Gilded Age' was also a time of gross inequalities, and speculation and over-production caused serious economic setbacks, particularly in 1873 and 1893, which led not only to industrial unrest but also to a search for new markets, particularly in

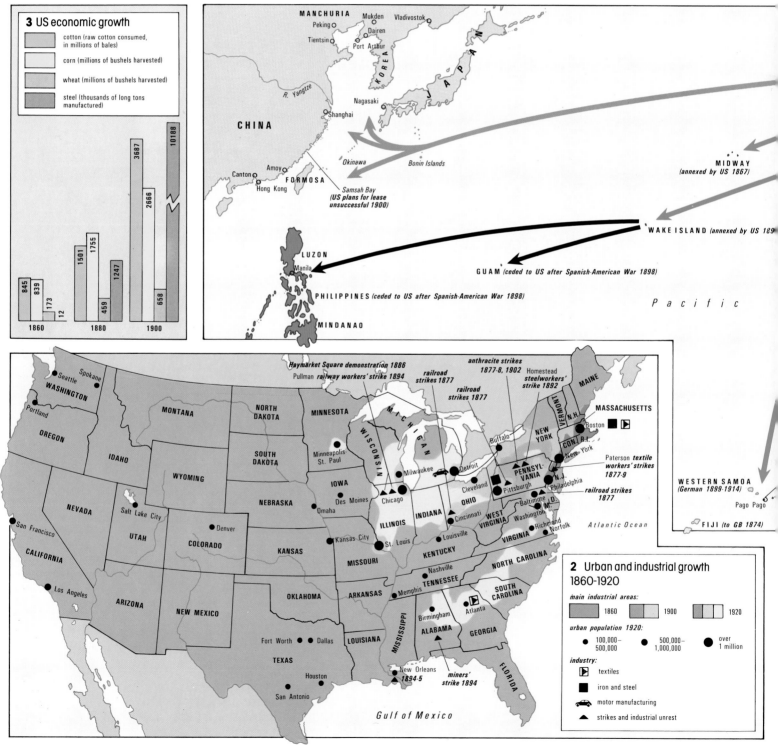

3 US economic growth

- cotton (raw cotton consumed, in millions of bales)
- corn (millions of bushels harvested)
- wheat (millions of bushels harvested)
- steel (thousands of long tons manufactured)

2 Urban and industrial growth 1860-1920

main industrial areas:
1860 1900 1920

urban population 1920:
- 100,000–500,000
- 500,000–1,000,000
- over 1 million

industry:
- textiles
- iron and steel
- motor manufacturing
- strikes and industrial unrest

eastern Asia. Already in 1867 the United States had annexed Midway Island as a Pacific base; in 1887 it secured Pearl Harbor. The other area of advance was the Caribbean and Latin America, where, by the Hay-Pauncefote agreement of 1901, Great Britain gave the United States a free hand. But the turning point came with the Spanish-American war of 1898, which made Cuba into an American protectorate and brought the Philippines – 'a stepping-stone to China' – under American rule (map 4). By 1914, when the Panama Canal was opened, the United States was the world's greatest industrial power. It was also, without fully realising it, involved in world politics. The way was prepared for the United States' entry into the First World War.

5 Population density in 1900

inhabitants per square mile:

- 0-2
- 2-6
- 6-18
- 18-45
- 45-90
- 90 and over

ALASKA
(purchased from Russia 1867)

QUEEN CHARLOTTE ISLANDS

UNITED STATES OF AMERICA

4 American expansion in the Pacific and Caribbean, 1867-1917

- US influence
- US possession
- US protectorate
- military action by US

HAWAIIAN ISLANDS
(annexed by US 1898)

MEXICO

PUERTO RICO
(ceded to US by Spain 1898)

VIRGIN ISLANDS

CUBA
Guantanamo

HAITI

DOMINICAN REPUBLIC

JAMAICA

BARBADOS

TRINIDAD

BRITISH HONDURAS

HONDURAS

GUATEMALA
EL SALVADOR

NICARAGUA

COSTA RICA

PANAMA

Panama Canal
(open 1914, Canal Zone leased to US)

COLOMBIA

VENEZUELA

Caracas

Caribbean Sea

1 The development of Canada, 1867-1920

- land occupied prior to 1851
- land occupied 1851-1871
- land occupied 1871-1901
- land occupied 1901-1921

population 1871:
- ☐ towns of 25,000 to 100,000 people
- ▣ towns of over 100,000 people

population 1911:
- ● towns of 25,000 to 100,000 people
- ● towns of over 100,000 people

ALBERTA
1905 — date of accession to Dominion of Canada

railways 1916:
- ——— Canadian Pacific Railway
- – – – Canadian Northern (Main Line)
- ······ National Transcontinental Railway
- ⬭ main industrial regions

BRITISH COLUMBIA 1871
ALBERTA 1905
SASKATCHEWAN 1905
MANITOBA 1870
ONTARIO 1867
QUEBEC 1867
NEW BRUNSWICK 1867
NOVA SCOTIA 1867
Prince Edward I. 1873
NEWFOUNDLAND 1949
LABRADOR to Newfoundland 1927

Hudson Bay

Australia and New Zealand from 1788

Although Australia and New Zealand were discovered by the Dutch explorer Tasman in 1642, colonisation only began after Cook hoisted the British flag at Botany Bay in 1770 (page 64). New South Wales served as a penal colony from 1788 to 1839, Van Diemen's Land (later Tasmania) from 1804 to 1853, and in 1829 the British government, fearing to be forestalled by the French, claimed the whole Australian continent. Fear of France also led to the annexation of New Zealand in 1840. But in both lands geographical obstacles, lack of exportable products, and, in the case of New Zealand, the bitter Maori wars between 1860 and 1871, made the early years of colonisation difficult. New South Wales was hemmed in by the Blue Mountains. Beyond the Great Dividing Range the country soon became arid and inhospitable. Coastal settlements at Perth (1829), Melbourne (1835), and Adelaide (1836) established

bridgeheads for exploration in the west (map 5), but as late as 1850 the total white population was only around 350,000, while in New Zealand it was still below 100,000 in 1860. Inducements to settle were few. Neither country was self-supporting, and early trade (chiefly seal products and sandalwood) was insufficient to pay for imports (map 4), and was further hampered by the East India Company's monopoly in the area.

The discovery of gold in New South Wales and Victoria in 1851 and in Otago (South Island) in 1861 initiated a new phase. Even more important was the rapid growth of sheep farming. In 1850 Australia sent 39 million lb. of wool to Great Britain. By 1879 the quantity had increased to 300 million lb. In New Zealand, where wool was largely a South Island product, exports rose from £67,000 in value in 1853 to £2,700,000 twenty years later. The development of the North Island, held back by the Maori wars, came later, after the introduction of refrigeration. Refrigeration made possible the large-scale export of frozen lamb from the South Island, but it also lay behind the growth of dairy farming in the

north, which now, stimulated by the exports trade in butter and cheese, drew ahead of the south in population.

Political development kept pace with economic growth. In 1855 New South Wales, Victoria, South Australia and Tasmania became self-governing colonies, followed by Queensland in 1859, and in 1901 joined together to form the Commonwealth of Australia. New Zealand, which had been divided in 1852 into six provinces, each with an elected council, became a united Dominion in 1876, after measures had been taken to safeguard the rights of the Maori population. Both dominions remained heavily dependent on primary exports. For long they enjoyed preferential treatment in the British market; but developments after 1945, particularly the British retreat from Asia, brought important changes. In 1952 both dominions joined for security with the United States in the ANZUS Pact, and when Great Britain entered the European Common Market (1973) and dismantled imperial preference, they were forced to diversify their economies and seek new markets. The process of reorientation is still continuing.

4 Early trade

Early trade (left)

1/Main route from Europe via Cape of Good Hope. First colonisation fleet to New South Wales 1788, mainly convicts and marines. By 1790, with arrival of second fleet, it was clear that the colonies would be reliant upon regular supplies from Europe.

2/Convict transport ships return to U.K. via New Zealand for timber, and Canton for tea or Calcutta for oriental goods.

3/Sydney-based ships to Pacific islands for sandalwood to trade for tea at Canton.

4/Sydney-based ships to Bass Strait islands for seal skins and oil (first major exports to U.K.). Seal fields soon exhausted. Eastern colony ports used as bases for American and British whaling ships, an industry developed by colonists from 1820s.

5/Sydney to Tahiti for pork for provisioning convicts.

6/Macassan fishermen to northern Australian coast to collect trepang (sea cucumbers) to trade with Chinese merchants.

7/Van Diemen's land grain to Sydney.

8/South Australian grain to eastern colonies.

9/South Australian grain to Europe. From 1840s wool and minerals, the basis of late nineteenth century trade with Europe.

1 The settlement and development of Australia

European nationalism
1815-1914

The flame of nationalism was kindled in Europe by the French revolution. In France itself the revolution forged a sense of national unity, and elsewhere, notably in Spain and Prussia, the humiliation of defeat and French occupation after 1807 produced a short-lived national reaction. For the most part, however, nationalism was confined to a narrow segment of the middle class. It was anathema to the ruling classes, and rarely touched working people. Polish peasants held aloof from the insurrections of 1831, 1846 and 1863; in Ireland only acute agrarian distress after 1877 lined them up behind the nationalists. Down to 1848 liberal and constitutional reform was the main demand, and it was against this, rather than nationalism, that the victorious powers set their faces after the fall of Napoleon at the Congress of Vienna in 1815. Their other main objective was to erect a barrier against a resurgence of revolutionary France. Hence their decision to transfer the Austrian Netherlands (later Belgium) to Holland, to install Prussia in Westphalia and most of the Rhineland, and to hand over the ancient republic of Genoa to Sardinia-Piedmont. As compensation for the loss of the Netherlands, Austria received the Venetian republic and the duchy of Milan, as well as indirect control of Parma, Modena and Tuscany. Sweden, which had to surrender Finland to Russia, was compensated with Norway.

The overriding objective of the great powers after 1815 was to uphold the Vienna settlement and to combat the threat of liberalism and nationalism, but by 1830, when a new wave of liberal and nationalist agitation broke out, the eastern and western powers were drawing apart. By destroying a common front, their divergence of interests enabled Greece (page 116) and Belgium to obtain independence, although in the latter case the territorial settlement, including the disposal of Limburg and Luxembourg was postponed until 1839 (map 5).

In Norway the forced union with Sweden aroused resentment similar to that felt in Belgium towards Holland. There was friction, but little active resistance, and eventually a Norwegian declaration of independence was accepted by Sweden (map 4). The course of events in Poland (1831, 1846) and in Italy, Germany and Hungary in 1848-49 was more eventful. Here nationalist agitation erupted in full-scale war; but the solidarity of the conservative powers and divisions among the nationalists themselves brought all to nothing.

What changed this situation was the rise of a new generation of statesmen. Louis Napoleon, emperor of France since 1852, Cavour, who became prime minister of Sardinia-Piedmont in the same year, and Bismarck, minister-president of Prussia after 1862, all toyed with nationalism, confident of their ability to use it for their own ends. These were not the ends of the liberals who had led the nationalist movements of 1848-49. Cavour's purpose was to ensure that Italian unification was carried out by and in the interests of Sardinia; hence his opposition to the famous Sicilian expedition of the patriot Garibaldi (1807-82) in 1860. Bismarck was determined to ensure that Germany was merged in Prussia, not Prussia in Germany. Both also realised that their objectives could only be achieved by war and diplomacy. Hence Cavour's alliance with France against Austria (1858) and Bismarck's wars of 1864, 1866 and 1870. The result was the unification of Italy (except for Venetia and the Papal State) in 1861 (map 3) and the unification of Germany in 1871 (map 2). Both were retrospectively endorsed by liberal nationalists, but neither satisfied the nationalism they aroused. Italy still laid claim to the Alto Adige, Fiume and Trieste. Bismarck's 'small German' solution, excluding Austria, disappointed those who hankered after a Greater Germany. Indeed, it was after 1870, when the problems of the multi-national Austro-Hungarian state came to the fore, that nationalist claims became loudest. The confusion of peoples and languages in eastern Europe (map 1) defied easy solutions and exacerbated the conflicts which led, step by step, to war in 1914.

5 Belgian independence 1830-39

United Netherlands 1815-31

boundary of German Confederation 1815

boundary of German Confederation 1839

4 The Scandinavian kingdoms

3 The unification of Italy, 1859-70

Kingdom of Sardinia in 1815

territory annexed 1859

territory annexed May 1860

territory annexed November 1860

territory annexed 1866

territory lost to France 1860

French from 1768, formerly Genoese

international frontier 1914

1 Peoples, languages and political divisions in the 19th century

— national frontiers 1914
- - - national frontiers in 1815 where different

▨ Romansch
▨ Macedonian Slavs

Atlantic Ocean

FINNS

NORWEGIANS

SWEDES

GREAT RUSSIANS

ESTONIANS

SCOTS

DANES

LATVIANS
LITHUANIANS

WHITE RUSSIANS

IRISH

ENGLISH

WELSH

DUTCH

POLES

UKRAINIANS

FLEMINGS
WALLOONS

G E R M A N S

CZECHS

BRETONS

SLOVAKS

FRENCH

AUSTRIANS

HUNGARIANS

SLOVENES

R O M A N I A N S

CROATS

BASQUES

S E R B S

BULGARIANS

SPANIARDS

CATALANS

I T A L I A N S

CORSICANS

PORTUGUESE

ALBANIANS

GREEKS

TURKS

2 The unification of Germany, 1815–71

North Sea

Baltic Sea

DENMARK

R. Niemen

Tilsit

SCHLESWIG

Schleswig
Kiel

Königsberg

HOLSTEIN
Lübeck

Rostock

Danzig

EAST PRUSSIA

MECKLENBURG

POMERANIA

WEST PRUSSIA

P R U S S I A

Hamburg

Stettin

OLDENBURG
Bremen

R. Elbe

Berlin

R. Warthe

R. Vistula

NETHERLANDS

H A N O V E R

Hanover

BRANDENBURG

POSEN

Amsterdam

Posen

The Hague

Münster

BRUNSWICK

R U S S I A

WESTPHALIA

ANHALT

Antwerp

Dortmund

P R U S S I A

Göttingen

Kassel

POLAND

Brussels

Düsseldorf

Leipzig

RHENISH

Breslau

BELGIUM

Aachen

Cologne

Erfurt

Dresden

S I L E S I A

PRUSSIA

Koblenz

WETZLAR
HESSE

THURINGIA

SAXONY

R. Oder

NASSAU

Frankfurt

Sedan
1870

Luxembourg

Darmstadt

Prague

Sadowa
1866

B O H E M I A

Prussians occupy Paris 1871

PALATINATE

Nuremberg

Verdun

Metz

LORRAINE

Nancy

Karlsruhe

R. Danube

Vienna

Strassburg

Stuttgart

WÜRTTEMBERG

B A V A R I A

FRANCE

ALSACE

HOHENZOLLERN

R. Rhine

BADEN

Ulm

Munich

R. Meuse

Basle

Constance

SWITZERLAND

A U S T R I A

▨ Prussia in 1815
▨ acquired by Prussia 1815-66
— boundary of German Confederation of 1815
- - - boundary of North German Confederation 1866
▨ Imperial territory of Alsace-Lorraine 1871
— boundary of German Empire 1871
◄--- Austro-Prussian forces attack Denmark 1864
◄— Prussian armies in the war with Austria 1866
◄— German armies in the Franco-Prussian war 1870-71

The European powers
1878-1914

After the unification of Germany and of Italy (page 114), it seemed for a time as though the major questions which had disturbed the peace of Europe since 1848 had been resolved. Bismarck, the architect of German unification, concentrated his efforts after 1871 upon building a system of alliances which would ensure the future of the new German Reich. The 'wild Junker' had become a conservative, anxious only to preserve what had been won; and his alliances were defensive. But the history of the next forty years is the story of how alliances, originally defensive and stabilising in intent, turned into an aggressive and destabilising system. Furthermore, the unification of Germany and of Italy, far from marking a halting place, opened up a hornet's nest of nationalist revindications. After 1870 the nationalist

movement which had agitated western Europe for forty years, spilled over into the Balkans; and the struggles of the Balkan peoples for independence (map 1) inevitably involved the powers who were their supporters or adversaries, particularly Russia and Austria-Hungary, which, after its exclusion from Germany and Italy after 1866, was essentially an eastward-looking Balkan power.

The evolution of the relations between the great powers between 1879, when Bismarck tried to reconcile his sympathies with a conservative Russia with support for Austria-Hungary, and 1914, when the whole precarious balance fell apart, is indicated diagrammatically on maps 2(a) to 2(f). Until the beginning of the new century the system worked reasonably well. Revolts in the Balkans between 1875 and 1878, culminating in Russian intervention and war with Turkey, thoroughly alarmed the powers; and after the Congress of Berlin (1878) Balkan affairs took a secondary place. Checked in Europe, Russia turned to central Asia and the Far

East, and during the first half of the period the dominant themes were Anglo-Russian rivalry in Asia and Anglo-French rivalry in Africa. What changed this situation was the decision of Germany under William II, particularly after Bülow became chancellor in 1900, to seek 'a place in the sun'. This was not unreasonable; but by now most places in the sun had been occupied, and German policy was seen as a threat by the established imperial powers. The result was the Anglo-French reconciliation (1904) and the Anglo-Russian reconciliation (1907). German 'world policy' also required a navy, resulting in the naval competition which soured Anglo-German relations between 1906 and 1912. After 1907 the Triple Entente with France and Russia became the lynch-pin of British policy, the only firm assurance against the German 'threat'. Germany, on the other hand, saw itself being 'encircled' by a hostile ring constructed by Great Britain.

The result was that the lines between the Triple Alliance and the Triple Entente were drawn tighter. Also

1 The Balkans, 1878-1913

- – – frontier of Ottoman Empire 1800

- proposed Bulgaria under Treaty of San Stefano 1878

- national frontiers after the Balkan wars 1912-13

Germany was driven closer to its only dependable ally, Austria-Hungary. When Austria annexed Bosnia-Herzegovina in 1908, Bülow lent full support, and Austro-Russian antagonism in the Balkans, hitherto suppressed, was rekindled. The climax was postponed until the outbreak of the Balkan wars in 1912. The aggrandisement of Serbia which resulted was viewed by Austria as an intolerable threat. Russia, on the other hand, could not leave Serbia in the lurch without losing credibility. The result was the stupendous build-up of armaments (diagram 3) as the grinding logic of the system came into play. When in 1914 the murder of the Austrian archduke Franz Ferdinand brought matters to a head, the combustible material was piled up which exploded in the First World War.

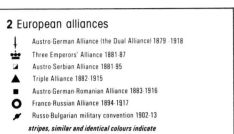

2 European alliances

- ↓ Austro-German Alliance (the Dual Alliance) 1879-1918
- ♔ Three Emperors' Alliance 1881-87
- ◩ Austro-Serbian Alliance 1881-95
- ▲ Triple Alliance 1882-1915
- ■ Austro-German-Romanian Alliance 1883-1916
- ○ Franco-Russian Alliance 1894-1917
- ⚑ Russo-Bulgarian military convention 1902-13

*stripes, similar and identical colours indicate
an entente or community of interests*

2a/The Dual Alliance: October 1879, resulted from the Balkan upheavals of 1875-8. When Russia attacked Turkey and imposed the Treaty of San Stefano, the Austro-Russian understanding of 1873 broke down. Bismarck's purpose in the Dual Alliance was to stabilise the situation. Germany could not afford to let Austria-Hungary succumb to a Russian attack; but the alliance was strictly defensive. It did not imply a common front against Russia, understanding with which was still a basic element in Bismarck's policy, still less a German commitment to underwrite Austrian ambitions in the Balkans. Nevertheless the Dual Alliance marked a turning point: the era of formal alliances had begun.

2b/Bismarck's system at its zenith: 1883. The formation of the Three Emperors' Alliance (1881) appeared to have restored stability in Eastern Europe. But the smouldering Austro-Russian antagonism continued, brought to a head again by the Bulgarian crisis of 1886-7. Alliances with Serbia (1881) and Romania (1883) sought to limit Russian influence in the Balkans. The Triple Alliance of Germany, Austria and Italy (1882) insured Austria against Italian attack in case of war with Russia. After the Three Emperors' Alliance broke down, Bismarck sought security by his Reinsurance Treaty with Russia (1887), while Austria joined in a 'Mediterranean agreement' with Britain, Italy and Spain against France and Russia.

2c/The 'New Course' in Germany: 1891. Even before Bismarck's fall in 1890, it was evident that his complicated system of alliances was running into difficulties. Russo-German relations deteriorated sharply after 1887 as a result of tariff and loan disputes. When the new German chancellor, Caprivi, dropped Bismarck's Reinsurance Treaty, renewed the Triple Alliance, and lined up with the 'Mediterranean entente', Russia replied by a military convention and alliance with France (1894). But the 'new course' was short-lived. After 1895 Germany saw more profit in co-operation with France and Russia in the Far East, while Austria-Hungary and Russia agreed (1897) to put Balkan problems on ice.

2d/The Anglo-French entente: 1904. The decision of William II and Bülow after 1897 to move from a continental, European to a 'world' policy challenged all three established imperial powers and brought about a major realignment. In 1902 France settled its long-standing dispute with Italy; in 1904 it reached a similar settlement with Great Britain. Germany's attempt to exploit Russia's weakness after the Russo-Japanese war and the 1905 revolution to prise apart the Franco-Russian alliance misfired. Franco-British ties were strengthened; Russia and England settled their colonial differences in 1907, and the three powers joined in the Triple Entente to counter and contain Germany.

2e/Europe after the Bosnian crisis: 1909. The Austrian annexation of Bosnia and Herzegovina, a response to the Turkish revolution of 1908, ended the Austro-Russian Balkan entente of 1897 and caused a major crisis in international relations. When Russia protested, Germany gave Austria full support, reversing Bismarck's defensive interpretation of the Dual Alliance, and forced Russia to back down. Henceforward Austria-Hungary and Russia were at loggerheads in the Balkans. Anglo-German relations also were at their nadir, a consequence of growing naval rivalry. The result was to consolidate the Triple Entente, particularly after the second Morocco crisis (1911), when Britain took the lead in opposing Germany.

2f/Europe on the eve of war: 1914. Between 1911 and 1914 the front between the Triple Alliance and the Triple Entente hardened. During the Balkan wars (1912-13), when Serbia, Greece and Bulgaria combined to drive Turkey out of Europe, the two groups still co-operated. But Austria was aghast at the consequent enlargement of Serbia and feared pro-Serb irredentism in its Slav provinces, and Germany was haunted by the spectre of encirclement. When, after the assassination of Franz Ferdinand at Sarajevo on 28 June 1914, Austria decided to punish Serbia and Berlin threw itself unreservedly behind Vienna, the system of alliances almost automatically led to general war.

The First World War
1914-1918

When the assassination of the Austrian heir-presumptive, Archduke Franz Ferdinand, by Bosnian terrorists at Sarajevo on June 28, 1914, sparked off the immediate sequence of events that led to the First World War, the European powers were already divided into heavily armed camps (page 116), and neither was prepared to risk diplomatic defeat. Germany already had its battle plan prepared: the famous Schlieffen Plan, drawn up in 1905, to trap and annihilate the French army by a great encircling movement through Belgium before France's Russian ally had time to mobilise. The expectation everywhere was for a short war, over by Christmas 1914, and only after this expectation proved false did the search for allies begin in earnest. Germany and

Austria were joined by the Ottoman Empire and Bulgaria, the Entente powers by Italy, Romania and Greece, and eventually by the United States (map 1).

The German strategy was very nearly successful and brought the German armies within 40 miles of Paris (map 2). It was frustrated by the unexpectedly rapid mobilisation of Russia, which invaded East Prussia and defeated the German 8th Army at Gumbinnen (August 20, 1914). Although the Russians were repulsed at Tannenberg (August 26–29), their offensive drew off German reserves, which helped the French and British armies in the west to halt the German advance in the battle of the Marne (September 5–8), while the Russians simultaneously inflicted a crushing defeat on Austria at Lemberg. The Schlieffen Plan had failed, Germany was forced to despatch troops to the east to prop up the Austrian front, and in the west the war

became a war of trenches, artillery, barbed wire and machine guns. Each side launched offensives, with sickening casualties, but without succeeding in advancing more than a few thousand yards. Railways could bring up reinforcements to the front before slow-moving advancing troops could make good any advantage they might have created. The question for both, by the end of 1915, was how to break the stalemate. The answer of the Entente, sponsored by Winston Churchill, was to attack Germany from the rear by campaigns in the Dardanelles and Mesopotamia (page 124), at Salonika, and, after Italy entered the war on May 23, 1915, against Austria on the Isonzo. All were failures. The German answer was to bring Great Britain to its knees by crippling losses at sea. The submarine campaign, initiated on February 1, 1917, was nearly successful, and only defeated when Lloyd George introduced the con-

voy system in May. But its result was to bring the United States into the war on the Entente side on April 6, 1917.

Even so, the German position was not hopeless. Huge losses in the Brusilov offensive of 1916 and economic chaos at home had broken the Russian fighting spirit, and the Russian revolutions of March and October 1917 (page 120) enabled Germany to transfer troops from the Eastern to the Western Front in the hope of victory before the United States could mobilise. On March 21, 1918,

1 The line-up of the Powers

Central Powers

Entente (Allied) Powers

neutral states

total mobilised forces

neutral states that later joined Central Powers, with date

neutral states that later joined Entente Powers, with date

killed and died (1914-1918)

* estimated figures

3 The war in Europe, 1914-18

major Central Powers offensives

major Allied offensives

major battles

battles costing over 250,000 killed

naval mutinies

army mutinies

food riots

naval bases

major naval battles

German raids on English coast

all battles, offensives, mutinies etc. coloured according to year:

1914   1916   1918

1915   1917

furthest German advance in the west, 1914

the trench line, November 1914

furthest Russian advance in the east, 1914-15

Russian front, November 1915

territory held by Central Powers, December 1917 (close in the west to the "Hindenburg line")

front line at time of Brest-Litovsk armistice between Germany and Russia December 1917

German penetration of Russia, February 1918

armistice line in the west, November 1918

railways

4 Allied shipping losses, 1914-18

figures in tons

Russia 183,000

Greece 346,000

US (while neutral) 56,000

US (while belligerent) 397,000

Italy 872,000

France 900,000

Great Britain 7,800,000

Hindenburg and Ludendorff launched their great offensive in the west (map 3). Once again it was a near success, but the Allied line held, and on July 18 the French commander Foch launched the counter-offensive which was to be the decisive campaign of the war. On September 29 Ludendorff acknowledged defeat. By now war weariness was rampant. Austria and Bulgaria were near to collapse; the British blockade had brought Germany to the edge of starvation; and the German government, fearful of a Bolshevik revolution, sued for an armistice. On November 11, 1918, fighting ceased. Over 8 million men had perished, as had three empires, the Tsarist, the Austro-Hungarian and the Ottoman. In retrospect the war of 1914–18 was the great European civil war, which destroyed the old European order, squandered Europe's human and material resources, and jeopardised its future. Few people realised in 1918 what had happened; but the age of European predominance was over and a new age of global politics had begun.

2 The German attack in the West, August 1914

→ German "Schlieffen Plan" to encircle Paris

→ actual route of German armies

→ Allied counter offensives

The Russian Revolution
1905-1925

Revolution came to Russia suddenly, but not unexpectedly, in the wake of the unsuccessful Russo-Japanese war of 1904–05 (page 126). Intensive industrialisation since 1890 had created a large, profoundly discontented urban proletariat, and it was they who spearheaded the revolution of 1905, although their revolt sparked off widespread unrest in the countryside (map 1). The Tsar was forced to grant a constitution, including a *duma*, or parliament, but by 1907 the government was back in full control. Nevertheless the 1905 revolution irreparably weakened the old order, and after 1912, following the shooting of strikers in the Lena goldfields in Siberia, a great new wave of social unrest swept the empire. Internally, Russia was in no position in 1914 to meet the challenge of the First World War; and when in the winter of 1916–17 economic dislocation, hunger and sheer incompetence brought the crisis to a head, the government capitulated almost without resistance. This was the February revolution of 1917, which placed power in the hands of liberal Duma politicians. But the Provisional Government's authority was circumscribed by the powerful Petrograd Council (or Soviet) of Soldiers' and Workers' Deputies, and it was also compromised by its commit-

ment to continue the war. When, in April, Lenin returned from exile in Switzerland, promising peace, land and bread, and demanding all power for the Soviets, its days were numbered. An attempt in September by the Commander-in-Chief, General Kornilov, to seize the capital miscarried when his troops rebelled, and on November 7 (October 25 by the old calendar) the Bolsheviks struck, arrested the Provisional Government, and assumed power in the name of the Soviets. This was the October, or Bolshevik, revolution.

The odds were weighted heavily against the new government. The overriding need was peace, and Lenin insisted, against strong opposition, on accepting the onerous terms imposed by Germany in the Treaty of Brest-Litovsk (March 1918). But immediately the Bolsheviks were faced with civil war and foreign intervention, as White Russian armies with British, French, Czech and other support, attacked the new republic (map 2). Lenin pinned his hope on war-weariness and revolution in the west (map 3) and on uprisings among subject peoples in the east (map 4), but to little avail. In Europe, particularly in Germany, revolutionary currents were strong between 1919 and 1923, but they were met by counter-revolutionary forces, including Hitler's National Socialists. However, foreign intervention and the threat of a White Tsarist restoration rallied support for the Reds, and by 1920 the civil war had been won. But the devastation was immense. Industrial production

in 1920 was down to one-seventh of the 1913 level, and shortages provoked a wave of strikes and riots, culminating in the Kronstadt naval mutiny (February 1921). Lenin's answer was the 'New Economic Policy' (NEP), in effect a relaxation of requisitioning and controls. The new policy worked: by the end of 1925 industrial production had regained its pre-war level. Furthermore, the overt hostility of the West relaxed. War with Poland, which had invaded Russia in 1920, was ended by the Treaty of Riga (March 1921), and at the same time a treaty of friendship was signed with Turkey. It was followed by the Rapallo Treaty with Germany (1922) and in 1924 by diplomatic recognition from Britain, France and other European countries.

After Lenin's death in 1924 and a period of disputed succession Lenin's eventual successor, Stalin, ousted Trotsky, with his policy of 'permanent revolution'. Stalin's policy of 'socialism in one country', implying large-scale industrialisation and a re-shaping of inefficient agriculture, placed Russia, at a terrible human cost, in the first rank of industrial and international powers. Inaugurated by the first Five Year Plan of 1928, in many respects it marked a sharp break with the revolution of 1917. But it was also a fulfilment of Lenin's work. Even at the time of Lenin's death Russia was backward and under-developed. By 1939, as Lenin foresaw, Bolshevism had become 'a world force', changing the course of history.

2 Russia in war and revolution

boundary of the Russian Empire, 1914

front between Russia and Central Powers, March 1917

principal towns where Bolsheviks took power, Nov. 1917-Feb. 1918 (dates in new calendar)

boundary of Russian territory occupied by Central Powers following the Treaty of Brest-Litovsk, March 1918

boundary of area controlled by the Bolsheviks, August 1918

eastern boundary of area controlled by the Bolsheviks, April 1919

area controlled by the Bolsheviks, October 1919

boundary of Soviet Territory, March 1921

boundary of areas controlled by anti-Bolshevik forces, May 1920

White Russian armies

non-Russian anti-Bolshevik forces

Barents Sea

Murmansk

**BRITISH
FRENCH
CANADIANS
ITALIANS
SERBS**

*White
Sea*

CANADIANS
AMERICANS

Archangel
17 Feb 1918

BRITISH
FRENCH

FINNS

Petrozavodsk
17 Jan 1918

N O R W A Y

S W E D E N

F I N L A N D

*independence of
Finland recognised
December 1917*

L. Onega

L. Ladoga

Helsinki

Kronstadt

Petrograd (Leningrad)
7 Nov 1917

*Kornilov's attack on
Petrograd September 1917*

Vologda
8 Feb 1918

Vyatka
8 Dec 1917

Perm
14 Nov 1917

*Nicholas II
and family shot
by Bolsheviks
July 1918*

Yekaterinburg
(Sverdlovsk)
8 Nov 1917

British fleet

Revel (Tallinn)
8 Nov 1917

Novgorod
27 Nov 1917

Kostroma
15 Dec 1917

Yaroslavl 9 Nov 1917

Izhevsk
9 Nov 1917

B O L S H E V I K R U S S I A

ESTONIA

LETTS

Pskov
15 Nov 1917

Baltic Sea

LATVIA

Riga

BALTIC
GERMANS

LITHUANIA

GERMANY
(E.PRUSSIA)

Vitebsk
9 Nov 1917

Smolensk
12 Nov 1917

Tver (Kalinin)
10 Nov 1917

Ivanovo
7 Nov 1917

Nizhny Novgorod
(Gorkiy)
10 Nov 1917

Kazan
8 Nov 1917

Kolchak 1918-19

Ufa
8 Nov 1917

CZECHS

Moscow
15 Nov 1917

Kaluga
11 Dec 1917

Tula
20 Dec 1917

Trans-Siberian Railway

Samara
9 Nov 1917

Minsk
7 Nov
1917

Mogilev
1 Dec 1917

Warsaw

Orel
14 Nov 1917

Tambov
13 Feb 1918

Penza
4 Jan 1918

Orenburg
31 Jan 1918

Brest-
Litovsk

P O L A N D   POLES

Gomel
12 Nov 1917

Voronezh
12 Nov 1917

Saratov
9 Nov 1917

Ural Cossack Army
1918-20

CZECHOSLOVAKIA

Zhitomir
22 Jan 1918

Kiev
8 Feb 1918

*Denikin
1919*

Poltava
19 Jan 1918

Kharkov
24 Dec 1917

**Don Cossacks
1917-19**

Tsaritsyn (Stalingrad)
(Volgograd)
27 Nov 1917

R. Don

R. Volga

HUNGARY

ROMANIANS

BESSARABIA

Yekaterinoslva
(Dnepropetrovsk)
11 Jan 1918

Novocherkassk
25 Feb 1918

Kishinev
10 Dec 1917

Nikolayev
27 Jan 1918

Rostov-on-Don
10 Nov 1917

R O M A N I A

Odessa
31 Jan
1918

Wrangel 1920

Cossacks

Astrakhan
7 Feb 1918

Sevastopol
29 Dec 1917

Simferopol
26 Jan 1918

Novorossiysk
14 Dec 1917

FRENCH

BRITISH

*Caspian
Sea*

B U L G A R I A

Black   Sea

Entente fleet

BRITISH

BRITISH

Georgians

1919-20

Mensheviks

Batum

Tiflis (Tbilisi)

Baku
15 Nov 1917

Krasnovodsk

Kars

BRITISH

T U R K E Y

Tabriz

BRITISH

1918-19

P E R S I A

Entente fleet

The Chinese Revolution
1911-1949

By 1911 the imperial government of China was thoroughly discredited, and it only needed an army mutiny at Wuchang to repudiate its authority (map 1). But the republic proclaimed in 1912, with Sun Yat-sen as its first president, was overwhelmed by its inherited problems, and within weeks Sun was displaced by Yuan Shih-k'ai, the most powerful general of the old regime. After Yuan's death in 1916 the government in Peking lost control and power passed into the hands of provincial warlords, whose armies caused untold damage

and millions of casualties. Compounding this misery were the expansionist policies of Japan, which had secured control of Shantung and Manchuria in 1915 (page 126), as well as the presence of foreign powers, based in the Treaty Ports, who interfered in Chinese politics and exploited the struggling Chinese economy.

In 1919, when the Paris Peace Conference refused to abrogate Japanese and other foreign privileges, this desperate situation exploded in a massive upsurge of Chinese nationalism, which found vent in the 4 May Movement of 1919, a spontaneous uprising of students and urban workers, which was the real starting point of the Chinese revolution. It provided a new constituency for Sun Yat-sen, who had taken refuge at Canton,

and in 1923 Sun reorganised his Nationalist (Kuomintang, KMT) Party, allied with the Chinese Communist Party (CCP, founded in 1921), and prepared to reunite the country. But Sun died in 1925, and it was Chiang Kai-shek, the Moscow-trained general of the KMT army, who led the great Northern Expedition of 1926 which aimed at the elimination of the warlords and the unification of the country (map 2). Helped by peasant and workers' uprisings along its route, it was astonishingly successful, and by April 1927 Chiang established his capital at Nanking. But the uneasy alliance of KMT and CCP could not hold, and in 1927 Chiang turned on his allies, massacring the Communists in Shanghai. Furthermore, the warlords were not entirely eliminated, and

Chiang's direct rule was limited effectively to the lower Yangtze (map 3). Finally, the Japanese, fearing the potential challenge from a reunited China, decided to reinforce their hold in the north. After 1931, when Japan overran Manchuria, Chiang had to meet simultaneously the Japanese threat from without and the Communist threat at home.

Chiang's purge had virtually eliminated the Communists in the cities, but peasant disaffection, arising from his failure to carry out land reform, provided them with new possibilities in the countryside. It was Mao Tse-tung who realised this, and his base at Chingkang Shan in a remote mountainous area was the main, though not the only, seedbed of the revitalised Com-

munist movement. KMT attacks drove Mao to Kiangsi where the most important Soviet was established and where the Communists ruled an area of several million people developing reform programmes as a peasant-based party rather than an urban, proletarian party on the Russian model. Further KMT attacks forced the Communists to abandon Kiangsi and it was on the famous Long March, to Yenan (map 4), where Mao gathered widespread support by his reform programmes and by spearheading resistance to the Japanese invasion, that his peasant-based wing of the party gained ascendancy. The result was that large areas of China passed under Communist control, while Chiang's government, which had withdrawn under Japanese

pressure to the remote fastness of Chungking, was unpopular and out of touch. This was the situation in 1945 after the defeat of Japan, though other factors, particularly the growing Soviet-American involvement, played a part. Negotiations for a political settlement broke down and in 1947 open civil war broke out. The Communists defeated the Nationalists in Manchuria and took Peking in January 1949 (map 5). The great battle around Suchow (November 1948–January 1949) opened the way south. On October 1, 1949, the People's Republic was proclaimed, and the Nationalists fled to Taiwan. But the civil war compounded the devastation of the previous decades and China's new rulers were left with a formidable task of reconstruction.

The Ottoman Empire

1800-1923

The Ottoman Empire gradually disintegrated between the beginning of the nineteenth century and the end of the First World War. Steady European economic and colonial penetration weakened the economy, and the success of the nationalist movements in the latter part of the century caused large areas either to break away or to fall effectively under foreign control.

Austria and Russia had been making inroads into the empire throughout the last decades of the eighteenth century; they were joined by France, whose expedition to Egypt in 1798 eventually resulted in the end of effective control from Constantinople and the creation of a dynasty by the Ottoman viceroy, Mohammed Ali Pasha, which lasted from 1805 to 1952. His son, Ibrahim Pasha, led expeditions to subdue the Wahabi rulers of Nejd, inaugurated a period of Egyptian rule over the Sudan, and conquered the whole area between what is now Turkey and Egypt between 1831 and 1839.

In the face of this and other challenges, the empire began a series of major reforms, first of its military establishment and then in the fields of law, education and administration. Two major edicts in 1839 and 1856 stressed the subjects' rights to equality and security of life and property. However, especially in the Balkans, the Powers' claims to be able to intervene on behalf of their protegés had the effect of encouraging the nascent nationalist movements; southern Greece, Bulgaria, Montenegro, Romania, and Serbia had all become independent by 1878.

At the same time France was making substantial inroads into North Africa, while Italy invaded Libya in 1911. There were also stirrings of discontent in other Arab provinces, particularly during the long and oppressive reign of Abdul-Hamid II (1876–1909), when ideas of autonomy gradually gained currency, encouraged by the revival of Arabic literature and campaigns to reform the Arab language. Opposition to Abdul-Hamid's rule culminated in the Young Turk revolution of 1908–09, but the policies pursued by the Young Turks alienated much of the Arab population, and contributed substantially to the Arabs' willingness to seek accommodation with Britain in the course of the war. They were to be disappointed, since the peace settlement put most of the Middle East firmly under British and French control. After Turkey's defeat the caliphate was abolished and a secular republic established.

Similar developments took place in Iran, where the Qajar dynasty (1779–1924) had faced constant Russian and British interference in their internal affairs, culminating in an agreement to divide the country into the spheres of influence of the two powers in 1907. However, the combination of foreign pressures and movements for reform within the country helped to arouse national consciousness and political awareness, and the Constitutional Revolution of 1905–1911 marked a major advance in political self-confidence and maturity.

**The Middle East and North Africa
1800–1923** (below)
Afghanistan Independent state under Durrani dynasty to 1842; remained independent despite Russian invasions and wars with Britain 1839–42, 1878–90, 1919.
Albania Ottoman province since 14th century; independent principality 1912; kingdom 1928–39.
Armenia Western part in Ottoman Empire, eastern part in Persia until Russian occupation 1804; independent republic 1918–1920; subsequently absorbed into Turkey and USSR.
Azerbaijan Part of Persia until early 19th century; partly under Russian occupation 1803–28; northern part independent republic 1918–1920; northern part incorporated into USSR after 1920.
Bahrain Independent sheikdom under al-Khalifa family since 1783; under British protection since 1820, formalised in 1892.
Bessarabia Ottoman province; Russian 1812–56; ceded to [Ottoman] Moldavia 1856; Russian 1878; Romanian since 1918.
Bosnia-Herzegovina Ottoman province since 15th century; Austrian administration after 1878; part of Yugoslavia since 1918.
Bukhara Independent khanate; Russian protectorate 1868; part of USSR since 1924.
Bulgaria Ottoman province since 14th century; given autonomy but partitioned 1878; independent kingdom 1908; present (1991) boundaries since 1919.
Daghestan Part of Iran; incorporated into Russia/USSR since 1859.
Dodecanese Ottoman since 16th century; occupied by Italy 1912; to Greece 1947.

Eastern Rumelia Ottoman province since 14th century; part of Bulgaria since 1885.
Georgia Independent kingdom under intermittent Persian control; incorporated into Russia 1801; independent republic 1918–20; part of USSR since 1920.
Greece Ottoman rule since 14th century; independent since 1833; enlarged by additions of Crete and Macedonia in 1913.
Hejaz Under Ottoman suzerainty since early 16th century but generally autonomous under Sharifs of Mecca until 1916; independent 1916–24; absorbed into Saudi Arabia 1925.
Iraq Formed from Ottoman provinces of Basra, Baghdad and Mosul 1920; under Hashemite monarchy 1921–58; British mandate 1920–32.
Kars and Ardahan Ottoman provinces since 16th century; to Russia 1878; in Armenian republic 1918–20; part of Turkey since 1920.
Khiva Independent khanate; Russian occupation 1873.
Kokand Independent khanate; Russian occupation 1876.
Kuwait Ottoman province under hereditary rule of Al Sabah family since c.1756; treaty of protection with Britain 1899–1961.
Lebanon Ottoman conquest 1516–17; Mount Lebanon ruled by independent

dynasties to 1840; given special status within the Ottoman Empire after civil war of 1860; under Ottoman Christian governors 1861–1915; enlarged and made a republic under French mandate 1920–1946.
Macedonia Ottoman province since 14th century; divided between Bulgaria, Greece and Serbia (later Yugoslavia) 1913.
Montenegro Ottoman province since 14th century but generally under autonomous rule; independent 1878; incorporated into Yugoslavia 1918.
Nejd Under Saudi family from 1746; occupied by Egypt for the Ottomans 1818–1822; Saudis regain control 1902; Kingdom of Saudi Arabia incorporating Hasa, Hejaz, Nejd, 1932; Asir added 1934.
Palestine Ottoman province since 16th century; British occupation 1917; assigned to Britain as mandate 1920–1947 with British obligation to facilitate creation of Jewish National Home.
Persia (Iran) Independent kingdom under Qajar Shahs 1779–1924; partition into British and Russian spheres of influence 1907; under Pehlevi dynasty 1924–79.
Qatar Autonomous sheikdom under al-Thani family; British protection 1916–1971.
Romania Formerly Ottoman provinces of Moldavia and Wallachia (since 14th

century); united 1861, independent 1878; enlarged to present (1991) boundaries with the addition of Bessarabia 1918.
Serbia Ottoman province since 14/15th century; autonomous since 1817; separate kingdom 1878; part of Yugoslavia since 1918.
Syria (Name formerly applied to whole area of modern Jordan-Lebanon-Palestine/Israel-Syria.) Ottoman province since 1516; British occupation 1917; Arab kingdom of Damascus 1918–20; French occupation and mandate 1920–1946; sanjak of Alexandretta ceded to Turkey 1939.
Transjordan Part of Ottoman province of Damascus; emirate under British mandate 1923–1946.
Tunisia Ottoman conquest 1574; virtually independent under Husainid dynasty 1705–1881; French conquest 1881; French protectorate 1881–1956.
Turkey Core of Ottoman Empire (early 14th century to 1923); Turkish Republic created 1924.
Yemen Local rulers belonging to Za'idi (Shi'i) sect; nominally part of Ottoman Empire since 1517; Aden occupied by Britain 1839; parts of south in treaty relations with Britain 1886–1954; independent state in north 1918.

zones of control
zones of influence
international frontiers 1914
frontier according to the Treaty of Sèvres 1920

4 The Greco-Turkish War, 1920-22

area under Greek control 1920
limit of Greek advance 1921
direction of Greek offensive 1921
boundary of Greek control 1921-22
direction of Turkish offensive 1922

Agreements between the Powers(*above*)
In 1907 parts of Persia became British and Russian spheres of influence (**1**). During the First World War, Britain, France, Italy and Russia made provisional arrangements to divide the Ottoman Empire; in 1915 Russia was given Constantinople, the Straits and the Dardanelles (**2**), France a sphere of influence in Syria and Cilicia (**3**) and Italy in south-west Turkey and the Dodecanese islands (**4**). Under the Sykes-Picot agreement (1916) Palestine was to be internationalised (**5**), Britain was to be given Mesopotamia (**6**), Haifa and Acre on the Mediterranean coast, and the area between (**7**); France gained Aleppo, Damascus, Mosul and their hinterlands (**8**); Russia gained north-west Anatolia, and parts of Kurdistan and Armenia (**9**); subsequently the Italians were promised most of south-west Anatolia (**10**). The British, seeking Arab support, promised Sharif Husain of Mecca a state extending over most of the Arab provinces of the Ottoman Empire. Finally, the Balfour Declaration of 1917 stated that Britain favoured 'the establishment of a national home in Palestine for the Jewish people.' In 1920, the Treaty of Sèvres gave Smyrna (Izmir) and its hinterland to Greece (**11**) and created autonomous states in Armenia and Kurdistan, although the rise of the Turkish Republic meant that the Treaty was never ratified. Most of the present boundaries of the area were agreed at the Lausanne Conference (1923)

1 The disintegration of the Ottoman Empire, 1805-1923

approximate frontiers in 1800
Ottoman Empire in 1800
frontiers after First World War

areas of rule or control:
British
French
Spanish
Italian
Russian

Independent sheikdom under Al Bu Said family since 1741; British protectorate 1891-1971

Small sheikdoms under British protection 1820s-1971

Aden port annexed by Britain 1839; treaties of friendship and protection between Britain and local rulers 1886-1954

2 The Middle East in the First World War, 1914-18

Ottoman Empire in 1914
under British Empire in 1914
under Russian Empire in 1914
Turkish forces
Russian forces
French forces
Allied forces
Arab forces with Col. T. E. Lawrence
area of Arab revolt against Ottomans
Turkish lines at time of surrender, 30 Oct, 1918
railways

1914 British Protectorate

Modern Japan, 1868-1941

The Tokugawa shogunate, established in 1609 (page 50), gave Japan two hundred years of peace and prosperity. But a generation before 1868 it was evident that internal tensions were building up and that the *bakufu* (or Shogun's government) in Edo was losing control. Peasant unrest and discontent among impoverished *samurai*, whose position had been undermined by the growth of a money economy, was compounded by British, Russian, French and American pressure for the opening of Japan to foreign trade. A period of complicated manoeuvring ensued, in which the four western feudal domains (*han*), Satsuma, Choshu, Tosa and Hizen, took the lead (map 1). The outcome was the so-called Meiji restoration, when the emperor, supported by dissident elements, moved from Kyoto to Edo, now re-named Tokyo (or eastern capital), displaced the Shogun, and took direct control of government.

The Meiji restoration of 1868 was in reality a revolution, carried out with the definite aim of modernisation and westernisation. The old feudal structure was replaced in 1871 by a modern system of prefectures. Samurai privileges were abolished (1873), though samurai from Choshu had a leading place in the new conscript army. A western style peerage (1884), cabinet government (1885) and a two-chamber parliament (1889) laid the foundations of political stability; a national education system was instituted (1872) providing teaching for 90 per cent of children by 1900. At the same time economic development was taken in hand (map 2). The first railway was opened in 1872, and by 1906 the main network was completed. Industrialisation proceeded more slowly, beginning effectively only at the end of the 1800s. By 1889 the number of cotton mills had risen from 3 in 1877 to 83, and by 1913 Japanese production dominated the home market and had a substantial foothold abroad, particularly in China. Nevertheless agriculture remained the main employment until after the First World War. The number employed in agriculture fell from 70 per cent of the population in the 1870s to 57 per cent in 1914, but still provided almost all the foodstuffs for a population which rose from 39 million in 1868 to 56 million in 1918.

International recognition of Japan's new status was nevertheless slow in coming. It had been forced in the 1850s to negotiate unequal treaties with the western powers, and it was not until 1894 that foreign consular jurisdiction was abolished and only in 1911 that Tokyo regained tariff autonomy. These concessions were a tribute to Japan's military successes, seen above all in the war with China (1894–95) and in the Russo-Japanese war (map 4). The first overseas ventures, in the Bonin and Ryukyu islands and in Taiwan, were undertaken primarily to still unrest at home, but in 1894 Japan embarked on a full-scale imperialist policy (map 3). Even so, it was forced by the European powers to return all its conquests except Taiwan; but the Anglo-Japanese treaty of 1902, inspired by mutual fear of Russia, was a turning point. In the war with Russia (1904–05), Japan's forces achieved a series of victories culminating in the fall of Port Arthur (January 1905), the battle of Mukden (February–March) and the destruction of the Russian Baltic fleet in the Tsushima Straits (May). After the war the two combatants rapidly reached agreement over a division of spheres of interest, which allowed Japan to annex Korea in 1910. It had embarked on the creation of a Japanese empire on the Asian mainland, and the war of 1914–18 and the Russian revolution (page 120) enabled it to gain a foothold in Shantung and Manchuria. Although once again western pressure compelled it to withdraw, Japan was recognised at the Peace Conference in 1919 as a major power with a permanent seat on the Council of the League of Nations.

During the 1920s Japanese policy veered between cooperation with the west and an inherent anti-foreign feeling, fed by a sense of discrimination. Until 1932 cooperation prevailed, but the impact of the Great Depression (page 130) swung the balance in the opposite direction, and, beginning with the advance into Manchuria in 1931, Japan set out to carve out an empire in East Asia. After the Japanese attack on the Chinese mainland in 1937, tension grew with the United States. The lines of the Second World War were already being drawn. When Germany defeated France and Holland in 1940, Japan's moment seemed to have arrived, and the advance into South-East Asia began (map 5). In spite of astounding initial successes (page 134), it was a gamble that failed. But paradoxically the failure, and the subsequent American occupation, propelled Japan even more decisively into the modern world than the Meiji restoration, socially authoritarian and backward-looking, had done.

1 Japan in 1868

- provincial borders
- Five highways
- extensions to the Five Highways
- secondary roads
- sea-routes
- ◆ important castle towns
- *feudal territories:*
- major Tokugawa domains
- major anti-Bakufu domains
- American, Russian, British and other naval visits

2 Industrialisation and economic growth, c. 1880-1922

town population 1918:
- ○ less than 50,000
- ◉ 50,000-100,000
- ⊕ 100,000-500,000
- ⊠ 500,000-1 million
- ■ over 1 million

- ——— railways in 1906
- – – – additions to railways 1906-1918
- main manufacturing areas
- KYOTO prefecture

minerals:
- ● coal
- C copper
- ▲ iron
- ▮ oil

industry:
- ceramics
- chemicals
- food
- machinery
- manufacturing industry
- metal
- shipbuilding
- textiles
- wood
- silk

3 The growth of the Japanese empire, 1872-1918

RUSSIA

SAKHALIN

KARAFUTO 1905

KURILE IS. 1875

MANCHURIA

Hokkaido

Changchun

SOUTH MANCHURIA

Sea of Japan

Pacific

KWANTUNG (leased territory 1905)

KOREA CHOSEN 1910

Honshu

Ocean

SHANTUNG

Tsingtao

J A P A N

Shikoku

Kyushu

CHINA

BONIN (OGASAWARA) IS. 1873

RYUKYU (LOOCHOO) IS. 1872

FUKIEN

Amoy

TAIWAN (FORMOSA) 1895

Japan's possessions at the end of 1875

territorial acquisitions 1894-1914

spheres of Japanese influence in 1918

4 The Russo-Japanese War 1904-05

MANCHURIA

R. Liao

JEHOL

Harbin

Chinese Eastern Railway

South Manchurian Railway

Changchun

Kirin

KIRIN

CHIENTAO

Vladivostok

(occupied by Russia 1897-1905)

FENGTIEN

Fushun

Mukden

Mukden, Feb-March 1905

Anshan

Liaoyang

CHINA

Hulutao

Newchwang

Shanhaikuan

Antung

R. Yalu

R. Tumen

Takushan

Pyongyang

Chinnampo

Wonsan (Gensan)

Port Arthur

Dairen (Dalny)

fall of Port Arthur, Jan. 1905

Liaotung Peninsula

R. Han

Kaesong

Sea of Japan

Chefoo

Weihaiwei

Inchon (Chemulpo)

Seoul (Keijo)

SHANTUNG

Kiaochow

Tsingtao

KOREA

Yellow Sea

Masampo

Pusan (Fusan)

Mokpo

Japan destroys Russian fleet May 1905

Port Hamilton Is.

Shimonoseki

Quelpart I.

Tsushima Strait

Sasebo

JAPAN

movements of Japanese forces 1904-05

railways in 1918

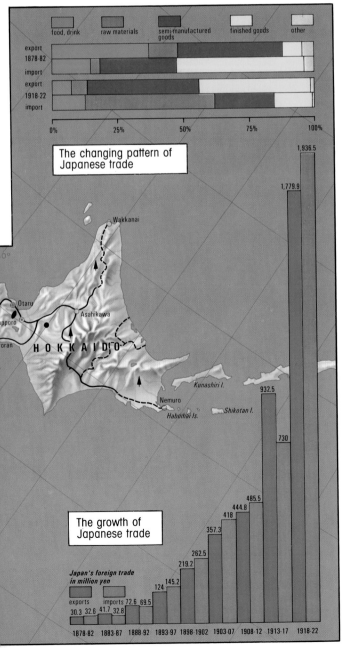

food, drink | raw materials | semi-manufactured goods | finished goods | other

export 1878-82
import
export 1918-22
import

0% 25% 50% 75% 100%

The changing pattern of Japanese trade

Wakkanai

Otaru

Asahikawa

HOKKAIDO

Kunashiri I.

Nemuro

Shikotan I.

Habomai Is.

The growth of Japanese trade

Japan's foreign trade in million yen

exports | imports

1,936.5

1,779.9

932.5

730

485.5

418 | 444.8

357.3

262.5

219.2

124 | 145.2

72.6 | 69.5

30.3 | 32.6 | 41.7 | 32.8

1878-82 | 1883-87 | 1888-92 | 1893-97 | 1898-1902 | 1903-07 | 1908-12 | 1913-17 | 1918-22

5 Japanese expansion, 1931-41

U S S R

Trans-Siberian railway

MANCHURIA

Manchukuo (Japanese Protectorate proclaimed 1933)

Nomonhan 1939

Japanese forces defeated by Red Army under Zhukov

MONGOLIA

Vladivostok

Changkufeng 1938

Mukden

Sea of Japan

KOREA

Russian support for China 1935

Yellow River (Huang Ho)

Peking (capital to 1911, from 1949)

Tientsin

Tokyo

J A P A N

C H I N A

1938

1932 1941

Yellow Sea

Nanking (capital 1912-37, 46-49)

Shanghai 1937

Ryukyu Is.

R. Yangtze

Nanchang

Chungking (capital 1937-46)

Amoy

Taiwan (Formosa)

INDIA

Swatow

7 Dec. 1941

Pacific Ocean

Burma Road

Canton 1938

Hong Kong

PHILIPPINE IS. (U.S.A.)

Mandalay

Hanoi 1940

Franco-Japanese agreement permitting occupation

Manila

BURMA

FRENCH INDO-CHINA

South China Sea

SIAM

under Japanese influence

Bangkok

1941

Saigon

Japan 1928

expansion to 1933

expansion to 1941

Chinese capitals

Japanese conflict with USSR

Japanese attacks

Japanese support for independence movements

Allied bases

European political problems, 1919-1939

The First World War shattered the equipoise of 1914. The long-term goal after 1918 was a return to 'normalcy', but it was always an illusion. Not merely had the collapse of the Habsburg Empire, the defeat of Germany and the Bolshevik Revolution completely altered the balance of power in Europe, but the pre-war economic equilibrium was also destroyed. All the victorious powers were in debt to the United States, and Great Britain, which had largely financed its allies, never fully recovered. These facts weighed heavily at the Paris Peace Conference in 1919, but the dominant fact was probably fear of the spread of revolution from Russia. This accounts for the relatively lenient treatment of Germany, which suffered only minor territorial losses, except for the restoration to the newly independent Poland of the lands seized in the partitions at the end of the eighteenth century. The real problem facing the peacemakers was the tangle of nationalities in Europe. Finland, Estonia, Latvia and Lithuania were detached as independent republics from Russia, which was not represented at the Conference, and Russia also lost Bessarabia to Romania and a large part of White Russia to Poland after the Russo-Polish war of 1920. However, the independent republics of White Russia, Georgia, Armenia and Azerbaijan were brought back into the Soviet Union in 1921 (map 1). The main beneficiary of the peace settlement was Romania, which, in addition to Bessarabia, acquired the Dobruja from Bulgaria and Transylvania from Hungary. But the projected dismemberment of Turkey was thwarted by the national revival under Mustapha Kemal Atatürk (page 124), and in 1923 the new republic was recognised by the Treaty of Lausanne.

The peace treaties left dissatisfied minorities everywhere, and there were widespread movements of refugees, the most extreme case being the wholesale exchange of populations negotiated after the Greco-Turkish war of 1920-22 (map 3). More important politically, they also created a lasting sense of injustice and discrimination. It was inconceivable that either Germany or Russia, once they recovered their strength, would accept a position of inferiority. In addition, there was the irredentism of Hungary, the country which had suffered most from the peace settlement, which was exploited, after 1927, by Mussolini's Fascist Italy, which hoped in this way to build up for itself a dominant position in the Danubian basin. Thus Europe was divided between revisionists and anti-revisionists, and the only hope for the latter was to support the status quo by a system of military pacts. France, with its alliances with Poland (1921) and Czechoslovakia (1924), underpinning the 'Little Entente' between Czechoslovakia, Yugoslavia and Romania (1921), was the heart and soul of the security system. It operated effectively until the Great Depression (page 130) and the instability it engendered in France, which undercut France's credibility among its East European clients. When Poland signed a Neutrality Pact with Germany in 1934, it marked the beginning of the collapse of the French security system.

The Locarno treaties (1925), whereby Germany recognised the post-war frontier settlements with France and Belgium, marked the end of the long years of frustration, civil disorder and conflict which had bedevilled Europe since 1918. Germany was welcomed back into the community of nations; so also, after 1925, was Soviet Russia. But the stabilisation of 1925-29 was more apparent than real. With the exception of Czechoslovakia, none of the new states of eastern Europe was economically viable, and the onset of the Depression exposed their weaknesses and left them a prey to German infiltration. When the slump in Germany threw up a mass nationalist movement headed by Adolf Hitler, who came to power in January 1933 (map 2),

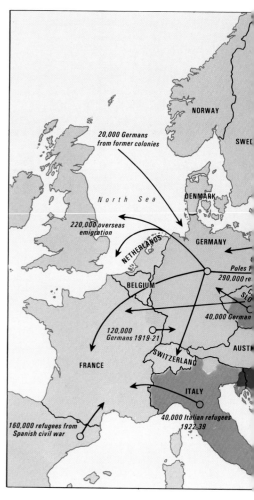

the post-war settlement came under a direct threat. Germany left the League and in 1936 remilitarised the Rhineland, destroying the Versailles and Locarno agreements. In 1936 civil war broke out in Spain, and Hitler and Mussolini both sent aid to the nationalist rebels of

Plebiscites and territorial disputes

1 plebiscite Feb. 1920: divided between Denmark and Germany

2 occupied by France, 1923-5

3 to Belgium 1919

4 to Belgium 1919

5 evacuated 1930, remilitarized 1936

6 League of Nations Mandate by plebiscite to Germany 1935

7 to France 1919

8 divided between Germany and Poland by plebiscite Mar. 1921

1 National conflicts and frontier disputes, 1919-36

—— German empire, 1914	—— British mandates	▢ new states
—— Austro-Hungarian empire, 1914	—— French mandates	▢ areas of dispute
—— Russian empire, 1914	▲ plebiscites held	▢ areas temporarily autonomous or independent
—— post-settlement frontiers		▢ areas under armed occupation
		▢ areas under League of Nations High Commissioners
		★ political disturbances

3 The refugee problem

- Germans
- Poles
- Czechs
- Slovaks
- Hungarians
- White Russians
- Ukrainians/Ruthenians
- Romanians
- Bulgarians
- Turks
- Albanians
- Macedonians
- Greeks
- Serbs/Montenegrins
- Bosnians
- Slovenes
- Croats
- Italians

1917-22 100,000, Russian refugees from Bolshevik Revolution

200,000, Latvians, Estonians, Lithuanians

Germans 1919-23

1,000,000 Poles

90,000 Germans

650,000 Russian refugees from Bolshevik Revolution

60,000 Greeks

200,000 Hungarians 1919-24

80,000 Turks 1913-39

50,000 Bulgarians

110,000 Turks 1913-39

350,000 Armenians 1914-23 to Europe

10,000 Bulgarians

300,000 Greeks

1,000,000 Greeks 1922-24

350,000 Turks

FINLAND · ESTONIA · LATVIA · LITHUANIA · POLAND · RUSSIA · UKRAINE · ROMANIA · Black Sea · BULGARIA · GREECE · YUGOSLAVIA

4 The Spanish Civil War, 1936-39

- Nationalist supply route
- Republican supply route
- 'International Brigade' operations
- main Nationalist attacks
- main Republican attacks
- Nationalist July 1936
- Nationalist October 1937
- Nationalist July 1938
- Nationalist Feb. 1939
- Republican Feb. 1939

FRANCE · PORTUGAL · ALGERIA · SPANISH MOROCCO · Mediterranean Sea

El Ferrol · Gijón · Santander · Guernica · La Coruña · Santiago de Compostela · Oviedo · Bilbao · San Sebastián · León · Burgos · R. Ebro · Zaragoza · Barcelona · Oporto · Valladolid · Belchete · Tarragona · *from Odessa* · Salamanca · Guadarramas · Guadalajara · Teruel · Minorca · Mahón · Madrid · Jarama · Castellón de la Plana · Palma · Majorca · Cáceres · Brunete · Toledo · Valencia · Ibiza · Formentera · Badajoz · Mérida · Albacete (International Brigade base) · Alicante · Lopera · Córdoba · *from Genoa* · Huelva · Seville · Granada · Almería · Cartagena · Cádiz · Málaga · Tangier · *from Hamburg*

General Franco. Spain had become bitterly divided between right and left following the establishment of a radical republican regime in 1931. The civil war was won by Franco after three years of savage fighting (map 4); the conflict sharpened European divisions between fascists, communists and democrats. Britain and France began to rearm in 1936, but war was unpopular at home. They sought to negotiate the crisis away. But Hitler's annexation of Austria in March 1938, and the threat to Czechoslovakia that followed, undermined European security. At Munich in September 1938 the West agreed to German occupation of the Czech Sudetenland. In March 1939 Hitler seized the rest of Czechoslovakia by force. In April Mussolini occupied Albania, and Hitler decided on war with Poland. The fragile balance of power gave way. Britain and France agreed in March 1939 to go to war if Hitler threatened European security again.

...ied occupation 1920-3, ...nexed by Lithuania 1923, ...onomous 1924, ...Germany 1939

...Germany July 1920

...Poland Dec. 1918

...artitioned between ...echoslovakia and Poland 1920

...Hungary 1921

...Austria 1920

...nexed by Poland 1920, ...Poland by plebiscite 1922

...Greece from Bulgaria 1919

...emilitarized 1924, remilitarized ...36

...eek-Bulgarian conflict, 1925

Caspian Sea · ...IJAN ...endent ...18-20 · Kurds 1919, 1922-7, 1931-2, 1935-6 · PERSIA · Baghdad 1936 · 1920, 1935 · Euphrates

2 Electoral performance of the Nazi Party in Sep. 1930 and Mar. 1933

Nazi % share of vote
- 50-59
- 40-49
- 30-39
- 20-29
- 10-19
- 0-9

1930 — Kiel · Rostock · Hamburg · Bremen · Hanover · Berlin · Stettin · Königsberg · Kassel · Cologne · Leipzig · Dresden · Breslau · Nuremberg · Stuttgart · Munich · GERMANY

1933 — Kiel · Rostock · Hamburg · Bremen · Hanover · Berlin · Stettin · Königsberg · Kassel · Cologne · Leipzig · Dresden · Breslau · Nuremberg · Stuttgart · Munich · GERMANY

5 German and Italian expansion, 1935-39

1. Czech territory given to Germany by Munich agreement Sept. 1938
2. Czech territory given to Hungary Nov. 1938
3. occupied by Hungary March 1939
4. Czech territory taken by Poland Sept. 1939
5. annexed by Germany 1938
6. plebiscite to join Germany 1935
7. Italian expansion
8. annexation of Memel March 1939

North Sea · Baltic Sea · Memel · LITHUANIA · NETHERLANDS · Danzig · R. Elbe · Berlin · R. Vistula · Warsaw · USSR · (reoccupied by Germany 1936) · Rhineland · GERMANY · R. Oder · POLAND · FRANCE · Saar · R. Rhine · Prague · CZECHOSLOVAKIA · Teschen · Munich · Vienna · Ruthenia · SWITZERLAND · AUSTRIA · Budapest · HUNGARY · ROMANIA · ITALY · YUGOSLAVIA · R. Danube · Adriatic Sea · Corsica · Rome · Sardinia · ALBANIA (annexed by Italy 1939) · Mediterranean Sea · Sicily

ERITREA · Addis Ababa · ETHIOPIA (conquered by Italy 1935-36) · ITALIAN SOMALILAND · KENYA · Mogadishu · Indian Ocean

→ Italian campaigns 1935-36

The Great Depression
1929-1939

After 1925 it appeared that the disorders of the post-war world had been overcome and a period of relative stability and prosperity had begun. The Great Depression quickly dispelled this illusion. Conventionally its starting point was the financial crash on Wall Street in October 1929; but this was only the manifestation of deeper weaknesses in the world economy. In the United States business was in trouble long before the crash. Worldwide, commodity prices had been falling since 1926, impairing the capacity of exporters such as Australia to buy products from Europe and the United States. The German economy also was faltering by 1928. However, more important than the causes of the depression were its consequences. These were almost instantaneous, although it was only after 1930 that dislocation reached its peak. Its most arresting manifestation was unemployment which reached record heights in 1932. In many industrial countries over a quarter of the labour force was thrown out of work. Industrial production fell to 53 per cent of its 1929 level in Germany and the United States, and world trade sank to 35 per cent of its 1929 value. Attempts to solve the problem only made things worse. As early as 1930 the United States imposed the Hawley-Smoot Tariff, the highest in its history. The United Kingdom responded in 1932 by negotiating the Ottawa Agreements, a series of preferential tariffs for the Commonwealth. Another expedient was competitive devaluation. After England left the Gold Standard in 1931, country after country followed suit and the result was the development of closed currency blocs (map 1), which inhibited international trade still further.

Economic nationalism fostered political nationalism, just as unemployment and the erosion of middle-class living standards fostered political extremism. The fall of the Hamaguchi government in Japan in 1931 marked the end of constitutional democracy and the beginning of Japanese aggression in Manchuria (page 126). In Germany, Brüning's deflationary policies, raising unemployment from under 3 million in 1930 to 6 million two years later, paved the way for Hitler. Hitler's accession to power in January 1933 was followed by Dollfuss's dictatorship in Austria, and eastern Europe, with the exception of Czechoslovakia, quickly followed suit (map 3). France remained precariously democratic until 1940, and in the United Kingdom, where a right-wing 'national' government won a huge majority in 1931, Mosley's fascist movement made little headway. But even here and in the United States, where F. D. Roosevelt was elected president in 1932 with a promise of a 'New Deal', fascist movements exercised considerable pressure (map 2). Only the Soviet Union, isolated from the world economy, was able to sustain economic growth (map 1) – a fact which was to be of cardinal importance after 1941. Roosevelt's New Deal made initial progress, but faltered after 1936 when a new phase of economic down-turn began. By 1939 the United States had not regained the level of industrial output of 1929, and only the Second World War, and the boost it gave to production pulled it out of depression.

The effects of the depression also hit the primary producing countries of Asia, Africa and Latin America. Here, as the crisis radicalised peasants and workers, nationalist and revolutionary movements gained new bases of support. In this respect, as in many others, the Great Depression was the catalyst of the modern world.

1 The world economy, 1929-39

major currency blocs:
- gold bloc
- yen bloc
- German-dominated exchange control area
- dollar area
- sterling area
- areas of shifting or dubious allegiance due to German-American rivalry

- areas of loose currency bloc allegiance

production indices:
- 1929 = 100
- 1930
- 1932
- 1934
- 1936
- 1938

3 Social unrest and political movements in Europe

political regimes:
- fascist
- repressive or conservative
- democratic

23.2 percentage of industrial workers unemployed 1932

major movements of protest and dissatisfaction:
- ◆ strike wave
- ▲ sitdown strike
- ■ riot, demonstration, or single strike
- ● right-wing activity

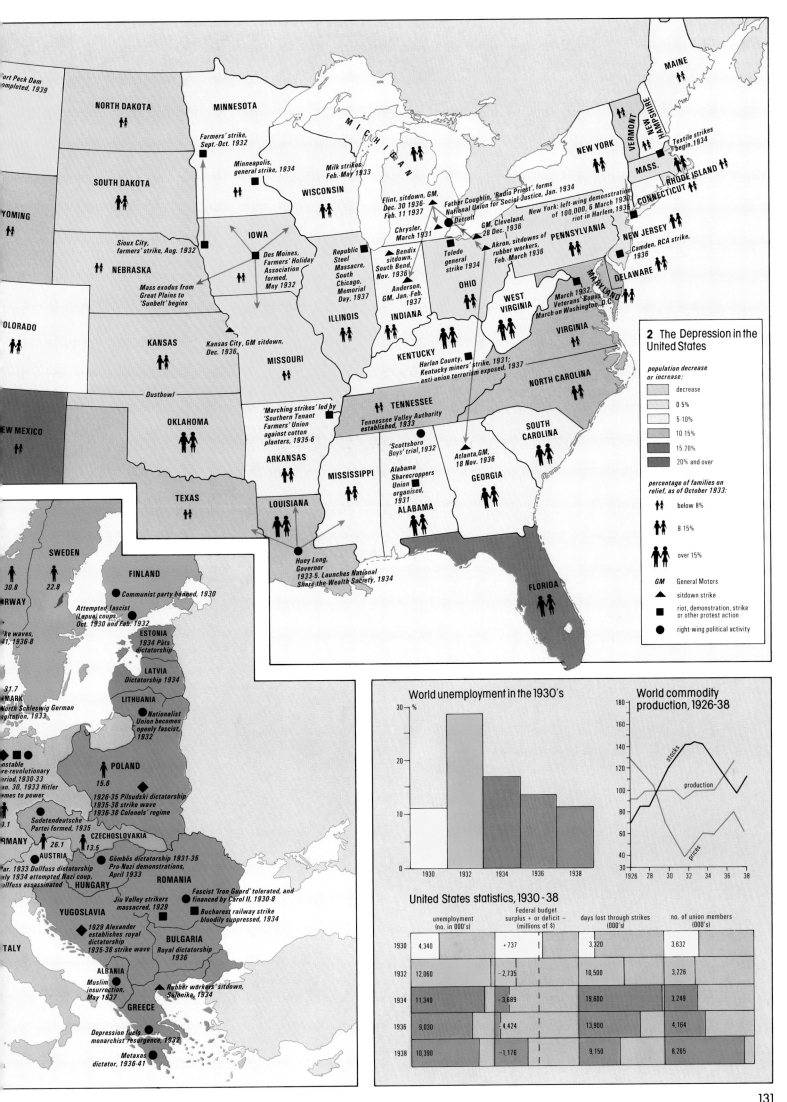

Fort Peck Dam completed, 1939

NORTH DAKOTA

MINNESOTA

MAINE

VERMONT

NEW HAMPSHIRE

Farmers' strike, Sept.-Oct. 1932

Minneapolis, general strike, 1934

Milk strikes Feb.-May 1933

NEW YORK

Textile strikes begin, 1934

SOUTH DAKOTA

WISCONSIN

MASS.

RHODE ISLAND

WYOMING

MICHIGAN

CONNECTICUT

Flint, sitdown, GM, Dec. 30 1936- Feb. 11 1937

Father Coughlin, 'Radio Priest', forms National Union for Social Justice, Jan. 1934

New York: left-wing demonstration of 100,000, 6 March 1930; riot in Harlem, 1935

IOWA

Chrysler, March 1931

Detroit

GM, Cleveland, 28 Dec. 1936

PENNSYLVANIA

NEW JERSEY

Sioux City, farmers' strike, Aug. 1932

Akron, sitdowns of rubber workers, Feb.-March 1936

Camden, RCA strike, 1936

NEBRASKA

Des Moines, Farmers' Holiday Association formed, May 1932

Republic Steel Massacre, South Chicago, Memorial Day, 1937

Bendix sitdown, South Bend, Nov. 1936

Toledo general strike 1934

DELAWARE

Mass exodus from Great Plains to 'Sunbelt' begins

Anderson, GM, Jan.-Feb. 1937

OHIO

WEST VIRGINIA

MARYLAND

March 1932, Veterans' Bonus March on Washington, D.C.

COLORADO

ILLINOIS

INDIANA

VIRGINIA

KANSAS

Kansas City, GM sitdown, Dec. 1936

KENTUCKY

Harlan County, Kentucky miners' strike, 1931; anti-union terrorism exposed, 1937

NORTH CAROLINA

MISSOURI

Dustbowl

NEW MEXICO

OKLAHOMA

'Marching strikes' led by 'Southern Tenant Farmers' Union against cotton planters, 1935-6

TENNESSEE

Tennessee Valley Authority established, 1933

SOUTH CAROLINA

ARKANSAS

'Scottsboro Boys' trial, 1932

Atlanta, GM, 18 Nov. 1936

TEXAS

MISSISSIPPI

Alabama Sharecroppers Union organised, 1931

GEORGIA

LOUISIANA

ALABAMA

Huey Long, Governor 1933-5. Launches National Share-the-Wealth Society, 1934

FLORIDA

2 The Depression in the United States

population decrease or increase:

	decrease
	0-5%
	5-10%
	10-15%
	15-20%
	20% and over

percentage of families on relief, as of October 1933:

below 8%

8-15%

over 15%

GM General Motors

▲ sitdown strike

■ riot, demonstration, strike or other protest action

● right-wing political activity

SWEDEN

FINLAND

30.8

22.8

Communist party banned, 1930

NORWAY

Attempted fascist (Lapua) coups, Oct. 1930 and Feb. 1932

ESTONIA

1934 Päts dictatorship

31.7

ke waves, 1, 1936-8

LATVIA

Dictatorship 1934

DENMARK

North Schleswig German agitation, 1933

LITHUANIA

Nationalist Union becomes openly fascist, 1932

nstable re-revolutionary period, 1930-33 an. 30, 1933 Hitler comes to power

POLAND

15.6

1926-35 Pilsudski dictatorship 1935-38 strike wave 1936-38 Colonels' regime

Sudetendeutsche Partei formed, 1935

GERMANY

26.1

CZECHOSLOVAKIA

13.5

AUSTRIA

ar. 1933 Dollfuss dictatorship ly 1934 attempted Nazi coup, ollfuss assassinated

Gömbös dictatorship 1931-35 Pro-Nazi demonstrations, April 1933

ROMANIA

Fascist 'Iron Guard' tolerated, and financed by Carol II, 1930-8

HUNGARY

Jiu Valley strikers massacred, 1929

Bucharest railway strike bloodily suppressed, 1934

YUGOSLAVIA

1929 Alexander establishes royal dictatorship 1935-38 strike wave

BULGARIA

Royal dictatorship 1936

ITALY

ALBANIA

Muslim insurrection, May 1937

Rubber workers' sitdown, Salonika, 1934

GREECE

Depression fuels monarchist resurgence, 1932

Metaxas dictator, 1936-41

World unemployment in the 1930's

	1930	1932	1934	1936	1938

World commodity production, 1926-38

stocks

production

prices

1926 28 30 32 34 36 38

United States statistics, 1930-38

	unemployment (no. in 000's)	Federal budget surplus + or deficit − (millions of $)	days lost through strikes (000's)	no. of union members (000's)
1930	4,340	+ 737	3,320	3,632
1932	12,060	− 2,735	10,500	3,226
1934	11,340	− 3,689	19,600	3,249
1936	9,030	− 4,424	13,900	4,164
1938	10,390	− 1,176	9,150	8,265

131

The War in the West
1939-1945

Hitler's accession to power in 1933 added a new dimension to international politics. He was held back at first by Germany's diplomatic isolation and by the need to put the shattered economy back on its feet. But by 1936 this phase was over. The re-occupation of the Rhineland, the denunciation of the Locarno treaties (page 128), the Rome-Berlin axis, and the anti-Comintern Pact with Japan, demonstrated the new thrust of German policy. Nevertheless Hitler hoped to get his way by threats and bluster rather than by war, and the unopposed annexation of Austria and the dismemberment of Czechoslovakia in 1938 seemed to prove him right. When in the following year he turned against Poland he expected that England and France would once again give way, and believed that the notorious Nazi-Soviet pact of August 23, 1939, would deter the Western powers from intervention. But this time Hitler miscalculated. When German

troops invaded Poland (September 1, 1939), England and France declared war, though they did nothing to aid the Poles.

For the first three years the German armies, with their *Blitzkrieg* strategy, were extraordinarily successful (map 1). After the fall of Poland Hitler halted, hoping that the Western powers would negotiate a compromise peace. Then, in April 1940, he launched his attack in the west, overran Denmark and Norway, and turned against France, which was knocked out of the war before the end of June. But the new Churchill government in London refused to concede defeat, and Hitler launched a major air offensive, intended to prepare the way for invasion. The victory of the Royal Air Force in the Battle of Britain forced him on September 17, 1940, to call off the projected invasion. Instead, Hitler decided to attack Soviet Russia. The directive for 'Operation Barbarossa' was issued in December 1940, the invasion of Russia launched on June 22, 1941. It nearly succeeded. Before the tide turned, German armies were outside Moscow and Leningrad and had overrun southern Russia to the

Black Sea and the Caucasus.

Meanwhile two other events intervened. One was the lack of success of Italy, which had entered the war in 1940, which forced Hitler, in 1941, to divert troops to conquer Yugoslavia and Greece and to reinforce the African front. Secondly the United States, entering the war in 1941 (page 134), supplied Britain and Russia with much needed arms and equipment, and also helped to defeat the German submarine campaign in the Atlantic (map 3). The British victory at El Alamein (October 1942), the subsequent capitulation of the Italian and German armies in Africa (May 1943), the Anglo-American invasion of Sicily and then Italy, and the fall of Mussolini (July 1943), were major Allied successes. But it was the great Russian victory at Stalingrad (January 1943) that was decisive. The Germans' last major offensive in the east at Kursk failed in July 1943. Thereafter they fought a stubborn defensive war (map 2), but after the Anglo-American landings in northern France (June 1944) and the opening of the Second Front, the ring was closed.

and the bases were lost for the 'secret weapons' which Hitler hoped would force the British to capitulate. The Ardennes offensive (December 1944) was a final attempt to break out in the west; but by now the Allies held the initiative. A major Soviet offensive against East Prussia opened in January 1945, and by April Berlin was under assault. On April 30 Hitler committed suicide, and on May 7 his successor, Admiral Doenitz, surrendered unconditionally. The costs were appalling: 15 million military and 35 million civilians had perished, 20 million of whom were Soviet citizens. Some 6 million Jews were exterminated in concentration camps or otherwise. Anglo-American saturation bombing reduced many German cities to rubble, and 25 million Russians were left homeless. Europe was in ruins, and already the differences between the victorious powers, which were to darken the post-war years (page 136), were visible.

1 The German advance, 1939-43

- Axis territory 1 September 1939
- Axis satellites
- Axis occupied
- ← German advances 1939 41
- ← Italian advances
- ← Axis attack on USSR 1941
- ← Axis advances in USSR 1942
- ← Allied forces
- cities severely damaged by bombing
- ⌐ airborne landings
- ←-- Allied withdrawals
- Soviet occupied territory 1939-40
- British Empire
- neutral powers

principal German concentration and extermination camps: ●

1	Auschwitz-Birkenau	7	Flossenbürg	14	Ravensbrück
2	Belzec	8	Gross Rosen	15	Sachsenhausen
3	Bergen-Belsen	9	Majdanek	16	Sobibor
4	Buchenwald	10	Mauthausen	17	Stutthof
5	Chelmno	11	Mittelbau	18	Theresienstadt
6	Dachau	12	Natzweiler	19	Treblinka
		13	Neuengamme		

3 The battle of the Atlantic, 1941-45

Allied shipping sunk by U Boats:
- · 3 Sept. 1939 – 6 Dec. 1941
- · 7 Dec. 1941 – 18 Sept. 1943
- ● 19 Sept. 1943 – 8 May 1945

Allied shore-based air cover by 1941
Allied shore-based air cover by 1945

2 The defeat of Germany, 1943-45

⬛ 'Grossdeutsches Reich' 1942

← Axis attacks

◄-- Axis withdrawal

✊ cities under heavy air attack

➡ Allied attacks

★ major battles with date

● commando raids

⚲ airborne landings

✊ partisan/resistance movements

↘ V1 launching sites

↘ V2 launching sites

NORWAY
1940-44

SWEDEN

Oslo

Stockholm

FINLAND

Petsamo
1944
1944

Murmansk
1944

1944

1944

1944

Helsinki

Lake Ladoga
1944

Vyborg

Narva
1944

Leningrad

Novgorod
1941-42

Dec. 1941 ★ Moscow

USSR

ESTONIA

LATVIA
Riga

Velikiye Luki

Rzhev

LITHUANIA
Kaunas

Vyazma
1942-43

Tula

DENMARK
Copenhagen
1940-44

Flensburg

Baltic Sea

E. PRUSSIA
Feb.-April 1945
Königsberg

Bialystok

Minsk
1944

Mogilev

Bryansk
1941-42

Orel

Lubeck

Hamburg

Stettin

Hanover

Bremen

Berlin
May 1945

Torgau

Dresden

May 1945

Prague

POLAND

Warsaw
1944-45
1941-44

R. Vistula

R. Bug

June-Aug. 1944 ★

Gomel

1943-44

June-Aug. 1943 ★ Kursk

Karkhov

Voronezh

R. Don

Stalingrad
★ *Nov. 1942-Feb 1943*

R. Volga

Astrakhan

1940-44

HOLLAND
Arnhem
Sept. 1944

Brussels

Dusseldorf
Cologne
Dec. 1944

Frankfurt

Metz

Mannheim

Stuttgart

R. Rhine

Munich

GERMANY

R. Oder

Lemberg

Tarnopol

SLOVAKIA
1944

Vienna
April 1945

AUSTRIA

Alps

SWITZERLAND

Milan

Trieste

R. Po

Genoa

1943-45

1944-45

Livorno

Florence

Rimini

Zara

Corsica

Sardinia

ITALY

taken June 1944
Rome

Anzio
Jan.-March 1944

Cassino
Jan.-March 1944

Naples

Salerno

Bari

Taranto

Messina

Sicily

Pantelleria

Malta

Mediterranean Sea

Crete
1941-45

HUNGARY
Budapest
1944-45

Debrecen

1945

Zagreb
1945

CROATIA

Sarajevo
1941-44

SERBIA
1941-44

MONTE-NEGRO

Belgrade

Kotor

ROMANIA

Ploesti

Bucharest

R. Danube

Transnistria

R. Prut
R. Dniester
R. Mss

Jassy

Odessa

BULGARIA

Sofia
1944

ALBANIA

GREECE
1941-44

Salonika

Athens

Istanbul

Ankara

UKRAINE

R. Dnieper

Kiev
Sept.-Oct. 1943 ★
1942-43

Krivoy Rog

Stalino

Kerch

Crimea

Sebastopol

Black Sea

Rostov

1942-43

1942-43

1942-43 ✊

Caspian Sea

Ordzhonikidze

Caucasus Mts.

Batum

TURKEY

Rhodes

Cyprus

SYRIA

IRAQ

IRAN

LEBANON

PALESTINE

TRANSJORDAN

SAUDI ARABIA

North Sea

Tunis
Bizerta
il-May 1943 ★

Feb.-May 1943

TUNISIA

Tripoli

LIBYA

Benghazi

El Agheila

Cyrenaica

Tobruk

Bardia

Jan.-June 1942

British offensive 23 Oct. 1942

Oct.-Nov. 1942 ★

El Alamein

Alexandria

Cairo

EGYPT

133

The War in Asia and the Pacific
1941-1945

Japanese expansionism in the 1930s was the product of a desire to achieve economic self-sufficiency, military security and a self-imposed leadership of eastern Asia (page 126). Japan after September 1931 overran Manchuria and then set about the reduction of its neighbouring provinces by overrunning much of China north of the Yangtze and sponsoring puppet regimes in its area of conquest. By 1941, Japan, with no possibility of militarily or politically ending the Chinese war, found its ambitions widening to include the European colonial empires in South-East Asia. These offered the raw materials and markets that would free Japan from an economic dependence upon an increasingly unfriendly United States. The latter's re-armament programmes were scheduled to near completion by 1944–1945; the prospect of future naval inferiority and the economic blockade imposed upon Japan after its occupation of Indo-China in 1940 prompted Japanese action. The attack upon the US Pacific Fleet at Pearl Harbor in December 1940 was an attempt to forestall American military preparation and thereby buy the time needed to secure and develop South-East Asia.

In challenging the United States Japan sought to fight the world's greatest industrialised power to a stalemate that would result in a negotiated peace which would recognise Japanese hegemony in eastern Asia. Within six months of the start of the Pacific war Japanese forces had conquered American, British and Dutch possessions throughout South-East Asia and had carried the war to the borders of India, to the waters that washed Australia and into the south-west Pacific (map 1). Yet in those months Japan failed to inflict a naval defeat sufficient to impair US military capacity and morale: indeed, in attempting to do so the Imperial Navy suffered a reverse in the Coral Sea in May 1942, the devastation of its front-line carrier force off Midway in June and crippling losses in the protracted Guadalcanal campaign of August 1942-February 1943. Thereafter, without the means to end the war that it had initiated, Japanese strategic mobility was rapidly eroded as the Imperial forces became obliged to fight defensively on widely separated fronts against a number of enemies (map 2). The United States no less slowly grew into a force that was able to sustain four major efforts: a devastatingly successful campaign against Japanese naval and merchant shipping; an 'island-hopping' strategy with amphibious forces that bypassed the major centres of Japanese resistance; an ultimately overwhelming carrier offensive that was to carry the war to the Japanese Home Islands; and a strategic air offensive, based upon the

Marianas, that was to shatter Japanese urban areas in the last six months of the war (map 3). By August 1945, when the US atomic bomb attacks upon Hiroshima and Nagasaki and the Soviet offensive in Manchuria enforced their surrender, the Japanese had been utterly exhausted and defeated. However, the brief Japanese colonial adventure had unleashed forces of revolutionary nationalism that were to shape events throughout eastern and South-East Asia over the next three decades.

3 The bombardment of Japan, 1945

area of industrial concentration
the 'Big Six' fire-raid targets
secondary fire-raid target
mine-laying target
naval bombardment
atomic bomb target

KOREA
Sea of Japan
Hokkaido
Shimonoseki Strait
East China Sea
Nagasaki 9 Aug.
Hiroshima 6 Aug.
Kyushu
Kobe
Shikoku
Osaka
Nagoya
Honshu
Linshoten Strait
Kawasaki
Yokohama
Tokyo
Pacific Ocean

SOVIET UNION
Sea of Okhotsk
Kamchatka
Komandorski Is.
Bering Sea
60
Soviet army attacks (9 Aug 1945)
Khabarovsk
Sakhalin
17 Aug 1945
Aleutian Is.
Attu Krska Amchitka
May-Aug 1943
MANCHURIA (MANCHUKUO)
10 Oct 1943
Japanese perimeter Oct 1944
Japanese perimeter March 1944
INNER MONGOLIA
Hokkaido
Kurile Is.
40
Peking
Dairen
Sea of Japan
JAPAN
ian Forces
se advance into Burma
Oct 1943
se offensive into NE India
ne 1944
offensive into Burma
ov 1944
e offensive in Yunnan
44-March 1945
n taken May 1945
CHINA
Tientsin
Seoul
KOREA
Pusan
East China Sea
Hiroshima 6 Aug 1945
Tokyo
Nagasaki 9 Aug 1945
Shikoku
Kyushu
Nanking
Shanghai
bombing attacks from 15 June 1944
Fighters cover and sweep over Japan from May 1945
Kunming
1944 Japanese Ichi-go Offensive
Chinese counter-offensive April-June 1945
Amoy
Okinawa
Direct air attack on Japan from Okinawa April to Aug 1945
Volcano Is.
Bonin Is.
Midway
Hawaiian Is.
Laokai
Hanoi
Formosa
Iwo Jima Feb-March 1945
20th Air Force maintains direct air attack on Japan from 24 Nov 1944-14 Aug 1945
Oahu-Pearl Harbor
20
Gulf of Hainan Tongking
Mandalay
SIAM
angoon
FRENCH INDO-CHINA
Hong Kong
Canton
Luzon landings Jan 1945
Manila
Philippine Is.
Battle of Philippine Sea. Japanese carrier aviation annihilated June 1944
Marianas
Saipan June 1944
Tinian
Pacific Ocean Area Forces
Bangkok
25 Oct 1944
Battle of Leyte Gulf. Heavy Japanese naval losses
Leyte
Guam July 1944
Eniwetok Feb 1944
Marshall Is.
Pnom Penh
Saigon
Mindoro Dec 1945
Leyte landing 20 Oct 1944
23/29 Oct 1944 Major defeat
Ulithi Sept 1944
Caroline Is.
Kwajalein Feb 1944
Majuro Jan 1944
Gulf of Siam
South China Sea
Mindanao May 1945
Zamboanga
Palau Sept 1944
Truk
Main fleet base of central Pacific. In effect abandoned by Japanese 1944
Christmas Is.
MALAY STATES
BRUNEI June 1945
Sulu Sea
Makin
Gilbert Is.
Kuala Lumpur
SARAWAK
Tarakan May 1945
Borneo
Morotai Sept 1944
Halmahera
Tarawa Nov 1943
Abemama
0
Singapore
Balikpapan July 1945
Sansapur July 1944
Sorong
Noemfoor July 1944
Biak May 1944
Hollandia
Manus Feb 1944
Admiralty Is.
Bismarck Arch.
Rabaul New Ireland
Green Is.
Ellice Is.
Sumatra
Dutch East Indies
Bandjarmasin
Celebes
Ceram
Amboina
Macassar
New Guinea
Wewak
New Britain
Bougainville Nov 1943
Russell Is.
Eastern Solomons
Palembang
Batavia
Java
Surabaya
Flores
Tanimbar Is.
Saidor Jan 1944
Buna
Solomon Is.
Tulagi
25/26 Oct 1942 Japanese forces repulsed
Battle of Santa Cruz Aug 1942
Guadalcanal some 50 actions 7 Aug 1942-9 Feb 1943
Java Sea
Sumba
Timor
Port Moresby
South Pacific Area Forces
Japanese perimeter Aug 1945
Timor Sea
Cape York
Darwin
17/25 Sept 1942 Japanese ground forces repulsed
Espiritu Santo
New Hebrides
Fiji Is.
20
2 The Allied counter-offensive
Allied advance
Allied air attack
Allied base
Japanese base
Japanese base bypassed or neutralised
atomic bomb target
battle
South-west Pacific Area Forces
Queensland
Coral Sea
New Caledonia
AUSTRALIA
Sydney
Melbourne

90 110 130 150 170 190

Europe after 1945

Europe emerged from the war of 1939-45 devastated and politically divided. Major territorial changes in the East, where Soviet frontiers were advanced approximately to the former Tsarist boundary and Poland was compensated with German territory up to the Oder-Neisse line, were accompanied by a vast movement of displaced persons, including over 12 million Germans (map 1). Germany and Austria were divided into occupation zones and placed under four-power control. But growing Soviet-American conflict after the abortive Potsdam conference (July-August 1945) undermined four-power cooperation, and the consolidation of the Soviet hold in eastern Europe accelerated the division of the continent into two armed camps, completed by the establishment of the North Atlantic Treaty Organisation (1949) and the Warsaw Pact Organisation (1955). In 1949 the three western zones of Germany became the German Federal Republic, while Moscow established the German Democratic Republic in the east.

Economic recovery in the West was stimulated by American aid under the Marshall Plan (1947), and after 1950 western Europe experienced an unprecedented economic boom. Simultaneously, the process of economic integration was initiated, which led in 1957 to the creation of the European Economic Community (EEC), though at first Great Britain remained outside, founding a rival organisation, EFTA (European Free Trade Association), and only joining the EEC with Denmark and Ireland in 1973 (map 4). In eastern Europe economic growth was slower but continuous, thanks to Stalinist methods of industrial and agricultural development. Harsh conditions led to widespread strikes and demonstrations in eastern Germany in 1953 and to national uprisings in Poland and Hungary in 1956, the latter, like the experiment in national communism in Czechoslovakia in 1968, brutally suppressed by Soviet troops. Nevertheless, after 1957 there was considerable

economic progress. East Germany and Romania forged ahead. Elsewhere, progress was sluggish and uneven, notably in Poland, where the formation, in 1979, of an active trade union movement, Solidarity, resulted in the imposition of martial law by 1981.

Steady economic growth helped to stabilise Europe politically. Parliamentary democracy flourished in most of western Europe. In 1954 West Germany was integrated into the western bloc, becoming a member of NATO. Austrian sovereignty was restored a year later. By the 1970s links between eastern and western Europe were much improved. At the European Security Conference in Helsinki in 1975 the post-war settlement of Germany and Poland was formally recognised, and a period of *détente* inaugurated. In the 1970s democracy finally triumphed in Spain, Portugal and Greece, paving the way for their eventual entry into the Common Market. During the 1980s ties between EEC members grew closer. In 1985 it was agreed that by 1992 a single market would be created for goods and services throughout the

Community. In 1991 at the Dutch city of Maastricht it was further agreed that the Community would work towards full monetary union and a pooling of foreign and defence policies, paving the way for far-reaching plans for political union.

While western Europe drew closer together, the eastern bloc rapidly disintegrated (map 2). Popular protest against economic stagnation and political repression, encouraged by the reform programme of Soviet leader Gorbachev, gathered momentum throughout eastern Europe. In 1989 one Communist regime after another crumbled, to be replaced by freely elected multi-party parliaments. East Germany was reunited with West Germany in October 1990. The following year, the Soviet Union collapsed as its western regions voted for independence, with the Baltic States, the Ukraine and Belarus all gaining independence that year. The remaining republics, plus the Ukraine and Belarus, agreed in December 1991 to establish a loose Confederation of Independent States (CIS). New links were forged between

1 Territorial change and population movements, 1945-49

- ～～～ border of Germany in 1937
- Allied control zones of Germany and Austria
- ◼◼ cities divided into four occupation zones
- annexed by Russia 1940–45
- states which became Communist 1945-48
- Yugoslav gains from Italy in 1945

peoples resettled, evacuated or expelled (with numbers):
- ◆▶ Germans
- Baltic peoples
- Finns driven from area bordering Russia
- Soviet nationals
- Russians forcibly repatriated
- Poles
- Czechs
- peoples settled by International Refugee Organisation

western and eastern Europe as the continent once again became a single entity.

The collapse of communism brought both political freedom and political instability. In some states the communists kept a grip on power by adopting democratic disguise. In others, including Russia, there developed a growing polarisation on ethnic, religious or ideological lines. Yugoslavia was the worst affected. Democracy brought the fragmentation of the federation. In 1991 Croatia and Slovenia won their independence. From 1992 to 1995 a brutal civil war, echoing the worst excesses of the Second World War, was fought between Bosnian Muslims, Serbs and Croats (map 3). A fragile peace was signed in November 1995, dividing Bosnia into separate states. Serbia was then plunged into political crisis as efforts were made to impose a virtual dictatorship.

In the European Community, which in 1993 became the wider European Union following the implementation of the Maastricht Treaty (1991), political nationalism became a significant voice again. Quasi-fascist parties in France, Austria and Italy broke the welfare-capitalist consensus of right and left that had dominated west European politics since the 1940s. Economic development was uneven, undermining efforts at monetary union. In 1992 the Exchange Rate Mechanism almost collapsed with the withdrawal of Britain and Italy. The aim of complete monetary integration and a single currency by 1999 forced several countries into harsh austerity programmes. The new Europe represents a profound paradox: on the one hand a general movement towards greater collaboration; on the other mounting evidence of extreme nationalism and political confrontation.

4 European economic blocs, 1947-97

- Benelux customs union, 1947

Council for Mutual Economic Assistance (COMECON)
- COMECON members 1949
- subsequent members

The European Free Trade Assocation (EFTA)
- EFTA members late 1972

The European Economic Area (EEA)
- EEA members April 1997
- borders 1997

The European Union (EU)
- EEC members 1957
- joined Jan. 1973
- joined Jan. 1981
- joined Jan. 1986
- admitted Oct. 1990
- joined Jan. 1995
- applied by April 1997 for EU membership (with year of application)
- YUGO. countries which broke up 1990-93

3 The Yugoslav civil war, 1991-5

- Croatia, June 1991
- overrun by the Yugoslav army and Croatian Serb forces by Dec. 1991
- Bosnia-Herzegovina, Mar. 1992
- secured by Yugoslav army and Bosnian Serb forces by Dec. 1992
- controlled by Bosnian Croat forces, Dec. 1992
- under Bosnian government control, Dec. 1992
- Croatian advances, Jan. 1993
- Federation of Bosnia and Herzegovina advances, Oct.-Nov. 1994
- Croatian and Federation of Bosnia and Herzegovina advances, spring 1995
- Bosnian Serb advances, summer 1995
- Croatian and Federation of Bosnia and Herzegovina advances, Aug.-Oct. 1995
- overwhelmingly or largely Muslim, 1991; no significant Muslim presence by 1996
- Autonomous Province of Western Bosnia, Sep. 1993-Aug. 1994
- remained under Serb control by Dayton agreement Nov.1995
- to be returned to Croatian control under Zagreb agreement
- UN designated "safe areas"

2 The collapse of communism, 1985-91

- Soviet-dominated Eastern Europe to 1989
- Soviet Union to 1991
- Yugoslavia to 1991
- other communist states to 1991
- united with the Federal Republic of Germany, 1990
- independent, 1991
- de-facto independent states, late 1991, on former territory of the Soviet Union, internationally unrecognized
- over-run by Yugoslav army, July-Dec. 1991
- borders, 1991

Mar. 1990: Congress of Estonia formed, declares Soviet rule illegal
Mar. 1991: referendum endorses independence
Aug. 1991: independence declared
Sep. 1991: independence recognized by USSR

1989: mass anti-communist demonstrations
Mar. 1991: referendum endorses independence
Aug. 1991: independence declared
Sep. 1991: independence recognized by USSR

1989: mass anti-communist demonstrations
Mar 1991: independence declared
Apr.-June 1990: economic embargo imposed by USSR
Sep. 1991: independence recognized by USSR

Mar. 1985: Mikhail Gorbachev becomes leader of Communist Party; initiates perestroika and glasnost, loosens Soviet control of satellite states
June 1991: Boris Yeltsin elected president of Russian Federation
Aug. 1991: hard-line communist coup against Gorbachev fails
Nov. 1991: Communist Party declared illegal
Dec. 1991: USSR dissolved

from 1985: Solidarity leads opposition to communism
June 1989: partially free elections
Sep. 1989: Solidarity-led government takes office
Jan. 1990: Communist Party dissolved
Oct. 1991: free elections

June 1989: Popular Front founded.
Aug. 1991: independence declared
Dec. 1991: founder member of CIS

from 1988: anti-government demonstrations
Nov. 1989: mass demonstrations end communist rule.
Apr. 1990: new constitution adopted; becomes a federation
June 1990: free elections

Sep. 1989: mass exodus of political refugees reach the West via Hungary; communist leadership in crisis
Oct.-Nov. 1989: widespread demonstrations against leadership
9 Nov. 1989: Berlin Wall breached
Mar. 1990: free elections
July 1990: currency union with West Germany
Oct. 1990: reunified with West Germany

1989: opposition mass-movements emerge
Aug. 1991: independence declared
Dec. 1991: referendum endorses independence; founder member of CIS

from 1987: communist regime relaxes control
Sep. 1989: allows East Germans to travel to the West
Oct. 1990: communist rule ends peacefully
Mar.-Apr. 1990: free elections

June 1989: Popular Front wins 75% of votes in election
Aug. 1991: independence declared

Dec. 1989: economic war between Belgrade government and Slovenia
Apr. 1990: free elections
June 1991: independence declared; Yugoslav army attempts to regain control of Slovenia
July 1991: Brioni Agreement ends fighting in Slovenia; Yugoslav army withdraws

Apr.-May 1990: free elections
Dec. 1990: Serbian-inhabited areas declare independence
June 1991: independence declared; fighting in Slovenia spreads to Croatia as Serbs attempt to extend territory in Croatia and Bosnia

Dec. 1989: mass demonstrations lead to armed uprisings and overthrow of Ceauşescu regime
June 1991: free elections
Nov. 1991: new constitution adopted

Nov. 1989: President Zhivkov removed from office
June 1990: free elections
July 1991: fresh elections following adoption of new constitution

Jan. 1990: state of emergency declared; Soviet troops intervene
Oct. 1991: independence declared

Nov. 1991: independence declared

Nov. 1988: mass demonstrations against Russification
Mar. 1991: referendum endorses independence
Apr. 1991: independence declared

Sep. 1989: economic embargo imposed by Azerbaijan
Sep. 1991: referendum endorses independence; independence declared

Sep. 1991: independence declared

1987: mass strikes against wage freeze and falling living standards; growing Serb militancy against minorities
July 1990: provincial autonomies abolished
1990-1: increasing tension between Belgrade government and Slovenia and Croatia

Jan.-May 1990: democratic reforms initiated by leadership
Mar. 1991: free elections

137

Retreat from empire
after 1947

The European empires of the nineteenth century (page 100) were still intact in 1939, though most German and Ottoman possessions had passed as League of Nations mandates to Britain, France and Japan. Nationalist unrest in the Middle East and Asia exposed the growing fragility of the empires in the 1930s. By the 1950s the demands for independence were irresistible.

None of the European powers surrendered its colonies voluntarily. France fought stubbornly to maintain control in Indo-China, and the Netherlands struggled to contain the nationalists in Java, who had proclaimed an Indonesian republic in 1945. Neither was successful. Vietnamese victory at Dien Bien Phu (1954) forced France to give way (page 148). In Indonesia the nationalists advanced step by step into Kalimantan, Celebes and the Moluccas, until by 1956 they controlled the whole of the former Dutch East Indies except West Irian, which they annexed in 1963 (map 2). The British, also, had no intention of abdicating their imperial position, but continual unrest

forced their hand and in 1947 India and Pakistan became independent (page 104), followed by Burma and Ceylon. Nevertheless Britain still clung to its base at Singapore, fought a long war against Malayan insurgents and resisted Indonesian attempts to annex Sarawak and Brunei. Only after 1967, when Aden was evacuated, did Britain abandon its presence east of Suez, except in Hong Kong, to be retained until 1997, its economic success being of great benefit to China.

Resistance to independence was strongest in colonies with a white settler population, or where there was substantial European investment. This was the situation in the Belgian Congo (Zaire) where, within days of independence, the province of Katanga, with its rich copper and uranium resources, seceded, resulting in prolonged civil war, only halted in 1965 when a government favourable to Western mining interests was set up (map 4). In Algeria, with a white population of one million, the bloodiest war of liberation was fought between 1954 and 1962, first in the countryside and then in the cities (map 3). But conflict was scarcely less bitter in Rhodesia, Kenya and the Portuguese colonies of Angola, Mozambique and Guinea-Bissau.

The British attempted to save the situation in the Rhodesias and Nyasaland by creating a Central African Federation (1953); but when Zambia and Malawi rejected this compromise (1964), Southern Rhodesia declared unilateral independence (1965) in order to ensure white predominance. But the collapse of the Portuguese empire in 1974 forced the Rhodesian government, now surrounded by black states, to cede control to the black majority and Zimbabwe was born in 1980.

By now the formal structures of European imperialism had been dismantled (map 1). In their place came different forms of association, the British Commonwealth and a special relationship between France and its ex-colonies. Britain showed in the Falklands War in 1982 that she was still prepared to fight on behalf of the few islands still directly ruled from London. Only in southern Africa did the white minority try to maintain traditional white rule. But even here pressure from popular democratic movements compelled change. Namibia won independence in 1990 and in South Africa the government abandoned 'apartheid' and in 1993 agreed to hold the first free multi-racial elections the following April.

3 The Algerian Civil War 1954-62

French administrative and military territories

French defensive frontier lines

2 Indonesia and Malaysia, 1945-65

- - → Indonesian confrontation with Malaysia
⟶ expansion of Indonesian Republic
▰ areas of unrest

Republic of Indonesia 1945

Indonesian states incorporated in Republic, with dates

Federation of Malaysia 1963

South China Sea

PHILIPPINES

MINDANAO

Pacific Ocean

SABAH
(British North Borneo)
claimed by Philippines 1962

BRUNEI

SARAWAK

1963-4

WEST IRIAN
(Dutch New Guinea)
annexed by
Indonesia 1963

Medan

1964

MALAYA

Kuala Lumpur

Singapore 1959

Borneo
KALIMANTAN
1950

CELEBES
(SULAWESI)
1950

MOLUCCAS
1950

SUMATRA

1964

1963-4

Bandjarmasin

Makasar

REPUBLIC OF SOUTH
MOLUCCAS suppressed by
Indonesia 1952

Palembang

Dutch-Indonesian conflict 1945-9

Indian Ocean

Jakarta
(Batavia)

Bandung

MADURA

JAVA

Jogjakarta

LESSER SUNDA IS.
1950

TIMOR 1950

PORTUGUESE
TIMOR
annexed by Indonesia
1976

an Sea

Algiers Feb.1959
Tizi-Ouzou   Bougie
chell   Collo Philippeville Bône
1954   3 Sétif 2 1955
GIERS   Constantine
Hodna Mts.   CONSTANTINE
1   1954
uled-Naïl Mts   March
1955
Aures Mts.   Feriana
El Oued   Oct.1955
Touggourt   TUNISIA
(independent
1956)
uat
ouvement National
gérien (MNA)
ug.1955, "invaded"
FLN Dec.1956
ERRITORIES   6
▲▲ Ouargla

areas of FLN (Front
de Libération Nationale)
activity, with date

6 wilayas, administrative areas
of FLN "shadow government"

oil fields   ▲▲▲

1 Decolonisation, 1947-90

▰ territories independent since 1947, with date

MPLA anti-colonial liberation organisations involved in armed struggle

colonies, protectorates and mandates prior to 1947:

○ British   ○ Spanish   ○ Australian
○ French   ○ Dutch   ○ South African
○ Belgian   ○ Italian   ○ New Zealand
○ Portuguese   ○ U.S.

□ dependent states, coloured accordingly

CHINA

TIBET
re-absorbed by China 1950;
autonomous region 1965

GHANISTAN

PAKISTAN
1947

NEPAL

BHUTAN

Anglo-Chinese agreement
1986 for reunification 1997,
with Hong Kong able to
retain its institutions for 50
years   Hong Kong

Macao

SIKKIM
annexed by India
1975

INDIA

1947

EAST
PAKISTAN
1947
(BANGLADESH
1971)

BURMA
1948

LAOS
1954

NORTH
VIETNAM
1954

insurrection against
French rule 1945-54

THAILAND

SOCIALIST
REPUBLIC
OF VIETNAM
unified 1976

CAMBODIA
1954

SOUTH
VIETNAM
1954

*South China
Sea*

PHILIPPINES 1946

Pacific Ocean

*Andaman Is.
(Indian)*

SRI LANKA 1948
called Ceylon until 1972

MALDIVES 1965

BRUNEI
1984   Sabah

MALAYA 1957 Communist guerrillas
1948-57

MALAYSIA
1963

SINGAPORE
1965   Sarawak

Sumatra

Borneo

Celebes

WEST
NEW GUINEA
to Indonesia 1963

PAPUA
NEW GUINEA
1975

Indian   Ocean

INDONESIA ○ 1949

Java

E. TIMOR
FRETILIN (to Indonesia 1976)

AUSTRALIA

Atlantic Ocean

Bahamas 1973

CUBA

Turks and Caicos Is.

HAITI

DOMINICAN
REP.

British Virgin Is.

Anguilla
St. Barthélemy
Antigua Barbuda
1981
St. Christopher
Nevis
1983

Puerto Rico
FALN

American Virgin Is.

BELIZE 1981
(formerly British
Honduras)

Jamaica 1962

Montserrat
Guadeloupe

St. Martin
Sint-Maarten

Dominica 1978

Martinique

Barbados
1966

HONDURAS

Aruba   Curaçao

St. Lucia 1979

St. Vincent 1980

Grenada
1974

Caribbean   Sea

Bonaire

Trinidad
and
Tobago
1962

NICARAGUA

PANAMA

COLOMBIA

VENEZUELA

New Ireland
New Britain 1975
(to Papua New Guinea)

Kiribati 1979 (formerly Gilbert Is.)

Nauru 1968

Jarvis I.

Pacific Ocean

Tuvalu 1978
(formerly Ellice Is.)

Solomon Islands 1978

Wallis and
Futuna Is.

Western Samoa 1962

American Samoa

Marquesas Is.

Vanuatu 1980
(formerly
New Hebrides)

Fiji 1970

Tonga 1970

Society Is.
Tahiti Is.

New Caledonia

Cook Is.

Gambier Is.

AUSTRALIA

Kermadec Is.

Pitcairn I.

Norfolk I.

Lord Howe I.

Asia and Africa after independence

The history of Asia and Africa since independence is one of chronic instability. Three factors stand out: first, the seizure of power by military leaders (Egypt 1952, Pakistan 1958, Ghana 1966, Indonesia 1967), with the aim (rarely successful) of abolishing corruption and stabilising the economy; second, the resurgence of long-standing regional, tribal and religious conflicts (Naga unrest in India, Kurdish revolts in northern Iraq, Turkey and Iran, nationalist uprisings among the Kachins, Mons, Shans and other 'hill peoples' in Thailand and Burma); finally persistent intervention by the great powers, particularly in the Middle East. Sino-Soviet rivalry lay behind the Vietnamese invasion of Cambodia and the Chinese invasion of Vietnam (1979). In Africa the United States and the Soviet Union inter-

vened in the Somali-Ethiopian war (1976–78), and France sent troops to Chad, and, with other Western powers, helped to quell the insurrection in Zaire in 1978. The attempted secession of Biafra (map 2), essentially a revolt of the Ibo people in eastern Nigeria against northern domination, was defeated by the federal government, with broad international backing. On the other hand, the secession of Bangladesh from Pakistan (1971) was successful, though only achieved with massive Indian military support.

Two countries alone were exceptions from the general pattern. Japan's progress, after the recovery of independence in 1951, was phenomenal. Maintaining close relations with the United States, successive governments concentrated on industrial development and new technology until in the 1970s Japan emerged as the world's third industrial nation (diagram 4). The case of China is more equivocal. Reconstruction after the Revolution (page 122) proceeded apace; but the

'Great Leap Forward' (1958–60) and the 'Cultural Revolution' (1966–68) brought not only political strife but also severe economic disruption and widespread massacre. After the death of Mao Tse-tung (1976) stability returned and there was wide-ranging economic reform, particularly in agriculture; China also became an industrial power. Countries around the Pacific Rim – South Korea, Taiwan, Singapore – made significant

economic progress in the 1970s and 1980s based on the cheap production of high-technology goods for the West. Elsewhere poverty remained endemic. In 1985 only 6 out of 47 African countries had an average annual income above $750 a head; only 10 out of 80 states in the whole region had an average annual income above $2,500.

Faced by the threat of internal disruption, governments everywhere looked

2 Nigeria and the Biafran War 1967-70

- Ibo heartland
- boundaries of the 12 States
- Biafra, declared 30th May, 1967
- effectively occupied by Biafra, 9th Aug. 1967
- Biafran offensive towards Lagos
- Nigerian offensives

to the great powers for support. Inevitably they were drawn into great-power politics. Iran, where the United States covertly helped the Shah's supporters to oust the nationalist Mossadeq in 1953, was one bastion of American influence in the Middle East until 1979 when Ayatollah Khomeini introduced revolutionary Islamic fundamentalism and a long war with Iraq ensued. The Jewish state of Israel, at war with its Arab neighbours

ever since its foundation in 1948 (map 3) received US support. The Soviet Union supported Syria and Egypt until the latter, after the Egyptian-Israeli war of 1973, turned to the United States for financial backing. This diplomatic revolution inaugurated a new phase. At Camp David in 1978 Egypt and Israel came to terms, but the rest of the Middle East remained in a constant state of crisis. From 1980 Iraq and Iran were at war for eight years;

Lebanon collapsed in civil war; in 1990 Iraq invaded Kuwait and was driven out by UN forces early the following year.

Democracy made significant gains in the whole area during the 1980s and 1990s (notably in Pakistan, the Philippines, Namibia, South Africa and Zambia) but elsewhere single party or military regimes were still the rule. Prospects for stability and an end to violence and political coercion remained uncertain.

1 Post-independence wars and revolutions

civil war

invasion

guerrilla activity

border dispute

Nationalist government of Mossadeq ... ved and Shah restored
9 Islamic revolution: overthrows Shah; ...mentalist state imposed
8 war with Iraq
Ayatollah Khomenei dies

... supports Baluchistani separatists ...akistan
... invaded by USSR; Amin killed, Karmal ...sident; resistance by Islamic guerrillas
... USSR withdraws
... post Suviet-backed regime ...ated by Islamic guerrillas

CHINA
1950 invasion of Tibet
1953-7 first Five-Year Plan
1958-60 Great Leap Forward; abandonment of Soviet model and beginning of Sino-Soviet dispute
1960 border conflicts with India and USSR
1966-8 Cultural Revolution; mobilization of Red Guards
1971 China admitted to United Nations
1972 Nixon visits; normalization of Sino-American relations
1976 death of Mao tse-Tung; political reorientation under Hua Guofeng and Deng Xiaoping, leading to the revival of private sector trade and production
1989 democracy demonstration by students in Peking crushed
1990 economic liberalisation accompanies new wave of political repression
1997 death of Deng Xiaoping

TIBET

INDIA
1962 Sino-Indian border war
1975-7 state of emergency proclaimed
1984 Sikh separatist uprising suppressed; Indira Gandhi assassinated
1991 Rajiv Gandhi assassinated
1995-7 radical religious movements undermine stability

PAKISTAN
1958 military coup by Ayub Khan
1965 border clashes with India and war over Kashmir
1977 military coup by Zia ul-Haq
1988 democratic elections; Bhutto prime minister
1996 Benazir Bhutto deposed

BANGLADESH
1971 secession from Pakistan;
1971-5 civil war
1975 murder of Shikh Mujib and military control
1991 democracy established

BURMA
1958, '62 military coups
1974 Socialist People's Republic inaugurated
1988 military coup
1990 pro-democracy protests lead to free elections; military refuse to recognise result
1995 opposition leader Aung San Suu Kyi released from house arrest

-75 Marxist insurgency by People's Democratic Republic ...emen defeated with British and Iranian help
...5 Islamic protest movement

...91 armed resistance to Ethiopian rule ...independence from Ethiopia

Selassie overthrown by army junta
-8 war with Somalia over border
-8 severe famine; Western aid
... civil war; Mengistu's communist regime overthrown

SRI LANKA
1958, '61 fighting between Sinhalese and Tamils
1971 government assumes emergency powers after rural guerrilla uprising; 1984 intercommunal rioting
1986-90 Indian intervention to crush Tamil rebellions

1948 Democratic People's Republic of Korea proclaimed
1950 invasion of South Korea
1994 death of dictator, Kim Il Sung, succeeded by son, Kim Jong II

NORTH KOREA

SOUTH KOREA
1948 Republic of Korea proclaimed
1950 Korean War (see page 148)
1961 military coup followed by dictatorship of Park Chung Hee (assassinated 1979); mounting opposition from 1974
1979 martial law (relaxed 1981)

JAPAN
1951 peace treaty with USA; end of occupation
1956 agreement with USSR ending state of war; cession of territories taken from Russia in 1905
1960 widespread demonstrations against security treaty, granting US military bases in Japan and Okinawa
1972 normalisation of relations with China
1974 trade disputes with US and EEC
1990 formal agreement with USSR to end 1945 war

OKINAWA
Occupied by US after 1945
1972 reverted to Japan

Seat of Chinese Nationalist government under Chiang Kai-shek since 1949
1958 territorial dispute with mainland China over Quemoy and Matsu
1996 China attempts military intimidation as Taiwan holds free elections

TAIWAN

1954 French withdrawal followed by civil war
1956-73 war between US-backed South and communist-backed North
1973 US withdraws all forces
1976 North and South Vietnam reunified under Viet-Minh rule
1978 invasion of Cambodia and border clashes with China
1979 Chinese invasion defeated
1986 liberal economic reforms

VIETNAM

LAOS
1953-73 civil war
1975 monarchy abolished; Pathet Lao seizes power
1986-91 programme of economic reforms restores free-market economy

THAILAND

CAMBODIA
1947 military takeover; guerrilla activity by Communist and minority groups since 1960
1976 border clashes with Cambodia
1988 democratic elections
1991 military coup
1992 democracy restored

PHILIPPINES
Communist and Muslim insurgency since 1968, erupting into civil war 1972-8
1986 Marcos regime ousted following general election; Aquino president
1992 Ramas succeeds as president

Mindanao
1970 monarchy abolished
1970-4 civil war; victory of Khmer Rouge who conduct massacre of civilians
1978 Vietnamese invasion overthrows Khmer Rouge
1989 Vietnamese forces withdraw
1993 democratic elections

MALAYSIA
1969 risings by Chinese minority groups
1975-8 Communist guerrilla activity
1989 Communist party ends war

IRIAN JAYA

INDONESIA
1967 Sukarno ousted by military coup; suppression of Communists
1976 resistance to Indonesia rule in E. Timor
1977-9 secessionist rising in Irian Jaya
1984 radical Islamic protest
1989-91 widespread democracy protests

E. Timor

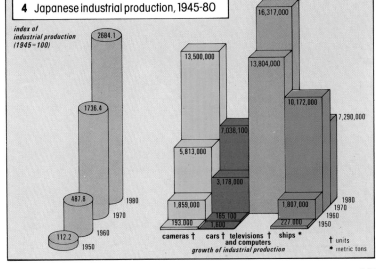

3 Israel and Palestine, 1947-95

Jewish state under UN partition plan for Palestine 1947

Israel after Arab invasion and War of Independence 1948

Israel conquests 1967

Egyptian re-conquests, and Israeli conquests 1973

350,000 from Europe
283,000 from M. East
Beirut
Tyre
LEBANON
Damascus
SYRIA
Golan Heights
Qunaytirah
Sea of Galilee
Haifa
Samaria
Tel-Aviv
Nablus
ISRAEL
R. Jordan
West Bank
Jaffa
Jerusalem
Amman
Jericho
Gaza
Hebron
Dead Sea
Gaza Strip
Judaea
Rafah
Beersheba
264,500 from N. Africa
Palestinian areas achieved autonomy, 1994/5
Mediterranean Sea
Port Said
Ismailia
Suez
Suez Canal
JORDAN
Negev
Giddi Pass
Mitla Pass
Sinai Peninsula
returned to Egypt 1981
Elat
Aqaba
SAUDI ARABIA
Abu Rudeis oilfield
Gulf of Suez
Gulf of Aqaba
Strait of Tiran
EGYPT
Sharm el Sheikh
Ras Muhammad
El Arish
Red Sea

population movements:
Jewish immigration 1948-64
Arab emigration 1948 (total 726,000)
Arab emigration 1967 (total 400,000)

4 Japanese industrial production, 1945-80

index of industrial production (1945=100)

2684.1
1736.4
487.8
112.2

16,317,000
13,500,000
13,804,000
10,172,000
7,290,000
7,038,100
5,813,000
3,178,000
1,859,000
1,807,000
193,000
185,100
1,600
227,000

cameras †   cars †   televisions † and computers   ships *

1980
1970
1960
1950

† units
* metric tons

growth of industrial production

Latin America since 1930

The world depression of 1930 (page 130) was a watershed in the history of Latin America. Heavily dependent on primary exports (map 2), all the republics were hit by the drop in world trade. Chile's exports fell by over 80 per cent between 1929 and 1933; those of Bolivia and Peru by 75 per cent. In Brazil coffee was burnt. Only oil-exporting Venezuela more or less weathered the storm. The result was widespread disillusion with the middle-class liberal or radical parties, themselves apparently helpless. In 1930 and 1931, 11 of the 20 republics south of the Rio Grande experienced revolutionary changes of government. In Mexico, where Cárdenas (1934–40) revived the land distribution policies of 1911, the shift was to the left, but the swing was mainly to the right, though not back to nineteenth century *caudillismo* (page 96), the social bases of which were being eroded by urbanisation and population movements (map 3). The new dictators were populists, appealing directly to the masses and cooperating with organised labour and the trade unions. They also introduced programmes of industrialisation, following Soviet or, more often, fascist models, to reduce dependence on overseas markets and hasten economic development.

Manufacturing industry was given a further boost by the Second World War, which cut off imported consumer goods and stimulated the industrial sector. But industrialisation made Latin America dependent upon imported capital goods, raw materials, technology and finance, creating enormous foreign debts. Multinational corporations exploited the cheap labour markets of Latin America without stimulating economic development. Social tensions arose from income concentration, unemployment, lack of opportunities and the presence of foreign interests. Social revolutions were attempted but frustrated in Guatemala, Bolivia and Chile (map 1), and this underlined the obstacles to change when economies are too narrowly based to sustain welfare programmes and when local élites are prepared to collaborate with the United States. Cuba from 1959 attempted to achieve social change, economic growth and freedom from the United States simultaneously. The revolution led to greater social equality and an improvement in the prospects of rural workers but it also involved a commitment to a repressive government and a dependence on the Soviet Union.

In the face of revolutionary change, many governments closed their ranks. With some support from the upper and middle classes, military governments in the south combined political repression with economic liberalisation. But by the late 1980s their policies had largely failed, and in the face of economic recession and popular protest the grip of the military was gradually eroded. Democracy made ground, even if generally under the watchful eye of the military and, especially in Peru, in the face of violent far-left revolutionary movements. Yet foreign debt, civil conflict, enormous poverty and widespread crime remained perennial barriers to effective stabilization.

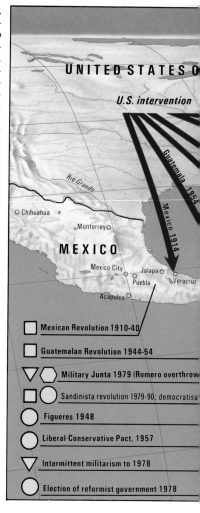

UNITED STATES O

U.S. intervention

Rio Grande

Chihuahua
Monterrey
MEXICO
Mexico City   Jalapa
Puebla
Acapulco   Veracruz

Guatemala 1954
Mexico 1914

☐	Mexican Revolution 1910-40
☐	Guatemalan Revolution 1944-54
▽ ⬡	Military Junta 1979 (Romero overthrow
☐ ◯	Sandinista revolution 1979-90; democratisa
◯	Figueres 1948
◯	Liberal-Conservative Pact, 1957
▽	Intermittent militarism to 1978
◯	Election of reformist government 1978

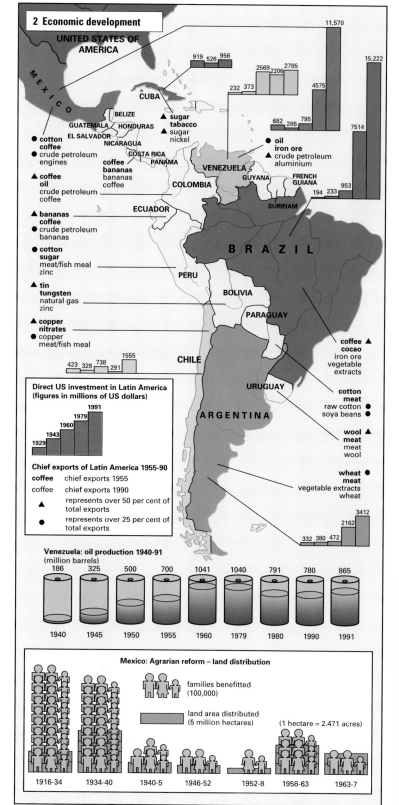

2 Economic development

UNITED STATES OF AMERICA

MEXICO

CUBA

▲ sugar
tabacco
▲ sugar
nickel

BELIZE
GUATEMALA HONDURAS
EL SALVADOR
NICARAGUA
COSTA RICA
PANAMA

● cotton
coffee
● crude petroleum
engines
▲ coffee
oil
crude petroleum
coffee
▲ bananas
coffee
● crude petroleum
bananas
● cotton
sugar
meat/fish meal
zinc
▲ tin
tungsten
natural gas
zinc
▲ copper
nitrates
● copper
meat/fish meal

coffee
bananas
bananas
coffee

VENEZUELA

● oil
iron ore
▲ crude petroleum
aluminium

COLOMBIA

GUYANA
FRENCH
GUIANA
SURINAM

ECUADOR

PERU

BOLIVIA

PARAGUAY

B R A Z I L

coffee ▲
cocao
iron ore
vegetable
extracts

cotton
meat
raw cotton ●
soya beans ●

wool ▲
meat
meat
wool

wheat ●
meat
vegetable extracts
wheat

CHILE

URUGUAY

A R G E N T I N A

919 526 956
232 373
2569 2206 2785
682 286 795
11,570
4575
15,222
7514
194 233 953
423 328 738 291 1555
332 380 472 2162 3412

Direct US investment in Latin America
(figures in millions of US dollars)

1929 1943 1960 1979 1991

Chief exports of Latin America 1955-90

coffee	chief exports 1955
coffee	chief exports 1990
▲	represents over 50 per cent of total exports
●	represents over 25 per cent of total exports

Venezuela: oil production 1940-91
(million barrels)

186	325	500	700	1041	1040	791	780	865
1940	1945	1950	1955	1960	1979	1980	1990	1991

Mexico: Agrarian reform – land distribution

families benefitted
(100,000)

land area distributed
(5 million hectares)

(1 hectare = 2.471 acres)

| 1916-34 | 1934-40 | 1940-5 | 1946-52 | 1952-8 | 1958-63 | 1963-7 |

UNITED STATES OF AMERICA

MEXICO

Mexico City

CUBA
HAITI
DOMINICAN REPUBLIC

BELIZE
GUATEMALA   HONDURAS
EL SALVADOR   NICARAGUA
COSTA RICA   PANAMA

Caracas

VENEZUELA   GUYANA   SURINAM

COLOMBIA
Bogotá

Quito
ECUADOR

B R A Z I L

PERU
Lima

BOLIVIA
La Paz

PARAGUAY
Asunción

Santiago
URUGUAY
Monte
Buenos Aire

C H I L E   A R G E N T I N A

Patagonia

Tierra del Fuego

urbanisation in 1970: %age of population living in cities of over 100,000 inhabitants

Argentina
Bolivia
Brazil
Chile
Colombia
Cuba
Ecuador
Guatemala
Honduras
Mexico
Nicaragua
Paraguay
Peru
El Salvador
Uruguay
Venezuela

1 Social and political movements, 1930-92

□ **Social revolution** Fundamental change (attempted or achieved) in economic and social structure by nationalist or Marxist movements

○ **Reformism** Moderate socio-economic change or modernisation by democratic or other process

☆ **Populism** Revolutionary change by dictatorships appealing to popular forces, especially urban labour

◇ **Christian Democracy** Radical socio-economic change by Christian Democrat parties

▽ **Militarism** Military dictatorship of the right, with or without social or modernising programme

⬡ **Indigenous guerrilla movements** Urban guerrillas from late 1960's following failure of Cuban-inspired rural guerrillas

Washington

Atlantic Ocean

ERICA

Grenada 1983

Dominican Republic 1916-24, 1965-66

Cuba 1921-23, 1933, 1961

Haiti 1915-34

Bahama Islands

Miami

Panama 1903-18, 1989

Havana

CUBA

Nicaragua 1912-33

Santiago

HAITI

DOMINICAN REPUBLIC

Dominica
Martinique
St. Lucia

Cuban Revolution 1959 □

BELIZE

GUATEMALA

Guatemala City

HONDURAS

St. Vincent

Cuban inspired guerrilla movements 1959 68

Barbados

Tobago
Trinidad

Grenada

US invasion 1983

Rómulo Betancourt 1945-48, 1959-64 ○
Carlos Andrés Pérez 1974-79

NICARAGUA

Managua

EL SALVADOR

San José

COSTA RICA

Panama City

PANAMA

Cartagena

Caracas

VENEZUELA

Rafael Caldera 1969-7; Luis Herrera Campins 1979; Jaime Lusinchi 1984 ◇

Georgetown
Paramaribo

GUYANA

SURINAM

Cayenne

FRENCH GUIANA

Getulio Vargas 1930-45, 1950-54 ☆
João Goulart 1961-64 ▽
Modernising militarism 1964

Civilian rule 1985; democratisation 1986 ○

COLOMBIA

Bogotá

Macapá

Belém

Fortaleza

Quito

ECUADOR

Guayaquil

Rio Negro

R. Amazon

Manaus

Gurupá

R. Purus

Recife

Piura

PERU

B R A Z I L

Salvador (Bahia)

Trujillo

Huánuco

Callao
Lima

Cuzco

Brasília

3 Population growth and change

middle class, as % of total population (1963):

▢ 5%-20%
▢ 20%-30%
▢ 30%-40%
▢ 40%-50%
▢ over 50%
▢ no available information

☆ **Radical militarism** 1968
○ **Return to civilian rule 1980**
President Fujimori suspends constitution 1992

Arequipa

La Paz

BOLIVIA

Sucre

Belo Horizonte

50% percentage of population engaged in agriculture (1963)

Antofagasta

PARAGUAY

Asunción

São Paulo

Santos

Rio de Janeiro ⬡

□ **Bolivian Revolution 1952-64**
□ **Che Guevara (killed 1967)**
▽ **Military 1980; democratisation 1982**
◇ **Eduardo Frei 1964-70**
□ **Salvador Allende (Popular Unity) 1970-73**
▽ **Pinochet 1973- free market economy**

San Miguel de Tucumán

Florianópolis

Military dictatorship Stroessner 1954 ▽
Rodriguez 1989

R. Uruguay

Porto Alegre

Copiapó

Santa Fé
Córdoba

URUGUAY

Rio Grande

Rosario

Fray Bentos

Montevideo

Batllismo 1903-33 ○

Valparaiso

ARGENTINA

Buenos Aires

Tupamaros ⬡

C

H

I

L

E

Mendoza

Santiago

Military 1973 ▽

Concepción

Bahia Blanca

Civilian rule 1985; democratisation 1986 ○

Valdivia

Osorno

Montoneros ⬡

Juan Domingo Perón 1943-55, 1973-4 ☆

Rawson

Military 1976-83 ▽

Democratisation and civilian rule 1983 ○

Mexico: population increase 1900-80

67.0
48.2
35.0
25.8
19.7
16.6
14.3
15.2
13.6

millions

70
60
50
40
30
20
10

Mexican Revolution | Post-Revolution

1900 10 20 30 40 50 60 70 80

Rio de Janeiro

P

a

t

a

g

o

n

i

a

Comodoro Rivadavia

Brazil: population increase 1920-80

120
100
80
60
40
20
0

millions

1920 1940 1950 1960 1970 1980

Santa Cruz

Falkland Islands (Islas Malvinas) occupied by Argentina 1982; occupation ended by UK Task Force June 1982

Tierra del Fuego

143

The United States from 1945

The years from 1940 to 1980 saw economic, demographic, and social changes in the United States that transformed the lives of its people. The agricultural, industrial, and service sectors of the economy reached unprecedented levels of productivity. Fewer farmers provided not only for a population which, by 1980, was overwhelmingly urban, but also a significant proportion of the world's production of major staples such as wheat, corn, and soya beans (diagram 5, A–C). Mechanisation (under 10 per cent of the cotton crop was harvested by machine in 1949, 96 per cent in 1969), greater yields from improved seed and fertilisers, and an intensely market-oriented and government subsidised system of sales and distribution made this possible. The economy at large grew at a comparable pace until the 1970s. The gross national product (in constant 1958 dollars) was $227.2 billion in 1940, $722.5 billion in 1970. The service sector expanded more rapidly than did manufacturing, and cities such as Atlanta and Houston in the South and South-west, and Los Angeles, San Francisco, and Denver in the West, became major centres of economic activity (map 4).

This economic growth was accompanied by massive flows of people both within and into the country. With the end of large-scale immigration in the 1920s and the relative immobility of the 1930s, it seemed as though the mobility of American life was over. But the armament build-up during the Second World War attracted many people to the old industrial centres of the Northeast and the Midwest, and to new plants elsewhere. Economic expansion after the war sustained these flows. Millions of blacks and whites left the Southern countryside for the East, the Midwest, and the far West: many more agricultural, industrial, and professional families moved to the West, the Sun Belt of the South and Southwest, and to burgeon-ing cities around the nation (map 1). An interstate system of highways totalling about 40,000 miles by 1980 facilitated the long-distance movement of people, and the rise of complex networks of residence and work (map 2). By 1980 only a third of the population lived in non-metropolitan areas.

About 10 million immigrants arrived in the US between 1950 and 1980 (map 1), plus millions more illegally. Perhaps the most dramatic social change was in the realm of race relations. Between 1940 and 1980 a centuries-old structure of formal, explicit racial discrimination against blacks and Asians all but disappeared. Minorities made major gains in education, income and social acceptance. But this revolution in race relations was not without strains. The massive black and Hispanic migration to American cities exploded in substantial urban riots during the troubled years of the 1960s (map 3). A further strain was imposed by the war in Vietnam, where US ground-troops were committed in large numbers from 1965 to 1973 (page 148). The war polarized American society and brought strong protests from abroad.

Vietnam also imposed serious strains on the American economy. From the late 1960s inflation and unemployment rose and in 1971 the dollar was devalued. High state spending also led to growing deficits. But during the 1980s, American confidence largely returned, taking its lead from President Reagan's promise to reverse economic decline and restore the country's world role. Military intervention in Grenada, Panama, Nicaragua (page 143) and the Middle East (page 141), coupled with the successful ending of the Cold War with the Soviet Union (page 148), provoked renewed national pride. A new consumer boom also produced economic revival, though at the cost of hugely increased deficits. Whatever the structural problems of the US economy, by the 1990s many Americans were persuaded that their country's liberal capitalism was still viable.

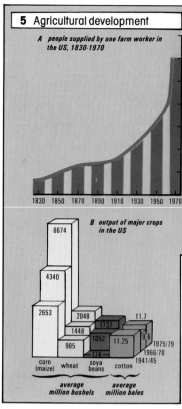

5 Agricultural development

A people supplied by one farm worker in the US, 1830-1970

1830 1850 1870 1890 1910 1930 1950 1970

B output of major crops in the US

6674
4340
2653 2048
1448 1737 11.7
1052 11.25 9.6 1975/79
985 174 1966/70
corn (maize) wheat soya beans cotton 1941/45

average million bushels | *average million bales*

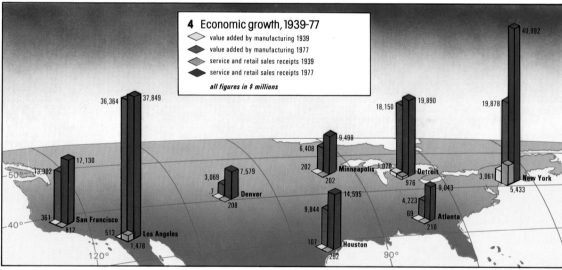

4 Economic growth, 1939-77

◇ value added by manufacturing 1939
◆ value added by manufacturing 1977
◇ service and retail sales receipts 1939
◆ service and retail sales receipts 1977

all figures in $ millions

36,364 37,849
17,130
13,302
3,069 7,579
.7 Denver 208
361 San Francisco
812
513 Los Angeles
1,478
202 6,408 9,498
202 Minneapolis
9,844 14,595
107 Houston
252
40,992
18,150 19,890
976 Detroit
1,070
4,223 9,043
69 Atlanta
210
3,061 19,878
5,433 New York

2 Growth of metropolitan areas 1940-75 (standard)

■ 1940
■ 1960
▨ 1975
— interstate highways 1980

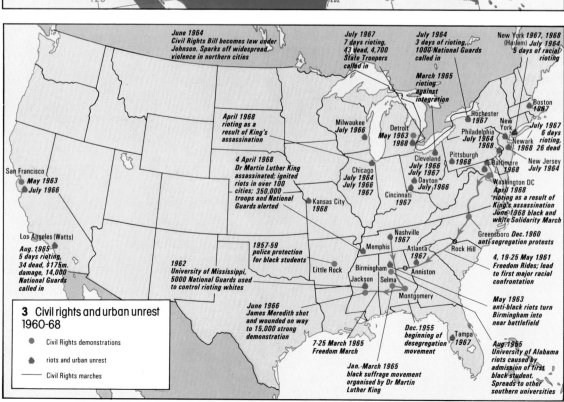

3 Civil rights and urban unrest 1960-68

● Civil Rights demonstrations
♦ riots and urban unrest
— Civil Rights marches

June 1964 Civil Rights Bill becomes law under Johnson. Sparks off widespread violence in northern cities

July 1967 7 days rioting, 43 dead, 4,700 State Troopers called in

July 1964 3 days of rioting, 1000 National Guards called in

New York 1967, 1968 (Harlem) July 1964 5 days of racial rioting

March 1965 rioting against integration

April 1968 rioting as a result of King's assassination

4 April 1968 Dr Martin Luther King assassinated; ignited riots in over 100 cities; 350,000 troops and National Guards alerted

Milwaukee July 1966
Detroit May 1963 July 1967
Rochester 1967
New York
Philadelphia July 1967 6 days
July 1964 1968
Newark rioting, 1968 26 dead
Cleveland July 1966 July 1967
Pittsburgh 1968
Baltimore 1968
New Jersey July 1964
Chicago July 1966 July 1966 1967
Dayton July 1966 1967
Cincinnati 1967
Washington DC April 1968 rioting as a result of King's assassination June 1968 black and white Solidarity March
Kansas City 1968

San Francisco May 1963 July 1966

Los Angeles (Watts) Aug. 1965 5 days rioting, 34 dead, $175m. damage, 14,000 National Guards called in

1957-59 police protection for black students

1962 University of Mississippi, 5000 National Guards used to control rioting whites

Nashville 1967
Memphis
Atlanta 1967
Greensboro Dec. 1960 anti-segregation protests
Rock Hill
4, 19-25 May 1961 Freedom Rides; lead to first major racial confrontation
Little Rock
Birmingham
Anniston
Jackson Selma
Montgomery

June 1966 James Meredith shot and wounded on way to 15,000 strong demonstration

7-25 March 1965 Freedom March

Jan.-March 1965 black suffrage movement organised by Dr Martin Luther King

Dec. 1955 beginning of desegregation movement

May 1963 anti-black riots turn Birmingham into near battlefield

Tampa 1967

Aug. 1955 University of Alabama riots caused by admission of first black student. Spreads to other southern universities

144

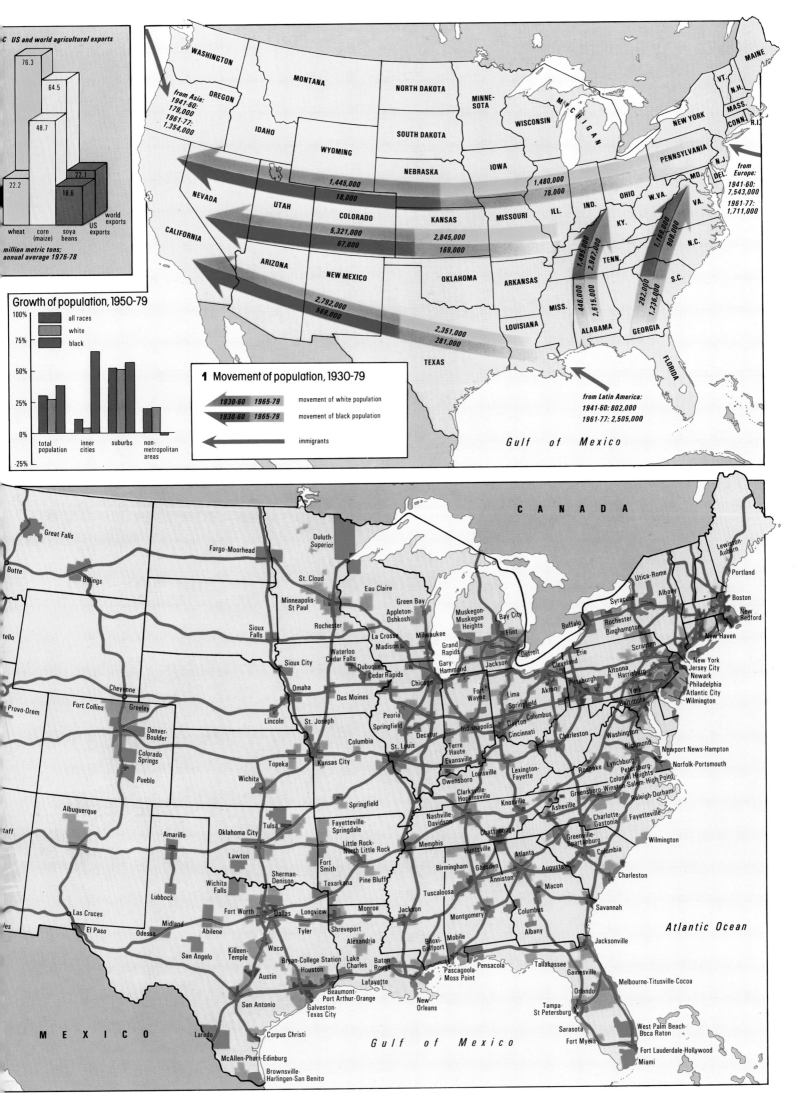

C US and world agricultural exports

76.3
64.5
48.7
22.2
22.1
18.6

wheat | corn (maize) | soya beans | world exports | US exports

million metric tons; annual average 1976-78

Growth of population, 1950-79

- all races
- white
- black

100%
75%
50%
25%
0%
-25%

total population | inner cities | suburbs | non-metropolitan areas

from Asia:
1941-60: 179,000
1961-77: 1,354,000

from Europe:
1941-60: 7,543,000
1961-77: 1,711,000

1,445,000
78,000

1,480,000
78,000

18,000

5,321,000
67,000

2,845,000
169,000

1,495,000
2,987,000

1,169,000
908,000

2,792,000
569,000

2,351,000
281,000

446,000
2,615,000

292,000
1,236,000

1 Movement of population, 1930-79

1930-60	1965-79	movement of white population
1930-60	1965-79	movement of black population
		immigrants

from Latin America:
1941-60: 802,000
1961-77: 2,505,000

Gulf of Mexico

CANADA

Atlantic Ocean

MEXICO

Gulf of Mexico

145

The Soviet Bloc
1928-91

By the time of Lenin's death in 1924 the new Bolshevik state had survived the perils of civil war and foreign intervention (page 120). The future character of the Soviet Union was decided principally by the policies introduced by Stalin after 1928: the forced collectivisation of agriculture and a series of Five-Year Plans for immense industrial growth. Both involved massive casualties from state terror or famine. The farm revolution claimed as many as five million victims, most of them in the Ukraine. By 1939 the rural population was smaller, but the harvest was 20 per cent higher; 30 million more were working in industry. Modernisation on this scale came at a high price. In the 1930s Stalin erected a harsh dictatorship, and a terror apparatus to rival Hitler's. An estimated eight to nine million people were murdered or imprisoned by 1939.

The war against Germany (page 132), in which approximately 28 million people perished, caused colossal devastation: 1,700 towns and 70,000 villages were destroyed. But major new industrial centres, such as the giant iron and steel complex at Magnitogorsk in the southern Urals, were beyond the reach of the German armies. During the war more than 2,500 important factories were

evacuated from the western areas to the Urals, Siberia or Kazakhstan. Reconstruction was necessary on a scale equal to the great industrialisation drive of the 1930s. In just three years industrial production was restored to pre-war levels. By 1950 the national product was twice as large as it had been in 1940. Much of the rebuilding was done with forced labour, supplied by a vast network of labour camps and colonies for political prisoners run by the GULAG. A brutal camp regime forced work out of 'dissidents', regular criminals and foreign prisoners. Millions died in the camps from hunger, neglect and overwork.

In occupied eastern Europe pro-Soviet regimes were installed everywhere, backed by the vast Red Army stationed throughout the region. The politics of Stalinism were gradually introduced, with forced modernisation, one-party rule and a regime of terror against anti-Communists of every kind. Stalin's death in 1953 brought a reaction against the system. In eastern Europe strikes and protests broke out, but were harshly suppressed. In the Soviet Union there developed a wave of de-Stalinisation following Khrushchev's denunciation of Stalin's methods (though not his goals) at the 20th Party Congress in 1956. The terror was relaxed, though not abandoned. Efforts were made to raise wages and improve living standards. The Cold War tension with the West eased temporarily.

Under Khrushchev (1955-64) there was a certain liberalisation of attitudes to culture and dissent.

Khrushchev's new strategy failed to work. The programme to open up the 'virgin lands' to expand grain output was damaged by soil erosion, and wheat had to be imported from Canada; living standards stagnated after 1959, and economic growth slowed; growing tension over Berlin, deteriorating relations with Mao's China and a crisis in Cuba in 1963 all pushed the economy back towards heavy spending on arms. Khrushchev's liberalisation politicies were blamed, and in 1964 the military and party leaders brought about his downfall. Under Brezhnev (1964-82) and Kosygin (1964-80) there was an abrupt reversal of direction. The economy was given more incentives, but under a closely-controlled central plan, and more consumer goods were produced

to stave off popular protest. The political and cultural liberalisation was reversed, and state power reasserted. In 1968 Soviet tanks destroyed the reform movement in Czechoslovakia. Throughout the Soviet bloc the police state became more extreme in response to the greater awareness amongst the population of what was on offer in the West.

By Brezhnev's death popular pressure for political and economic reform was growing. A cautious start was made under his successor, Andropov (1982-84). But under Gorbachev (1985-91) the pace quickened dramatically. Paradoxically, reform highlighted the country's economic weaknesses and opened the way for nationalist protest and greater pressure for democracy throughout the Soviet bloc (see map 2). In 1989 the Communist regimes in Eastern Europe collapsed one after another following waves of popular

1 Communist Eastern Europe to 1985

- Soviet zone of occupation in Austria, 1945-55
- Iron Curtain, 1948
- frontier incidents, 1950-2
- frontier finalized by GDR-Polish treaty, 1950
- Balkan Pact, 1954 (not functional from 1955)
- Nato members from 1955
- Warsaw Pact from May 1955
- Soviet troop deployments in Hungary, 1956
- participated in invasion of Czechoslovakia, 1968
- Warsaw Pact troop deployments in Czechoslovakia, 1968
- mass exodus of refugees
- uprisings, 1953
- uprisings, 1956
- mass protests, 1968
- mass protests and strikes, 1970-85
- frontiers, 1950

violence, to be replaced by democracy (limited in places) and a rush to embrace liberal capitalism. In the Soviet Union the embattled Communist Party conceded major political and economic reforms. The Union itself began to disintegrate, and the economy entered deep crisis. In August 1991 conservative Communists tried to stage a coup to prevent the collapse of Stalin's legacy. It failed, but the coup hastened the final disintegration of the Soviet Union as the many national republics, led by the Baltic states, rushed to take over their own affairs. In December the Union was formally dissolved to be replaced by a Confederation of Independent States, dominated by Russia, the largest national unit. The revolution of 1917, with conspicuous irony, had failed to win the support of those very masses in whose name Lenin had launched it 74 years before.

5 The Soviet economy 1950-85

year	steel (million tons)	coal (million tons)	exports (billion roubles)	cars (thousands)	televisions (thousands)
1950	27.3	261	1.6	65	12
1960	65.3	509	5.0	139	1726
1970	116.0	624	11.5	344	6682
1980	148.0	716	49.6	1327	7528
1985	155.0	726	72.7	1332	9371

4 Agricultural land and land tenure 1940-79

year	state farms	collectives	sown area (mill. ha.)	farm workers (mill.)	population (mill.)
1940	4,000	237,000	150.6	18.7	194
1950	5,000	124,000	146.3	20.5	179
1960	7,000	45,000	203.0	17.1	212
1970	15,000	34,000	206.7	14.4	242
1975	18,000	29,000	217.7	13.5	253
1979	21,000	26,000	217.3	12.8	262

2 Collectivization and population movements, 1923-39

principal areas of collectivization

- 2-10% of all farms collectivized by 1928
- 25-50% of all farms collectivized by 1933
- 50-70% of all farms collectivized by 1933
- 70-85% of all farms collectivized by 1933
- principal famine areas, 1932
- *Kraslag* labour camp administration zone
- corrective labour camps, 1932
- frontiers, 1930

city populations by census of Jan. 1939

(in thousands)
over 1 million / 500-1,000 / 250-500 / 100-250 / 50-100

population by census of Dec. 1926 — growth of population Dec. 1926 to Jan. 1939

3 Principal ethnic groups of the Soviet Union, 1989

- Slav
- Turkic
- Caucasian
- Finno-Ugric
- Moldavian
- Baltic
- Iranian
- others

ASSR autonomous Soviet Socialist Republic
SSR Soviet Socialist Republic
AO autonomous Okrug
AD autonomous district

The nationalities of the Soviet Union, 1989

Russians 53.19%	Poles 0.41%	Uzbeks 6.12%
Latvians 0.54%	Moldavians 1.23%	Tajiks 1.55%
Lithuanians 1.10%	Ukrainians 16.18%	Kazakhs 2.98%
Estonians 0.38%	Mordvins 0.42%	Kirghiz 0.93%
Belorussians 3.78%	Turkmen 1.00%	Chuvash 0.31%

Tatars 2.44%	Jews (scattered) 0.51%
Bashkirs 0.53%	Germans (scattered) 0.75%
Georgians 1.46%	others 3.73%
Armenians 1.70%	
Azerbaijanis 2.49%	

The Cold War from 1947

With the elimination of Germany, Japan and Italy and the weakening of Great Britain and France in the Second World War, the USA and the USSR emerged as the two 'super-powers'. The Cold War symbolized their political and ideological confrontation. Conflict was already visible before the end of the war. In view of the US monopoly of the atom-bomb and the potential threat it implied for the USSR, Stalin decided, after the failure of the Potsdam Conference (July-Aug. 1945), to consolidate Soviet control in eastern Europe (page 136). In reply, the USA built up the defence of western Europe, with the formation of the North Atlantic Treaty Organisation (NATO) in 1949.

Starting as a conflict over central Europe and divided Germany, the Cold War soon developed into a global confrontation. In October 1949 the Communists triumphed in the Chinese civil war. Communist insurgency bubbled up in Vietnam, Malaya and Indonesia; in North Korea, the product of a division agreed by the powers in 1945, a Communist regime was installed in 1948. It was here that the first serious conflict of the Cold War was fought, when North Korea tried to bring the south into the Communist bloc by force. For the United States the Korean War (1950) was evidence of a world-wide Communist conspiracy, although, in fact, the Chinese only intervened when the American advance to the Yalu river seemed to threaten their security (map 2); but American policy hereafter was to 'contain' the Communist powers by a series of encircling alliances. NATO was followed by SEATO (South-East Asia Treaty Organisation, 1954) and the Baghdad Pact (1955), converted into CENTO (Central Treaty Organisation) in 1959. By this time the USA had over 1400 foreign bases, including 275 bases for nuclear bombers, in 31 countries around the Soviet perimeter (map 1). Meanwhile the USSR had acquired nuclear weapons (A-bomb 1949, H-bomb 1953), and when it launched the first space satellite (Sputnik) in 1957, a new dimension was added. Although the intercontinental ballistic missile (ICBM) did not make the American bases obsolete, it meant that, in the event of nuclear war, each of the two superpowers could attack the other's cities directly. The resulting 'nuclear stalemate' enforced a gradual reappraisal.

There were other contributory factors. The monolithic blocs were showing signs of strain, evidenced on the Soviet side by Polish and Hungarian uprisings (1956) and growing signs of a Sino-Soviet rift. In western Europe, France under General de Gaulle rejected American political leadership after 1958. Furthermore, the Baghdad Pact, far from increasing security in the Middle East, divided it into hostile camps, opening it, after

America declined to finance the Aswan high dam and after the Suez War (1956), to Soviet influence (map 4). For the USA the Cuban revolution (1959) posed more immediate problems. When, after an unsuccessful attempt by US-supported dissidents to unseat Fidel Castro, the USSR sent nuclear missiles to Cuba, war seemed imminent, until Krushchev agreed (Oct. 26 1962) to their removal (map 5). But in Indo-China, where the US had refused in 1954 to endorse the settlement of the long anti-colonial war against France (page 138) and had set up a counter-revolutionary regime in Saigon, the situation remained tense. In the end the US was forced to intervene directly, and by 1968 some 543,000 American ground troops, as well as substantial naval and air forces, were committed. But this failed to defeat the guerrilla tactics of the Vietnamese National Liberation Front (map 3), and in 1973, with the US economy under severe pressure, President Nixon called a halt. In 1972 Nixon signed the first SALT treaty limiting nuclear armaments, but after the Soviet invasion of Afghanistan (1979) a new arms race began, culminating in the controversial US 'Star Wars' programme. A new era of super-power co-operation began under Reagan and Gorbachev, which led to agreement to reduce nuclear arsenals. Soviet withdrawal from Afghanistan and from eastern Europe, and joint agreement on a re-unification of Germany in 1990 brought the 'classical' Cold War to an end.

2 The Korean War, 1950-3

2) Chinese intervention Oct. 1950

3) UN maximum advance 24 Nov. 1950

US task force 77

5) armistice line 27 July 1953

38th Parallel

landing of US X Corps 15 Sep. 1950

4) Chinese and North Korean maximum advance 25 Jan. 1951

1) North Korean advance 15 Sep. 1950

3 The war in Vietnam, 1957-73

- controlled by the NLF
- controlled by the Saigon government
- contested areas
- ✳ Tet offensive, 1968

4 The Middle East during the Cold War, 1955-68

Soviet arms and financial aid to Iraq after 1958 revolution

Soviet aid to Syria from 1955

US 6th fleet

American landings in Lebanon 1958

American aid to Israel

3) left Baghdad Pact 1958

Soviet aid to build Aswan dam and assistance 1955-73

decline of British influence:
1) evacuation of Canal Zone 1954 and abortive invasion 1956
2) dismissal of General Glubb 1956
3) Iraqi revolution, assassination of Nuri es-Said 1958
4) withdrawal from Aden 1967

- members of Baghdad Pact
- countries opposed to Baghdad Pact
- major pipelines of the Iraq Petroleum Company and Aramco
- ▲ major oil fields
- areas occupied by Israel after the 1967 war

1 The Cold War, 1948-87

members of Rio Pact, 1948

founding members of NATO, 1949

later NATO members (with date)

dependencies occupied by NATO members, 1954

non-NATO members of Baghdad Pact and/or SEATO, 1955

● principal overseas US military bases, (1962)

● principal overseas Soviet military bases

states and dependencies with defence treaties with, and/or offering military facilities to, NATO, 1962

Soviet-led communist camp, 1954

Warsaw Pact members and allies, 1985

members of the conference of non-aligned states, 1987

frontiers, 1987

5 The Cuban missile crisis, 1962

US blockade zone

range of Soviet missiles

Soviet missile and jet bomber bases

US Air Force base

US naval base

149

The world towards the millennium

For forty years after 1945 the world was dominated by the rival blocs headed by the United States and the Soviet Union and by confident expectations of increasing economic growth. From the mid-1980s both collapsed. The disappearance of the USSR and prolonged recession transformed the world.

The collapse of the Soviet system and the conclusion of the Cold War at the close of the 1980s were initially welcomed as an end to tyranny. Hopes that east and west would converge and democracy and economic liberalism triumph worldwide were widespread. These expectations were soon dashed. The global economy, in part adversely affected by the economic ruin of the former Soviet bloc, grew only fitfully. Massive international debt, particularly in the developing world, inhibited growth in Africa and Latin America. The developed economies of Europe and America grew slowly, but had high levels of unemployment, and welfare bills so large that they continue to threaten financial stability. Only in the area of fastest growth, the Pacific Rim, did the economy continue to boom (map 1). The so-called 'Tiger' economies of Asia now produce a large proportion of the world's exports, and provide a good deal of its industrial investment. The economic balance in the new millennium will continue to shift away from the old heartlands of industrialisation.

The gap between rich and poor worldwide continued to widen. The economic and political stability of much of the developing world continued to be threatened by high population growth, persistent famine, high incidence of disease (including AIDS, most of whose sufferers are to be found in Africa) and economic stagnation. The only success story in Africa came in the south. In 1994 the white minority in South Africa finally gave way to a democratically elected black government led by Nelson Mandela. South Africa still has the highest per capita income on the African continent.

Hand in hand with a sense of economic uncertainty there developed a declining confidence in the state and its political institutions. This was seen most clearly in the collapse of the Soviet Union, the civil war in Yugoslavia and the rise of political and religious extremism in India, the Middle East and even in parts of Europe. Confidence in the rule of law was further undermined by widespread evidence of political corruption, particularly in Japan, Italy and much of the former Soviet bloc. A strident popular nationalism has contributed to the crisis of state: Czechs and Slovaks set up two different states in 1993, Chechen rebels defied the Russian army for two years until they won autonomy in 1997 and, in Ireland, Kurdistan, Zaire and a dozen other countries, nationalist conflicts persist.

The crisis of legitimacy was also evident in the spread of organised crime and 'warlordism'. The most striking example was the spread of the illicit trade in drugs. By 1992 this was worth an estimated $500 billion, and provided relative prosperity in countries such as Bolivia and Colombia, where prospects for more normal trade development were poor. In turn, the drug trade provoked further layers of criminality in the laundering of drug earnings and in rising crime rates in the developed world.

Elsewhere warlords emerged in areas where legitimate central government had broken down or where corruption on a vast scale came to replace the more normal operation of the market. In Somalia, in Lebanon, in the former Yugoslavia, in Afghanistan and in much of Central Asia the rule of law disintegrated amid violent conflict between rival gangs using terror to gain economic advantage. The spread of violence of this kind also helped fuel a growing refugee problem. In 1992 there were an estimated 38 million refugees across the world, most living in makeshift camps with little food or medical aid. Much of the progress made in the 1980s in the promotion of human rights was reversed. State terror, private corruption and local brigandage were still the lot of a large fraction of the world's population.

The international order inevitably altered in this climate of uncertainty. Despite the ending of the Cold War and subsequent scaling down of their nuclear arsenals by the US and the states of the former Soviet Union (page 148), the spread of nuclear weapons remained an acute concern. The struggle for control of the former Soviet arsenal was a source of continuing tension while other states, notably Israel, Pakistan and North Korea, already possessed or were poised to develop their own nuclear weapons. China, meanwhile, which had weathered the collapse of the Soviet Union with apparent impunity, found itself the new superpower of Asia. With vast military resources and an economy growing faster than that of any other industrial power's, its elevation underlined the rapidly increasing might of east Asia, an apparently decisive tilt in the balance of world power.

For all its problems, there are also signs in the 1990s of a growing international collaboration. The United Nations, particularly under Secretary-General Boutros Boutros-Ghali (1991-96), has come to play a more active role in areas of

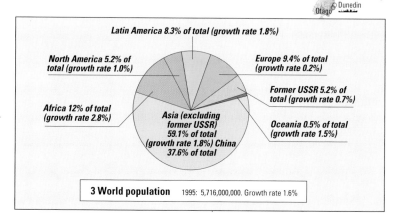

3 World population 1995: 5,716,000,000. Growth rate 1.6%

Latin America 8.3% of total (growth rate 1.8%)

North America 5.2% of total (growth rate 1.0%)

Europe 9.4% of total (growth rate 0.2%)

Former USSR 5.2% of total (growth rate 0.7%)

Africa 12% of total (growth rate 2.8%)

Asia (excluding former USSR) 59.1% of total (growth rate 1.8%) China 37.6% of total

Oceania 0.5% of total (growth rate 1.5%)

crisis (the Gulf War, Somalia, Bosnia, Rwanda) than it did in the 1980s . In 1992 at Rio de Janeiro an 'Earth Summit' was convoked to tackle issues of global environmental damage, in particular the threat of global warming produced by rising industrialisation and declining forestation. The international economy is also governed by close collaboration between the major economies, and through numerous multi-national economic blocs and large multi-national firms, who think of markets and production in global terms (map 2). On the eve of the new millennium the world order is very different from the bi-polar system built on the ruins of the Second World War. It is a world poised between economic stabilisation and political collaboration on the one hand, and nationalism, religious extremism, state decline and economic crisis on the other.

4 Infant mortality and life expectancy

Infant mortality (deaths per 1000 live births)

	1955	1995

GHANA 138 / 81
USA 26 / 8
MEXICO 54 / 35
CHILE 120 / 13
INDIA 100 / 81
JAPAN 40 / 5
FRANCE 39 / 7
USSR/RUS. 60 / 21
FED. 113 / 9
YUGO.

Life expectancy at birth (years)

GHANA 38.00 / 55.50
USA 69.50 / 75.50
MEXICO 38.00 / 70.50
CHILE 51.00 / 69.00
INDIA 31.50 / 62.50
JAPAN 67.50 / 79.00
FRANCE 70.50 / 79.00
USSR/RUS. 68.00 / 70.50
FED. 58.00 / 71.50
YUGO.

ALASKA
Anchorage
Seward

CANADA

Port Alberni
Vancouver
Seattle
Tacoma
Portland
Pacific City
Oakland
San Francisco
Los Angeles
Long Beach
San Diego

USA

4.7 / 2.6 / 2.3

Hawaii
Honolulu

MEXICO

2 The world economy and economic groups

- ten largest economies
- ten largest GDP per capita
- ten smallest GDP per capita
- 1,800% stock markets: highest percentage growth 1983-93
- stock markets: ten largest capitalizations
- OECD headquarters of financial organizations

- North American Free Trade Area (NAFTA)
- Common Market of the Southern Cone (Mercosur)
- Central American Common Market (CACM)
- Economic Community of West African States (ECOWAS)
- Organization for Economic Co-operation and Development (OECD)

- Organization for Petroleum Exporting Countries (OPEC)
- Southern African Development Community (SADC)
- Association of South East Asian Nations (ASEAN)
- Organization of African Unity (OAU)
- Organization of American States (OAS)
- European Union (EU)
- European Economic Area (EEA)

NORWAY $26,300
SWEDEN $24,800
FINLAND
EST.
LAT.
LITH.
DENMARK $26,600
IRE. UK
$1,152 bn
$463 bn
NETH. $1,000 bn
GERMANY $1,900 bn $23,600
POLAND
BELARUS
LUX.
BEL.
CZECH. REP.
SLOV.
UKRAINE
OECD Paris
$35,600
FRANCE $1,300 bn
AUSTRIA
SWITZ.
Basle
HUNGARY
ROMANIA
6,300%
$1,100 bn
Vienna OPEC
YUGO.
BULGARIA
PORTUGAL
SPAIN $500 bn
$456 bn
Bank for Int'l Settlements
ITALY
$272 bn
$36,400
GREECE

see inset map above

ICELAND
$24,000

RUSSIAN FEDERATION $3,900 bn

CANADA
$600 bn
$327 bn

$6,400 bn
World Trade Org. World Bank Washington

USA
$5,224 bn
$24,800
$23,600
BERMUDA

MEXICO
5,200%

KAZAKHSTAN
MONGOLIA
TURKEY
MOROCCO
ALGERIA
LIBYA
EGYPT
IRAQ
IRAN
AFGHAN.
PAKISTAN
$600 bn
CHINA $385 bn
$3,000 bn $31,500
JAPAN
1,800%
BHUTAN
NEPAL
SOUTH KOREA
HONG KONG
1,800%
SAUDI ARABIA
$111
$156
INDIA $165
TAIWAN
$169
SRI LANKA
THAILAND
VIETNAM
PHILIPPINES
5,900%
VENEZ. GUYANA
COLOMBIA
2,100%
ECUADOR
MAURITANIA
MALI
NIGER
CHAD
SUDAN
$63
YEMEN $78
ETHIOPIA
SOMALIA
MALAYSIA
INDONESIA
6,900%
28,000%
PAPUA NEW GUINEA
PERU
BRAZIL
$500 bn
GUINEA
SIERRA LEONE $145
NIGERIA
IVORY COAST
GHANA GABON
ZAIRE
CAMEROON
KENYA $102
TANZANIA $94
BOLIVIA
PARAGUAY
ZAMBIA
ANGOLA
MADAGASCAR
AUSTRALIA
CHILE
2,100%
NAMIBIA
MOZAMBIQUE $81
BOTSWANA
$217 bn SOUTH AFRICA $220 bn
ZIMBABWE
URUGUAY
ARGENTINA
2,000%
NEW ZEALAND

151

Acknowledgements

ACKNOWLEDGEMENTS AND BIBLIOGRAPHY

We have pleasure in acknowledging the following:
Map 5, page 76, is based, with kind permission, on map 2, page 107 in *Grosser Atlas Zur Weltgeschichte*, Westermann
Map 5, page 111, is based, with the kind permission of George Philip & Son Ltd, on page 215 of *The New Cambridge Modern History Atlas* H.C. Darby, H. Fullard (eds.)

Among the large number of works consulted by contributors, the following contain valuable maps and other data that have been particularly useful:

I. History Atlases

Atlas zur Geschichte 2 vols. Leipzig 1976
Bazilevsky, K.V., Golubtsov, A., Zinoviev, M.A. *Atlas Istorii SSR*, Moscow 1952
Beckingham, C.F. *Atlas of the Arab World and the Middle East*, London 1960
Bertin, J. (et al) *Atlas of Food Crops*, Paris 1971
Bjørklund, O., Holmboe, H., Røhr, A. *Historical Atlas of the World*, Edinburgh 1970
Cappon, L. (et al) *Atlas of Early American History*, Chicago 1976
Darby, H. C., Fullard, H. (eds.) *The New Cambridge Modern History* vol. XIV: Atlas, Cambridge 1970
Davies, C.C. *An Historical Atlas of the Indian Peninsula*, London 1959
Engel, J. (ed.) *Grosser Historischer Weltatlas* 3 vols. Munich 1953–81
Fage, J.D. *An Atlas of African History*, London 1958
Gilbert, M. *Russian History Atlas*, London 1972
Gilbert, M. *Recent History Atlas 1860–1960*, London 1966
Gilbert, M. *First World War Atlas*, London 1970
Gilbert, M. *Jewish History Atlas*, London 1969
Hazard, H.W. *Atlas of Islamic History*, Princeton 1952
Herrmann, A. *Historical and Commercial Atlas of China*, Havard 1935
Herrmann, A. *An Historical Atlas of China*, Edinburgh 1966
Jedin, H., Latourette, K.S., Martin, J. *Atlas zur Kirchengeschichte*, Freiburg 1970
Joppen, C., Garrett, H.L.O. *Historical Atlas of India*, London 1938
Kinder, H., Hilgermann, W. *DTV Atlas zur Weltgeschichte* 2 vols. Stuttgart 1964
Matsui and Mori *Ajiarekishi chizu*, Tokyo 1965
May, H.G. (ed.) *Oxford Bible Atlas*, Oxford 1974
Nelson's Atlas of the Early Christian World, London 1959
Nelson's Atlas of World History, London 1965
Nihon rekishi jiten Atlas vol., Tokyo 1959
Palmer, R.R. (ed.) *Atlas of World History*, Chicago 1965
Paullin, C.O. *Atlas of the Historical Geography of the United States*, Washington 1932
Ragi al Faruqi, I. *Historical Atlas of the Religions of the World*, New York 1974
Roolvink, R. *Historical Atlas of the Muslim Peoples*, London 1957
Schwartzberg, J.E. (ed.) *A Historical Atlas of South Asia* Chicago 1978
Shepherd, W.R. *Historical Atlas*, New York 1964
Toynbee, A.J., Myers, E.D. *A Study of History, Historical Atlas and Gazetteer*, Oxford 1959
Treharne, R.F., Fullard, H. (eds.) *Muir's Historical Atlas*, London 1966
Van der Heyden, A.M., Scullard, H.H. *Atlas of the Classical World*, London 1959
Wesley, E.B. *Our United States . . . . its History in Maps*, Chicago 1977
Westermann *Grosser Atlas zur Weltgeschichte*, Brunswick 1978
Whitehouse, D. & R. *Archaeological Atlas of the World*, London 1975
Wilgus, A.C. *Latin America in Maps*, New York 1943

II. General Works

Ahzweiler, H. *L'Asie Mineure et les Invasions Arabes*, Revue Historique 1962
Ajayi, J.F.A., Crowder, M. *History of West Africa* vols. 1 & 2 London 1974
Allchin, B. & R. *The Birth of Indian Civilisation*, London 1968
Australia, Commonwealth of, Department of National Development, *Atlas of Australian Resources*
Barraclough, G. *Medieval Germany*, Oxford 1938
Basham, A.L. *The Wonder that was India*, London 1967
Beresford, M. *New Towns of the Middle Ages*, London 1967

Berney, M. (ed.) *Australia*, Sydney 1965
Bloch, M. *Les Caractères Originaux de l'Histoire Rurale Française*, Oslo 1931
Boisselier, J. *La Statuaire du Champa*, Paris 1963
Bury, J.B., Cook, S.A., Adcock, F.E. (eds.) *The Cambridge Ancient History*, Cambridge 1923–
Bury, J.B., Gwatkin, H.M., Whitney, J.P. (eds.) *The Cambridge Medieval History*, Cambridge 1911
Chang, K.C. *The Archaeology of Ancient China*, New Haven & London 1968
Cheng Te-k'un *Archaeology in China*, Cambridge 1959
Churchill, Winston S. *The Second World War*, London 1948–53
Coedès, G. *Les Etats Hindouisés de l'Indochine et d'Indonésie*, Paris 1964
Cook, M.A. (ed.) *A History of the Ottoman Empire to 1730*, Cambridge 1974
Cresswell, K.A.C. *A Short Account of Early Muslim Architecture*, Oxford 1958
Crowder, M. *West Africa under Colonial Rule*, London 1968
Cumberland, K.B. *Aotearoa Maori: New Zealand about 1780*, Geographical Review no. 39
Curtin, P. de A. *The Atlantic Slave Trade*, Wisconsin 1969
Dalton, B.J. *War and Politics in New Zealand 1855–1870*, Sydney 1967
Darby, H.C. (ed.) *An Historical Geography of England before AD 1800*, Cambridge 1936 & 1960
Despois, J., Raynal, R. *Géographie de l'Afrique du Nord*, Paris 1967
Dyos, H.J., Aldcroft, D.H. *British Transport*, Leicester 1969
East, W.G. *The Geography behind History*, London 1965
East, W.G. *An Historical Geography of Europe*, London 1966
Edwardes, M. *A History of India*, London 1961
Evans, B.L. *Agricultural and Pastoral Statistics of New Zealand 1861–1954*, Wellington 1956
Ferguson, J. *The Heritage of Hellenism*, London 1973
Fisher, C.A. *South-East Asia*, London 1964
Fletcher, A. *Tudor Rebellions*, London 1968
Fowler, K. *The Age of Plantagenet and Valois*, New York 1967
Fourquin, G. *Histoire Economique de l'Occident Médiéval*, Paris 1969
Ganshof, F.L. *Etude sur le Développement des Villes entre Loire et Rhin au Moyen Age*, Paris–Brussels 1943
Geelan, P.J.M., Twitchett, D.C. (eds.) *The Times Atlas of China*, London 1974
Gernet, J. *Le Monde Chinois*, Paris 1969
Grousset, R. *The Empire of the Steppes: A History of Central Asia*, New Brunswick N.J. 1970
Guillermaz, J. *Histoire du Parti Communiste Chinois*, Paris 1968
Hall, D.G.E. *A History of South-East Asia*, London 1968
Harlan, J.R. *The Plants and Animals that Nourish Man*, Scientific American 1976
Harlan, J.R., Zohary, D. *The Distribution of Wild Wheats and Barleys*, Science 1966
Hatton, R.M. *Europe in the age of Louis XIV*, London 1969
Henderson, W.O. *Britain and Industrial Europe 1750–1870*, Liverpool 1954
Hopkins, A.G. *Economic History of West Africa*, London 1973
Inalcik, H. *The Ottoman Empire: The Classical Age 1300–1600*, London 1973
Jeans, D.N. *An Historical Geography of New South Wales to 1901*, Sydney 1972
Kennedy, J. *A History of Malaya 1400–1959*, London 1962
Kjölstad, T., Rystad, G. *5000 år: Epoker och utvecklingslinjer*, Lund 1973
Konigsberger, H., Mosse, G.L. *Europe in the sixteenth century*, London 1968
Langer, W.L. *An Encyclopedia of World History*, London 1972

La Roncière (et al) *L'Europe au Moyen Age*, Paris 1969
Lattimore, O. *Inner Asian Frontiers of China*, New York 1951
Lyashchenko, P.I. *History of the National Economy of Russia to the 1917 Revolution*, New York 1949
Majumdar, R.C. *The Vedic Age*, Bombay 1951
Majumdar, R.C. *History and Culture of the Indian People, Age of Imperial Unity*, Bombay 1954
Macmillan's Atlas of South-East Asia, London 1964
McBurney, C.B.M. *Proceedings of the British Academy LXI* 1975
McIntyre, W.D., Gardner, W.J. *Speeches and Documents on New Zealand History*, Oxford 1970
McNeill, W.H. *A World History*, New York 1971
Meinig, D.W. *On the Margins of the Good Earth*, New York 1962, London 1963
Mellaart, J. *The Neolithic of the Near East*, London 1975
Ministry of Works *A Survey of New Zealand Population*, Wellington 1960
Miquel, A. *L'Islam et sa Civilisation*, Paris 1968
Morrell, W.P., Hall, D.O.W. *A History of New Zealand Life*, Christchurch 1957
Moss, H. St. L.B. *The Birth of the Middle Ages*, Oxford 1935
Mulvaney, D.J. *The Prehistory of Australia*, London 1975
Mussett, L *Les Invasions: Les Vagues Germaniques*, Paris 1965
Musset, L. *Les Invasions: Le Second Assaut contre l'Europe Chrétienne*, Paris 1971
The National Atlas of the United States of America, Washington DC 1970
Neatby, H. *Quebec, The Revolutionary Age 1760–1791*, London 1966
New Zealand Official Yearbook, Wellington 1893–
Ogot, B.A. (ed.) *Zamani, A Survey of East African History*, London 1974–1976
Oliver, R., Fagan, B. *Africa in the Iron Age c.500 BC– AD 1400*, Cambridge 1975
Oliver, R., Atmore, A. *Africa since 1800*, Cambridge 1972
Ostrogorsky, G. *History of the Byzantine State*, Oxford 1956
Parker, W.H. *An Historical Geography of Russia*, London 1968
Pitcher, D.E. *An Historical Geography of the Ottoman Empire*, Leiden 1973
Piggott, S. *Prehistoric India to 1000 BC*, London 1962
Sanders, W.T., Marino, J. *New World Prehistory: Archaeology of the American Indian*, Englewood Cliffs, N.J. 1970
Saum, L.O. *The Fur Trader and the Indian*, London 1965
Seltzer, L.E. (ed.) *The Columbia Lippincott Gazetteer of the World*, New York 1952
Simkin, C.F. *The Traditional Trade of Asia*, Oxford 1968
Smith, C.T. *An Historical Geography of Western Europe before 1800*, London & New York 1960
Smith, W.S. *The Art and Architecture of Ancient Egypt*, London 1965
Snow, D. *The American Indians: their Archaeology and Prehistory*, London 1976
Stavrianos, L.S. *The World to 1500*, Englewood Cliffs, N.J. 1975
Stein, Sir Aurel *Travels in Central Asia*, London 1935
Stratos, A.N. *Byzantium in the seventh century*, Athens 1965
Tarn, W.W. *Alexander the Great*, Cambridge 1948
Tate, D.J.M. *The Making of South-East Asia*, Kuala Lumpur 1971
Thapar, R. *A History of India*, London 1967
The Times Atlas of the World, Comprehensive Edition, London 1980
Toynbee, A.J. (ed.) *Cities of Destiny*, London 1967
Toynbee, A.J. *Mankind and Mother Earth*, Oxford 1976
U.S. Strategic Bombing Survey, Summary Report (Pacific War), Washington 1946
Van Alstyne, R.W. *The Rising American Empire*, Oxford 1960
Van Heekeren, H.R. *The Stone Age of Indonesia*, The Hague 1957
Wadham, S., Wilson, R.K., Wood, J. *Land Utilization in Australia*, Melbourne 1964
Watters, R.F. *Land and Society in New Zealand*, Wellington 1965
Wheatley, P. *The Golden Khersonese*, Kuala Lumpur 1961
Wheeler, M. *Early India and Pakistan to Ashoka*, London 1968
Willey, G. *An Introduction to American Archaeology* vols. 1 & 2 Englewood Cliffs, N.J. 1970
Williams, M. *The Making of the South Australian Landscape*, London 1974
Wilson, M., Thompson, L. *Oxford History of South Africa* vols. 1 & 2 Oxford 1969, 1971

INDEX

1 HISTORICAL PLACE NAMES

Geographical names vary with time and with language, and there is some difficulty in treating them consistently in an historical atlas, especially for individual maps within whose time span the same place has been known by different names. We have aimed at the simplest possible approach to the names on the maps, using the index to weld together the variations.

On the maps forms of names will be found in the following hierarchy of preference:

a English conventional names or spellings, in the widest sense, for all principal places and features, e.g., Moscow, Vienna, Munich, Danube (including those that today might be considered obsolete when these are appropriate to the context, e.g., Leghorn)

b Names that are contemporary in terms of the maps concerned. There are here three broad categories:

i names in the ancient world, where the forms used are classical, e.g., Latin or latinized Greek, but extending also to Persian, Sanskrit, etc.

ii names in the post-medieval modern world, which are given in the form (though not necessarily the spelling) current at the time of the map (e.g., St. Petersburg before 1914, not Leningrad).

iii modern names where the spelling generally follows that of *The Times Atlas of the World*, though in the interests of simplicity there has been a general omission of diacritics in spellings derived by transliteration from non-roman scripts, e.g., Sana rather than Şana'ā'.

2 THE INDEX

The index does not include every name shown on the maps. In general only those names are indexed which are of places, features, regions or countries where 'something happens', i.e., which carry a date or symbol or colour explained in the key, or which are mentioned in the text.

Where a place is referred to by two or more different names in the course of the atlas, there will be a corresponding number of main entries in the index. The variant names in each case are given in brackets at the beginning of the entry, their different forms and origins being distinguished by such words as *now, later, formerly* and others included in the list of abbreviations (*right*).

'Istanbul (*form.* Constantinople, *anc.* Byzantium)' means that the page references to that city on maps dealing with periods when it was known as Istanbul follow that entry, but the page references pertaining to it when it had other names will be found under those other names.

Places are located generally by reference to the country in which they lie (exceptionally by reference to island groups or sea areas), this being narrowed down where necessary by location as E(ast), N(orth), C(entral), etc. The reference will normally be to the modern state in which the place now falls unless (a) there is a conventional or historical name which conveniently avoids the inevitably anachronistic ring of some modern names, e.g., Anatolia rather than Turkey, Mesopotamia rather than Iraq, or (b) the modern state is little known or not delineated on the map concerned, e.g., many places on the Africa plates can only be located as W., E., Africa, etc.

Reference is generally to page number/map numbers (e.g., 118/1) unless the subject is dealt with over the plate as a whole, when the reference occurs as 118-19 (i.e., pages 118 and 119). All entries with two or more references have been given sub-headings where possible, e.g., Civil War 129/4. Battles are indicated by the symbol ✕. References to names of persons, treaties, etc., occurring in the text are followed by the abbreviation T. e.g. 'Alexander the Great 22T'.

Though page references are generally kept in numerical order, since this corresponds for the most part with chronological order, they have been rearranged occasionally where the chronological sequence would be obviously wrong, or in the interests of grouping appropriate references under a single sub-heading.

All variant names and spellings are cross-referenced in the form 'Bourgogne (Burgundy)', except those which would immediately precede or follow the main entries to which they refer. The bracketed form has been chosen so that such entries may also serve as quick visual indications of equivalence. Thus Bourgogne (Burgundy) means not only 'see under Burgundy' but also that Burgundy is another name for Bourgogne.

3 ABBREVIATIONS

a/c	also called
AD	Autonomous District
Alb.	Albanian
anc.	ancient
AR	Autonomous Region
Ar.	Arabic
a/s	also spelled
ASSR	Autonomous Soviet Socialist Republic
Bibl.	Biblical
Bulg.	Bulgarian
C	Century (when preceded by 17. 18 etc.)
C	Central
Cat.	Catalan
Chin.	Chinese
Cz.	Czech
Dan.	Danish
Dut.	Dutch
E	East(ern)
Eng.	English
Est.	Estonian
f/c	formerly called
Finn.	Finnish
form.	former(ly)
Fr.	French
f/s	formerly spelled
Ger.	German
Gr.	Greek
Heb.	Hebrew
Hung.	Hungarian
Indon.	Indonesian
Ir.	Irish
Is.	Island
It.	Italian
Jap.	Japanese
Kor.	Korean
Lat.	Latin
Latv.	Latvian
Lith.	Lithuanian
Mal.	Malay
med.	medieval
mod.	modern
Mong.	Mongolian
N	North(ern)
n/c	now called
Nor.	Norwegian
n/s	now spelled
NT	New Testament
obs.	obsolete
OT	Old Testament
Pers.	Persian
Pol.	Polish
Port.	Portuguese
Rom.	Romanian
Russ.	Russian
S	South(ern)
s/c	sometimes called
Som.	Somali
Sp.	Spanish
S. Cr.	Serbo-Croat
SSR	Soviet Socialist Republic
Sw.	Swedish
T	text
Turk.	Turkish
Ukr.	Ukrainian
US(A)	United States (of America)
var.	variant
W	West(ern)
Wel.	Welsh
WW1	The First World War
WW2	The Second World War

Aachen (Fr. Aix-la-Chapelle anc. Aquisgranum) W Germany Frankish royal residence 34/4; industrial development 98/2; WW1 119/3

Aargau Switzerland Reformation 75/1

Aarhus (n/s Århus) Denmark bishopric 38/2; archbishopric 52/3

Abal Takalik E Mexico Mayan centre 12/2

Abasgia region of Caucasus 43/1

Abbasid Caliphate 40/2

Abbasids Muslim dynasty 40/2, 3

Abbeville N France 17C revolt 77/2

Abd al Kadir Algerian leader 102T

Abdera NE Greece Greek colony 19/4

Abemama Gilbert Is captured by Japanese 134/1; retaken by US 135/2

Abenaki NE Canada Indian tribe 63/1

Abhisara NW India kingdom 23/3

Abilene C USA cow town 94/1

Abipon Argentina Indian tribe 63/1

Abkhaz ASSR Caucasus 147/3

Abodrites Germany tribe 33/5, 34/4, 54/2

Aboukir Bay Egypt ✕ 87/2, 90/2

Abreu Portuguese explorer 65/2

Abr Nahr Syria province of Achaemenid Empire 20/5

Abrotonum (Sabrata)

Abu Bakr First Caliph 41/1

Abu Rawash Lower Egypt pyramid 17/3

Abu Salabikh C Mesopotamia Sumerian site 16/2

Abu Simbel Upper Egypt New Kingdom temple 21/1

Abu Sir Lower Egypt pyramid 17/3

Abydus W Turkey Persian War 23/1; Dorian colony 19/4; Byzantine Empire 43/1

Abydus Upper Egypt 17/3; 21/1

Abyssinia (now Ethiopia) 101/2

Acadia (Nova Scotia)

Acancéh E Mexico Mayan site 12/2

Acapulco Mexico early trade 66/1

Acarnania country of ancient Greece 18/3

Accho (Acre)

Accra Ghana early European settlement 61/2

Aceh (Atjeh)

Achaea (a/s Achaia) early Greek state 18/3; 19/4; 22/1; Roman province 31/3

Achaemenid Empire Persia 24T, 20/5

Achaia (Achaea)

Açores (Azores)

Acragas (Lat. Agrigentum mod. Agrigento) Sicily Dorian colony 19/4

Acre (OT Accho NT Ptolemais Fr. St. Jean-d'Acre Heb. Akko) Palestine 21/4; Levantine city 21/1; Muslim reconquest 40/3; early trade 58/3

Actium W Greece ✕ 31/3

Acton SE USA ✕ 95/2

Adab Mesopotamia Sumerian site 16/2

Adal E Africa early state 60-61

Adamgarh C India site 9/1

Adana W Turkey Byzantine Empire 42/2; 43/1; revolt against Ottoman rule 48/2; Ottoman Empire 124/1

Ad Dawhah (Doha)

Addis Ababa Ethiopia Italian penetration 103/3

Adelaide S Australia founded 113/1; industry 108/1

Aden S Arabia early trading centre 25/1; Muslim trade 58/3; early trade with China 58/3; early church 38/1; Portuguese in 64/1; early town 67/1; Ottoman Empire 125/1; taken by British 101/2; British base 138/1

Aden Protectorate (successively renamed Protectorate of South Arabia, Federation of South Arabia, People's Republic of South Yemen, People's Democratic Republic of Yemen; now part of United Yemen)

Adichanallur S India site 9/1

Admiralty Islands S Pacific Japanese attack 135/1

Adowa N Ethiopia ✕ 103/3

Adramyttium (mod. Edremit) W Turkey 43/3

Adrar W Africa rock painting 10/1

Adrar Bous SE Algeria early site 11/1

Adrar Tiouiyne SE Algeria early site 11/1

Adrianople (anc. Adrianopolis mod. Edirne) W Turkey Byzantine Empire 43/1, 3; Ottoman centre 49/1; occupied by Greece 128/1

Adrianopolis (mod. Edirne Eng. Adrianople) W Turkey archbishopric 27/2

Adriatic Sea Mycenaean trade 18/2

Adulis Red Sea Iron Age site 11/1; early port 25/1, 60/1

Adyge AR Caucasus 147/3

Adzhar ASSR Caucasus 147/3

Aegates islands S Italy ✕ 31/2

Aegean Mycenaean settlement 19/1

Aegospotami (Turk. Karaova Suyu) NW Turkey ✕ 23/2

Aegyptus (mod. Egypt) Roman province 31/3

Aelana (a/c Aela, mod. Aqaba) Roman Empire 25/2

Aelia Capitolina (mod. Jerusalem) Judaea Roman city 25/2

Aenus (mod. Enez) W Turkey Aeolian colony 19/4

Aeolians early people of N Greece 18/3

Aequii early people of C Italy 30/1

Aesernia (mod. Isernia) C Italy Latin colony 30/1

Aethelred II of England 36T

Aetolia ancient country of C Greece 18/3; 22/1, 3

Afars and Issas, French Territory of (form. French Somaliland now Republic of Djibouti)

Afghanistan under Abbasid sovereignty 41/2; independent sultanate 125/1; Soviet base 149/1; invaded by USSR 141/1; economy 151/2

Africa early man 3/3; agricultural origins 6/2, 11/1; early cultures 11/1; Portuguese exploration 64/1; early trade 58/3; early European voyages of discovery 65/2; European expansion and trade 66/2, 67/1; early empires 60-61; European penetration 103/3; slave trade 60-61; colonial empires 100/2; anti-colonial resistance 138/1; modern political developments 140/1; economy 151/1

Africa (mod. Tunisia and Libya) Roman province 31/3, 4; conversion to Christianity 26/1; Byzantine province 42/1

Afrikaners 102T

Aga-Buryat Mongol AD E USSR 147/3

Agade Mesopotamia early city 17/4

Agadès (var. Agadez) W Africa early site 11/1; 58/3, 60-61

Agathe (mod. Agde) SW France Ionian colony 19/4

Agde (Agathe)

Aggersborg N Denmark circular fortification 52/3

Aghlabids Muslim dynasty of Tunisia 40/2

Agincourt (mod. Azincourt) N France ✕ 56/5

Aglar (Aquileia)

Agra N India mutiny 104/1

Agram (Zagreb)

Agrigentum (Gr. Acragas mod. Agrigento) Sicily Roman Empire 24/2, 31/3

Agrippa II kingdom of 26/3

Aguascalientes state of C Mexico 97/1

Aguntum (mod. San Candido) N Italy bishopric 26/2

Ahar NW India site 9/1

Ahicchatra N India 9/1; 29/4

Ahmadabad (Ahmedabad)

Ahmedabad (n/s Ahmadabad) W India industry 105/3

Ahvenanmaa (Åland Islands)

Aichi prefecture of C Japan 126/2

Aidan, St. 38/3

Aigues-Mortes S France Mediterranean trade 59/2; Huguenots 74/3

Aigun NE China treaty port 107/4

Ain Jalut Palestine ✕ 40/2, 46/1

Air W Africa rock painting 11/1

Aire NW France fort 80/1

Aisne river NE France WW1 118/3

Aistulf Lombard ruler 32T

Aix (or Aix-en-Provence anc. Aquae Sextiae) S France archbishopric 34/4; St Bartholomew Massacre 74/3; parlement 80/1

Aix-la-Chapelle (Aachen)

Aix-la-Chapelle, Treaty of 86T

Aizu N Japan 126/1

Ajanta C India Buddhist site 27/1

Ajayameru (mod. Ajmer) C India 29/4

Ajmer (form. Ajayameru) N India British rule 104/1; industry 105/3

Ajnadain Palestine ✕ 41/1

Akan W Africa early state 60/1

Akaroa S Island, New Zealand early French colony 112/2

Akhisar (Thyatira)

Akhtiar (Sevastopol)

Akita town and prefecture of N Japan 126/2

Akjoujt W Africa early site 10/1

Akkad Mesopotamia 17/3

Akkerman (from 1946 Belgorod-Dnestrovskiy anc. Tyras Rom. Cetatea Alba) S Russia Ottoman conquest 49/1

'Akko (Acre)

Akkoyunlu Muslim dynasty of Anatolia 49/1

Akrotiri S Aegean early settlement 19/1

Aksai-Chin district of N Kashmir territorial dispute with China 105/5

Akşehir (Philomelium)

Aksu (a/s Aqsu) Sinkiang trade 25/1; Muslim insurrection against China 106/1

Aktyubinsk Kazakhstan 84/3

Alabama state of SE USA Civil War 93/5; Depression 131/2; population 145/1

Alaca Hüyük C Anatolia Hittite city 21/1

Alacaluf Indian tribe of S Chile 63/1

Alagoas state of E Brazil 97/1

Alalakh (a/c Atchana) Syria Mycenaean trade 18/2; Mitannian city 21/1

Alalia (or Aleria) Corsica Ionian colony 19/4

Alamgirpur India stone age and Harappan site 9/1, 5

Åland Islands (Finn. Ahvenanmaa) SW Finland neutralised 128/1

Alans (Lat. Alani) E and W Europe, Africa tribal movements 32/2

Alarcos S Spain ✕ 37/4

Alaric I King of Visigoths 32/2

Alaşehir (Philadelphia)

Alashiya (mod. Cyprus) under Hittite Empire 20/2

Alaska state of USA purchase from Russia 84/3, 111/4; Pacific Rim 150/1

Alaungpaya King of Burma 70T

Alawites minority sect of W Syria political disturbance 128/1

Alba Fucens C Italy 30/1

Alba Iulia (anc. Apulum Hung. Gyulafehérvár Ger. Karlsburg) Romania Mithraic site 26/1

Albania Black Death 57/1; principality 116/1; Ottoman province 124/1; Muslim insurrection 130/3; territorial dispute with Greece 128/1; annexed by Italy 129/5; WW2 132-3; COMECON 137/4; Cold War 149/1; end of Communism 137/2

Albania ancient country of Caucasus 31/3

Albany (form. Fort Orange) NE USA seized by English 67/3

Albany W Australia founded 113/1

Albazinsk SE Siberia founded 84/2

Alberta province of Canada 111/5

Albertville (now Kalémié) E Belgian Congo 138/4

Ålborg N Denmark megalithic flint mine 15/3

Albret region of SW France 72/2

Albuquerque Portuguese empire-builder 70T

Alcalá S Portugal Megalithic tomb 14/3

Alcibiades Athenian leader 23/2

Alemanni tribe of C Europe 32/2, 34/1

Alemannia SW Germany part of Frankish Empire 34/4, 35/2

Alençon N France fief annexed by France 72/2; provincial capital 80/1

Alep (Aleppo)

Aleppo (anc. Beroea a/c Yamkhad Fr. Alep Ar. Halab) Syria Mitannian city 21/1; bishopric 39/1; Byzantine Empire 43/1; early trade 58/3; conquest by Ottomans 49/1; French occupation 125/3

Aleria (Alalia)

Alessandria N Italy Lombard League 55/3; Signorial domain 56/3

Aleut tribe of Alaska 63/1

Aleutian Islands W Alaska to USA 84/3; attacked by Japanese 134/1; retaken by Americans 135/2

Alexander's Empire 22/3

Alexander the Great 22T

Alexandreschata (Alexandria Eschata)

Alexandretta (mod. Iskenderun) E Turkey Achaemenid Empire 21/5; ceded to Turkey 128/1

Alexandria (Ar. Al Iskandariyah) Egypt spread of Christianity 26/1; Alexander's route 22/3; Roman Empire 25/2, 31/3; Christian centre 27/2, 39/1, 4; trade 58/3, 61/2; Arab conquest 41/1; conquered by Ottomans 49/1

Alexandria NW India Alexander's route 23/3

Alexandria (mod. Gulashkird) S Persia Alexander's route 23/3

Alexandria (mod. Ghazni) Afghanistan Alexander's route 23/3

Alexandria (later Merv since 1937 Mary) C Asia 23/3

Alexandria ad Caucasum Afghanistan Alexander's route 23/3

Alexandria Arachoton (mod. Qandahar Eng. Kandahar) Afghanistan Alexander's route 23/3

Alexandria Areion (mod. Herat) Afghanistan Alexander's route 23/3

Alexandria Eschata (a/c Alexandreschata) C Asia Alexander's route 23/3

Alexandria Prophthasia (mod. Farah) Afghanistan Alexander's route 23/3

Alexandria Sogdiana NW India Alexander's route 23/3

Alexandria Troas W Anatolia Roman Empire 31/3

Alexios I Byzantine Emperor 42T

Al Fas (Fez)

Alfonso VI of Léon and Castile 36T

Alger (Algiers)

Algeria economy under French rule 108/1; Ottoman province 124/1; French invasion 103/3; French colonisation 101/1, 103/3, 102/5; immigration from France 108/2; civil war 138/3; under Vichy control 132/1; independence 138/1; political development 140/1; OPEC 151/2

Algiers (Fr. Alger Sp. Argel Ar. Al Jaza'ir anc. Icosium) N Algeria Mediterranean trade 58/3; Corsair city 61/2; Ottoman rule 48/2; Allied landing WW2 132/2

Algonquin Indian tribe of C Canada 63/1

Al Hadhr (Hatra)

Al Hudaydah (Hodeida)

Ali fourth Caliph 41/1

Alice Springs C Australia 113/1

Aligarh N India mutiny 104/1

Ali Kosh W Persia early farming site 7/4

Ali Murad NW India Harappan site 9/5

Alişar Hüyük C Anatolia Hittite city 21/1

Al Iskandariyah (Alexandria)

Al Jaza'ir (Algiers)

Aljubarrota Portugal ✕ 56/1

Al Khalil (Hebron)

Allahabad NE India Indian mutiny 104/1; industry 105/3

Allahdino NW India pre-Harappan site 9/5

Allenstein (Pol. Olsztyn) W Poland acquired by Germany after plebiscite 128/1

Al Madinah (Medina)

Al Makkah (Mecca)

Almalyk Mongolia bishopric 39/1

Almanza Spain ✕ 81/5

Al Mawsil (Mosul)

Almería S Spain early agriculture 6/2; Mediterranean trade 36/2

Almohads Muslim dynasty and empire of North Africa 40/2; 60/1

Almoravids Muslim dynasty of Morocco 40/2; North African empire 36/2

Alpes Cottiae Roman province, France/Italy 30/3

Alpes Maritimae Roman province, France/Italy 30/3

Alpes Poeninae Roman province, France/Italy 30/3

Banat region of Hungary/Romania/Yugoslavia conquered by Habsburgs 78/3
Banbury C England Industrial Revolution 98/1
Ban Chiang N Thailand early site 7/2, 8/3
Ban Chiang Hiang C Thailand Neolithic site 8/3
Bancorna Wales early bishopric 26/2
Banda Islands East Indies early trade 70/3
Bandar Abbas (form. Gombroon) SW Persia Ottoman siege 48/2
Bandarawela Bridge Ceylon site 9/1
Bandjarmasin (n/s Banjarmasin) S Borneo trade centre 71/2
Bangalore S India industry 105/3
Banghazi (Benghazi)
Bangka island off E Sumatra Dutch settlement 71/2
Bangkok (Thai. Krung Thep) S Thailand early trade centre 71/2; captured by Japanese 135/1
Bangladesh (form. East Pakistan or East Bengal) 141/1
Bangor N Ireland monastery 38/2, 3
Bangor-is-y-coed Wales monastery 38/3
Banjarmasin (Bandjarmasin)
Banjul (Bathurst)
Ban Kao SW Thailand earl site 8/3
Ban Na Di N Thailand Neolithic site 8/3
Bannockburn C Scotland ✕ 53/6, 56/4
Bannu (form. Edwardesabad) NW Pakistan industry 108/1
Bañolas N Spain site of early man 3/3
Banpo (Pan-p'o)
Ban Prasat N Thailand Neolithic site 8/3
Bantam (form. Banten) Java Islamic town 40/5; early trade 70/1, 3; sultanate under Dutch control 71/4
Banten (Bantam)
Bantu peoples of Africa early movements 10T, 60T
Banzart (Bizerta)
Bapaume NW France fort 80/1
Bar region of NE France/W Germany Burgundian possession 72/2; duchy 78/1
Bara-Bahau SW France Palaeolithic art 5/3
Baragunda C India site 9/1
Baranovichi (Pol. Baranowicze) W Russia WW1 119/3
Barbados island of West Indies settled by English 66/4; British colony 86/1, 97/1; independence 139/1 (inset)
Barbuda island of West Indies settled by English 66/4
Barca Libya Dorian colony 19/4; ✕ 20/5
Barcelona (anc. Barcino) NE Spain Mediterranean trade 36/2, 59/2, 3; urban revolt 57/1; 18C urban development 82/4; ✕ 90/1; Civil War 129/4
Barcelonette SE France fort 80/1
Barcino (mod. Barcelona) NE Spain early bishopric 26/2
Bardaa NW Persia early archbishopric 39/1
Bardia (n/s Bardiyah) Libya WW2 133/2
Barduli (Barletta)
Bareilly N India mutiny 104/1
Barents, Willem explorer 65/2
Barguzinsk (now Barguzin) SC Siberia founded 84/2
Bari (anc. Barium) S Italy Magyar occupation 37/1; captured by Normans 36/2
Barium (Bari)
Barletta (anc. Barduli) S Italy medieval city 55/3
Barmen-Elberfeld (since 1930 Wuppertal) W Germany industrial development 99/2
Barnard Castle N England ✕ 73/4
Barnaul C Asia founded 84/2
Barnsley C England Industrial Revolution 98/1
Baroda C India industry 108/1
Bar-sur-Aube C France medieval fair 58/1
Barygaza (mod. Broach n/s Bharuch) NW India trading centre 25/1
Basel (Basle)
Bashkirs Turkic people of C Russia 85/1; ASSR 147/3
Basingstoke S England Industrial Revolution 98/1
Basle (Fr. Bâle Ger. Basel) Switzerland medieval trade 58/1; Reformation 75/1; bishopric 78/1
Basque Provinces N Spain reconquest by Castile 37/4
Basque Republic N Spain autonomy 128/1
Basques people of N Spain and SW France 34/1; 35/2, 115/1
Basra (Ar. Al Basrah) Mesopotamia early archbishopric 39/1; ✕ 41/1; trade 59/3; Ottoman conquest 48/2; British control 125/2; WW1 125/2
Bassano N Italy ✕ 91/1
Bassein Burma early trade centre 71/2
Bassein (Port. Baçain) W India Portuguese settlement 66/2
Bassia NE India site 9/1
Bass Strait SE Australia land bridge 5/2; early trade 113/4
Bastar former state of C India 105/3
Basti district of N India ceded to Britain 87/3
Bastidas, Rodrigo explorer 64/3
Basutoland (now Lesotho) S Africa British protectorate 102/2, 4, 5
Batanea district of Judaea 26/3
Batavi tribe of the Netherlands 30/3
Batavia (form. Sunda Kalapa, since 1949 Jakarta f/s Djakarta) Java early trade 66/2; Dutch control 71/4; occupied by Japanese 134/1
Batavian Republic (mod. Netherlands) state established by French Revolution 89/3
Bath W England Industrial Revolution 98/1
Bathurst SE Australia founded 113/1

Bathurst (now Banjul) Gambia, W Africa 102/1
Bato Caves C Philippines early site 8/3
Baton Rouge S USA ✕ 93/5
Batu Buruk E Malaya Neolithic site 8/3
Batu Khan Mongol leader 46T
Batum (n/s Batumi) Caucasus British occupation 121/2
Bautzen E Germany ✕ 91/1
Bavaria (Ger. Bayern) conversion to Christianity 38/3; part of Frankish Empire 35/2, 4, 55/3; Wittelsbach territory 72/1; Reformation 75/1; Electorate 79/1; German Empire 115/2; customs union 98/3; Confederation of the Rhine 91/4; short-lived soviet republic 120/3
Bawit Egypt monastery 38/1
Baxter Springs C USA cow town 94/1
Bayern (Bavaria)
Bayonne (anc. Lapurdum) SW France 18C financial centre 82/4; 80/1
Bayreuth S Germany margraviate 79/1
Bayrut (Beirut)
Beachy Head S England Dutch naval victory 81/4
Beans Store C USA cow town 94/1
Bear Island Spitsbergen discovered 65/2
Béarn region of SW France under English rule 52/2; acquired by France 72/2
Bear Paw Mountains C USA ✕ 95/2
Bear Valley W USA mining site 94/1
Beas Valley NW India site 9/1
Beaucaire S France medieval fair 59/2
Beaulieu S England Industrial Revolution 98/1
Beaumaris N Wales castle 53/7
Beauvais N France 17C revolt 77/2
Beaver NW Canada sub-arctic Indian tribe 63/1
Beç (Vienna)
Becan E Mexico Mayan site 12/2
Bechuanaland (now Botswana) country of S africa British protectorate 102/2, 103/5
Bedcanford S England ✕ 33/3
Bédeilhac SW France Palaeolithic art 5/3
Bedford S England Industrial Revolution 98/1
Begram (a/s Bagram, anc. Kapisa) Afghanistan early trading 25/1
Beidha NW Arabia early farming site 7/4
Beira SE Africa Portuguese occupation 103/3
Beirut (anc. Berytus Fr. Beyrouth Ar. Bayrut) Lebanon Mediterranean trade 58/3; political disturbances 128/1
Belarus (f/c Belorussia, White Russia) independence 137/2
Belfast S Africa ✕ 103/4
Belfort E France fort 80/1
Belgian Congo (form. Congo Free State now Zaire) colony 100/2, 102/5; independence 138/1
Belgica Roman province of NE France 30/3
Belgium (form. Spanish Netherlands or Southern Netherlands) independence 114/5; industrial revolution 99/2; colonial empire 100/2; WW1 118-119; acquisition of Eupen and Malmedy 128/1; economic and social development 1929-39 130/1; WW2 132/1, 2; EU 137/4, 151/2; NATO 149/1
Belgorod S Russia founded 85/1; early bishopric 38/2
Belgorod-Dnestrovski (Akkerman)
Belgrade (anc. Singidunum S. Cr. Beograd) C Yugoslavia ✕ 46/1; Ottoman conquest 48/2; WW1 119/3; 132-133
Belize city of C America founded by British 66/3, 69/3
Belize (form. British Honduras) 142/1, 2, 3; independence 139/1 (inset)
Bellary district of S India ceded to Britain 87/3
Belleau Wood NE France WW1 118/3 (inset)
Belorussia (a/s Byelorussia f/c White Russia n/c Belarus) independence after WW1 129/2; SSR 147/3
Beloye Ozero N Russia monastery 38/2
Belzec S Poland concentration camp 132/1
Bemba tribe of Rhodesia 61/2
Benares (anc. Kasi now Varanasi) N India 87/3
Bender (mod. Bendery Rom. Tighina) S Russia Ottoman conquest 48/2
Bendigo SE Australia goldfield 113/1
Benevento (anc. Beneventum) C Italy dukedom under Byzantine Empire 42/1
Beneventum (mod. Benevento) C Italy Roman Empire 30/1, 3
Bengal country of E India spread of Islam 41/4; under Mughal Empire 48/2; medieval trade 59/3; under British rule 87/3, 104/1, 105/3; Partition between India and Pakistan 105/5
Benghazi (anc. Berenice Ar. Banghazi) Libya Italian occupation 103/3; WW2 132/1
Benguela Angola Portuguese settlement 61/2
Benin early state of Nigeria 60-61
Benin (form. Dahomey) country of W Africa independence 138/1
Benkulen Sumatra trading post 71/2
Bensington S England ✕ 35/3
Bentheim W Germany county 79/1
Bent's Fort C USA fur station 94/1
Beograd (Belgrade)
Beothuk Newfoundland Indian tribe 63/1
Berar C India tribal territory 105/3
Berbera (anc. Malao) Somalia Muslim colony 60/1; British occupation 103/3
Berbers people of NW Africa 45/1; attack Roman Africa 32/1
Bere Welsh stronghold 53/7
Bernice Red Sea early trading port 24/1

Berenice (mod. Benghazi) Libya city of Roman Empire 24/2, 31/3; early bishopric 26/2
Berezina river W Russia ✕ 91/1
Berezov (now Berezovo) W Siberia founded 84/2, 85/1
Berg W Germany Reformation 74/4, 75/1; duchy 79/1
Bergama (Pergamum)
Bergamo (anc. Bergomum) N Italy medieval city 55/3
Bergen Norway bishopric 38/2; Hanseatic trading post 59/2; WW2 132/1
Bergen (Mons)
Bergen-Belsen N Germany concentration camp 132/1
Bergues NE France fort 80/1
Bering, Vitus explorer 65/4
Beringia N Pacific landbridge 4/1
Bering Strait N Pacific European discovery 65/4
Berlin Germany Hanseatic city 59/2; WW1 119/3; Communist uprising 120/3; WW2 132/2; Berlin Wall 146/1; Cold War 149/1
Bermuda British colony in W Atlantic 100/2; economy 151/2
Bern (Fr. Berne) Switzerland early canton 54/5; Reformation 75/1
Bernicia ancient kingdom of NE England 33/3, 35/3
Bernifal SW France Palaeolithic art 5/3
Beroea (mod. Veroia) N Greece bishopric 27/2
Beroea (Aleppo)
Berry region of C France French Royal domain 52/2, 72/2; province 80/1
Bersham N England Industrial Revolution 98/1
Berytus (mod. Beirut) Lebanon Roman Empire 25/2, 31/3; early bishopric 26/2
Besançon (anc. Vesontio) E France archbishopric 34/4; medieval fair 59/2; gained by France 81/4; fort 80/1
Beshbalik W Mongolia 47/1, 3
Besigheim W Germany Mithraic site 26/1
Bessarabia region of Romania/Russia acquired by Russia 85/1; Ottoman province 124/1; lost to Romania 128/1; regained by Russia 121/2
Beth Katraye SE Arabia early bishopric 39/1
Bethlehem Palestine bishopric 26/2
Beth-shan Palestine Levantine city 21/1
Béthune N France fort 80/1
Beverley NE England Industrial Revolution 98/1
Bewdley W England Industrial Revolution 98/1
Beyrouth (Beirut)
Bhabra (Bairat)
Bhagatrav NW India Harappan site 9/5
Bhagrapir E India site 9/1
Bharatpur district of N India communal riots 104/4
Bharuch (Broach)
Bhongir C India site 9/1
Bhonsla state of C India 87/3; alliance with Britain 87/2 (inset)
Bhota (mod. Tibet) 29/4
Bhutan Himalayan kingdom 105/3, 107/4, 139/1; economy 151/2
Biache-Saint-Vaast NE France site of early man 3/3
Biafra E Nigeria civil war 140/2
Biak island of NW New Guinea captured by Allies 135/2
Big Bell W Australia gold town 113/1
Big Hole NW USA ✕ 95/2
Big Mound N USA ✕ 95/2
Bigorre region of SW France under English rule 52/2; independent fief 72/2
Bihać N Bosnia-Herzegovina civil war 137/3
Bihar state of E India under British control 104/1, 105/3; civil disobedience 104/4
Bílá Hora (White Mountain)
Bilbao N Spain 18C financial centre 82/4; Civil War 129/4
Billungmark district of N Germany 55/1
Bilma W Africa early trade 60-61
Biloxi S USA fur station 94/1
Bilston C England Industrial Revolution 98/1
Bilzingsleben E Germany site of early man 3/3
Bindon S England ✕ 33/3
Bingen W Germany Mithraic site 26/1
Binh Dinh (Vijaya)
Birbhanpur E India site 9/1
Bird Creek C USA ✕ 95/2
Birkenhead N England Industrial Revolution 98/1
Birmingham C England 18C industry 82/4; Industrial Revolution 98/1; bombed in WW2 132/1
Birmingham SE USA industry 109/1; civil unrest 144/4
Bisa tribe of C Africa 61/2
Bishopbridge E England Industrial Revolution 98/1
Bishop's Stortford S England Industrial Revolution 98/1
Bismarck, Prince von 114T, 116T
Biterrae S France bishopric 26/2
Bithynia ancient country of NW Anatolia 19/4, 22/3, 4; Byzantine Empire 43/1
Bithynia and Pontus Anatolia Roman province 31/3
Bitlis E Anatolia Byzantine Empire 43/1
Bitolj (n/s Bitola Turk. Monastir) S Yugoslavia Ottoman control 48/1
Bituricae C France archbishopric 26/2
Biysk Russ. C Asia founded 84/2
Bizerta (anc. Hippo Zarytus Fr. Bizerte Ar. Banzart) Tunisia under Abbasids 40/2; WW2 132/2
Bjerre N Denmark megalithic flint mine 15/3

Burnt Corn SE USA ✕ 95/2

Bursa (anc. Prusa later Brusa) W Anatolia Byzantine Empire 42/4; centre of Ottoman state 49/1

Burundi (form. Urundi) country of C Africa native state 61/2; independence 138/1; political development 140/1. See also Ruanda-Urundi

Burwell E England Industrial Revolution 98/1

Bury N England Industrial Revolution 98/1

Buryat-Mongol ASSR E USSR 147/3

Buryats Mongolian tribe 47/1

Bury St Edmunds E England Industrial Revolution 98/1

Bushy Run NE USA ✕ 95/2

Bussa W Africa reached by Mungo Park 102/1

Buto Egypt early urban centre 16/1

Button, Sir Thomas explorer 64/1

Buxar NE India site 9/1; ✕ 87/2 (inset)

Buxentum (Gr. Pyxous a/s Pyxus) S Italy Roman colony 30/1

Byblos (mod. Jubail) Syria early trade 17/4; Mycenaean trade 18/2; Phoenician city 19/4; Levantine city 21/1; Alexander's route 22/3

Byelorussia (Belorussia)

Bylany Czechoslovakia site 15/1

Bylot, Robert explorer 64/1

Byzantine Empire (a/c East Roman Empire) 30T; 36/2, 37/1, 40/2, 41/1, 42-43; conflict with Seljuks 41/2

Byzantium (Eng. Constantinople mod. Istanbul) E Thrace Dorian colony 19/4; Peloponnesian War 23/2; Roman Empire 24/1, 2; Achaemenid Empire 20/5

Cabeço da Arruda C Portugal megalithic tomb 14/1

Cabinda coastal district of SW Africa occupied by Portuguese 103/3

Cabral, Opero Portuguese explorer 64/2

Cacaxtla C Mexico early site 12/2

Cáceres W Spain Civil War 129/4

Cachar district of E India annexed by British 104/2, 105/3

Cacheu W Africa Portuguese settlement 60/2

Caddo S USA Indian tribe 63/1

Cádiz (anc. Gades) SW Spain reconquered from Muslims 37/1; trading port 82/4; naval base 87/2; Civil War 129/4

Caen N France 80/1; French Revolution 89/2; WW2 132/1, 2

Caere (mod. Cerveteri) C Italy Etruscan city 19/4

Caerleon (Isca)

Caernarvon (Wel. Caernarfon anc. Segontium) N Wales castle 53/7

Caesaraugusta (mod. Zaragoza Eng. Saragossa) N Spain Roman Empire 24/2, 30/3; early archbishopric 26/2

Caesarea C Israel Roman Empire 25/2, 31/3; early archbishopric 27/2; town of Judaea 26/3

Caesarea (mod. Cherchell) N Algeria Roman Empire 30/3

Caesarea (a/c Caesarea Cappadociae, mod. Kayseri) C Anatolia early archbishopric 27/2; Roman Empire 31/3; Byzantine Empire 43/1

Caesarodunum (Tours)

Caesaromagus (Chelmsford)

Cagliari (Carales)

Cahokia C USA early site 12/3; French post 67/3; fur station 94/1

Caiguá forest Indian tribe of S Brazil 63/1

Cairns E Australia early settlement 113/1

Cairo (Fr. Le Caire Ar. Al Qahirah and Al Fustat - Old Cairo) Egypt Muslim conquest 49/1; early trade 58/3, 61/2; captured by Ottomans 49/1; Ottoman Empire 48/2

Cajamarca C Andes site 12/4, 5

Cajamarqilla C Andes site 12/5

Cajon Pass SW USA 94/1

Calabria region of S Italy part of Kingdom of Naples 56/3

Calagurris (mod. Calahorra) N Spain Roman Empire 30/3

Calais N France 100 Years War 56/5; WW1 118/3; WW2 132/2

Calcutta E India trade 67/2; British settlement 66/2; industry 105/3; naval mutiny 105/4

Çaldıran (a/s Chaldiran) E Turkey ✕ 49/1

Caldy Islands S Wales monastery 38/3

Caledonia (Scotland)

Cales C Italy Latin colony 30/1

Calgary W Canada growth 111/1

Calico Hills W USA early site 5/2

Calicut (a/c Kozhikode) SW India trade 59/3, 67/1; industry 105/3

California state of SW USA ceded by Mexico 97/1; Depression 130/2; population 145/1

Callao Peru trade 66/1

Callatis Bulgaria Ionian colony 19/4

Calleva (mod. Silchester) S England Roman Empire 30/3

Callipolis (mod. Gallipoli) S Italy Greek colony 19/4

Calne SW England Industrial Revolution 98/1

Calusa Indian tribe of SE USA 63/1

Camarina Sicily Dorian colony 19/4, 23/2

Cambaluc Mongolia early bishopric 39/1

Cambodia (known formally as Democratic Kampuchea earlier Khmer Republic) early sites 8/3; temple kingdoms 51/2; invaded by Siam and Vietnam 71/2; French protectorate 101/2; independence 139/1; Vietnamese war 148/3; political development 141/1

Cambous S France early settlement 14/2

Cambrai N France Burgundian possession 73/3; WW1 118/3 (inset)

Cambria (mod. Wales) expansion of Christianity 38/3

Cambridge E England castle 36/3; Industrial Revolution 98/1

Camden SE USA ✕ 92/1

Cameroon (f/s Cameroons, Cameroun Ger. Kamerun) country of W Africa German colony 100/1, 102-103; independence 138/1; OAU 151/2

Campa forest Indian tribe of S America 63/1

Campania region of C Italy Roman Empire 30/1

Camp David Agreement 140T

Campeche province of S Mexico 97/1

Camulodunum (mod. Colchester) S England Roman Empire 24/2, 30/1

Cana (a/s Cane) S Arabia early port 24/1

Canada early trade 68/5; Confederation 101/1; development 110-111; NATO 149/1; economy 109/1, 151/2; Pacific Rim 150/1

Canadian Pacific Railway 111/1

Çanakkale (f/s Chanak) W Turkey Greco-Turkish War 125/4

Çanakkale Boğazi (Dardanelles)

Canal de Briare N France 80/1

Canal Royal S France 80/1

Canary Islands Portuguese exploration 64/1; on early trade routes 66/1; Spanish sovereignty 87/1, 138/1

Canaveral, Cape (for a short time called Cape Kennedy) SE USA 65/3

Canberra SE Australia capital territory 113/1

Candamo N Spain Palaeolithic art 5/3

Çandar (a/c Kastamonu) early emirate of N Anatolia 49/1

Candelaria W Cuba Soviet missile site 149/5

Candida Casa S Scotland monastery 38/3

Çankırı (Gangra)

Cannae S Italy ✕ 31/2

Canterbury (anc. Durovernum ecclesiastical Lat. Cantuaria) S England monastery 38/3; Industrial Revolution 98/1

Canterbury S Island, New Zealand 112/2

Cantigny NE France WW1 118/3 (inset)

Canton S China trade 25/1, 59/3; treaty port 107/4; captured by Japanese 127/5

Canton River S China first European visit 65/2

Cantuaria (mod. Canterbury) archbishopric 26/1

Canusium (mod. Canosa di Puglia) S Italy Roman Empire 30/1

Canute the Great 38/2, 53/4

Caparcotna Palestine Roman Empire 25/2

Cap Blanc SW France Palaeolithic art 5/3

Cape Artemisium (mod. Gr. Artemision) E Greece ✕ 22/1

Cape Bojador NW Africa ✕ 60/2

Cape Breton Island E Canada French possession 86/1

Cape Coast Castle (a/c Cape Coast) Ghana early British settlement 60/2 (inset)

Cape Colony S Africa early settlement 60T; captured by British from Dutch 87/2; British colony 102-103 (inset)

Cape Finisterre NW Spain ✕ 90/3

Capeletti N Algeria cattle domestication 11/1

Cape of Good Hope S Africa first European voyage 65/2; Dutch settlement 61/2

Cape Province S Africa established by Dutch East India Co. 61/2

Cape St Vincent S Portugal ✕ 90/3

Cape Town South Africa Dutch settlement 61/2

Cape Verde Islands W Africa Portuguese exploration 60/2; Portuguese sovereignty 100/1; independence 138/1

Capitanata region of C Italy part of Kingdom of Naples 56/3

Caporetto N Italy WW1 ✕ 119/3

Cappadocia (Pers. Katpatuka) country of E Anatolia Alexander's Empire 22/3; independent state 22/4; Roman province 31/3; Byzantine province 42/2, 43/1

Capsa (mod. Gafsa) Tunisia Roman Empire 30/3

Capua S Italy Mithraic site 26/1; Roman Empire 24/2, 31/3

Caracas Venezuela colonised 69/3

Carajá forest Indian tribe of C Brazil 63/1

Carales (mod. Cagliari) Sardinia Roman Empire 30/3; archbishopric 26/2

Carapito N Portugal megalithic tomb 14/3

Carchemish (Turk. Karkamiş) E Anatolia 20/2, 21/1

Cardiff S Wales Industrial Revolution 98/1

Caria (Pers. Karka) country of W Asia Minor Persian province 21/1

Carib Indian tribe of Caribbean 63/1

Caribbean early voyages of discovery 65/3; European settlement 66/1; colonial expansion 69/3; US involvement 111/4, 142/1

Carinthia (Ger. Kärnten) province of S Austria Frankish duchy 54/1; medieval German Empire 55/3; acquired by Habsburgs 56/2, 78/3; Habsburgs duchy 79/1; 128/1

Carlisle N England rebellion against Henry VIII 73/4; Industrial Revolution 98/1

Carmana (Kirman)

Carmania country of E Persia 23/3, 29/4

Carnatic (a/c Karnataka) coastal region of SE India 87/2

Carniola (Ger. Krain) region of Austria/Yugoslavia medieval Germany 55/3; acquired by Habsburgs 56/2, 78/3; Habsburg duchy 79/1

Carnuntum ancient town of Austria Mithraic site 26/1; Roman Empire 24/2, 31/3

Carolina N America British settlement 67/3

Caroline Islands C Pacific German sovereignty 101/2; captured by US from Japanese 135/2

Carolingian Empire (Frankish Kingdom)

Carpathos (It. Scarpanto) island of E Mediterranean colonisation 19/1

Carpi N Italy ✕ 81/5

Carreg Cennen S Wales castle 53/7

Carrier sub-arctic Indian tribe of NW Canada 63/1

Carson City W USA mining site 94/1

Cartagena (anc. Carthago Nova) SE Spain naval base 87/1; Civil War 129/4

Carteia S Spain Roman Empire 30/3

Carthage (Lat. Carthago) Tunisia Stone Age site 11/1; Phoenician colony 19/4; Roman Empire 24/2, 30/2, 3; early archbishopric 27/2; Byzantine reconquest 32/1; Muslim conquest 40/1

Carthago Nova (mod. Cartagena) SE Spain Roman Empire 24/2, 30/2, 3, 32/3; archbishopric 26/2

Cartier, Jacques French explorer 64/2

Cascades NW USA ✕ 95/2

Cashel Ireland bishopric 26/2

Casimir I king of Poland 72/1

Caspian Gates N Persia Alexander's route 22/3

Cassano N Italy ✕ 81/5

Cassel N France ✕ 81/4

Cassino C Italy WW2 133/2

Castellón de la Plana E Spain Civil War 129/4

Castiglione N Italy ✕ 91/1

Castile region of Spain at time of Reonquista 36/2; acquired by Habsburgs 72/1

Castillo N Spain Palaeolithic art 5/3

Castillo de Teayo Mexico Aztec town 62/2

Castle Cavern S Africa Iron Age site 11/1

Castoria N Greece Byzantine Empire 43/3

Castra Regina (mod. Regensburg form. Eng. Ratisbon) C Germany Roman fort 24/2

Castulo (mod. Cazlona) S Spain Roman Empire 30/3

Catalans people of NE Spain 115/1

Catalonia (Sp. Cataluña Cat. Catalunya) region of NE Spain reconquest by Aragon 37/4; under French rule 90/1; autonomous 128/1

Catana (mod. Catania) Sicily ally of Athens 23/2; Roman Empire 31/3; medieval German Empire 55/3

Catanzaro S Italy WW1 119/3

Catawba Indian tribe of SE USA 63/1

Cattaro (mod. Kotor) E Adriatic WW1 119/3

Caucasus early urban settlement 16/1; Muslim expansion 41/1

Cawahib forest Indian tribe of W Brazil 63/1

Cawnpore (n/s Kanpur) N India Indian Mutiny 104/1; civil unrest 104/4

Cayapó forest Indian tribe of C Brazil 63/1

Cayenne French Guiana colonisation 69/3

Çayönü E Anatolia early farming site 7/4

Cazlona (Castulo)

Ceará NE Brazil Confederation of the Equator 97/1

Cebu island of C Philippines Spanish control 67/1

Cedar Creek C USA ✕ 95/2

Cedar Mountain SE USA ✕ 93/5

Cefalù (anc. Cephaloedium) Sicily medieval German Empire 55/3

Celebes (Indon. Sulawesi) island of East Indies Muslim expansion 40/5; occupied by Japanese 134/1; state of Indonesia 139/2

Celenderis S Anatolia Ionian colony 19/4

Celts tribe of W Europe, France 19/4; expansion 15/5

Cempoala Mexico Aztec town 62/2; on Cortés' route 68/1

Cenomani early people of N Italy 30/1

CENTO treaty organisation 148T

Central African Federation (Northern Rhodesia, Southern Rhodesia, Nyasaland)

Central African Republic (form. Central African Empire form. Ubangi-Shari) independence 138/1; political development 140/1

Central India Agency Indian states under British control 104/1, 105/3

Central Provinces (now Madhya Pradesh) state of central India 105/3

Ceos (mod. Kea) island of the Aegean colonisation 19/1

Cephaloedium (Cefalù)

Cephalonia (mod. Kefallinia) island of the Ionian Byzantine Empire 43/3; Venetian territory 48/1

Cerdagne (Sp. Cerdaña) region of France and Spain Habsburg territory 80/1

Cerdicesford S England ✕ 33/2

Ceredigion district of Wales 53/7

Cerebon (Cheribon)

Cerigo (anc. Cythera, mod. Kithira) island of S Greece Venetian territory 48/1

Cerkes (Circassia)

Cernăuţi (Czernowitz)

Cerro de Trinidad C Andes early site 12/4

Cerveteri (Caere)

Cēsis (Wenden)

Český Těšín (Teschen)

Cetatea Alba (Akkerman)

Ceuta (Ar. Sebta) Spanish enclave in N Morocco Spanish occupation 100/2

Ceylon (anc. Taprobane, Sinhala or Lanka a/c Saylan, Sarandib) Graeco-Roman finds 25/1, 29/4; under British rule 87/3; Buddhism 105/3; independence 139/1; adopted title Republic of Sri Lanka 139/1; political developments 141/1

Mladec Czechoslovakia site of early man 3/3
Mlu Prei Cambodia early site 8/3
Moab ancient country of Middle East 21/2
Mobile S USA fur station 94/1; ✕93/5
Moçambique (Mozambique)
Moçâmedes Angola Portuguese settlement 103/3
Moche C Andes site 12/4
Modena (anc. Mutina) N Italy Mithraic site 26/1; Lombard League 55/3; Republican commune 56/3; Renaissance Italy 73/5; unification of Italy 114/3
Modoc plateau Indian tribe of NW USA 63/1
Moesia region of Balkans district of Byzantine Empire 43/1
Moesiae late Roman province of Greece 31/4
Moesiae Inferior Roman province of the Balkans 31/3
Moesiae Superior Roman province of the Balkans 31/3
Mogadishu (n/s Muqdisho It. Mogadiscio) Somalia Muslim colony 60/1; early trade 58/3; Italian occupation 103/3
Mogador (now Essaouira) Morocco Iron Age site 11/1
Mogilev W Russia Hanseatic trade 59/2; WW1 119/2; WW2 133/2
Mogonticaum (mod. Mainz) W Germany Roman Empire 24/2, 30/3
Mohács Hungary ✕48/2
Mohammed founder of Islam 40T, 41/1
Mohave Indian tribe of SW USA 63/1
Mohenjo-Daro N India early urban settlement 9/1, 16/1; Harappan site 9/5
Mohi Hungary ✕46/2
Moira Baths C England Industrial Revolution 98/1
Mojos forest Indian tribe of S America 63/1
Mokhlos E Crete Mycenaean settlement 19/1
Mokpo S Korea Russo-Japanese war 127/4; 1950-53 War 148/2
Moldavia (Turk. Boğdan Rom. Moldova) region of Romania/Russia Hungarian 56/2; under Ottoman control 49/1; occupied by Russia 91/1; part of Romania 116/1; SSR 146/2
Moldova (f/c Moldavia) independence from USSR 137/2
Molino Casarotto NW Italy farming site 15/1
Mollwitz (Pol. Malujowice) SW Poland ✕79/2
Molodovo W Russia Palaeolithic art 5/3
Molotov (Perm)
Moluccas (Indon. Maluku Dut. Malukken form. Spice Islands) islands of E Indies Muslim expansion 70/1; European discovery 70/3; early Portuguese trade 67/1; Dutch control 71/2; independent republic 139/2
Molukken (Moluccas)
Mombasa Kenya Muslim colony 60-61; early trade 61/2, 66/2; British occupation 100/3
Monamore SW Scotland megalithic tomb 14/3
Monastir (S. Cr. Bitolj Maced. Bitola) S Yugoslavia WW1 119/3
Monastiraki Crete palace site 19/1
Mondovi NW Italy ✕90/1
Monemvasia (It. Malvasia) S Greece Byzantine Empire 43/3; Ottoman conquest 48/2
Mongol Empire 46-47
Mongolia (form. Outer Mongolia) 33/1; under Turkish Empire 33/1; unification of Mongol tribes 47/1; Chinese incursions under Ming 51/4; Chinese protectorate 106/1; autonomy 107/4; Russian sphere of influence 101/2; People's Republic 120/4; limit of Japanese expansion 127/5; Soviet base 149/1
Mong-tseu (Mengtze)
Monmouth W England Industrial Revolution 98/1
Mons (Dut. Bergen) Belgium WW1 118/3, 119/2
Mons people of S Burma early kingdom 51/2
Montagnais-Naskapi subarctic Indian tribe of NE Canada 63/1
Montana state of NW USA Depression 130/2; population 111/5, 145/1
Montauban S France 80/1; French Revolution 89/2
Mont Cenis SE France Hannibal's route 30/2; pass 58/1
Montdidier NE France WW1 118/3 (inset)
Monte Albán C Mexico early site 13/1; Zapotec centre 62/2
Monte Circeo Italy site of early man 3/3
Montenegro (S. Cr. Crna Gora) region of S Yugoslavia independent state 116/1; under Ottoman rule 124/1; 19C alliances 117/2; WW1 118-9; forms part of Yugoslavia 128/1; WW2 133/2
Montenotte N Italy ✕90/1
Montereau N France ✕90/1
Monte Verde S Chile early site 5/2
Montezuma I Aztec emperor 62T
Montezuma II Aztec emperor 62T
Montferrat Renaissance Italy 73/5
Montgaudier SW France Palaeolithic art 5/3
Montmaurin S France site of early man 3/3
Montmirail N France ✕90/1
Montpellier S France Genoese trade 36/2
Montreal (Fr. Montréal) E Canada capture of French fort by British 86/1; industry 111/1
Montserrat island West Indies English settlement 66/4; British colony 139/1 (inset)
Mooloya Estate C Ceylon political disturbance 104/4
Moravany Czechoslovakia Palaeolithic art 5/3
Moravia (Czech. Morava Ger. Mähren) region of C Czechoslovakia occupied by Poland 51/2; medieval German Empire 55/3; acquired by Bohemia 56/2; Hussite influence 57/1; acquired by Habsburgs 71/1, 78/3; Reformation 75/1; Margravate 79/1; forms part of Czechoslovakia 129/2

Mordva people of C Russia 44/1, 45/2, 85/1; conquered 44/3
Mordvinian ASSR W USSR 147/3
Morea (a/c Peloponnese) region of S Greece Byzantine Empire 43/3; conquered by Ottomans 48/1
Morelos province of C Mexico 97/1
Moreton Bay E Australia penal colony 113/1
Morgarten E Switzerland ✕54/5
Mori W Japan clan territory 51/3
Morioka N Japan 126/1
Mormon Bar W USA mining site 94/1
Mormon Trail N USA settlers' route 94/1
Morocco (Fr. Maroc Sp. Marruecos) under Almohads 60/1; Sharifian dynasties 61/2; Spanish conquest 103/3; independent sultanate 124/1; independence 138/1; conflict with Algeria 140/1; US bases 149/1
Morotai island N Moluccas, E Indies captured by Allies 135/2
Mortsani Slav tribe of E Europe 54/2
Moscha (a/s Moskha) S Arabia early trading centre 25/1
Moscow (Russ. Moskva) W Russia early bishopric 38/2; city of Vladimir-Suzdal 45/2; early trade 58/3; 18C urban development 83/4; captured by Napoleon 91/1; urban growth 146/2; WW1 119/3; Bolshevik seizure of power 121/2; WW2 132-3
Moshesh tribe of S Africa 103/2
Moskha (Moscha)
Moskva (Moscow)
Mosquito Coast C America English settlement 66/4; to Nicaragua 97/1
Mossel Bay S Africa Portuguese exploration 64/1
Mossi early states of W Africa 60-61
Mostar S Bosnia-Herzegovina Ottoman Empire 49/1; civil war 137/3
Mosul (Ar. Al Mawsil) Iraq early archbishopric 39/1; Muslim conquest 41/1; Ottoman Empire 49/1; WW1 125/2; oilfield 150/4
Mound City USA Hopewell site 12/3
Moundville SE USA site 12/3, 62/4
Mount Isa N Australia copper 113/1
Mount's Bay SW England megalithic axe factory 14/3
Mouri W Africa early Dutch settlement 60/1 (inset)
Mousehold Heath E England ✕73/4
Mozambique (form. Portuguese East Africa Port. Mocambique) early trade 66/2; Portuguese settlement 66/2; Portuguese colony 101/1, 103/3; independence 138/1; political development 140/1; economy 151/2
MPLA Angolan guerrilla movement 138T/1; 140/1
Mtskheta Caucasus early archbishopric 27/2
Muchic Andean Indian tribe of S America 63/1
Mudraya Libya satrapy of Achaemenid Empire 20/5
Mud Springs C USA ✕95/2
Mughal Empire India 41/4, 48/2
Mukden Manchuria capital of Manchuria 106/1; treaty town 107/4; Russo-Japanese war 127/4; Japanese occupation 127/5
Multan district of NW India Muslim conquest 41/4, 4; industry under British rule 105/3
München (Munich)
Mundurucú forest Indian tribe of N Brazil 63/1
Munich (Ger. München) S Germany in Thirty Years War 77/5; industrial development 98/2; WW1 119/3; WW2 133/2
Munster SW Ireland Presidency 73/4
Münster N Germany bishopric 79/1
Muqdisho (Mogadishu)
Murad I Ottoman ruler 48T; 49/1
Murad II Ottoman ruler 48T; 49/1
Murban United Arab Emirates oilfield 151/4
Murcia region of S Spain reconquest by Castile 37/4
Murfreesboro SE USA ✕93/3
Murmansk N Russia Allied occupation 121/2
Muroma E Slav tribe of C Russia 44/1
Murom-Ryazan early principality of C Russia 45/2
Muroran N Japan 126/2
Murviedro (Saguntum)
Murzuk Libya early trade 61/2; Barth's journey 102/1
Musang Cave N Philippines Neolithic site 8/3
Muscat (Ar. Masqat) town and district of SE Arabia early trade 58/3; Ottoman siege 48/2
Muscat and Oman (now Oman) SE Arabia British protectorate 125/1
Muscovy early principality of W Russia 48/2, 85/1
Mutina (mod. Modena) N Italy Roman Empire 24/2, 30/1, 31/3
Muziris S India early trade 25/1
Mwenemutapa early state of SE Africa 61/2
Mycale W Anatolia ✕20/5, 22/1
Mycenae ancient city of S Greece 16/1, 18/2, 19/1
Mylae (mod. Milazzo) Sicily Roman Empire ✕30/2
Mylasa (mod. Milas) SW Anatolia Alexander's route 22/3
Myos Hormus ancient port on Red Sea 25/2
Myra S Anatolia Byzantine Empire 42/2
Mysia ancient country of W Anatolia 22/3
Mysore (now Karnataka) region of S India alliance with Britain 87/2 (inset); state under British rule 104-5
Mytilene (a/s Mitylene) island of Aegean ceded to Greece 116/1
Mzilikazi tribe of S Africa 102/2

Nabateans ancient people of Palestine 26/3
Nabha N India Sikh demonstrations 104/4
Näfels Switzerland ✕54/5
Nagano city and prefecture of C Japan 126/2
Nagappattinam (Negapatam)
Nagasaki W Japan early European trade 67/1, 66/2; industry 126/2; bombed by US 135/2, 3
Nagidus S Anatolia Greek colony 19/4
Nagorno-Karabakh autonomous district of Azerbaijan 147/3; occupied by Armenia 137/2
Nagoya C Japan 126/2, 135/3
Nagpur C India 104/4, 105/3
Nahuatl Indian tribe of C Mexico 63/1
Naimans Mongolian tribe 47/1
Nairobi Kenya occupied by British 103/3
Naissus (mod. Niš) S Yugoslavia Roman Empire 24/2; bishopric 27/2
Najd (Nejd)
Najran SW Arabia early bishopric 39/1
Nakhichevan ASSR Caucasus 147/3
Nakhon Pathom S Thailand Hundu-Buddhist remains 51/2
Nakhom Ratchasima C Thailand Vietnam war 148/1
Nambicuara forest Indian Tribe of W Brazil 63/1
Namibia (form. South West Africa, earlier German South West Africa) German colony 101/2, 103/3; independence from South Africa 138/1, 140/1; OAU 151/2
Namsos C Norway WW2 132/1
Namur Belgium Burgundian possession 73/3; town of Spanish Netherlands 77/1; WW1 119/2
Nanchang S China Ming provincial capital 51/4; under warlord control 122/2; anti-Nationalist insurrection 123/4; occupied by Japanese 127/5
Nanchao (mod. Yunnan) SW China independent kingdom 50-51
Nan Chihli E China Ming province 51/4
Nancy E France ✕73/3; WW1 119/2
Nanhai S China Han Commanderie 29/3
Nanking N China Ming provincial capital 51/4; treaty port 107/4; Nationalist capital 122/2; occupied by Japan 127/5
Nanning S China treaty port 107/4
Nantes NW France Scandinavian settlement 37/1; 17C revolt 77/2; trading port 83/5; centre of French Revolution 89/2; industrial development 98/2
Nantwich C England ✕76/4
Nanyueh SW China independent kingdom 28/2
Napata Egypt Iron Age site 11/1; fortress 21/1
Napier N Island, New Zealand founded 112/2
Naples (anc. Neapolis It. Napoli) Mediterranean trade 58/3, 82/4; industrial development 99/2; WW2 133/2
Naples, Kingdom of Black Death 57/1; to Aragon 72/1; acquired by Habsburgs 72/1; to Austria 81/5; satellite of France 91/1; unification of Italy 114/3
Napoleon Emperor of France 90-91
Napoli (Naples)
Naqada Upper Egypt 17/3
Nara C Japan Buddhist site 27/1; prefecture 126/2
Narbo (mod. Narbonne) S France Roman Empire 24/2
Narbonensis (a/c Gallia Narbonensis) Roman province of S France 30/3
Narbonne (anc. Narbo) S France Muslim conquest 40/1; medieval trade 58/1
Nariokotome E Africa site of early man 3/3
Naroch Lake W Russia WW1 ✕119/3
Narosura E Africa early site 11/1
Narragansett Indian tribe of NE USA 63/1
Narraganset Fort NE USA ✕95/2
Narva Estonia, W Russia 1905 Revolution 120/1; WW2 133/2
Narvik N Norway WW2 132/1
Narym W Siberia founded 84/2
Naseby C England ✕76/4
Nashville SE USA ✕93/5
Nashville Road C USA settlers' route 94/1
Nassau principality of C Germany 79/1; Reformation 75/1; unification with Germany 115/2
Natal province of S Africa annexed by Britain 103/2; British colony 103/4
Natchez S USA Indian tribe 63/1
Natchez Trace S USA settlers' route 94/1
Natchitoches S USA fur station 94/1
Natick NE USA Protestant mission 94/1
National Road C USA settlers' route 94/1
Nations, Battle of the (Leipzig) E Germany ✕90/1
NATO 137/3, 148T
Naucratis Egypt Iron Age site 11/1; Greek colony 19/4
Nauru island W Pacific independence 139/1 (inset)
Nautaca (mod. Karshi) C Asia on Alexander's route 23/3
Navajo Indian tribe of SW USA 63/1
Navarino (Pylos)
Navarre (Sp. Navarra) region of N Spain/SW France kingdom 37/4; acquired by Habsburgs 72/1; acquired by France 80/1
Navas de Tolosa S Spain ✕40/2
Navpaktos (Lepanto)
Naworth Castle N England ✕73/4
Naxos Sicily in Mycenaean world 18/2; Greek colony 19/4
Nazca Andean Indian tribe of S America 63/1
Nazlet Khatir S Egypt site of early man 3/3

Parpalló E Spain Paleolithic art 5/3

Parsa (a/c Persis) S Persia satrapy of Achaemenid Empire 21/5

Parthenopean Republic S Italy state established by French Revolution 89/3

Parthia ancient country of N Persia 22/3, 4

Parthians ancient people of the Caucasus 31/3

Pasargadae SW Persia Alexander's route 23/3; ✕25/5

Passau SE Germany bishopric 35/4, 38/2, 3, 79/1

Passchendaele NW Belgium WW1 ✕118/3 (inset)

Passi di Corvo S Italy farming site 15/1

Patagonia region of S Argentina 97/1

Pataliputra (mod. Patna) NE India trading centre 25/1

Patara SW Anatolia Greek colony 19/4; early bishopric 27/2

Patavium (mod. Padova Eng. Padua) N Italy Roman Empire 24/2

Pathet Lao Laotian Communist movement 140/1

Patna (Pataliputra)

Patras (mod. Gr. Patrai anc. Patrae) S Greece Byzantine Empire 43/1

Pattala NW India limit of Alexander's journey 23/3

Pau SW France seat of intendant 80/1

Paul, St. journeys 27/2

Paulis (now Isiro) NE Belgian Congo Congo crisis 138/4

Pavia (anc. Ticinum) N Italy Lombard League 73/5; medieval trade 58/1; Signorial domination 56/3

Pavlov Czechoslovakia Palaeolithic art 5/3

Pavón Mexico early site 12/3

Pawnee plains Indian tribe of C USA 63/1

Paya Indian tribe of C America 63/1

Pearl Harbor Hawaii bombed by Japanese 134/1

Pechenegs tribe of Ukraine 43/3, 44/1, 45/2

Pechenga (Petsamo)

Pecherskaya Lavra Ukraine monastery 38/2

Pech-Merle SW France Palaeolithic art 5/3

Pechora tribe of N Russia 85/1

Pécs (Ger. Fünfkirchen) S Hungary uprising 1956 146/1

Pecsaete tribe of early England 33/3, 35/3

Pedra Branca S Portugal megalithic tomb 14/3

Pedra Coberta NW Spain megalithic tomb 14/3

Pedra Furada Brazil early site 5/2

Peebles county of C Scotland acquired by Edward III 56/4

Pegu early state of S Burma, Buddhist site 27/1; peripheral Mongol control 47/1; early trade 71/2

Pei Chihli NE China Ming province 51/4

P'ei-li-kang (a/s Peiligang) NE China early settlement 8/2

Peipus, Lake (Russ. Chudskoye Ozero Est. Peipsi Järv) W Russia ✕45/2

Peking (form. Mong. Khanbalik) N China early trade 59/3; Ming capital 51/4; warlord attacks 22/1; Japanese occupation 127/5; industry 108/1

Pelew (Palau)

Pella Palestine early bishopric 27/2

Pella Macedonia 20/5, 22/3

Peloponnesian War 23/2

Peloponnesus (Eng. Peloponnese a/c Morea) region of S Greece 18-19

Pelusium N Egypt Alexander's Empire 22/3; Roman Empire 25/2, 31/3

Pelym W Siberia founded 84/2

Pemaquid NE USA ✕95/2

Pemba island Tanzania Muslim colony 60/1

Pembina N USA fur station 94/1

Pembroke S Wales Scandinavian settlement 37/1; WW1 118/3

Penang state of Malaya British possession 71/5; WW2 134/1

Peninj E Africa site of early man 3/3

Peninsular War 90/1

Pennsylvania state of E USA colony 67/3, 92/1; Civil War 93/5; depression 131/2; population 111/5, 145/1

Pennsylvania Road NE USA settlers' route 94/1

Penobscot NE USA founded 67/3

Pensacola SE USA Spanish post 67/3; fur station 94/1

Penuel Palestine ancient capital 21/2

Penydarran S Wales Industrial Revolution 98/1

Penza C Russia founded 85/1; 1905 Revolution 121/1; Bolshevik seizure 121/3

Pepin King of Franks 34T

Pequot Fort NE USA ✕95/2

Perak state of Malaya 71/5

Perath Mesopotamia early archbishopric 27/2

Perche N France fief 72/2

Pereslavets SW Russia 45/2

Pereyaslavl Ukraine bishopric 38/2; early principality 45/2

Pereyaslavl N Russia town of Vladimir-Suzdal 45/2

Pergamum (Gr. Pergamon Turk. Bergama) W Anatolia Roman Empire 24/2, 31/3; early bishopric 27/2

Perge S Anatolia early archbishopric 27/2

Périgord region of C France English possession 52/2; annexed to France 72/2

Perinthus SE Europe Greek colony 19/4

Perlis state of Malaya tributary to Siam 71/5

Perm (1940-57 called Molotov) C Russia founded 85/1; Bolshevik seizure 121/2

Permians people of N Russia 38/2, 45/2

Pernambuco (now Recife) Brazil early Portuguese territory 66/1; Confederation of the Equator 96/1

Perpignan S France fort 80/1

Perryville SE USA ✕93/5

Persepolis Persia early trade 25/1; Alexander's Empire 23/3; Achaemenid Empire 21/5; Muslim conquest 41/1

Persia (now Iran) war with Greece 22/1; Achaemenid Empire 21/5; attacked by White Huns 32/1; expansion of Christianity 39/1; Muslim conquest 41/4; under Abbasid sovereignty 41/2; Mongol conquest 46-7; Safavid Empire 49/1; independent kingdom 125/1; British and Russian spheres of influence 125/3

Persian Gulf (a/c Arabian Gulf or The Gulf) WW1 125/2; oil 151/4

Persis (a/c Fars, Parsa) S Persia Alexander's Empire 23/3

Peru Spanish colonisation 66/1, 69/2; independence 97/1; war with Chile 97/4; political developments 142-3; economy 151/2

Perusia (mod. Perugia) N Italy Roman Empire 30/1, 31/3

Pesaro (Pisaurum)

Peshawar Pakistan industry under British rule 105/3; capital of NW Frontier Agency 105/5

Pesto (Posidonia)

Peterborough E England Industrial Revolution 98/1

Petersfels SW Germany Palaeolithic art 5/3

Petra Jordan Roman Empire 25/2, 31/3; early archbishopric 27/2

Petralona Greece site of early man 3/3

Petřkovice Czechoslovakia Palaeolithic art 5/3

Petrograd (before 1914 St. Petersburg since 1924 Leningrad) WW1 119/3; Russian Revolution 121/2

Petropavlovsk (now Petropavlovsk-Kamchatskiy) Russ. Far East founded 84/2

Petsamo (Russ. Pechenga) NW Russia Russian conquest from Finland 133/2

Pettau (Poetovio)

Pevkakia E Greece Mycenaean settlement 19/1

Pfalz (Palatinate)

Pfalz-Sulzbach W Germany principality 79/1

Phaistos Crete Mycenaean site 19/1

Phalaborwa SE Africa Iron Age site 11/1; 60/1

Phanagoria S Russia Greek colony 19/4

Phan Rang S Indo-China Hundi-Buddhist temple 51/2

Phaselis SW Anatolia Greek colony 19/4

Phasis Caucasus Greek colony 19/4; Roman Empire 33/1

Phazania (mod. Fezzan) region of S Libya 31/3

Philadelphia (mod. Alaşehir) W Anatolia early church 27/2

Philadelphia (Amman)

Philadelphia E USA founded 67/3; industry 109/1

Philiphaugh S Scotland ✕76/4

Philippi N Greece Roman Empire 27/2

Philippines early sites 8/3; spread of Islam 40/5; early trade 67/1; Spanish conquest 71/2; acquired by US 102/2, 110/4; occupied by Japanese 127/5, 134/1; retaken by Americans 135/2; independence 139/1; political development 141/1; US bases 149/1; industry and economy 150/1, 151/2

Philippine Sea ✕135/2

Philippopolis (mod. Plovdiv Turk. Filibe) Bulgaria Roman Empire 31/3; Byzantine Empire 43/1; Ottoman Empire 48/1

Philistia ancient country of Middle East 20/2

Philomelium (mod. Akşehir) C Anatolia Byzantine Empire 43/3

Phnom Laang Cambodia early site 8/3

Phnom Penh Cambodia 70/1, 71/2; Vietnam war 148/3

Phocaea W Anatolia Greek colony 19/4

Phocis ancient territory of C Greece 18/3

Phoenicia at time of Greeks 19/4, 21/2; Roman province 31/3

Phoenicians move into Africa 11/1

Phrygia ancient country of W Anatolia 19/4, 22/3; Byzantine Empire 43/3

Phylakopi S Aegean early settlement 14/2; Mycenaean palace sites 19/1

Piacenza (anc. Placentia) N Italy Lombard League 55/3; Signorial domination 56/3; medieval fair 59/2

Piauí state of NE Brazil 97/1

Picardy (Fr. Picardie) region of N France annexed from Burgundy 72/2, 80/1; WW1 118/3 (inset)

Picentes early tribe of N Italy 25/1

Pictavi W France early bishopric 26/2

Picton S Island, New Zealand railway 112/1

Picts early tribe of Scotland 32/1, 38/3

Piedmont (It. Piemonte) region of N Italy 88/3, 114/3

Pigs, Bay of Cuba CIA invasion 149/5

Pilos (Navarino, Pylos)

Pilsen (Cz. Plzeň) Czechoslovakia industrial development 99/2

Pima Indian tribe of N Mexico 63/1

Pindal N Spain Palaeolithic art 5/3

Pinega N Russia town of Novgorod Empire 45/2

Pinkie Scotland ✕73/4

Pinsk W Russia town of Turov-Pinsk 45/2

Piombino N Italy Duchy 73/5; French rule 91/1

Piqillacta C Andes early site 12/5

Pi-Ramesse Lower Egypt Egyptian city 21/1

Piro forest Indian tribe of S America 63/1

Pisa (anc. Pisae) N Italy medieval city 55/3; Mediterranean trade 36/2, 58/1; raids and conquests 36/2; Republican commune 56/3

Pisae (mod. Pisa) N Italy Roman Empire 30/1, 31/3; bishopric 27/2

Pisaurum (mod. Pesaro) N Italy Roman colony 30/1

Piscataway Fort NE USA ✕95/2

Pisidia ancient country of C Anatolia 22/3, 43/1

Pistoia (anc. Pistoriae) N Italy medieval city 55/3

Pitcairn Island C Pacific British colony 139/1 (inset)

Pithecusa S Italy Greek colony 19/4

Pit River W USA ✕94/2

Pittsburgh E USA industry 109/1, 110/2

Pityus Caucasus Greek colony 19/4; early bishopric 27/2

Pizarro, Francisco Spanish explorer 68/2

Placentia (mod. Piacenza) N Italy Latin colony 30/1

Plassey E India ✕87/2 (inset)

Plataea C Greece ✕20/5, 22/1

Plate River (Sp. Rio de la Plata) Argentina explored 64/2

Plevna (now Pleven) Bulgaria WW1 119/3

PLO Palestinian nationalist movement 140T

Pločnik S Yugoslavia early settlement 14/2

Ploeşti Romania WW2 133/2

Plovdid (Philippopolis)

Plussulien NW France megalithic axe factory 14/3

Plymouth SW England naval base 87/1; Industrial Revolution 98/1; WW1 118/3; WW2 132/1

Plymouth NE USA founded 67/3

Plzeň (Pilsen)

Poço da Gateira S Portugal megalithic tomb 14/3

Podolia region of S Ukraine acquired by Lithuania 56/2

Poduca S India early port 25/1

Poetovio (mod. Ptuj Ger. Pettau) N Yugoslavia Mithraic site 27/1; Roman Empire 31/3

Pohai (Kor. Parhae mod. Manchuria) NE China early state 51/1

Pohang S Korea 1950-53 war 148/2

Point of Rocks C USA ✕94/2

Poitiers (anc. Limonum) C France ✕34/4, 40/1, 56/5; 17C revolts 77/2; seat of intendant 80/1

Poitou region of W France French Royal domain 52/2; province of France 80/1

Pola (mod. Pula) N Yugoslavia Roman Empire 31/3; WW1 119/3

Polabii Slavic tribe of N Germany 54/1, 2

Poland conversion to Christianity 38/2; under Boleslav Chrobry 52/1; Mongol invasion 46/2; union with Lithuania 56/2; Black Death 57/1; Empire of Casimir IV 72/1; acquired by Russia 85/1; agriculture and peasant emancipation 82/1; Reformation 75/1; Partitions 79/4; revolt against Russia 88/1; WW1 119/3; independence after WW1 120/3; territorial disputes 128-1 128/1, 131/3; WW2 132/1; territorial changes 136/1; Comecon 137/4; Warsaw Pact 149/1; mass protests and strikes 1970-85 146/1; end of Communist rule 137/2

Poles post-WW1 migration to Poland 128/3; post-WW2 migration to West 136/1

POLISARIO W Sahara guerrilla movement 138/1, 140/1

Polish Corridor 128/1

Polotsk W Russia early city and principality 45/2; Hanseatic trading post 59/2

Polovtsy tribe of C Russia 44-5

Poltava Ukraine town of Pereyaslavl 45/2; industry and urban growth 84/4; 1905 Revolution 120/1; Bolshevik seizure 121/2

Polyanye Slav tribe of the Ukraine 44/1

Polynesia islands of C Pacific early settlement 10/2

Pomerania (Ger. Pommern Pol. Pomorze) region of N Europe acquired by Poland 52/1; medieval German Empire 55/3; acquired by Prussia 78/2; Reformation 75/1; unification of Germany 79/1, 115/2

Pomerania, East part of Germany 79/1

Pomerania, Swedish ceded to Prussia 114/4

Pomerania, West to Sweden 77/3

Pomeranians Slav tribe of N Europe 54/2

Pomerelia (Ger. Pommerellen) region of N Europe occupied by Teutonic Knights 54/4, 56/2

Pomo Indian tribe of NW USA 63/1

Pompeiopolis S Anatolia Roman Empire 31/3

Ponce de León Spanish explorer 64/3

Pondicherry (Fr. Pondichéry) SE India French settlement 66/2; captured by British 87/2 (inset); French enclave 105/3

Pondo region of SE Africa British administration 102/2

Pons Saravi E France Mithraic site 26/1

Ponthieu region of NE France under English rule 52/2; Burgundian possession 73/3

Pontia (mod. Ponza) W Italy Latin colony 30/1

Pontianak W Borneo Dutch settlement 71/2

Pontica region of E Anatolia 39/4

Pontnewydd N Wales site of early man 3/3

Pontus district of N Anatolia 19/4; Roman province 31/4; Byzantine Empire 43/1

Ponza (Pontia) island C Italy Mithraic site 26/1

Poona W India industry 108/1

Populonia N Italy Etruscan city 19/4, 30/1

Porkkala S Finland Soviet leased territory returned to Finland 146/1

Porolissensis Roman province of E Europe 31/3

Porolissum Romania Roman Empire 31/3

Portage la Prairie (Fort La Reine)

Port Arthur (Chin. Lushun Jap. Ryojun) Manchuria ceded to Russia and Japan 83/3, 107/4; Russo-Japanese war 127/4

Port Arthur (now Thunder Bay) C Canada growth 111/1

Port Arthur Tasmania penal settlement 113/1

Port Augusta S Australia settlement 113/1

Port Chalmers S Island, New Zealand 113/1

Port Elizabeth SE Africa British settlement 102/2, 103/3

Port Essington N Australia founded 113/1
Port-Francqui (now Ilebo) C Belgian Congo 138/4
Port Hedland W Australia early settlement 112/1
Port Hudson S USA X92/5
Portland S England WW1 118/3
Portland SE Australia founded 113/1
Port Lincoln S Australia settlement 113/1
Port Macquarie SE Australia penal settlement 113/1
Port Moresby SE New Guinea Allied base WW2 134/1, 135/2
Porto Novo SE India X87/2
Port Pirie S Australia settlement 113/1
Port Royal Jamaica British naval base 86/1
Port Said N Egypt Egyptian-Israeli war 141/3
Portsmouth S England naval base 87/1; Industrial Revolution 98/1; WW1 118/3
Portsmouth NE USA settlement 67/3
Portugal (anc. Lusitania) Jewish migration 39/4; Muslim conquest 40/1; reconquest 37/4; voyages of discovery 64-65; expansion overseas 66-7, 69/2; colonial empire 101/2; WW1 118-9; EU 137/1; NATO 149/1; US bases 149/1; economy 150/2
Portuguese East Africa (now Mozambique) 87/2, 101/2
Portuguese Guinea (now Guinea-Bissau) W Africa Portuguese colony 100/2; independence 138/1
Portuguese Timor E Indies annexed by Indonesia 139/1, 2
Porus early kingdom of NW India 23/3
Posidonia (later Paestum Mod. Pesto) S Italy Greek colony 19/4
Potaissa Romania Roman Empire 24/2
Potawatomi Indian tribe of C USA 63/1
Potentia (mod. Potenza Picena) N Italy Roman colony 30/1
Potidaea N Greece Dorian colony 19/4
Potosí Peru Spanish silver mine 66/1
Pouey-Mayou SW France megalithic tomb 14/3
Powhatan Indian tribe of E USA 63/1
Powys district of Wales 33/3, 57/1
Poynings Law English rule in Ireland 72T
Poznań (Ger. Posen) W Poland mass protests and strikes 1970-85 146/1
Pozzuoli (Puteoli)
Prague (Cz. Praha) Czechoslovakia bishopric 38/2; medieval trade 58/1; Hanseatic trade 59/2; industrial development 98/2; Communist coup 136/4; Russian occupation 1968 146/1
Praia das Maças C Portugal burial site 14/2
Prambanan C Java Hindu-Buddhist temple 51/2
Pravdinsk (Friedland)
Preanger district of Java Dutch control 71/4
Předmostí Czechoslovakia site of early man 3/3 Palaeolithic art 5/3
Pressburg (Cz. Bratislava) C Czechoslovakia X37/1
Preston N England X76/4; Industrial Revolution 98/1
Prestonpans S Scotland Industrial Revolution 98/1
Pretoria S Africa on Boer trek 102/2; X103/4
Preussen (Prussia)
Preussisch-Eylau (Eylau)
Preveza C Greece X48/2
Primorskiy Kray (Maritime Province)
Prince Edward Island (form. St. Jean) island of E Canada joins Dominion 111/1
Prince's Town Ghana early French settlement 60/2 (inset)
Principe island W Africa Portuguese settlement 61/2. See also São Tomé and Principe
Prizren Serbia WW1 119/3
Prome C Burma Buddhist site 27/1
Provence region of S France Frankish Empire 34/4, 35/2; medieval German Empire 55/3; Arabs expelled 36/2; annexed to France 72/1, 2; revolts 77/2; province of France 80/1
Providence NE USA founded 67/3
Provins C France medieval fair 58/1
Prusa (mod. Bursa) W Anatolia Byzantine Empire 43/1
Prussia (Ger. Preussen) region of E Germany conquest by Teutonic Knights 54/4; Reformation 75/1; Duchy 77/3; opposition to Napoleon 91/4; unification of Germany 115/2
Przemyśl Austria-Hungary WW1 119/3
Pseira E Crete Mycenaean settlement 19/1
Pskov W Russia town of Novgorod Empire 85/1; Hanseatic trading post 59/2; acquired by Muscovy 73/1
Pteria (mod. Boğazköy) C Anatolia X20/5
Ptolemaïs Egypt Roman Empire 31/3
Ptolemaïs (mod. Tulmaythah lt. Tolmeta) Libya Roman Empire 31/3; early archbishopric 27/2
Ptolemaïs (Eng. Acre mod. 'Akko) Palestine early archbishopric 27/2
Ptuj (Poetovio)
Puebla C Mexico early Spanish city 66/1; province 97/1
Pueblo Indian tribe of SW USA 13/1, 63/1
Pueblo Bonito SW USA site 62/4
Puelche Indian tribe of Argentina 63/1
Puerto Rico W Indies Spanish settlement 66/4; conquered by US 97/1
Pugachev uprising Russia 85/1, 89T
Puig Roig NE Spain megalithic tomb 14/3
Pukow E China British influence 107/4
Pundra region of E India 29/4, 5
Punic Wars 30/2
Punjab region of NW India Muslim expansion 41/1, 4, 87/3; state of British India 104/1, 105/3; partition between India and Pakistan 105/5

Puri district of NE India cession to Britain 87/3
Pusan (Jap. Fusan) S Korea Russo-Japanese war 127/4; 1950-53 war 148/2
Pushkari W Russia site of early man 3/3
Putaya Libya satrapy of Achaemenid Empire 20/5
Puteoli (mod. Pozzuoli) C Italy Roman colony 31/1; Roman Empire 24/2
Puto Shan mountain E China Buddhist site 27/1
Pyatigorsk Caucasus 85/1
Pydna C Greece X22/4
Pygmies people of C Africa 60/1, 2
Pylos (a/s Pilos lt. Navarino) SW Greece Mycenaean palace site 19/1; Levantine port 21/1
Pyongyang (Jap. Heijo) N Korea Russo-Japanese war 127/4; 1950-53 war 148/2
Pyramid Lake W USA X94/2
Pyramids, Battle of the Egypt 90/2
Pyrgi C Italy Roman colony 30/1
Pyrgos E Crete Mycenaean site 19/1
Pyu S Burma Buddhist kingdom 50/1
Pyxous, Pyxus (Buxentum)

Qadisiya S Mesopotamia X41/1
Qafzen NE Egypt site of early man 3/3
Qandahar (Kandahar)
Qasr Ibrim Upper Egypt fortress 21/1
Qatar sheikhdom of Persian Gulf 125/1
Qatna Syria Mesopotamia 20/2, 21/1
Qishan (Ch'i-shan)
Quadi Germanic tribe 30/3
Quanterness N Scotland megalithic tomb 14/3
Quban Upper Egypt fortress 21/1
Quebec city, E Canada capital of New France 67/3; captured by British 86/1; population 111/1
Quebec province, E Canada 164/5; joins Confederation 101/1; economic development 111/1
Quechua Andean Indian tribe of S America 63/1, 3
Queen Adelaide Province SE Africa 102/2
Queensland state of NE Australia 101/1, 113/1
Quelimane Mozambique Portuguese settlement 103/3
Quemoy island SE China Nationalist outpost 141/1, 149/1
Quentovic (a/s Quentowic) N France 34/4; Vikings 37/1
Querétaro state of C Mexico 97/1
Quetta Pakistan 105/3
Quiberon Bay W France X87/1
Quierzy N France Frankish royal residence 34/4
Quilon S India early trade 59/3
Qui Nhon S Vietnam 1945-75 war 148/3
Quiriguá E Mexico Mayan site 12/2
Quito Ecuador Inca Empire 63/3, 68/2; colonised 69/3

Rabaul Papua New Guinea Japanese base in WW2 135/2
Rabbath Ammon (Amman)
Rabih's State C Africa 103/3
Radimichi W Russia E Slav tribe 44/1
Rae Bareli district of N India civil disobedience 104/4
Rafah (anc. Raphia) Sinai Egyptian-Israeli war 141/3
Raffles Bay N Australia settlement 113/1
Rages (Rai)
Ragusa (now Dubrovnik) W Yugoslavia Byzantine Empire 43/1; Venetian conquest 36/2; Reformation 75/1; Ottoman vassal republic 48/1
Rai (anc. Rhagae Bibl. Rages Gr. Europus) N Persia early archbishopric 39/1; Muslim conquest 41/1; Mongol conquest 46/1; early trade 58/3
Rainy Lake (Fort Pierre)
Rajasthan (form. Rajputana-Agency) state of N India 105/5
Rajputana region of NW India Mughal conquest 48/2; in alliance with Britain 105/3
Rajputana Agency (now Rajasthan) state of British India 105/3
Rakka (anc. Nicephorium) Syria 49/1
Raleigh E USA X93/5
Rameses III pharaoh 18T
Ramillies Belgium X81/5
Ramla Palestine X41/1
Ramsey E England Industrial Revolution 98/1
Ramshög S Sweden megalithic tomb 15/3
Rangiriri N Island, New Zealand X112/3
Rangoon (anc. Dagon) Burma Buddhist site 27/1; early trade centre 71/2; occupied by Japanese 134/1; retaken by British 134/2
Rangpur NW India Harappan site 9/5
Ranians E Germany Slavonic tribe 54/2
Ranjit Singh territories of Lahore, NW India 104/1
Rann of Kutch region of W India boundary disputes with Pakistan 105/5, 141/1
Raphanea Syria Roman Empire 25/2
Raphia (Rafah)
Ras Hafun Somalia Muslim colony 60/1
Ras Shamra (anc. Ugarit) Syria Mycenaean trade 18/2
Rataria Bulgaria early archbishopric 27/2
Ratisbon (Ger. Regensburg) S Germany X91/1
Ravenna N Italy Roman Empire 24/2; early archbishopric 26/2; exarchate 42/1; captured by Venice 36/2; medieval city 56/3

Ravensberg N Germany Burgundian possession 73/3; county 79/1
Ravensbrück N Germany concentration camp 132/1
Reading S England Industrial Revolution 98/1
Reate (mod. Rieti) N Italy Roman Empire 30/1
Rechitsa W Russia town of Turov-Pinsk 45/2
Recife (Pernambuco)
Recuay early people of C Andes 12/4
Redarii N Germany Slav tribe 54/2
Redwood Ferry E USA X95/2
Reformation 74-75
Regensburg (anc. Castra Regina obs. Eng. Ratisbon) S Germany bishopric 38/2, 79/1; Frankish royal residence 35/4
Reggio (a/c Reggio di Calabria anc. Rhegium) S Italy Norman conquest 36/2; Ottoman siege 48/2
Reggio (a/c Reggio Emilia anc. Regium Lepidum) N Italy Republican commune 56/3
Regina C Canada growth 111/1
Regium Lepidum (Reggio Emilia)
Reichenau S Germany monastery 34/4
Reii S France early bishopric 26/2
Reims (Rheims)
Remedello N Italy burial site 14/2
Remi (mod. Rheims) N France early bishopric 26/2
Rennes NW France 17C revolt 77/1; French Revolution 89/2
Rethel NE France independent fief 72/2
Réunion (form. Bourbon) island Indian Ocean French colony 101/2
Reval (Russ. Revel mod. Est. Tallinn) NW Russia German colonisation 54/4; Hanseatic city 59/2; Swedish Empire 77/3
Rewardashur Persia early archbishopric 27/2, 39/1
Rhaetia (mod. Switzerland) Roman province 30/3
Rhagae (Per. Rai Bibl. Rages Gr. Europus) N Persia Alexander's Empire 23/3
Rhegium (mod. Reggio di Calabria) N Italy Greek colony 19/4, 23/2; Roman Empire 24/2, 31/3
Rheims (Fr. Reims anc. Durocortorun later Remi) N France sacked by Vandals 37/1; archbishopric 34/4; X91/1; industrial development 98/2; WW1 118/3; WW2 132/2
Rheinland (Rhineland)
Rhenish Prussia W Germany unification of Germany 115/2
Rhesaenae E Anatolia Roman Empire 25/2
Rhine, Confederation of the Napoleonic creation 91/1
Rhineland (Ger. Rheinland) region of W Germany remilitarised 128/1, 129/5
Rhode Island state of NE USA colony 67/3; Depression 131/2; population 111/5, 145/1
Rhodes (mod. Gr. Rodhos Lat. Rhodus lt. Rodi) island SE Aegean in Mycenaean world 18/2; Greek state 19/4; archbishopric 27/2; X41/1; under Knights of St John 49/1; Ottoman conquest 48/2. See also Dodecanese
Rhodesia (form. Southern Rhodesia, now Zimbabwe) British colony 101/2; independence (UDI) 138/1
Rhodus (mod. Gr. Rodhos Eng. Rhodes) island SE Aegean Roman Empire 24/2, 31/3
Ribe Denmark archbishopric 52/3
Rich Bar W USA mining site 94/1
Richmond N England rebellion against Henry VIII 73/4
Richmond E USA burned 93/5; industry 109/1, 110/2
Ricomagus (Riom)
Riete (Reate)
Riga Latvia, NW USSR founded by Teutonic Knights 54/1; Hanseatic city 59/2; early trade 58/3; Swedish Empire 77/3; short-lived Communist control 121/2; WW2 133/2;
Rijkholt S Holland megalithic flint mine 15/3
Rimini (anc. Ariminum) N Italy Lombard League 32/4, 54/3; Signorial domination 56/3; WW2 133/2
Rio Barbate Spain X40/1
Rio de Janeiro Brazil colonised 69/3; state 97/1; guerrilla activity 143/1
Rio de la Plata (mod. Argentina) early Spanish colony 69/3; vice-royalty in rebellion against Spain 88/1
Rio de Oro (later Spanish Sahara now Western Sahara) NW Africa Spanish colony 100/2, 103/3
Rio Grande do Norte state of N Brazil Confederation of the Equator 97/1
Rio Grande do Sul state of S Brazil 97/1
Riom (anc. Ricomagus) C France seat of intendant 80/1
Rio Muni (a/c Spanish Guinea now Equatorial Guinea) W Africa Spanish colony 102/5
Rio Negro state of W Brazil 97/1
Ripabianca C Italy farming site 15/1
Ripon N England Industrial Revolution 98/1
Rivoli N Italy X91/1
Roc des Sers SW France Palaeolithic art 5/3
Rochdale N England Industrial Revolution 98/1
Rochefort W France naval base 80/1
Rochford E England Industrial Revolution 98/1
Rockhampton E Australia early settlement 113/1
Rocroi NE France X74/4
Rodez region of S France 72/2
Rodhos (Rhodes)
Rodi (Rhodes)
Rogoźnica (Gross-Rosen)
Rogue River W USA X94/2
Rohri N India Harappan site 9/5
Rojadi N India Harappan site 9/5
Roma (Rome)
Romagna region of N Italy unification of Italy 114/3

Süntel N Germany ✕34/4
Sun Yat-sen Chinese president 122T
Suomussalmi C Finland WW2 132/1
Surabaya (Dut. Soerabaja) Java trading centre 71/2 occupied by Japanese 134/1
Surakarta district of Java Dutch control 71/2
Surashtra early state of W India 29/4
Surat NW India Mughal port 59/3; Ottoman siege 48/2; industry 105/3
Surgut W Siberia founded 84/2
Surinam (Dut. Surinam form. Dutch Guiana) country of S America 142-3
Susa SW Persia early urban settlement 16/2, 17/4; Assyrian Empire 20/2, 3; Alexander's route 22/3; Persian Royal Road 21/5
Susiana (a/c Elam mod. Khuzistan) region of SW Persia province of Alexander's Empire 22/3
Susquehanna Indian tribe of NE USA 63/1
Sussex early kingdom of S England 35/3, 38/3
Sutkagan-Dor NW India Harappan site 9/5
Sutrium N Italy Latin colony 30/1
Suvar E Russia early town 45/2
Suzdal C Russia town of Vladimir-Suzdal 45/2
Sverdlovsk (until 1924 and again from 1991 Yekaterinburg) C Russia 147/2
Swabia (Ger. Schwaben) region of S Germany province of medieval German Empire 55/1, 3
Swakopmund SW Africa German settlement 103/3
Swanscombe England site of early man 3/3
Swansea S Wales Industrial Revolution 98/1
Swartkrans S Africa site of early man 3/3
Swatow S China treaty port 107/4; Japanese occupation 127/5
Swaziland country of SE Africa British protectorate 101/1, 103/4; independence 138/1
Sweden conversion to Christianity 38/2; Viking expansion 37/1; emergence as a state 53/5; Black Death 57/1; Union of Kalmar 72/1; Reformation 75/1; empire in the Baltic 77/3; losses to Russia and Prussia 114/4; industry 98/2; loss of Denmark and Norway 114/4; 20C economic and socio-political development 131/3; EU 137/1; economy 151/2
Swift Creek/Santa Rosa Group early Indians of USA 12/3
Swindon W England Industrial Revolution 98/1
Swiss Confederation (a/c Helvetia) formation 54/4
Switzerland medieval cantons 54/5; Reformation 75/1; Industrial Revolution 98/2; neutral in WW1 118/1; EFTA 137/2; economy 150/1; WW2 132/1
Sybaris S Italy Greek colony 19/4
Sydney SE Australia founded 113/1; Allied base in WW2 135/2
Sydney Nova Scotia growth 111/1
Syene (mod. Aswan) Upper Egypt 38/1
Sykes-Picot Agreement 125/3
Sylhet district of Bengal votes to join Pakistan 105/5
Synnada W Anatolia early archbishopric 27/2; Byzantine Empire 43/1
Syracusa (a/s Syracusae mod. Siracusa Eng. Syracuse) Sicily Greek colony 19/4; Roman Empire 24/2, 31/3; ✕31/2; bishopric 27/2; Byzantine Empire 43/1; Norman conquest 36/2
Syria earliest settlements 7/2; centre of ancient civilisations 16-17; Mitannian cities 21/1; at time of Alexander 22/3; expansion of Christianity 38/1; Arab conquest 41/1; Ottoman province 124/1; WW1 125/2; WW2 132/1; independence 138/1; French control 125/3, 128/1; war with Israel 141/3; Soviet base 149/1
Syriam S Burma early trade centre 71/2
Syrmia (S. Cr. Srem Hung. Szerém Ger. Sirmien) district of Austria-Hungary now part of Serbia WW1 119/3
Syzran C Russia founded 84/2
Szczecin (Stettin)
Szechwan province of W China under Ming 51/4; Manchu expansion 106/1; Taiping rebellion 107/3; politically fragmented 122/2; Nationalist control 123/3
Szeged S Hungary uprising 1956 146/1
Szemao SW China treaty town 107/4
Szerém (Syrmia)
Sztutowo (Stutthof)

Taanach N Palestine Levantine city 21/1
Tabasco state of S Mexico 97/1
Tabennesis Egypt monastery 38/1
Tabert Algeria Arab conquest 40/1
Tábor Moravia Hussite centre 57/1
Tabora E Africa Livingstone's travels 20/1
Tabriz NW Persia early archbishopric 39/1; occupied by Mongols 46/1; early trade 58/3; conquered by Ottomans 48/2, 49/1
Tabun Israel site of early man 3/3
Tadcaster N England Industrial Revolution 98/1
Tadmekka NW Africa early town 60-61
Tadmor (Palmyra)
Taegu S Korea 1950-53 war 148/2
Taejon S Korea 1950-53 war 148/2
Taganrog Crimea acquired by Muscovy 85/1; industry 85/4; 1905 Revolution 120/1
Taghaza NW Africa trans-Saharan trade 60-61
Tagliacozzo C Italy ✕55/3

Tahiti island S Pacific Polynesian settlement 10/2; European discovery 65/4
T'ai-hsi-ts'un (a/s Taixicun) N China Shang city 8/4
Taiwan (a/c Formosa) Mesolithic sites 8/2; early settlements 8/2; contested by Dutch and Spanish 71/2; rising of aboriginals 106/1; acquired by Japan 107/4, 123/3, 127/3; seat of Chinese Nationalist government 141/1; economy 150/1, 151/2
Taixicun (T'ai-hsi-ts'un)
Taiyuan N China T'ang city 50/1; Ming provincial capital 51/4; French railway 107/4
Tajiks people of C Asia 146/2, 147/3
Tajikistan C Asia independence 151/4
Takeda C Japan clan territory 50/3
Takedda NW Africa trans-Saharan trade 60/1
Takla Makan Desert 25/1
Takoradi W Africa early Dutch settlement 60/2 (inset)
Takruo early empire of W Africa 60/1
Takua Pa S Thailand Hindu-Buddhist remains 51/2
Talas river C Asia ✕41/1
Talavera C Spain ✕90/91
Ta-li C China site of early man 3/3
Tal-i Ghazir W Persia early city 16/2
Tal-i Malyan W Persia early city 16/2
Tallinn (Ger. Reval Russ. Revel) Estonia SSR 137/2
Talladega SE USA ✕95/2
Tamanrasset S Algeria Saharan trade 61/2; French occupation 103/3
Tamar (Palmyra)
Tamaulipas state of N Mexico 97/1
Tambov C Russia founded 85/1; 1905 revolution 120/1; Bolshevik seizure 121/2
Tamluk (a/c Tamralipta) E India early trade centre 25/1
Tamsui N Taiwan early treaty port 107/4; Anglo-French attacks 107/2
T'an E China Chou domain 9/6
Tana S Russia Mongol conquest 47/4; early trade 58/3
Tanais S Russia Greek colony 19/4
Tanana sub-arctic Indian tribe of Alaska 63/1
Tananarive (n/s Antananarivo) Madagascar centre of Merina kingdom 103/3
Tancáh E Mexico Mayan centre 12/2
Tanganyika (form. German East Africa now part of Tanzania) independence 138/1; political development 140/1
T'ang Chi-yao Chinese warlord 122/2
Tangier (a/c Tangiers Fr. Tanger Sp. Tánger Ar. Tanjah anc. Tingis) Morocco international control 103/3
Tanguts tribe of S Mongolia 47/1
Tanis (a/c Avaris) Lower Egypt 21/1
Tanjah (Tangier)
Tanjore district of S India ceded to Britain 87/4
Tannenberg (Pol. Stębark) E Prussia ✕Teutonic Knights defeated 54/4; ✕WW1 119/3
Tannu Tuva (now Tuvinskaya ASSR) C Asia Russian protectorate 107/4, 120/4
Tantu E China Western Chou site 9/6
Tanyang E China Han commanderie 29/3
Tanzania (formed by amalgamation of Tanganyika and Zanzibar) 140/1; economy 151/2. See also German East Africa
Tao C China Western Chou domain 9/6
Taochow W China Ming military post 51/4
Taoism 27/1
Taoudenni NW Africa French occupation 103/3
Taprobane (Ceylon)
Tara W Siberia founded 84/2
Tarabulus al Gharb (Tripoli)
Tarabulus ash Sham (Tripoli)
Tarahumara Indian tribe of N Mexico 63/1
Tarakan NE Borneo Allied landing in WW2 135/2
Taranaki (a/c New Plymouth) province of N Island, New Zealand 112/2
Taranto (anc. Tarentum) S Italy Saracen occupation 37/1
Tarapacá S Peru acquired by Chile 97/4
Tarasco Indian tribe of C Mexico 63/1
Tarawa Gilbert Islands, S Pacific ✕135/2
Tarentaise SE France archbishopric 34/3
Tarentum (mod. Taranto) S Italy Greek colony 19/4; Roman Empire 24/2, 30/1, 31/3
Tarim Basin C Asia occupied by China 50/1, 106/1
Tarnopol (now Russ. Ternopol) E Austria-Hungary WW1 113/3; WW2133/2
Tarnow (now Pol. Tarnów) E Austria-Hungary WW1 119/3
Tarquinii (later Corneto mod. Tarquinia) C Italy Etruscan city19/4
Tarracina (earlier Anxur mod. Terracina) C Italy Roman colony 30/1
Tarraco (mod. Tarragona) NE Spain Greek colony 19/4; 24/2, 30/3
Tarraconensis Roman province of N Spain 30/3
Tarragona (anc. Tarraco) NE Spain Civil War 129/4
Tarsus S Anatolia early city 16/1; early trade 17/4; Assyrian Empire 17/4; Mycenaean bead 21/1; Hittite city 21/1; Alexander's route 22/3; Roman Empire 43/1
Tărtăria N Romania early settlement 14/2
Tartars (a/s Tatars) Turkic people of E Russia 47/1, 84/2, 146/3
Tartu (Dorpat)
Taruga C Africa Iron Age site 11/1
Tarvisium (Treviso)

Tashkent Russ. C Asia Alexander's journey 23/3; Mongol conquest 47/4; centre of Bolshevik activity 120/4; growth 147/2
Tasmania (until 1856 Van Diemen's Land) island state of SE Australia settlement and development 113/1 (inset
Tassili Massif N Africa rock painting 11/1
Tatanagar NE India industry 108/1
Tatarstan (f/c Tatar ASSR) in USSR 147/3; autonomous republic of Russian Federation 137/2
Tatars (Tartars)
Tatung N China early bishopric 39/1; Ming frontier defence area 51/4
Tauchira Libya Greek colony 19/4
Taung S Africa site of early man 3/3
Taunum W Germany Mithraic site 26/1
Taurasia (Turin)
Ta-wen-k'ou (a/s Dawenkou) NE China early settlement 8/2
Taxila NW India early trading centre 25/1; Alexander's route 23/3
Tayadirt N Morocco megalithic tomb 14/3
Taymyr AR N Siberia 147/3
Tazoult (Lambaesis)
Tbilisi (Tiflis)
Tchad (Chad)
Teate (mod. Chieti) C Italy Roman Empire 30/1
Tebessa (Theveste)
Teheran (Pers. Tehran) C Persia 124/1
Tehuelche Indian tribe of S Argentina 63/1
Te Ika-a-Maui (North Island)
Tekke SW Anatolia region of Ottoman Empire 49/1
Tel-Aviv C Israel 141/3
Tell Abu Hureira Syria early farming site 7/4
Tell Agrab Mesopotamia Sumerian site 16/2
Tell Asmar (Eshnunna)
Tell Aswad N Mesopotamia Sumerian site 16/2
Tell Brak E Syria early farming village 7/4; Mitannian city 21/1
Tell el-'Ubaid S Mesopotamia Sumerian site 16/2
Tell es-Sa'idiyeh Palestine Levantine city 21/1
Tell-es-Sawwan Mesopotamia early farming village 7/4
Tell Halaf C Mesopotamia early farming village 7/4
Tellicherry SW India English settlement 66/2
Telloh C Mesopotamia Sumerian site 16/2
Tell Ramad Lebanon early farming site 7/4
Tell Tayinat NW Syria Mitannian city 21/1
Tell 'Uqair N Mesopotamia Sumerian site 16/2
Tell Wilaya C Mesopotamia Sumerian site 16/2
Telo Martius (Toulon)
Tembu region of SE Africa 103/2
Temesvár (Timişoara)
Tempsa S Italy Roman colony 30/1
Tenasserim district of S Burma British control 71/2; annexed by British 104/2
Tenetehara forest Indian tribe of NE Brazil 63/1
Teng N China Chou domain and city-state 9/6; warring state 28/1
Tengyueh SW China treaty town 107/4
Tennessee state of SE USA Civil War 93/5; Depression 131/2; population 111/5, 145/1
Tenochtitlán Mexico Aztec capital 62/2; conquest by Spaniards 68/1
Teotihuacán early culture of C America 12/2
Tepehuan Indian tribe of N Mexico 63/1
Tepe Yahya S Persia early settlement 16/1
Tepic state of N Mexico 97/1
Te Porere N Island, New Zealand ✕112/3
Terebovl W Russia town of Galich 45/2
Teremembé forest Indian tribe of NE Brazil 63/1
Terezín (Theresienstadt)
Tergeste (mod. Trieste) N Italy Roman Empire 30/3
Ternate Moluccas, East Indies Islamic town 70/1; Portuguese settlement 70/3
Ternifine Algeria site of early man 3/3
Terracina (Tarracina)
Terranova di Sicilia (Gela)
Tertry N France ✕34/4
Teruel E Spain Civil War 129/4
Teschen (Cz. Těšín or Česky Těšín Pol. Cieszyn) city and district divided between Poland and Czechoslovakia 128/1; Czech part retaken by Poland 129/5
Teshik-tash C Asia site of early man 3/3
Těšín (Teschen)
Tete Mozambique Portuguese settlement 61/2; Stanley's travels 102/1
Teutonic Order Baltic 45/2; conquest of Prussia 54/4; territory lost to Poland 72/1
Teverya (Tiberias)
Te Wapounamu (South Island)
Tewkesbury W England Industrial Revolution 98/1
Texas state of S USE independent 97/1; Depression 131/2; population 111/5, 145/1
Texel I and II N Netherlands English/Dutch naval battles 81/3
Teyjat SW France Palaeolithic art 5/3
Thailand (f/c Siam) early Iron and Bronze Age sites 8/3; Theravada Buddhism 70/1; US bases 149/1; political developments 141/1; economy 150/1; 151/2. See also Siam
Thais people of SE Asia, expansion 51/2

Tuchi N China T'ang prefecture 50/1

Tucson SE USA on trail West 94/1

Tugursk Russ. Far East founded 84/2

Tukh (a/c Nubt) Upper Egypt pyramid 17/3

Tukharistan region of C Asia Chinese protectorate 50/1

Tukulti-Ninurta I King of Assyria 20/3

Tula Mexico Toltec centre 62/2

Tula C Russia 147/2

Tulagi Solomon Islands US base in WW2 135/2

Tulmaythat (Ptolemaïs)

Tulúm Mexico fortified site 62/2

Tumasik (now Singapore) Malaya 51/2

Tumbes Andean Indian tribe 63/1

Tunes (Tunis)

T'ung SE China Western Chou domain 9/6

Tungirsk SE Siberia founded 84/2

Tungusy people of Siberia 84/2

Tunhsi Western Chou site 9/6

Tunhwang W China early trade and silk route 25/1; Buddhist site 27/1; conquered by Han 28/2

Tunis (anc. Tunes) N Africa early trade 58/3; acquired by Habsburgs 72/1; Ottoman conquest 48/2, 61/2; French occupation 103/3

Tunisia under the Almohads 60/1; autonomy under Ottoman Empire 124/1; French protectorate 103/3; under Vichy control 132/1; WW2 132/2; independence 138/1

Tupinambá forest Indian tribe of E Brazil 63/1

Turckheim W France ✕81/4

Turfan NW China silk route 25/1; administrative centre of Later Han 28/2

Turin (It. Torino anc. Taurasia later Augusta Taurinorum) N Italy Lombard League 55/3; 18C urban development 83/4; ✕81/5

Turinsk W Siberia founded 84/2

Turkestan region of C Asia spread of Buddhism 27/1; during T'ang Empire 50/1; Chinese protectorate 106/1

Turkey on break-up of Ottoman Empire 124/1; war with Greece 125/4; Greek occupation of west 128/1; neutral in WW2 132/1; applies to join EU 137/4; Baghdad Pact and NATO 148/1, 149/1. See also Anatolia, Asia Minor, Ottoman Empire

Turkmen tribe of C Asia, conquered by Russia 84/3, 147/3

Turkmen SSR C Asia 147/3

Turkmenistan C Asia independence 151/4

Turks tribes on China's northern borders 50/1; invasion of Anatolia 41/2; movements after WW1 129/3. See also Ottoman Empire

Turks and Caicos Islands W Indies British colony 100/2

Turnhout Belgium medieval fair 58/1, 59/2

Turnu-Severin (Drobetae)

Turones (mod. Tours) C France archbishopric 26/2

Turov-Pinsk early principality of W Russia 45/2

Turukhansk C Siberia founded 84/2

Tuscany (It. Toscana) region of N Italy medieval German Empire 55/3; unification of Italy 114/3

Tuscararas SE USA ✕94/2

Tustrup N Denmark megalithic tomb 15/3

Tutchone sub-arctic tribe of NW Canada 63/1

Tutub (mod. Khafajah) N Mesopotamia Sumerian site 16/2

Tuva ASSR C Asia 147/3

Tuvalu (form. Ellice Islands) C Pacific British colony 193/1 (inset)

Tver (1931-91 Kalinin) W Russia early town of Vladimir-Suzdal 45/2

Two Sicilies kingdom 114/3

Tyana C Anatolia early bishopric 27/2; Byzantine Empire 43/3

Ty Isaf S Wales megalithic tomb 14/3

Tynedale N England Franchise of 56/4

Tyras (mod. Akkerman since 1944 Belgorod-Dnestrovskiy Rom. Cetatea-Alba) S Russia Roman Empire 31/3

Tyre (anc. Tyrus Ar. Sur) Lebanon early trade 17/4, 18/2; Phoenician city 19/4; Levantine city 21/1; besieged by Alexander 22/3; Roman Empire 25/2; early archbishopric 27/2; Crusades 40/3

Tyrol (Ger. Tirol It. Tirolo) region of W Austria medieval German Empire 55/3; acquired by Habsburg 78/3; County 79/1; peasant revolt 88/1; South Tyrol to Italy 128/2

Tyrus (Eng. Tyre Ar. Sur) Lebanon Roman Empire 25/2, 31/3

Tyumen C Russia founded 84/2; on railway to east 84/3

Tzintzuntzán Mexico Tarascan site 62/2

Tz'u-shan (a/s Cishan) N China early settlement 8/2

Uan Muhaggiag SW Libya early site 11/1

Ubangi-Shari (Oubangui-Chari, Central African Republic)

Udaipur former state of C India 104/1

Udinsk S Siberia founded 84/2

Udmurty people of C Russia 85/1; ASSR 147/3

Udon Thani N Thailand Vietnamese war 148/3

Udyana region of NW India 29/4

Uesugi E Japan clan territory 51/3

Ufa C Russia founded 85/1

Uganda British protectorate 101/2, 103/3; independence 138/1; political development 140/1

Ugarit (mod. Ras Shamra) ancient city of Syria 16/1; Mitannian city 21/1

Uighurs Turkic tribe of C Asia 47/1, 50/1

Ujiji C Africa meeting of Livingstone and Stanley 102/1

Ukraine post-WW1 independence 1917 128/1; WW2 132-3; industrial development 84/4; SSR 147/2

Ukrainians people of S Russia, emigration to West 129/3, 147/5; independence from USSR 137/2

Ulan Bator (Mong, Ulaanbaatar form. Urga) Mongolia 120/4

Ulithi island of C Pacific US base in WW2 135/2

Ulm S Germany ✕90/1

Ulster province of N Ireland early kingdom 73/4

Ulu Leang East Indies Neolithic site 8/3

Ulyanovsk (Simbirsk)

Umatilla NW USA ✕94/2

Umayyads Muslim dynasty, Caliphate 34/4, 40/1

Umbrians Italic tribe of C Italy 30/1

Umma Mesopotamia Sumerian city 16/2, 17/4

Unao N India Indian Mutiny 104/1

UNITA Angolan guerrilla movement 138T, 140/1

United Arab Emirates (form. Trucial States earlier Trucial Oman, Trucial Coast) federation of sheikhdoms, Persian Gulf creation 138/1

United Arab Republic name given to the union of Egypt and Syria 1958-61 retained by Egypt after dissolution until 1972

United Kingdom socio-political development 131/3; EU 137/4; NATO 149/1; economy 151/2. See also England, Scotland, Wales, Great Britain, Ulster

United Netherlands 79/1

United Provinces (a/c Dutch Republic) occupied by France 81/4

United States Thirteen Colonies and revolutionary war 86/1; War of Independence 92/1; industrialisation 110/2, 109/1; westward expansion 94/1; Indian wars 95/2; railway development 95/3; Civil War 92/3; population 111/5; Great Depression 130/3; 20C economic and industrial development 144-5; WW2 in Asia and Pacific 135/1; WW2 against Axis in West 132-3; involvement in Latin America 111/4, 143/1; in Cold War 148-9; NATO 148/1; Pacific Rim 150/1; economy 151/2

Unsan N Korea 1950-53 war 148/2

Unterwalden original Swiss canton 54/5

Upper Burma annexed by British 104/2

Upper Emigrant Trail S USA settlers' route 94/1

Upper Palatinate S Germany Reformation 75/1

Upper Silesia (Ger. Oberschlesien, Pol. Górny Śląsk) divided between Germany and Poland 128/1

Upper Volta (Fr. Haute-Volta n/c Burkina) country of W Africa independence 138/1; economy 150/1

Uppland E Sweden early kingdom 53/5

Uppsala E Sweden bishopric 38/2

Ur (of the Chaldees) S Mesopotamia early farming village 7/4; Sumerian city 17/2, 4

Urals mountains industrial region of USSR 147/1

Urartu (mod. Armenia) state of ancient Near East 20/4

Urbs Vetus (Volsinii)

Urewe E Africa Iron Age site 11/1

Urfa (Edessa)

Urga (mod. Ulan-Bator Mong. Ulaanbaatar) Mongolia seat of Lamaistic patriarch 106/1

Urgench C Asia Muslim trade 59/3

Uri original Swiss canton 54/5

Uruguay part of Brazil 97/1; independence 97/1; political development 143/1; industry and economy 142/2, 3; 151/2

Uruk (a/c Erech) Mesopotamia early farming village 7/4; Sumerian city 17/2, 4

Üsküb (S. Cr. Skoplje, Maced. Skopje) Yugoslavia Ottoman Empire 116/1

U.S.S.R. formation 120-1, 128/1; fighting against Japan 135/1; WW2 132-3; labour camps 147/2; constituent republics 146/2; nationalities 147/3; Communism overthrown 137/2; Comecon 137/4; Warsaw Pact 149/1; dissolved 137/2

Ust-Kutsk C Siberia founded 84/2

Ust-Orda Buryat-Mongol AD E USSR 147/3

Ust-Vilyuysk E Siberia founded 84/2

Ust-Vym N Russia bishopric 38/2

Utah state of W USA ceded by Mexico 97/1; Depression 130/3; population 111/5, 145/1

Ute Indian tribe of SW USA 63/1

Utica Tunisia Stone Age site 11/1; Punic city 19/4; Roman Empire 30/2

U Tong S Thailand Hindu-Buddhist remains 51/2

Utrecht (anc. Trajectum) Holland bishopric 38/3; Burgundian possession 73/3; province of Dutch Republic 77/1

Uttar Pradesh (form. United Provinces) state of N India 105/5

Uttoxeter C England Industrial Revolution 98/1

Uvja (a/c Elam) W Persia province of Achaemenid Empire 21/5

Uxii ancient tribe of W Persia 22/3

Uxmal E Mexico Mayan centre 12/2

Uzbeks people of C Asia 147/3

Uzbek SSR C Asia 147/3

Vagarshapat (since 1945 Echmiadzin) Armenia early archbishopric 27/2

Vaisali W Burma Hindu-Buddhist remains 51/2

Valencia (anc. Valentia) E Spain bishopric 38/2; reconquered by Aragon 37.4; 18C urban development 82/4; Muslim minority 75/1, ✕90/1; Civil War 129/4

Valentia (mod. Valence) S France bishopric 26/1

Valentia (Valencia)

Valladolid N Spain Lutheran minority 75/1; Civil War 129/4

Valley Road NE USA settlers' route 94/1

Valmy NE France ✕89/2

Valois region of NE France 72/2

Valona (anc. Avlona Turk. Avlonya now Alb. Vlorë) S Adriatic Ottoman town 48/2

Vancouver W Canada growth 111/1

Vandals Germanic tribe, invasion of Europe and N Africa 32/1, 2; 34/1

Van Diemen's Land (mod. Tasmania) early trade 113/4

Vanga ancient country of E India 29/4

Varangians Russia Viking raiders 44T/1

Varna (anc. Odessus 1949-57 Stalin) E Bulgaria burial site 14/2; ✕49/1

Vasiliki E Crete Mycenaean settlement 19/1

Vasio S France bishopric 27/2

Vassily III king of Muscovy 72/2

Vatsa early kingdom of N India 29/4

Vaud Switzerland Reformation 75/1

Veletians Slav tribe of NW Europe 55/1

Velia (Elea)

Velikiye Luki W Russia WW2 133/2

Velitrae C Italy Latin colony 30/1

Velsuna (Volsinii)

Vendée region of W France 80/1; uprising 89/2

Vendôme region of NW France 72/2

Venetia (It. Venezia) region of N Italy exchanged for Austrian Netherlands 78/3, 88/3; unification of Italy 114/3

Venetian Empire (Venice)

Venetian Republic NE Italy 79/1. See also Venice

Venezuela European discovery 65/3; independence 97/1; US influence 111/4; political development 143/1; economy 142/2, 3; OPEC 151/2

Venice (It. Venezia anc. Venetia) expansion into Adriatic and Aegean 37/4; Reformation 75/1; republican commune 56/3; early trade 58/3; Black Death 57/1; 18C financial centre 82/4; WW1 119/3

Ventspils (Windau)

Venusia (mod. Venosa) C Italy Latin colony 30/1

Vera Cruz E Mexico modern province 97/1

Vercelli N Italy Lombard League 55/3; Signorial domination 56/3

Verdalpino E Spain farming site 15/1

Verden N Germany bishopric 79/1

Verdun E France annexed to France 72/2; WW1 119/3 (inset)

Verdun, Treaty of 35/5

Vereeniging, Peace of Boer War 102T/4

Verkhne-Angarsk S Siberia founded 84/2

Verkhne-Kolymsk E Siberia founded 84/2

Verkholensk S Siberia founded 84/2

Verkhoturye W Siberia founded 84/2

Verlaine Belgium Palaeolithic art 5/3

Vermandois region of NE France Royal domain 52/2; Burgundian possession 73/3

Vermont state of NE USA Depression 131/2; population 111/5, 145/1

Vernyy (since 1921 Alma-Ata) Russ. C Asia industry 147/1

Veroia (Beroea)

Verona N Italy Roman Empire 24/2; Lombard League 55/3; Signorial domination 56/3; 18C financial centre 82/4

Verrazzano Italian navigator 65/2

Versailles N France 80/1

Vértesszőllős Hungary site of early man 3/3

Verulamium (mod. St. Albans) S England Roman Empire 30/3; bishopric 26/2

Vesontio (mod. Besançon) E France Roman Empire 30/3; archbishopric 26/2

Vetulonia C Italy Etruscan city 19/4

Via Appia (Eng. Appian Way) C Italy Roman road from Rome to Brindisi 30/1

Via Flaminia (Eng. Flaminian Way) C Italy Roman road from Rome to Rimini 30/1

Via Valeria C Italy Roman road 30/1

Viborg (Vipuri, Vyborg)

Vibo Valentia S Italy Latin colony 30/1

Vicenza N Italy Lombard League 55/3

Vichy France satellite state of Germany in WW2 132/1

Vicksburg S USA ✕92/5

Victoria state of SE Australia settlement and development 113/1

Videha ancient kingdom of E India 29/4

Vidin W Bulgaria Ottoman Empire 49/1

Vienna (anc. Vindobona Ger. Wien form. Turk. Bec) Austria siege of 48/2

Vienne (mod. Vienne) S France Roman Empire 30/3; archbishopric 26/1

Vientiane Laos trading centre 71/2

Vietnam 1945-75 war 148/3; unification of north and south 141/1; Soviet base 149/1. See also North Vietnam, South Vietnam, Indo-China

Viipuri (Sw. Viborg Russ. Vyborg) SE Finland captured by Russia 132/1

Vijaya (mod. Binh Dinh) S Indo-China capital of Champa Kingdom 51/2

Vikletice W Czechoslovakia burial site 14/2

Vila Nova de São Pedro C Portugal early settlement 14/2